RENSERI
RENSERI
Radio TV
BØKER
PAPIR
TASEN APOTEK
70

SKO
MAKERI

20

232

ARCHITECTURE AND WELFARE
Scandinavian Perspectives

Thordis Arrhenius
Ellen Braae
Guttorm Ruud (eds.)

ARCHITECTURE AND WELFARE
Scandinavian Perspectives

Birkhäuser

CONTENT

INTRODUCTION

Scandinavia consistently occupies the top of global happiness rankings. The Scandinavian "happiness" or well-being is often associated with democratic values, generous social welfare, socio-economic equality, and high levels of social and institutional trust.[1] Welfare policies in Scandinavia have traditionally addressed the whole population rather than targeting specific social groups or classes, generating inclusive welfare based on universal principles. In Denmark, Norway, and Sweden, the strong position of labor movements in the 1930s enabled political agreements between labor and capital in the three countries, which was essential for postwar developments of social democratic welfare states.[2] In these developments, architecture and planning were central. Scandinavian architects engaged politically in shaping society, and the 1930 Stockholm Exhibition launched modern architecture as a politically transformative force.[3] A common Scandinavian culture and history constituted the backdrop for Scandinavian cooperation, seen in the exchange of ideas between architects and planners from the three countries during the Second World War.[4] In the immediate postwar years, under a period of rapid modernization and economic development, new neighborhoods of affordable housing, cultural and social buildings, commercial centers, and supporting infrastructure were built across Denmark, Norway, and Sweden. This development was part of the physical realization of welfare state policies, translating Scandinavian social democratic ideals of universal welfare—or "welfare for all"—into space.

Despite the common perception that Denmark, Norway, and Sweden's universal approach to welfare transformed them into the world's most comprehensive, advanced, and successful welfare states, this political and spatial legacy is today being contested. Against a backdrop of increasing spatial segregation and rising inequality rates in the Scandinavian welfare states, the concept of "welfare for all" no longer enjoys the public and political consensus it did in the postwar years. Postwar architecture and planning, once seen as a medium of universal welfare, inclusion, and political participation, is now often associated with its opposites: alienation, exclusion, and isolation.[5]

In response to such contrasting and conflicting narratives, this publication examines the complex interrelationships between, and changes within, architecture and welfare in Scandinavia. We evoke four types of *formations*—which we understand as actions and processes that contribute to forming architecture-welfare relationships—namely, "Formations and Materializations," "Networks and Actors," "Debates and Critiques," and "Reconceptualizations and New Formations." These (plural) categories serve to differentiate, contest, challenge, and elaborate on the social democratic regime and the Nordic welfare state model. Through them, we aim

1 See Frank Martela et al., "The Nordic Exceptionalism: What Explains Why the Nordic Countries Are Constantly Among the Happiest in the World," in *World Happiness Report 2020*, ed. John F. Helliwell et al. (New York: Sustainable Development Solutions Network, 2020), 128–45.

2 According to the Danish sociologist Gøsta Esping-Andersen, the more comprehensive nature of social democratic regimes lies in the power of the labor movements in challenging capitalist interests and conservative ideas. See Gøsta Esping-Andersen, *The Three Worlds of Welfare Capitalism* (Cambridge, UK: Polity Press, 1989), 71.

3 See Eva Rudberg, *Stockholms-utställningen 1930: modernismens genombrott i svensk arkitektur* [Stockholm Exhibition 1930: the breakthrough of modernism in Swedish architecture] (Stockholm: Stockholmia, 1999). For the political role of Norwegian architects in the late 1930s, see also Anne-Kristine Kronborg's contribution in this volume.

4 See Espen Johnsen's contribution in this volume.

5 For analyses of the history of associating postwar architecture with problems, see contributions by Guttorm Ruud, Mikkel Høghøj, and Jennifer Mack in this volume.

to describe multiple, complex, changing formations of architecture and welfare within Scandinavia's nation states, with all of their social, cultural, and political similarities and differences. We present multiple interpretations of architecture and welfare, evoking a spatial, geographic, social, and temporal plurality that allows for a richer understanding of the physical, present-day welfare city and its architecture. These analyses provide insights into, and an overview of, the complex intersections that occur between architecture and welfare, offering essential support for future solutions, which necessarily must build on—and thus understand—what is already here. Moreover, the volume contains three visual essays, which each shed light on the complex realities of the welfare states in ways that are not easily summarized or integrated, thereby adding to a differentiated understanding and perception of architecture and welfare in Scandinavia. The book concludes with a reflection on the future of architecture and welfare, suggesting new fields of investigation and research.

FORMATIONS AND MATERIALIZATIONS

The formation of relationships between social values, populations, and physical materializations is essential to the development of welfare state architectures. The production of citizenship plays a particularly pivotal role in such processes. In "Formations and Materializations," a sociomaterial and political perspective is applied to three national contexts, each with their own sets of social values, social groups, and types of materializations.

Thordis Arrhenius analyzes welfare state housing through the case of the Swedish large-scale housing estate Navestad, which was designed and constructed in Norrköping between 1968 and 1972. Navestad's enormous, double ring-shaped housing complex, made of industrially produced concrete panels, was radically transformed and partly demolished at the end of the millennium as part of an extensive project to improve its sustainability. Arrhenius describes the stages of physical transformation of the estate's development, analyzing how such projects are perceived, redesigned, and advertised, and how ideologies and ideas of welfare are interchanging with architecture over time.

Often, Scandinavia is associated with playful innocence and the idea of happy childhoods, which has also become a cultural export. Martin Søberg interrogates this image through the Danish pedagogical ideology of *skrammellegepladsen* (the "junk playground"), where sand and scraps are the mediums for children's education in the welfare state. Søberg outlines how essential welfare concepts such as democracy, community, collaboration, production, and education were developed through children's constructions, which contrasted with the surrounding, more controlled, architectural environments of the housing estates.

Continuing with the theme of leisure, Beata Labuhn describes how mountain cabins form an essential part of Norwegian lifestyle and welfare perception. Norwegian leisure patterns have changed since the 1950s and while leisure itself results from welfare policies that ensure that the general population can afford vacations, this chapter sheds new light on transformations in the planning and use of mountain cabins. Examining the planning discussions surrounding Norwegian mountain areas in the 1960s, the history of the Norwegian mountain cabin unfolds as a complex story of the individual and collective aspects of these second-home landscapes and their transformation in line with a distinctively individualistic and privatized form of well-being.

NETWORKS AND ACTORS

Formations are not merely spatial; the professional networks of architects and planners constitute formations of welfare state architecture in their own right. These actors establish an often-invisible infrastructure that has long been neglected in the research of postwar welfare architecture. However, as the contributions in this part of the book reveal, such networks and actors exert influence well beyond the domain of architecture and the axis that joins state and citizen—a key characteristic of the Nordic Model.

Espen Johnsen argues that postwar architecture is often considered a nationally isolated phenomenon, generally evoking matters of identity and regional character and frequently being analyzed from within a national narrative. Nevertheless, Scandinavian postwar architecture and welfare share a common ground in the meetings, collaborations, and networks which emerged between architects in neutral Sweden during the Second World War, even if they were consequently interpreted in different ways by the countries involved.

Another formation of Scandinavian ideas was the "export" of the Swedish ideas of housing and housing policies. Frida Rosenberg describes the Swedish welfare state from an American perspective by outlining the visits of the famous "houser" Catherine Bauer to Sweden. Rosenberg thus highlights the extensive international networking that moved ideas between the contrasting ideological contexts and welfare regimes of Scandinavia and the United States.

Welfare state architecture also entailed crucial redefinitions of the role and responsibility of the architect. Returning to the formation of Norwegian welfare state housing policies in the 1930s, Anne-Kristine Kronborg describes how socialist architects in Norway engaged not only in their own professional environments but also in political networks, becoming political actors directly involved in public information and developing policies for housing.

The formation of the Swedish building industry is central to understanding the Swedish welfare state. Matthew Ashton and Erik Stenberg remind us that before today's perceptions of concrete as an environmentally challenging material, historical attempts were made to combine the industrial production of prefabricated concrete panels with a sophisticated interest in fine-art concrete objects. Ashton and Stenberg describe the duality of concrete as a welfare state material in Sweden (with references to Norway), understanding concrete not only as a medium that conveys social agendas and messages of technological prowess, and materializes economic rationalities, but also a vehicle of technological, social, cultural, and artistic experimentation.

DISCOURSES AND CRITIQUES

Spatial and professional formations are accompanied by discursive formations in mass media, public debates, and professional critiques. The sociopathological critique and mass media public discourses of the satellite towns in the Nordic countries that circulated around 1970 form a historical background that, beyond its role in the neoliberal transformation of such areas, continues to influence how architects, planners, and others see and talk about these types of buildings and urban neighborhoods today.

Across Scandinavia, a certain stigma is attached to the architecture and planning of the welfare state. Guttorm Ruud notes the ways in which territorial stigma was created through the critique of satellite town environments built in the late 1960s and early 1970s. In particular, he addresses a special issue of the *Sinnets Helse* (Health of the mind) magazine, known as "the Stovner report," which fueled mass media outrage and determined how this place and its inhabitants—primarily children—were to be perceived. By tracing and reframing the outcries of "children in crisis" and the critique of their living environment in this infamous report, another side of welfare and the Norwegian satellite towns emerges.[6]

A related media discourse is described by Mikkel Høghøj, who examines the creation of a new social group—"the youth"—and their association with the urban spaces of postwar welfare state housing estates, in a move that laid the groundwork for today's tendency to link certain social groups and behaviors to specific environments.

Criticism of modern suburbs has tended to land in simplistic representations of inhabitants' lives, needs, and desires, and polemic rhetorical forms. Addressing a series of reports on three modern Swedish suburbs, Jennifer Mack questions the methodological aspects of this research and makes a case for the critique of their conclusions—which, much like in Norway, had lasting effects on the public perception of modernist suburbs and housing areas.

While mass media was essential for influencing public opinion, the architectural discourse was crucial for professional reflection. Parallel to the public critical discourse was a professional debate that addressed the roles and responsibilities allocated to the architects of the welfare state. Christina Pech describes the Swedish debate in 1972 around the radio program *Det stora sveket* (The great betrayal), which claimed that welfare state architects had betrayed their social ideals.[7]

A similar Norwegian architectural analysis of the "betrayal" of the postwar generation of architects is described by Martin Braathen. Addressing the declaration of a crisis in the discipline that was issued by Marxist architects in the 1970s, Braathen considers the generational politics of architectural critique. In particular, he notes how the young Marxists of the 1970s targeted their socialist forebearers, the architects of the 1930s, who abandoned their positions of class critique to instead become social democrats and build satellite towns.[8] Not only do Pech and Braathen place welfare state architecture in another historical light, but they also actualize the discussion of architects' role and social responsibility.

6 This is described in more detail in Guttorm Ruud, "Sites of Crisis. Histories of the Satellite Town" (PhD diss., The Oslo School of Architecture and Design, 2021).
7 See Christina Pech, *Arkitektur och motstånd: Om sökandet efter alternativ i svensk arkitektur 1970–1980* [Architecture and resistance: On the search for alternatives in Swedish architecture 1970–1980] (Stockholm: Makadam, 2011).
8 For an extensive discussion of Marxist architectural critique in Norway, see Martin Braathen, "The Magician and the Shoemaker—Debates on Open Form and Marxist-Leninism in Norway around 1970" (PhD diss., NTNU, 2019).

9 For an extensive discussion on this topic, see Erik Sigge, "Architecture's Red Tape: Government Building Construction in Sweden, 1963–1973." (PhD diss., Stockholm, KTH, School of Architecture and the Built Environment, 2017).

RECONCEPTUALIZATIONS AND NEW FORMATIONS

Together, these materializations, actors and networks, and debates and critiques constitute the foundations of a number of contemporary transformations and reconceptualizations of welfare state architecture and planning. The changes that followed these "formations" included neoliberal deregulations and privatizations, which were often destructive to postwar notions of "welfare" and its architectures. Importantly, contemporary neoliberal tools and methods were often developed from within welfare state politics, through guidelines, regulations, and procedures for urban analysis. Historical notions of welfare are thus paradoxically embedded in neoliberal policies. In this complex and contradictory reality, new and creative interpretations, analyses, interventions, and perspectives are critical to the tasks of renewing, reimagining, rediscovering, and suggesting social potential in relation to welfare state architectures, cities, and landscapes.

Writing about postwar large-scale housing estate landscapes in Denmark, Ellen Braae argues that recent transformations of these areas have led to the exhaustion of their common spaces. She investigates the transformation of Farum Midtpunkt, a housing estate built in the 1970s, and theorizes the concepts of relational public spaces and their publicness searching for adequate ways to understand the role of these estates' omnipresent open spaces. In a commentary on the urban ideals of the ghetto policies, she presents an innovative analytical framework that makes it possible to see existing sociospatial qualities in a new light, a move which might inform current and future transformations.

Criticizing the transition from buildings for education to buildings as financial instruments and profitable entities, Erik Sigge addresses the example of Akademiska Hus, a Swedish state-owned property manager. This enterprise, Sigge argues, offers a prime example of the neoliberalization of an architecture originally meant to facilitate Swedish welfare policies.[9]

The development of the welfare city contradicts idealized, static notions of the "welfare city" as something belonging to the past. After outlining a history of the concept, Tom Nielsen emphasizes the complexity and heterogeneity of the Danish welfare city as it is embedded in the historic urban fabric, emphasizing the importance of imagining possible ways forward toward new urban versions.

Specific forms of the Danish city have been packaged and exported as recipes for "the good life" and "livability." Addressing the Finnish implementation of Jan Gehl's Danish model for urbanity, Leonard Ma considers how "welfare" and "well-being" are exported and transformed into instruments of urban economic development, revealing affinities between neoliberal politics and welfare urbanism.

VISUAL REPRESENTATIONS

Three photographic essays act as dividers between the book's parts, providing perspectives and angles that problematize the visual formations of Scandinavian welfare state architecture. These essays show that architectural imagery is neither obvious nor simple; rather, it conveys complex and contradictory messages, commenting on, contrasting, and illuminating idealized representations.

Aysha Amin's photographs of a transformed Danish housing estate evoke feelings of loss, but also of memory. The images are part of a search for the past that, while suggestively creating an emotional engagement with a seemingly abandoned and decaying physical environment, also offer a powerful critique of the rejection of welfare state architecture—not necessarily because of its architectural qualities but because of this environment's function as a setting for lived experience.

John Håkansson's close-up photographs of Swedish postwar suburbs contrast with monumental, heroic, or dystopic portrayals of mass housing. His photos challenge the emphasis on systems, repetition, and scale that are often present in the presentation of Swedish postwar architecture, as well as the rhetorical associations such imagery contain. The almost tactile surfaces in his photographs, which may be interpreted as formal abstractions or direct and everyday experience, remind us of more intimate features of the suburbs he visits.

For Ane Hjort Guttu, the visualization of satellite towns in the Norwegian welfare state confronts the impossibility of creating new imagery since every image appears to have already been photographed.[10] According to Guttu, we are so used to the historical photographs from architectural photographers and newspaper reportages depicting different postwar narratives (from heroism to critique) that alternative portrayals become almost unthinkable. Translated into the discourse of architecture and welfare, Guttu's photography thus suggests the difficulties of challenging established narratives and coming up with new interpretations, as one is always in danger of inadvertently reinforcing existing preconceptions instead of criticizing and challenging them.

WELFARE FUTURES

This book comes out of the research network *Nordic Models of Architecture and Welfare* (hosted by KTH Royal Institute of Technology in Stockholm). Along the way, this research environment has connected several research projects, including *Reconfiguring Welfare Landscapes*, WELLAND (University of Copenhagen); Spaces of Danish Welfare (Royal Danish Academy in Copenhagen), *Forming Welfare* (Royal Danish Academy), *Restoring the Welfare State* (Oslo School of Architecture), *Architecture in the Making: Architecture as a Making Discipline and Material Practice* (Chalmers, KTH, and LTH in Sweden), *Architecture in Effect: Rethinking the Social in Architecture* (KTH), and *The Architecture of Deregulations: Politics and Postmodernism in Swedish Building 1975–1995* (KTH). These projects have produced a number of edited anthologies, including Deane Simpson, Kirsten Marie Raahauge, Katrine Lotz, and Martin Søberg's 2022 *Architectures of Dismantling and Restructuring: Spaces of Danish Welfare, 1970–Present*; Kenny Cupers, Helena Mattsson, and Catharina Gabrielsson's 2020 *Neoliberalism on the Ground: Architecture and Transformation from the 1960s to the Present*; Sten Gromark, Jennifer Mack, Roemer van Toorn, Hélène

10 For photographic representations of the Norwegian satellite town, see also: Ane Hjort Guttu, "Å bo i drabantby" [Living in a satellite town], *Byggekunst: The Norwegian Review of Architecture* 87, no. 3 (2005): 20–31.

Frichot, Gunnar Sandin, and Bettina Schwalm's 2018 *Architecture in Effect: Volume 1: Rethinking the Social in Architecture, Volume 2: After Effects*; Katrine Lotz, Deane Simpson, Kirsten Marie Raahauge, Kjeld Vindum, Mette Jerl Jensen, and Jannie Rosenberg Bendsen's 2017 *Forming Welfare*; Jorge Otero-Pailos, Erik Fenstad Langdalen, and Thordis Arrhenius's 2016 *Experimental Preservation*; and Helena Mattsson and Sven-Olov Wallenstein's 2010 *Swedish Modernism: Architecture, Consumption, and the Welfare State*.[11]

Although this book is part of a long series of discussions, projects, and publications, it is not meant to be conclusive—we aim to raise questions and challenge assumptions, inspire further research, and inform architectural and planning practice in contemporary welfare cities. In line with this aim, two research network members, Helena Mattsson and Deane Simpson, provide an independent reflection that adds new perspectives, raises new questions, and discusses future directions for research on the developing spatialities of the welfare state. They begin by addressing geographical exceptionalism and geographical bounding and close by expanding the notion of welfare to a planetary scale, ultimately transcending the Scandinavian perspective.

Thordis Arrhenius
Ellen Braae
Guttorm Ruud

11 Deane Simpson et al., eds., *Architectures of Dismantling and Restructuring: Spaces of Danish Welfare, 1970–Present* (Baden: Lars Müller Publishers, 2022); Kenny Cupers, Helena Mattsson, and Catharina Gabrielsson, eds., *Neoliberalism on the Ground: Architecture and Transformation from the 1960s to the Present* (Pittsburgh: University of Pittsburgh Press, 2020); Sten Gromark et al., *Architecture in Effect: Volume 1: Rethinking the Social in Architecture, Volume 2: After Effects* (New York, NY: Actar Publishers, 2018); Katrine Lotz et al., eds., *Forming Welfare* (Copenhagen: Danish Architectural Press, 2017); Jorge Otero-Pailos, Erik Fenstad Langdalen, and Thordis Arrhenius, eds., *Experimental Preservation* (Baden: Lars Müller Publishers, 2016) Helena Mattsson and Sven-Olov Wallenstein, *Swedish Modernism: Architecture, Consumption, and the Welfare State* (London: Black Dog Publishing, 2010).

1 FORMATIONS AND MATERIALIZATIONS

Thordis Arrhenius

MONUMENTALITY AND MASS HOUSING IN SWEDEN

The Transformation of a Model

In 2015, the Swedish Police Authority introduced a new classification of neighborhoods (*bostadsområden*) into "vulnerable," "particularly vulnerable," and "especially vulnerable." The classification into different *stages* of vulnerability was based on the inhabitants' socioeconomic status, unemployment rate, and reported criminal activity in the area. With few exceptions, the housing areas classified were built between 1965 and 1974 and were part of Sweden's so called *Miljonprogram* (Million Program), a state-initiated program aiming to stimulate the building of affordable housing to a good standard for the general public. The Police Authority's report stated that the typical urban layouts of a Miljonprogram area, with its traffic separation, green commons, and clearly defined enclaves of houses, made it hard and dangerous or even impossible for the police to carry out their work—the call to take action was urgent.[1]

Identifying housing areas with particular needs and expected problems, which in turn are to be met and solved through extraordinary measures and strategies (often involving the reconfiguration and transformation of the built environment) suggests intriguing parallels with the Danish *Ghettoplan* ("Ghetto" package) from 2018.[2] However, in terms of this book's topic, architecture and welfare, I want to emphasize the explicit use of *housing typologies* and *urban form* as indicators of societal problems and criminality by a Swedish state authority. Several postwar mass housing estates built during the Miljonprogram era (1965–74) have been identified as vulnerable, and since the mid-1980s, subject to ambitious state-funded area-based interventions aiming to support their transformation and change. Under the name of modernization, sustainability, and restoration, Miljonprogram areas have been rebuilt and reconfigured to a larger or smaller extent. The scale of the public and market-led investment involved in such initiatives cannot be ignored. They suggest new types of political engagement in mass housing, involving new forms of financialization and architectural aesthetics, together with an explicit withdrawal from the universal tradition of Swedish housing policy established in the immediate postwar years—i.e., the aim of providing high-quality housing for all regardless of location or region.[3]

In the late 1970s, a shift in housing politics emerged as overarching national housing programs were exchanged for locally initiated, area-based interventions. In this essay, I navigate this shift by closely reading the material history of the large-scale mass housing project Navestad in the industrial city of Norrköping in central Sweden. I trace the materialization and dematerialization of the housing estate from its first manifestation as an architectural scale model in 1968 to its transformation into New Navestad in 2003. Pinpointing in this narrative three central policy documents in the history of housing politics in Sweden—*Bostadscociala Utredningen* (1945),

1 "Utsatta områden – sociala risker, kollektiv förmåga och oönskade händelser" [Vulnerable areas—social risks, collective capacity and unwanted incidents] (Stockholm: Polismyndigheten, Nationella operativa avdelningen, December 2015). See also "Riktade statsbidrag för socioekonomiskt utsatta områden" [Targeted government grants for socioeconomically vulnerable areas] (Stockholm: Riksrevisionen, 2020). For a study of vulnerable areas, see Manne Gerell et al., eds., *Att vända utvecklingen: från utsatta områden till trygghet och delaktighet* [Reversing the trend: from deprived areas to safety and inclusion] (Malmö Universitet, 2020), 59–67.

2 See *Ét Danmark uden parallelsamfund – Ingen ghettoer i 2030* [One Denmark without parallel societies—no ghettoes by 2030] (Copenhagen: Økonomi og indenrigsministeriet, 2018). For a critical discussion of the racial and punitive consequences, see: "Disguised Racism: Denmark's discriminatory, punitive and counterproductive Ghetto Package" (Euro-Med Monitor, February 2022). https://euromedmonitor.org/en/article/4898/Disguised-Racism:-Denmark's-discriminatory,-punitive-and-counterproductive-Ghetto-Package.

3 Erling Annaniassen and Bo Bengtsson, *Varför så olika? nordisk bostadspolitik i jämförande historiskt ljus* [Why so different? Nordic housing policy in a comparative historic light] (Malmö, Égalité, 2006), 160–66, see also Kristian Berg, "Det stora bostadsbyggandet" [The large-scale construction of housing], in *Rekordåren: en epok i svenskt bostadsbyggande* [The record years: an era in Swedish housing construction], ed. Thomas Hall (Karlskrona: Boverket, 1999), 24–30.

Karl-Erik Anebäck, director of Norrköpings Hyresbostäder, with a plan drawing of Navestad housing estate, pictured in the 1968 promotion pamphlet for the estate.

Architectural scale model of Navestad displayed at a press conference at the Norrköping municipality's public housing association, Norrköpings Hyresbostäder, in 1968.

4 *Navestad Bostadskomfort i Fritidsmiljö* [Navestad Residential comfort in a leisure environment] (Norrköping: Stiftelsen Norrköpings Hyresbostäder, 1968).

5 Lennart Bergentz, *Vi byggde Norrköping* [We built Norrköping] (Norrköping: Norrköpings byggmästareförening, 1993), 72–77.

6 Original quote in Swedish: "Idealbostaden, finns den? Och hur ska den vara beskaffad? De flesta människor har en vision av hur den egna bostaden bör se ut. En del drömmer om villan-markbostaden, för andra är bostaden i höghuset den ideala bostadsformen. Behoven och önskemålen skiftar, det är så många faktorer som påverkar valet av bostad, men alla vill ha en bostad, som är välplanerad, komfortabel och lättskött. [...]. Den koncentrerade men samtidigt omväxlande bebyggelsen, som anpassats efter den vackra naturen, har utformats för att passa den moderna människans krav på bostadskomfort i fritidsmiljö. I Navestad kommer att beredas plats för alla kategorier av människor, ensamstående och familjer, pensionärer och barn, för alla måste det finnas utrymme. Karl-Erik Anebäck, Norrköpings Stads Stiftelse Hyresbostäder." The quote, signed by *Karl-Erik Anebäck,* is extracted from the introduction of the presentation folder *Navestad Bostadskomfort i Fritidsmiljö*, 2.

Miljonprogrammet (1965), and *Kretsloppsmiljarden* (1995)—I speculate that Navestad operated as a *model* (an exemplar, pattern, or ideal that materialized in paper, concrete, and even rubble) revealing the changing nature, of the intersection between architecture, politics, and finance in the Swedish welfare model.

Built in 1968–72 to meet an acute housing shortage, Navestad was planned as two gigantic housing rings, each containing nearly a thousand housing units, complemented by an extensive field of 360 densely placed, low-rise, single-family homes.[4] A large and ambitious site-specific art project was part of the project, as was a novel building system of prefabricated concrete panels.[5] With its mix of high-rise and low-rise, as well as its ambitious public art project and high-quality architecture, Navestad constitutes one of the most extensive and elaborate public housing projects to be built in Sweden in the postwar period. However, suffering from a high level of vacancies and low demand, the estate was perceived as a failed project even before its completion in 1972, and at the turn of the new millennium, after a series of renovations and alterations had already taken place, Navestad was subject to an extensive "turn-around" project that radically transformed its architecture and halved the number of housing units. Despite these massive investments in the estate, Navestad was, and still is, identified by the Swedish Police Authority as a typical "vulnerable area" associated with social unrest, criminality, and low attractiveness. How, then, in terms of the specific history of the Navestad housing estate, has the interconnection of welfare and architecture played out?

THE MODEL: MASS HOUSING IN SWEDEN

> The ideal home—does it exist? And what should it be like? Most people have a vision of what their own home should look like. Some dream of a ground-level villa; for others, a residence in a high-rise building is the ideal housing form. Needs and desires change; however, while many factors affect the choice of a home, everyone wants a home that is well-planned, comfortable, and easy to maintain.... The concentrated and varied buildings, adapted to the beautiful natural landscape, have been designed to suit modern man's demands for residential comfort in a leisure environment. In Navestad, space will be provided for all categories of people—singles and families, pensioners and children—there must be room for everyone.[6]
>
> — Karl-Erik Anebäck,
> Norrköpings Stads Stiftelse Hyresbostäder

The room was crowded when the architectural scale model of Navestad was first revealed to the public in February 1968 at the headquarters of Norrköpings Stads Stiftelse Hyresbostäder (the municipality of Norrköping's association for rental housing). The housing association had invited the press to a preview of its most ambitious and large-scale mass housing project to date, and the interest was overwhelming. A snapshot shows serious-looking men in suits squeezing around the large model, pointing and discussing. Among the men, two women angle toward the model table, trying to get a glimpse. The ladies appear to be vividly engaged in discussion

7 Ahlin would collaborate with a local architect, Boris Sjön, in the development and execution of the Navestad housing estate. See further Pär Eliaeson, "Exemplet Navestad" [The Navestad example], *Tidskriften Rum*, October 2000, 30–33.

8 Björn Fontander, "Jättehus för 250 miljoner ger bostäder åt 6000" [Giant building worth 250 million provides housing for 6,000], *Dagens Nyheter*, February 13, 1968.

with Eric Ahlin, the architect behind the scheme, and his colleague Boris Sjön.[7] Present in the room is also the renowned and outspoken director of Norrköpings Hyresbostäder, Karl-Erik Anebäck, as well as representatives from Norrköpings Panelfabrik (the Norrköping concrete panel factory) and the concrete company Skånska Cementgjuteriet AB, which would not only build Navestad but later become the multinational global construction giant Skanska.

The national and local press closely followed the evolution of the Navestad housing project from the initial planning proposals in 1968 to its inauguration in 1972. On February 13, 1968, a full-length article was published in the daily liberal paper *Dagens Nyheter* with the headline "Jättehus för 250 miljoner ger bostäder åt 6000" (Gigantic building worth 250 million provides housing for 6,000), describing the high stakes surrounding the Navestad project. In the piece, journalist Björn Fontander notes that even before the project had been presented to the public, a stream of architects and delegations from different municipalities had visited Norrköpings Hyresbostäder's head office to view this impressive model of a project that would solve Norrköping's housing shortage in one go. The article describes the project, with its two large circular housing blocks—"each big enough to house the Colosseum of Rome"—as "futuristic." Within the outer housing rings, each 270 meters in diameter, an inner housing circle was planned. Between the inner and outer circle, a car-free street was raised over an undercroft garage that provided direct underground access to emergency and service vehicles. Impressed, Fontander stated that all households would be provided with parking for one to two cars and that the garage would be accessed directly by elevators from the housing units. The car-free street should be lined with trees, and instead of cars, playgrounds and sandpits would be arranged for smaller children, who could easily be surveyed from the balconies of the spacious dual-aspect apartments (which generally comprised of two bedrooms, a large living room, and a spacious well-equipped kitchen). All the entrances to the houses were oriented toward this calm, car-free street, and each of the three sections of the circular ring also opened up to form a small piazza where kindergarten and schools were located. The inner courtyard, on the other hand, Fontander notes, was planned for the older children laid out as a large, open common with several sports fields, including a circular ice rink. Fontander goes on to underline that beyond the courtyards, the rolling landscape of Vinsta forest offered further recreational spaces for winter and summer sports. In addition, where the two housing circles met, he tells the reader, a comprehensive service center with shops, schools, a swimming pool, a youth center, and a church would provide residents with everything they needed, including (although not yet confirmed) a "local police station British style."[8]

A month later, the left-wing tabloid paper *Aftonbladet* reported on the new housing scheme in Norrköping with a slightly different emphasis. Illustrated with a full image of the Navestad model and with the poetic headline "Att bo mellan trånga och vida rum" (To live between narrow and wide spaces), the article praised Navestad for the new and unconventional, strategy of combining formalism with functionality:

> The urban plan can be seen as a return to formalism in city planning. But it is a new kind of formalism, unrelated to the old façade arrangements, rather a product of functionalist ideas free from conventional thinking. … The urban plan creates a tension between intimacy and vastness. With varying building heights within its large circles, it meets the requirements for sunlight and creates an interesting rhythm. The difference between the Navestad project and previous circular buildings is primarily this spatial tension, this movement.[9]

The Swedish national press's engagement in this local mass housing project is noteworthy. As Sweden's first distinctly industrial city, Norrköping had a long history of precarious housing conditions and extreme housing shortages. From the mid-1800s onward, Norrköping grew to become Sweden's third-largest city, succeeding Stockholm as the country's leading center for textile production. The city, however, was famous not only for its prosperous textile industries but also for having one of the worst housing situations in Sweden, and even in Europe. Sweden's intense economic development in the postwar years had created not only a severe shortage of housing but also of labor. Providing affordable housing was thus not only a matter of caring for the less privileged and the poor but also a means to attract industrial workers to move to the city.[10] The lack of workforce, soaring building costs, and a real shortage of affordable housing were pressing issues in Norrköping, just as they were in Sweden in general at this time, and the housing issue engaged the political establishment on both the right and the left. The national press eagerly followed the Social Democratic-dominated Norrköping's ambition to develop a viable and cost effective model for housing the masses.

The dominant model for providing affordable mass housing in Sweden in the first part of the twentieth century was a cooperative housing model based on a membership system and collective savings toward a home. Well-known cooperative housing associations such as Hyresgästernas Sparkasse- och Byggnadsförening (HSB), founded in 1923, and Riksbyggen, founded in 1941, are still active today. Cooperatives generally build housing for private ownership but also maintain a stock of rental housing.[11] However, with the Socialdemokratiska arbetareparti (SAP, the Social Democratic Workers' Party) in power from 1932, a new model for mass housing started to take form, wherein rental housing would dominate.[12]

1945: A GOVERNMENT REPORT ON HOUSING —*BOSTADSSOCIALA UTREDNINGEN*

To survey the pressing housing situation in Sweden, a national housing study, *Bostadssociala utredningen* (The social housing investigation) was initiated in 1933. After more than a decade of thorough housing research, the study culminated in two final reports, one delivered in 1945 and one in 1947, which advanced the groundbreaking proposal that municipalities should be given extended rights to plan and control housing provision through a form of "planning monopoly."[13] This radical—and not uncontroversial—proposition would transform the provision of housing in Sweden and open the

9 Original quote in Swedish: "Stadsplanen kan sägas vara en återgång till formalismen i stadsbyggandet. Men det är en ny slags formalism som ingenting har med de gamla kulissuppställningarna att göra utan är en produkt av funktionalistiska idéer befriade från slentriantänkande. […] Stadsplanen ger en spänning mellan intimitet och stor rymd. Med olika hushöjder i de stora cirklarna klarar man kravet på solbelysning och får en intressant rytm. Skillnaden mellan Navestads projektet och tidigare byggda cirkelhus är framförallt detta rumsliga spänningsförhållande, denna rörelse." Torsten Frendberg, "Att bo mellan trånga och vida rum" [To live between narrow and wide spaces], *Aftonbladet*, March 5, 1968.

10 Lars Kvarnström, Dan Malmström, and Hans Nilsson, "Befolkning och boende" [Population and housing], in *Norrköpings historia: 1900-talet*, ed. Hans Nilsson (Linköping: Centrum för lokalhistoria, Linköpings universitet, 2000), 22–93.

11 Annaniassen and Bengtsson, *Varför så olika?* 160–66.

12 Formally, the Swedish Social Democratic Workers' Party, SAP (*Sveriges socialdemokratiska arbetareparti) is* usually referred to as the Social Democrats (Socialdemokraterna).

13 SOU (1945:63) *Slutbetänkande avgivet av Bostadssociala utredningen. Del 1. Allmänna riktlinjer för den framtida bostadspolitiken. Förslag till låne- och bidragsformer* [Final report of the Social housing survey. Part 1. General guidelines for future housing policy. Proposals for loan and grant schemes] (Stockholm: Socialdepartementet, 1945). See also Berg, "Det stora bostadsbyggandet."

way for the establishment of *allmänyttan* (non-profit housing associations) under the purview of the country's municipalities.[14] To control escalating building costs, the report recommended that *allmänyttan* build and develop housing entirely under their own administration, wholly acting as contractor developers. The new role allocated to municipal housing associations—now planners, developers, and builders—would significantly increase the rate and volume of production of affordable public housing in Sweden.[15]

The period initiated by the release of the Bostadssociala utredningen final report is, in the Swedish context, often referred to as *rekordåren* (the record years), alluding to the unprecedented volume of housing that was constructed in the form of single-family houses, row houses, and more extensive mass housing estates across Sweden. A quarter of the country's housing stock was built in 1950–75, in its totality constituting a significant national architectural heritage.[16]

The new role of the municipality in providing and building up a new stock of housing was paralleled by the extensive demolition of the older residential buildings in towns and cities across Sweden, including in Norrköping, in the 1960s. The demolition and slum clearance programs in both the inner cities and in more rural contexts were driven by concerns that the older housing stock, with its poor standards, would remain on the market as a less expensive alternative to new construction projects, undermining the ambition to raise the standard of housing and make it affordable for all.[17] Understood in this context, the recommendations of Bostadssociala utredningen established the logic for a new radical housing politics that aimed to avoid speculation by providing enough, or even a surplus of, affordable high-standard housing—in fact, to build so much housing that the shortage, the lack, would be erased and a market driven by speculation on housing shortage would be undermined.[18]

SERVING SOCIETY; THE CIVIC ARCHITECT

With its pressing housing shortage, Norrköping was among the first cities to follow the recommendations of the Bostadssociala utredningen. The year after the first report was presented, 1946, Stiftelsen Norrköpings Hyresbostäder, was founded and the first initiative to build municipal public housing was initiated with the housing area of Såpkullen. Located on the city's edge, four tower blocks were to provide housing for nurses and doctors from the nearby hospital.[19] The young Stockholm architect Eric Ahlin won the open architectural competition for the apartment towers together with Bo Ringers.[20] Having graduated only two years earlier, Ahlin had worked for Bostadsstyrelsen (the National Board of Housing), a new state authority for housing research established through the Bostadssociala utredningen.[21]

Informed by the new housing policies that emerged from the report, Ahlin wrote an article in *Byggmästaren* (the Swedish architectural review) pointing to the acute need to provide housing for the industrial worker and discussing necessary strategies for such a development. In the article, "Industrins Bostadsproblem" (The industry's housing problem), Ahlin argued that providing affordable housing for industrial workers was too crucial for Sweden's

14 For a comprehensive history of "allmännyttan," see Klas Ramberg, *Allmännyttan: välfärdsbygge 1850–2000* [Public housing: welfare building 1850–2000] (Stockholm: Byggförlaget, 2000).
15 The report also opened the way for powerful new collaborations between private and public actors. See Thord Strömberg, "Historien om bostadsmarknades politisering: socialdemokraterna och bostadsfrågan" [The history of housing market politicization: social democrats and the housing question], in *Socialdemokratins samhälle: SAP och Sverige under 100 år* [The society of social democracy: SAP and Sweden over 100 years], ed. Klaus Misgeld et al. (Stockholm: Tiden, 1989), 145–67.
16 Thomas Hall, ed., *Rekordåren: en epok i svenskt bostadsbyggande* [The record years: an era in Swedish housing construction] (Karlskrona: Boverket, 1999).
17 Martin Grander, "Allmännyttan och jämlikheten: Svensk bostadspolitik vid vägskäl?" [Public housing and equality: Swedish housing policy at a crossroads?"], Research report (Stockholm: SNS, 2020), 64. https://mau.diva-portal.org/smash/record.jsf?pid=diva2:1453153.
18 Strömberg, "Historien om bostadsmarknadens politisering," 145–67.
19 The tower blocks were planned as part of a larger housing area built by the housing cooperation HSB and primarily intended for larger families, but Såpkullen charted for a broader group in society. See Ramberg, *Allmännyttan: välfärdsbygge 1850–2000,* 115–19.
20 Ahlin won the competition with his equally young colleague, the architect Bo Ringers. They collaborated on several housing projects in Stockholm during the 1950s.
21 "Bostadspolitiken: svensk politik för boende, planering och byggande under 130 år" [Housing policy: Swedish housing, planning and construction policy over 130 years] (Karlskrona: Boverket 2007), 61–62.

industrial development to be left to the market. Similarly, the old system, whereby industry provided housing for its workers, must be revised. In the pressing housing situation, Ahlin argued that the most critical task was to create good, affordable housing for a flexible workforce that was free to follow the work rather than depend on employers for accommodation.[22] Housing as a necessary infrastructure for developing a prosperous modern industrial society informed Ahlin's argument. The provision of good, healthy, comfortable housing to everyone, everywhere, was a key to welfare and industrial development, he suggested.[23]

By winning the competition for Såpkullen in 1946, Ahlin would start a long-lasting collaboration with Norrköpings Hyresbostäder that would last over four decades. After designing Såpkullen's tower blocks on the west side of Norrköping, Ahlin was commissioned to take part in developing several new neighborhoods in primarily the southern part of Norrköping, where a total of nearly 12,000 dwellings were to be built between 1946 and 1972.[24] The swathe of public housing stretching out into the rolling open landscape for half a Swedish mile was concluded with the Navestad housing rings, which can be understood, in all their magnitude and monumentality, as the crescendo of Norrköpings Hyresbostäder and Ahlin's oeuvre in Norrköping.

THE FACTORY: PRODUCTION, INDUSTRIALIZATION, AND MASS HOUSING

With several estates built and the first part of the larger-scale housing estate of Hageby under construction, the Norrköpings Hyresbostäder rental housing association looked to increase and rationalize housing production even further. In 1964, the association formed a joint company, Norrköpings Byggelement, together with the leading concrete producer in Sweden, Skånska Cementgjuteri. With a factory producing concrete panels locally, the association took a step further in their role as developers, commissioning and building houses for the municipality and delivering building materials through a private-public partnership. With prioritized building rights on land owned by the city, Norrköpings Hyresbostäder now occupied a dominant position in relation to Norrköping's housing market. Their collaboration with a private construction firm was, however, politically complex in a municipal government dominated by the Social Democratic party, as was their commitment to limiting the need for manual construction labor; these factors contributed to its dynamic director, Karl-Erik Aneback, losing his previously strong position in municipal politics.[25]

The establishment of the concrete factory was preceded by extensive research and visits to international factories producing concrete panels. Norrköpings Hyresbostäder again commissioned Ahlin; together with the engineer Arne Johansson, a professor of construction at the Royal Institute of Technology in Stockholm, he was to develop a new method and production system for precast concret panels.[26] The system developed by Ahlin and Johnsson, the so-called *Norrköpingsmodellen* (The Norrköping model), was based on predefining a catalog of elements in measurements and sizes that could be combined in various configurations. Room-sized

22 Eric Ahlin, "Industrins bostadsproblem" [The industry's housing problem], *Byggmästaren*, no. 8 (1945): 132.

23 For the Såpkullen project, Ahlin put forward the innovative idea for a "stretchy" apartment by organizing the floorplan so that the bedroom had an individual entrance, allowing the tenants to expand or shrink their homes according to their economic situation. Såpkullen, with its "stretchy" apartments, was presented two years after in Eric Ahlin "Västra Såpkullen i Norrköping. Ett kommunalt bostadsprojekt" [Västra Såpkullen in Norrköping. A municipal housing project], *Byggmästaren*, no. 22 (1947): 318.

24 Lars Sandell, ed., *Hyresbostäder: 1946–1996* (Norrköping: Hyresbostäder i Norrköping, 1996), 77–96.

25 Bergentz, *Vi byggde Norrköping*, 73.

26 Bergentz, *Vi byggde Norrköping*, 72. For the history of concrete precast panel systems, see Erik Stenberg, "D4-gruppen 1955–1961: Pioneers of the Swedish Post War Panel Era," in *Flying Panels: How concrete panels changed the world*, ed. Pedro Ignacio Alonso and Hugo Palmarola (Berlin: DOM Publishers Berlin, 2019), 210–38. Published in conjunction with an exhibition of the same title, organized by and presented at ArkDes—The Swedish Centre for Architecture and Design, October 18, 2019–March 1, 2020.

Designed by Erik Ahlin, this housing estate in Norrköping was the first to be built in prefabricated concrete panels, delivered by Norrköpings Panelfabrik. The panels had a relief pattern by the silversmith Sigurd Persson and curved concrete balconies. Photograph by Sune Sundahl for the magazine *Betongindustrin*, 1964.

Navestad's housing estate under construction in the winter of 1969. The new industrial building methods that Erik Ahlin and Arne Johansson developed for Norrköpings panel fabrik allowed for construction during the winter. Note the snow on the concrete panels and building cranes.

27 Erik Stenberg, ed., *Structural Systems of the Million Program Era,* (Stockholm: KTH School of Architecture, 2013), 67, and Thordis Arrhenius and Marcelo Rovina Torres, eds., *RE/07* (Stockholm: KTH School of Architecture, 2024), 34–49. https://remasterstudio.com/re-07/.

28 Bergentz, *Vi byggde Norrköping*, 73.

29 Bergentz, *Vi byggde Norrköping*, 72–73.

30 Original quote in Swedish: "Vid detaljprojekteringen kommer stor omsorg att ägnas fasadutformningen och samarbete med konstnärer beträffande detaljer att ske." Quote from Bo Sylvan, *Einar Höste* (Lund: Signum, 2005), 61.

outer walls, slabs, and stairs served as the load-bearing structure, while parallel interior walls separated spaces into rooms. Openings such as windows and doors were standardized and pre-fitted in the factory. To achieve the concentric shapes, such as those required by the scheme for Navestad, the slab panels were tilted to maintain the system of rectangular façade panels when creating more complex forms. The visible joints between the façade panels and the floor slab were designed to lock when stacked into each other, rationalizing the building process and allowing for soundproofing and ventilation of the structure through the open joint. Overall, the Norrköping model was technologically advanced and driven by meticulous attention to detail, allowing for both variations and repetition within the system.[27]

The first area where the industrially produced concrete panels were used was in South Hageby, next to Navestad, through a custom-made town plan drawn by Ahlin, who also designed a large part of the housing stock. Featuring separated traffic systems, the plan was adapted to accommodate the tracks for the cranes that would lift the concrete elements. Skånska Cementgjuteriet cast the foundations on-site, but the frame came in ready-cast elements directly from the nearby factory, Norrköpings panelfabrik.[28]

TECHNOLOGY AND ART

In developing a new system for precast building elements in concrete, Ahlin cooperated not only with engineers but also initiated a strong collaboration with artists to explore the possibilities of mass production. Using different aggregates and concrete mixes to create variations of surfaces on the precast façade elements, the experiments started with large-scale concrete panels for Hageby's shopping center, executed in nearly classical geometrical forms, and continued in the Hageby housing area in Porten, where a white, marble-mixed concrete that reflected the light was used. The façade panels were cast using a flatbed mold with relief pattern inlays designed by the industrial designer and silversmith Sigurd Persson.[29] The result was a richly ornamented façade that, together with elegantly curved balcony fronts in smooth white concrete, suggested an architecture far from the frugal functionalism associated with mass housing in Sweden.

While the experimental use of factory-produced precast panels in Hageby suffered from initial technical problems, including leakage and yellowing concrete, ambitions remained high. With the factory up and running, the planning of the next large-scale housing complex, Navestad, with its two double rings of housing, would take the method of building complex forms with precast panels and the integration of art and architecture to a new level. The city plan for Navestad, dated June 28, 1966, states that the development should have an extra-high level of architectural refinement; in particular, "specific care will be taken in designing the façade and collaboration with artists regarding façade details will take place."[30]

At an early stage in the planning process for Navestad, Ahlin started to collaborate with Arne Jones, an established artist who had made several significant public artworks in Sweden. Jones was already familiar to Norrköping; in 1961, his sculpture *Spiral åtbörd*, a rotating spiral in aluminum sheeting, was installed in front of

Norrköping's leading art museum, generating a vivid discussion on the role of public art.[31] In collaboration with Ahlin, Jones made several sketch models of Navestad, studying the composition of the circular building volumes and how light and shadow were distributed on the curved façades. In an interview in 1996, Ahlin emphasized Jones' fundamental impact on the project's sculptural composition in the landscape.[32] Jones also attended to the architectural details of the houses. He designed the balconies, which, with their trapezoidal plan and light-colored concrete with a half-moon pattern, created a distinct modulation of the façade. Further and more significantly, in collaboration with Ahlin, Jones elaborated on the repetition and stacking of individual housing units in the composition of the overall façades, integrating art into the building system in a novel way. When the individual room-sized façade units, ornamented with a fluted pattern designed by Jones, were stacked together, they created giant pilasters on the façade, a form of mass ornament that bestowed a sense of monumentality to the project. The public art commissioned for Navestad underlined this theme of repetition, using identical industrially produced parts that, together, formed a larger, unique, and monumental whole.[33]

In 1967, Norrköping's art museum and Norrköpings Hyresbostäder launched a competition for the public art in Navestad. Jones was represented in the jury, and the renowned artist Einar Höste won with his large-scale proposal, *Genomgående skålform* (Continuous bowl shape).[34] Höste's proposal went beyond the competition brief, which asked for three squares to be adorned with individual art pieces, to instead incorporate the whole colossal housing ring in his scheme. The jury's motivation for the first prize read: "This proposal is ambitiously conceived and adheres to the fundamental architectural concept of Navestad."[35]

Höste's sculpture was composed of 57 sculptural elements evenly distributed along the pedestrian street between the circular structures, with a particular concentration in two of the three squares. Each element consisted of a sandblasted, gently concave, rhomboid aluminum plate supported by aluminum square columns of varying heights, ranging from 3 to 13 meters. The individual sculptural elements of the work were strategically placed to collectively form fragments of an enormous bowl, with its center situated in the heart of the housing ring.[36] The artwork also included outdoor furniture, playgrounds, paving, and ornamental details for planting boxes and the children's sandpits all designed by Höste in collaboration with both Jones and Ahlin. Like the architecture of the housing rings, Höste's and Jones' art was built of individual compositional fragments that, together through their arrangement in space, formed a larger whole: a colossal sculpture. Indeed the integration of art and architecture, functionality and form, dominated both the conception and the production of Navestad's mass housing project. As suggested by the architect and critic Pär Eliaeson, one of the few who has studied the formal composition of Navestad's architecture in more detail, the public art in Navestad, with its allusions to the monumental architectural qualities of the numerical organization of the two double-housing rings, took on mythical, almost cosmic, dimensions.[37] Although today it is both altered and neglected, Höste's sculpture in Navestad remains one of Sweden's most comprehensively executed public artworks.[38]

31 Arne Jones' abstract sculpture *Spiral åtbörd* created a vivid public debate about the elitism of modern art, but when Norrköping's main department store, Spiralen (the Spiral), used Jones' sculpture as its logotype, *Spiral åtbörd* caught the public imagination and has since been used in various ways as a symbol for the city of Norrköping. See "Spiral åtbörd, Arne Jones (1914–1976)," Norrköpings konstmuseum, accessed October 4, 2024, https://www.norrkopingskonstmuseum.se/offentlig-konst/spiral-atbord-1961-arne-jones-1914-1976/.

32 Eric Ahlin is interviewed in a study of Navestad from 1998 by the architects Nilsson Samuelsson and Pär Eliaeson. This is one of the very few instances in which the collaboration between Jones and Ahlin has been documented and confirmed by Ahlin. See Nilsson Samuelsson and Pär Eliaeson, "Exemplet Navestad – arkitektur och politik i Sverige 1998" [The example of Navestad—architecture and politics in Sweden 1998], accessed October 4, 2024, http://pe-ark.com/navestad1998/exempel/.

33 There is sparse information on how the collaboration between Jones and Ahlin took place. However, according to the art historian and later director of Norrköping Art Museum Bo Sylvan, Jones was deeply involved in the design of façade details. See Sylvan, *Einar Höste*, 59–74. Several study models of Navestad can be found in Västernorrland museum's Arne Jones collection.

34 "Tävlan om ordnande och konstnärlig utsmyckning av tre torgmiljöer" [Competition for the organization and decoration of three squares], announcement in several national papers including *Göteborgsposten*, October 2, 1967. see also Kristian Romare, *Tre torg i Navestad* [Three squares in Navestad] (Norrköping: Norrköpings museum, 1968).

35 Original quote in Swedish: "Detta förslag är stort tänkt och fullföljer den arkitektoniska idé som ligger till grund för Navestad." Cited in Sylvan, *Einar Höste*, 62.

36 Sylvan, *Einar Höste*, 59–74.

37 Eliaesson, "Exemplet Navestad," 30–33.

38 Einar Höste and Arne Jones were both part of the exhibition Konst i Betong [Art in concrete] at Modern Museum in 1964. See the catalogue for the exhibition: Pontus Hultén and Olle Rinman, *Konst i betong* [Art in concrete] (Stockholm: Moderna Museet, 1964).

The first of the two housing rings in Navestad was finished in 1971. The local photographer Lennart Jansson followed the evolution of the housing estate from laying the foundation to the first tenants moving in. These images show the pedestrian lane between the housing rings, which featured playgrounds, sandpits, and artwork designed by Einar Höste and Arne Jones.

The pedestrian lane between the low-rise and high-rise buildings in Navestad with balconies and entrances. Part of Einar Höste's monumental artwork can also be seen. Photograph by Lennart Jansson, 1971.

In 1972, when the second housing ring in Navestad was completed, Lennart Jansson started documenting how the children played in the open spaces. The inner circular courtyard, with its sports fields, newly planted trees, and landscaped grounds, functioned as a large open playground for older children.

1965: A NATIONAL HOUSING PROGRAM —MILJONPROGRAMMET

Navestad was realized as part of *Miljonprogrammet*—the program guiding the construction of one million housing units across Sweden between 1965 and 1974. On a national level, the program was part of a state effort to control an overheated building market, where the shortage of housing and construction workers kept inflating the cost of building.[39] Even before the program was launched, the rate of housing production in Sweden was high—nearly on the same level as in the years after the program was established. While the cost targets formulated in the 1945 Bostadssociala utredningen had mainly been reached by the mid-1950s, the housing shortage persisted.[40] Low, regulated rents, in combination with continued strong urbanization rates, had created growing housing queues that were increasingly burdensome for the ruling Social Democratic party, which was accused of creating a *kö-samhälle* (a society of queues), where you had to line up for welfare.[41]

A new governmental investigation, *Bostadsbyggnadsutredningen* (The residential building investigation), was appointed in 1957; led by the influential housing researcher Lennart Holm, the investigation estimated that to meet demands for higher-quality housing, a minimum of 1.5 million housing units needed to be constructed between 1960 and 1975. The previous standard of two rooms and a kitchen for a family of four, further, should be raised to three rooms and a kitchen. The investigation's final report, *Höjd bostadsstandard* (Raised building standards), published in 1965, emphasized the role of rationalization and industrialization in tackling the increasing construction costs associated with higher spatial standards, and the report is often seen as the beginning of Miljonprogrammet, although this name was coined later. Following the report's release, every year between 1965 and 1974, the Swedish Parliament granted loans for around 100,000 homes.[42]

The state loans targeting the building of housing benefited large projects of over 1,000 units which used a single building system, encouraging rationalization and industrialization. This affected the structure and size of the organizations that executed the work. The rationalization of the building industry not only limited demand for construction workers in terms of skills and numbers but also created several large-scale building companies, which controlled and steered the market between them. Previously to the Miljonprogram, smaller developers had dominated. Typically, building sites brought together craftsmen with different skills who often traveled long distances and lived in temporary accommodation, constituting an unruly and unpredictable workforce. Equally important, although less noted, construction was typically seasonal work; with the new industrially produced building system, production could take place all year round, speeding up construction times and evening out demand for manual labor between seasons.[43]

It has been suggested that it was not the number of housing units but the restructuring of the building sector that was the most significant and long-lasting effect of the Miljonprogram, a shift which continues to resonate within the structure of Swedish construction industry today. The program was part of the cementing of a financially driven housing policy and a building industry colored

39 Olof Eriksson, *Byggbeställare i brytningstid: bostadssektorn och statligt byggande under miljonprogramsperioden* [Building clients at a time of change: the housing sector and state construction during the Million Program period] (Stockholm: Statens råd för byggnadsforskning, 1994), 157–66.

40 Based on an industrial worker salary, the aim was that the rent for a family should not be more than 20 percent of the family income. Hall, *Rekordåren: en epok i svenskt bostadsbyggande*, 25.

41 See Berg, "Det stora bostadsbyggandet," 24–30.

42 SOU (1965:32) *Höjd bostadsstandard* [Raised building standards] (Stockholm: Prisma, 1965), 32. See also Eriksson, *Byggbeställare i brytningstid*, 47–78.

43 Alan Skarne, *Med kran och krok* (Stockholm: Ohlsson & Skarne Byggförlag, 1987), 11–24. See also Eriksson, *Byggbeställare i brytningstid*, 157–61.

by corporatism and characterized by building monopolies.[44] The objective to rationalize the Swedish building industry, implemented through the building loan system—where the state stood for the financial risk, while the building industry stood for quick and effective delivery—was, however, highly successful in terms of the numbers of units produced: within less than ten years, the shortage of housing was turned into a surplus.

SLEEP FACTORY

In June 1971, the daily newspaper *Dagens Nyheter* returned to Norrköping to report on the progress of the Navestad housing project.[45] It dedicated an entire spread to the housing scheme. In contrast to the newspaper's 1968 article, a new critical stance against industrial building and large-scale mass housing can be discerned. *Dagens Nyheter*'s initial overwhelming enthusiasm for the utopian housing scheme of Navestad was replaced by a suspicion of social failure, exploitation, and corruption. Under the double-edged headline "Cirkelrund sovfabrik intressantast i Sverige" (Circular sleep factory Sweden's most interesting), the journalist Mert Kubu, who often reported on housing issues under the mocking pseudonym *husbocken* (the old house borer), was clear in his judgment:

> The most exciting district in Sweden right now is undoubtedly Navestad on the outskirts of Norrköping. One can like the circular houses, which accommodate 5,700 inhabitants. One can dislike them. But you won't be indifferent after walking between the houses in the alleys. Among all the ugly, boxy and boring concrete neighborhoods that have sprung up in recent years, Navestad is undeniably an attempt at innovation.[46]

Although impressed by the architecture, Kubu expresses hesitation about the new mass-produced suburbs that tend to be, as the headline suggests, reduced to "sleep factories." However, the critique of Navestad does not stop there; the journalists suggest that the large mass housing project generates new "foreign" social problems unfamiliar to the Swedish welfare state. A more disturbing headline in the Norrköping spread foreshadowing later dominant narratives of segregation and racism: "Bostad i 'Harlem' väntar invandrare" (A home in "Harlem" awaits immigrants), which reported that:

> Norrköping risks being given its own Harlem—a district where social problems will pile up. Around one in three inhabitants of the not-yet-finished Navestad is an immigrant. Investigations show that 30 percent of the population in the northern ring is dependent on social benefits. Norrköping's citizens frown at the circular suburb. The neighborhood is left behind for the poor and the immigrants.[47]

Yet another headline hints at political corruption: "Byggkungarna bestämmer i Norrköping" (Constructions bosses run Norrköping). As an industrial working-class city where the Swedish Social Democrats had traditionally occupied a dominant position, Norrköping was often associated with strong class antagonisms. However, the

44 See, for example, the argument developed in Helena Mattsson, "Where the Motorways Meet: Architecture and Corporatism in Sweden 1968" in *Architecture and the Welfare State,* ed. Mark Swenarton, Tom Avermaete, and Dirk van den Heuvel (London: Routledge, 2015), 155–75.

45 Under the main headline "DN synar Norrköping" [DN investigates Norrköping], we find three articles on page 23–24 together with statistics and images reporting on the building of Navestad by the journalists Mert Kubu and Reinhard Kruse: "Cirkelrund sovfabrik intressantast i Sverige," "Bostad i 'Harlem' väntar invandrare," and "Byggkungarna bestämmer i Norrköping," *Dagens Nyheter,* June 8, 1971.

46 Original quote in Swedish: "Den intressantaste stadsdelen i Sverige just nu är helt säkert Navestad i utkanten av Norrköping. Man kan tycka bra om de cirkelrunda husen som rymmer 5700 invånare. Man kan tycka illa om dem. Men likgiltig blir man inte efter en promenad i gränderna mellan husen. Bland alla de fula dussinstadsdelar i fyrkantig betong som vuxit upp under de sena åren är onekligen Navestad ett försök till nytänkande." Mert Kubu, "Cirkelrund sovfabrik intressantast i Sverige," *Dagens Nyheter,* June 8, 1971.

47 Original quote in Swedish: "Norrköping hotar att få ett eget Harlem en stadsdel där de sociala problemen hopas. Omkring var tredje invånare i det ännu inte färdigbyggda Navestad är invandrare. Utredningar visar att 30 procent av befolkningen i den helt färdiga norra ringen är socialhjälpsberoende. Det etablerade Norrköping rynkar på näsan åt den cirkelrunda förorten. Stadsdelen 'blev över' åt fattiga och åt invandrare." Reinhard Kruse, "Bostad i 'Harlem' väntar invandrare," *Dagens Nyheter*, June 8, 1971.

articles suggest another reality where the Social Democratic Party-controlled municipality collaborated with, or was even steered by, private capital and cooperations:

> It is the private builders, the developers, the big bosses of HSB and Riksbyggen who decide how the town plans should look and how the land should be distributed in Norrköping. Oddly enough, the political parties have placed them all at the spoils of power (*maktens köttgrytor*) in Norrköping's building and urban planning committees. There, cases are handled according to the law under the greatest confidentiality—to "prevent land speculation." [48]

Taken together, the articles associate the mass production of pub lic housing not with welfare and well-being but with estrangement, exploitation, and corruption.[49]

THE MARKET: RESTORATION AND INVESTMENT

The close alliance between the building industry and housing politics had made possible the provision of high-quality, affordable housing to the masses as outlined by the Social Democrats in 1967: "Society's housing provision should be to ensure that the *entire population* is offered healthy, spacious, well-planned, and suitably equipped homes of good quality at reasonable costs." [50]

When the Millionprogram ended in 1974, there was more than enough affordable housing for all. However, this saturated housing market was now understood to affect the building industry and the labor market negatively. The housing politics of the Miljonprogram had produced a new generation of privately owned corporate construction companies, yet had removed the driving force that created them: the overproduction of housing removed the very market dynamic that these companies grew to fill. In a Fordist welfare state, characterized by a close alliance between industry and politics, between capital and state, surplus production was equally as problematic as empty shelves. Another housing issue emerged, not in terms of lack of provision but in terms of overproduction. From the point of view of municipalities around the country, vacancies and unwanted housing areas were becoming the new housing issue to engage in. *Allmännyttan*—both as a political concept and as a housing provider to the general public—was plunged into crisis.

FROM HOUSING SHORTAGE TO HOUSING SURPLUS

During the final construction phase of the second ring in Navestad, the housing situation in Norrköping had gone from one of acute shortage to that of surplus; a global recession was in the offing, and locally, the decline of the Swedish textile industry had caused Norrköping to slip in relative size and lose its status as an industrial city. In 1970, the last textile factory was shut down in the center, and the same year, as part of an ambitious regeneration of the town from a craft-based industry to a knowledge-based industry, a new university campus was established in the old industrial area

48 Original quote in Swedish: "Det är privatbyggarna, fastighetsmäklarna, HSB- och Riksbyggenpamparna som bestämmer hur stadsplaner skall se ut och hur marken skall fördelas i Norrköping. Märkligt nog har partierna placerat dem vid maktens köttgrytor i Norrköpings byggnadsnämnd och i fastighetsnämnden. Där behandlas ärenden enligt lag under största sekretesskydd – för att "förebygga markspekulation." Mert Kubu and Reinhard Kruse, "DN synar Norrköping," *Dagens Nyheter*, June 8, 1971.

49 The DN articles suggest that it is the developers that steer the development of the city—as representatives on building and planning committees, developers get access to confidential information that they use to increase their profit. In the popular local narrative, this strong alliance between private developers and the municipality has been coined as "the spirit of Norrköping," see Mats Granberg, *Norrköpingsandan: Texter från Norrköpings Tidningar* [The spirit of Norrköping: Texts from Norrköpings Newspapers] (Norrköping: Norrköpings stadsbibliotek, 2012), 7–10.

50 Original quote in Swedish (italics by author): "Samhällets mål för bostadsförsörjningen bör vara att hela befolkningen skall beredas sunda, rymliga, välplanerade och ändamålsenligt utrustade bostäder av god kvalitet till skäliga kostnader." Proposition 1967:100 angående riktlinjer för bostadspolitiken, cited in Hall, *Rekordåren: en epok i svenskt bostadsbyggande*, 30.

Navestad Housing Estate in Norrköping with the surrounding landscape of Vinsta forest, photographed by Joakim Kröger in 2000, just before the demolition and renovation of the estate started. The housing blocks closest in the image were lowered from eight to four floors.

As a research project, the architects Pär Eliaeson and Nilsson Samuelsson lived for three months in Navestad in 1998 to document the housing estate before the renovation began in 2000. The photograph shows the view from their apartment toward Vinsta forest.

Navestad housing estate with its green mature landscape and large trees. Photograph by Pär Eliaeson and Nilsson Samuelsson, 1998.

51 Bergentz, *Vi byggde Norrköping*, 75.
52 Sandell, *Hyresbostäder 1946–1996*, 77–96.

in the core of Norrköping. Now, the focus in the municipality went from building mass housing on the outskirts to regenerating Norrköping's city core.

After the extensive Navestad project, Norrköpings Hyresbostäder experienced financial problems and needed to be heavily subsidized by the municipality. In 1972, the concrete factory closed, and the private-public venture between Skånska Cementgjuteriet and Norrköpings Hyresbostäder ended. The housing associations' dire economic situation was partly a result of vacant flats in Navestad (the area was fully occupied only during a short period in the mid-1980s) but also partly caused by reduced building activity.[51] Since its establishment in 1946, Norrköpings Hyresbostäder has dominated the real estate market in Norrköping, enjoying beneficial state loans for housing, financial assets, and turnover generated through building projects. With its factory closed and with hardly any new building activity, Norrköpings Hyresbostäder's income now primarily had to come from rent. As a regulator of the rental housing market and a non-profit housing company, Norrköpings Hyresbostäder had traditionally aimed to keep rents low; besides making it even harder to fill increasing vacancies, raising rents was a controversial option. In this pressed economic situation, the upkeep and maintenance of the Norrköpings Hyresbostäder housing was put on hold, and the new utopian housing schemes soon became shabby and worn.

THE REAL ESTATE MARKET AND PUBLIC HOUSING

In the 1980s, Stiftelsen Norrköpings Hyresbostäder was transformed from a non-profit association into a limited company (Hyresbostäder i Norrköping AB) to be run as an ordinary real estate company owned by the municipality. In contrast to commercial companies, however, and since it had previously been a non-profit housing association, Hyresbostäder i Norrköping AB had no liquid capital investments at its disposal. To commence operations and raise capital, it started to sell off extensive parts of its housing stock to private developers. The main focus within Hyresbostäder now was making their remaining tenement housing attractive in a housing market where both private and social landlords had vacancies. The slogan of Hyresbostäder shifted to *Konsumenten i centrum* (the consumer at the center) and in the new, competitive rental housing market, architectural transformations, and stylistic visual changes would become tools to generate interest and attraction in relation to a "hard-to-sell" product.[52]

Hyresbostäder i Norrköping's transformation from a non-profit association to a profit-making real estate company was part of a larger systemic shift in Swedish economic politics that, in the end, would fundamentally alter the role of *allmänyttan* as society's main provider of affordable, high-standard housing for the general public. In 1992, a coalition government of Liberals and Social Democrats formulated a new overarching housing policy based on freedom of choice. A previous tax reform, popularly named *Århundrades skattereform* (the tax reform of a century) implemented in 1990–91, had lowered individual income tax to provide households more freedom to decide over their disposable income. The lost tax

53 Grander, *Allmännyttan och jämlikheten: Svensk bostadspolitik vid vägskäl?*, 64. See also: Bo Bengtsson, "Allmännyttan och bostadspolitiken i går, i dag, och i morgon – institutionella förutsättningar i förändring" [Public housing and housing policy yesterday, today, and tomorrow – changing institutional conditions], in *Nyttan med allmännyttan*, ed. Tapio Salonen (Stockholm: Liber 2015), 25–47.

54 See Martin Granders definition of public housing and the regimes of housing: Martin Grander, "For the Benefit of Everyone? Explaining the Significance of Swedish Public Housing for Urban Housing Inequality" (PhD diss., Malmö University, 2018), http://urn.kb.se/resolve?urn=urn:nbn:se:mau:diva-7437.

revenue was partly financed with decreased state subsidies for public housing. For *allmännyttan*, the reform led to a 50 percent nominal rent increase over three years in the early 1990s.[53]

In reality, the increase in housing costs for tenants caused a reduction in disposable income and, particularly amongst lower-income groups, less economic freedom rather than more. With raised rents, households with stable incomes opted for home ownership. With favorable tax reductions, owning your house was now an economically affordable and more economical option for an industrial worker than renting in *allmännyttan*. The mass housing estates of the Miljonprogram, which since the recession and the vacancies of the 1970s had acquired a bad reputation, were now the prevailing option for groups that, for different reasons, could not obtain a mortgage (the elderly, the young, the unemployed) or those that were not included in the welfare system (guest workers, immigrants, and refugees). Regardless of their architectural form and urban layout—large scale or low scale, high-rise or low-rise, individual dwellings or mass housing—the socioeconomic and racial segregation of the Milljonprogram housing areas was now fully in the making.

The most significant change to *allmänyttan* was the phasing out of state-subsidized loans, which removed the financial advantages and unique position that municipal housing associations had gained in 1945. With the same financing conditions as other players in the housing market, the associations' role in providing good, affordable housing for all was over, and with this, the general idea of affordable housing as part of welfare politics.[54]

1995: STATE FUNDING FOR SUSTANABILITY IN HOUSING: KRETSLOPPSMILJARDEN

It is, however, also crucial to note that although state housing subsidies were phased out, they were replaced by a new financial and political engagement in public housing. In the 1990s, as part of the *new economy*, state initiatives in public housing shifted from establishing grand national programs such as Miljonprogrammet based on universal principles of welfare to supporting local projects addressing particular problems in defined areas. As explained previously, the Swedish state had neither invested nor built public housing directly, but rather through an elaborate set of qualified and interest-controlled loans, it had steered investment in housing toward specific goals and numbers. Now, state funding for public housing was open to competitive bidding by municipalities, which in turn formed public-private partnership teams to develop business cases for the destination of state funds. To be able to bid successfully, you had to identify problems urgent enough to attract the funding. "Relevance" and "impact" became essential terms in this endeavor.

One of the larger state funds specifically targeting Miljonprogram areas was *Kretsloppsmiljarden* (The sustainability billion), established by the Social Democratic government in 1995. Although only 30 years had passed since the Miljonprogram was launched, areas built during the program were identified as urgently needing renovation. As part of an employment package directed toward the building industry, one billion SEK (Swedish kronor, equivalent 100

55 Propositionerna 1995/96:207 and 1995/96:222.

56 Kretsloppsmiljarden Propositionerna 1995/96:207 and 1995/96:222. See also Åsa Vifell, "Kretslopsmiljarden och de lokala investeringsprogrammen. Framgång för miljön – nederlag för förvaltningsmodellen" [The Kretslopsmilarden and the local investment programs. Success for the environment—failure for the governance model], in *Processer i Regeringskansliet – sex fallstudier*, SCORE reports (Stockholm: SCORE, 2001), 51–78.

57 For the effect and evaluation of the Lokala investeringsprogrammet (Local Investment program) on the million program areas see: Sonja Vidén and Marina Botta, *Bostadsförnyelse och miljöåtgärder med stöd av lokala investeringsprogram: Hållbar utveckling i 50–60–70-talens bostadsområden"* [Housing renewal and environmental measures with the support of local investment programs: Sustainable development in the residential areas of the 50s, 60s and 70s], final report for the FoU project "Hållbar utveckling i 50-, 60 och 70-talens bostadsområden – 'gröna' mål möter mark, hus och människor" (Stockholm: Arkitekturskolan KTH, 2006). See also Sonja Vidén, "Vård och förändring av hus och utemiljöer" [Care and alteration of buildings and outdoor environments], in *Rekordåren: en epok i svenskt bostadsbyggande*, ed. Thomas Hall (Karlskrona: Boverket, 1999), 133–94.

58 In 2025, Norrköping municipality and Norrköpings Hyresbostäder are planning to alter Navestad's community space and shopping areas; the latter is to be transformed into a recycling center that is open to the public and the former is to be moved into one of the housing rings, where, at a significant cost, housing was converted into offices in the 1990s (which today lies vacant).

59 For an informed discussion of the shift toward the bottom up and activation of local society in Swedish politics and urban theory, see Magnus Dahlstedt, "The Politics of Activation: Technologies of Mobilizing 'Multiethnic Suburbs' in Sweden," *Alternatives* 33, no. 4 (October, 2008): 481–504, https://doi.org/10.1177/030437540803300405.

million EUR) were allocated to adapting existing buildings' building practices in line with concepts of sustainability and renovation.[55] Grant applications for Kretsloppsmiljarden were intended to include educational and research-orientated aspects, as well as to support knowledge transfer between projects. However, these aspects were challenging to deliver, as the funds were also subject to competition between municipalities. Applying for funding was complex, as the definition of outcomes and results were vague and hard to decipher. Intriguingly, the government itself approved and evaluated applications for the Kretsloppsmiljarden, diverging from a long tradition in Sweden of delegating such decisions to expert groups or dedicated departments with concrete knowledge of the field.[56] Kretsloppsmiljarden, as a state initiative to invest in and support mass housing, stood in stark contrast to both Bostadssociala utredningen and Miljonprogrammet with their strong focus on scientific expertise and universal application. Now, the knowledge and expertise should grow from an area's local and specific needs and problems. In 1998, the ambitions of the Kretsloppsmiljarden were broadened in the "Lokal investeringsprogrammen" (local investment programs). The programs now included a total of 7.2 billion SEK (700 million EUR) and would have a fundamental impact on steering the transformation and rebuilding of the Miljonprogram-era housing area through economic incentives supporting local private-public partnerships.[57]

RESTORING THE WELFARE STATE: FROM MILLION PROGRAM TO BILLION PROJECT

Change is an integral part of Navestad's material history, from the completion of the first housing ring in the 1970s to the renovation project that took place in the first decades of the new millennium and through to today (2025), the housing estate has been characterized by the continuous transformation of its built structures.[58] From its inauguration in 1972, several more or less long-lived initiatives, led by various combinations of public actors and local interest groups, worked to alter the negative image of the estate to make it more attractive, initially at a relatively modest scale. Participatory projects, primarily involving tenants living on the estate, aimed to stimulate social interactions between new and old tenants. Norrköpings Hyresbostäder supported a local newspaper combining user information and news stories about the estate.[59] This was followed by a series of alterations of the apartment layouts, to make larger units into smaller ones in order to attract students, and single households. These minor, often bottom-up alterations, driven by local forces, had an effect: in the mid-1980s, the estate was fully occupied for the first time. However, in 1987, funded by a dedicated state grant toward renovation and rebuilding, a more extensive restoration of the common areas was initiated. The open public spaces of the inner courtyards and the surrounding landscape were subdivided to create private front gardens, and individual allotment gardens in the surrounding fields were made available. In the same spirit, the housing block's exposed ornamented concrete panels were painted over in different pastel colors, dividing the circular housing areas into "slices of cake," where each wedge was allocated a dedicated housing steward. The individual housing units were also changed at this time, but now with a focus on creating larger apartments with the argument that a better mixture between small and more significant flats could provide more variation and attract new tenants. Another project aimed toward diversification was a larger investment to rebuild part of the unrented housing blocks into offices for state institutions to introduce workplaces in the area. However, these more substantial changes did not increase interest in moving into the estate, and the number of vacant apartments began to rise. The municipal reorganization in the early 1990s, based on a purchaser-provider model with a competitive situation between different municipality units, made collaborations and local initiatives harder to coordinate, and toward the 1990s, local engagement in Navestad started to fade out, and many initiatives and collaborations ended.[60]

With an increasing number of vacant flats, the need for a more comprehensive approach to the problems faced by Navestad was identified by Norrköping municipality, and in the mid-1990s, under the name Nya Navestad (New Navestad), an ambitious "turn-around" project was launched with the objective to raise state and private funding.[61] Under the banner of sustainability, Nya Navestad was to finally and conclusively transform the estate's architecture through partial demolition and configuration.[62] The overall aim was to lower the scale of the building and open up the estate to the surrounding areas. In the original scheme, building heights varied between eight and three stories to maximize the sunlight access for apartments and create variations and a play of shadows on the façade. The highest blocks were oriented toward the motorway and the north, while the lower blocks were oriented south to allow views of the open landscape and the Vinsta forest and recreation area. Ahlin's and Jones' formal composition was driven by the idea of creating rhythm by way of differences between open and closed spaces; the alleys leading into the central courtyard from the exterior were deliberately narrow and intimate to emphasize the large open spaces within.

Intending to scale down the estate, the Nya Navestad project transformed the site-specific and ecological values (the maximizing of sunlight) of the Navestad project. By cutting down the high-rise, eight-story apartment blocks that aligned the higher blocks with the lower ones, a more uniform layout was created. Similarly, the housing rings were divided into smaller housing blocks. This radical and expensive alteration cut them in half to make more prominent entrance points into the protected inner space. This resulted in a more substantial visual presence of the motorway and changed the acoustic environment; the aim of excluding traffic noise in the inner courtyards was undermined, as was the original compositional idea of the architect of creating a closed shared neighborhood space in the inner rings.

This shift between variation and repetition was also altered regarding the individual housing units. The original layout and distribution of the 1972 project aimed to equalize quality among individual units. All flats had double-aspect views, sunlight, and balconies. The Nya Navestad project, on the other hand, strove to create variation through difference. An added pitched roof and rooftop apartments, clad with wood and with generous private

60 At the end of the Balkan war, the estate Navestad was temporarily turned into a refugee camp, with displaced people being housed in the vacant apartments. Many of the refugees found a permanent home in the estate which facilitated integration into the Swedish society. For an account of rebuilding and alterations prior to *Nya Navestad* see Sandell, ed., *Hyresbostäder 1946–1996*, 77–96. For the planning process leading to *Nya Navestad* see Katja Ketola, "I mötet mellan projekt och process: om samverkan och tillit i förnyelse av ett bostadsområde" [The meeting between the project and the process] (Lic.diss., Chalmers tekniska högskola, 2000).

61 Granberg, *Norrköpingsandan: Texter från Norrköpings Tidningar*, 7–10.

62 See the argument on governmentality, sustainability, and participatorial processes when establishing the *turn-around* project of Navestad 1998 in Sophia Lövgren, "Att skapa ett framtidens folk: governmentality och miljödiskurs i modern svensk bostadspolitik: miljonprogramsområdet Navestad" [To create the future people: Govermentality and environmental discourse in modern Swedish housing policy: the suburban area of Navestad] (PhD diss., Linköpings universitet, 2002). See also Åsa Bråmå, *Går det att vända utvecklingen i utsatta bostadsområden?: exemplet Navestad/Ringdansen i Norrköping* [Is it possible to reverse the trend in vulnerable residential areas? The example of Navestad/Ringdansen in Norrköping], CSK report (Centrum för kommunstrategiska studier, Linköpings universitet, 2011).

In 2003, the balcony façade was replaced with a glass-fronted design and external rainwater pipes replaced the fluted pilasters ornament. Photographed by John Håkansson in 2023.

The scaled-down Nya Navestad, with its lower housing block in orange and a single sculpture fragment previously belonging to Einar Höste's large-scale sculpture *Skålform* was photographed by John Håkansson in 2023.

Navestad's original ornamental concrete panels and balcony fronts were replaced in 2003 with a smooth plaster façade in various colors. Photographed by John Håkansson in 2023.

63 Vidén and Botta, *Bostadsförnyelse och miljöåtgärder med stöd av lokala investeringsprogram*, 77–81.

64 Kjell Löfberg and Henrik Witt, "Miljard lyfter miljonförort," *Dagens Nyheter*, Oktober 19, 2003.

terraces, introduced an unfamiliar hierarchy between the existing housing units. Now, some flats were more exclusive than others. Yet overall, the changes introduced made the housing area more uniform, and anonymous. The sculptural expression of the façade was toned down; the triangular-shaped concrete balcony fronts, with their ornamented half-moon pattern designed by Arne Jones, were exchanged for transparent off-the-shelf glass.

The recladding of the façade to add insulation covered the exposed concrete panels and the different textures and grains of their ornamented surfaces. Altogether, these alterations exchanged the sculptural concrete panel expression and rich large-scale ornamentation for a smooth, undecorated plaster façade in various pastel colors—pink and warm yellow. In one way, this referred stylistically back to the early history of social housing from the 1920s, the minimal ornamentation of which had signaled simplicity and economy of means in contrast to the heavy façade ornamentation of the nineteenth century. On the other hand, the new, smoothly rendered façade aesthetics, in combination with transparent glass balconies, related Navestad to contemporary commercial housing from the 1990s. The estate looked more ordinary and newer, although it was still large and repetitive.

This lengthy and total makeover was completed in 2003 at the impressive cost of one billion Swedish kronor (100 million EUR), quadrupling the original construction cost of 250 million Swedish kronor. The Nya Navestad project received 260 million in direct governmental grants from Kretsloppsmiljarden, and a consortium of private developers, and the municipality stood for the rest.[63] In the local press, Navestad was nicknamed "the Billion Program."[64] In this state-sponsored rebuilding, the initial 2,000 housing units were reduced to around 1,000, partly by combining smaller flats into bigger ones but mainly through demolition. When the Swedish State, for the first time, invested directly in public mass housing at this scale, it was not to provide more housing but to provide *less*.

THE RUIN: THE LEGACY OF A MODEL

In all its complexity, Navestad illustrates the history of housing the masses in Sweden. The conception, materialization, and dematerialization of its monumental structures reveals the potency of the intersection between architecture, politics, and finance in the Swedish welfare model—and how it has changed. The 1945 Bostadsociala utredningen had argued for the establishment of non-profit municipality-driven housing associations with the argument that the market, in the end, could not produce enough affordable housing in time. The market was driven by demand, and only a lack of housing generated the incentive to start building. Therefore, the market was always "late," and as Ahlin argued in his 1945 article on the housing question, this delay hindered a working, modern industrial society.

When Navestad was completed in 1972, Ahlin was interviewed by the left-wing tabloid paper *Aftonbladet* regarding the philosophy and future of public housing. His response emphasized the need for community and well-being when building housing, and he argued strongly for variation, good services, and shared spaces, all of which had been central to Ahlin in the planning of Navestad. However, when asked about the future of public housing, Ahlin interestingly argued that the notion of a permanent home of one's own might soon be outdated:

> If you look more generally at the living environment of the future, I think that people's attachment to a particular home will become weaker. This has to do with people changing jobs and occupations several times during their working life. The labor market is becoming more mobile geographically. In such a society it will not be so practical or self-evident to commit to a self-owned home. Instead of ownership, a rental mindset breaks through. We are witnessing a "rental revolution" that drastically changes the relationship between people and objects.[65]

Ahlin echoes the rhetorics advanced by the radical architects who initiated Bostadssociala utredningen in the first place in the 1930s.[66] In the model for housing the masses put forward in the housing investigation, the home was imagined not as an investment object floating on a speculative market, nor as a place of belonging and permanence, but rather as one of convenience and service: a neutral background to a life lived. Access to a healthy, affordable home was like free health services, education, and social security, one of several keys to a modern welfare society of independent, equal individuals.

The opening iconic image of the Swedish architectural manifesto of 1931 *acceptera*, titled "Individen och massan" (The Individual and the Mass) summarizes this utopian dream of an architecture that is not about individual expression or class identification or difference but about being of use, of *allmännytta* ("useful to all").[67] A well-planned architecture that, in its functionality and reticent beauty, would work for everyone—rich or poor, young or old. Yet, looking in the rearview mirror, this ideological and radical objective of freeing the home from vested desires and speculation was short-lived. In the neoliberal reality of Sweden today, public housing is part of the economic toolbox of municipalities. Housing, as well as other welfare buildings such as schools and libraries, are part of a real estate game wherein property is bought and sold in line with the directives of the municipality's yearly budget. Indeed, housing is no longer an infrastructure supporting industrialization but, in itself, an industry driving a market.

Yet the sturdy remnants of the political idea of architecture *as* welfare are still with us. If the political model for housing is lost, its material manifestations still work hard and—despite their worn surfaces—still serve us. The impressive and monumental circular housing ring of Navestad and its adjacent low-rise carpet of terraced housing still constitute a durable, even magnificent, welfare architecture heritage. It still provides homes of a good standard to thousands of Norrköping's citizens from far and near. Under the peeling, light pastel-colored façade of the 1990s renovation, giant fluted pilasters worthy of a palace of another era may once again be rediscovered. To great wonder, in the alleys between the rings, a sculpture park of cosmic dimensions may one day be unearthed, and with it, the question of how a previous society could afford such investments in public art and architecture.

65 Original quote in Swedish: "Ser man mera allmänt på framtidens bomiljö så tror jag att människornas bindning till en viss bostad blir svagare. Det hänger blanda samman med de stora förändringarna inom arbetslivet med arbets- och yrkesbyten flera gånger under en människas yrkesliv. Arbetsmarknaden blir mera rörlig också rent geografiskt. I ett sådant samhälle blir det inte så praktiskt eller självklart att binda sej vid en självägd bostad. I stället för ägande bryter ett hyrestänkande igenom. Vi får en 'hyresrevolution' som på ett drastiskt sätt ändrar förhållandet mellan människor och föremål." Eric Ahlin quoted in Ragnar Amrén, "Arkitekten, hur ska vi bo i framtiden?," *Aftonbladet*, February 20, 1972.

66 See SOU (1935:2) *Bostadssociala utredningen* (Stockholm: Socialdepartementet, 1935) and Eva Rudberg, *Uno Åhrén: en föregångsman inom 1900-talets arkitektur och samhällsplanering* (Stockholm: Statens råd för byggnadsforskning, 1981).

67 Gunnar Asplund et al., *acceptera* (Stockholm: Tiden, 1931), 2.

Individen och massan . . .

Det personliga eller det allmängiltiga?
Kvalitet eller kvantitet?
— en olöslig frågeställning, ty vi kan icke komma ifrån kollektivitetens faktum lika litet som vi kan komma ifrån individens fordran på självständigt liv.
Problemet heter i våra dagar:
kvantitet *och* kvalitet, massa *och* individ.
Det är nödvändigt att söka lösa det även i byggnadskonsten och konstindustrin.

"The Individual and the Masses." Cover image of the Swedish modernist manifesto *acceptera* from 1931 written by Gunnar Asplund, Wolter Gahn, Sven Markelius, Greger Paulsson, Eskild Sundahl, and Uno Åhren as a response to the critique of the 1930 Stockholm Exhibition and its modern architecture.

Martin Søberg

DANISH PLAYGROUNDS AND THE FORMATION OF THE WELFARE CITIZEN

During the interwar and postwar decades, Danish playgrounds were intended to contribute to the formation of productive, creative, and democratic welfare citizens. They would gain increasing attention and financial support by municipalities and the state along with the professionalization of childcare as part of social and educational welfare measures. Since then, the emphasis has shifted from children's constructive and creative play, emulating the sort of play one would find amongst children in the countryside, to children's experiences and development of competences, thereby resonating with a growing appreciation of the agency of architecture as part of the experience economy and the neoliberalization of society.[1] Beyond the ideas of "the good life," which sustained previous versions of the Nordic welfare society, ideas of individuality and "good experiences" have become prevalent. Each child should be allowed to express and unfold her or his "potential," rather than confining to a predetermined figure of an ideal welfare citizen—or perhaps this is precisely the figure of a new, updated version of the ideal Nordic welfare citizen.

By the turn of the twenty-first century, the integration of play and nature resulted in so-called "nature playgrounds," which could either be playgrounds built with natural materials or playgrounds which provided experiences and activities related to nature. In 1997, Friluftsrådet (The Danish outdoor council) organized an ideas competition on nature playgrounds and stated that "Children should have experiences of nature as a natural part of their everyday life, for instance in the nature playground, even though this never can or should replace the experience of the real forest, beach, or field!"[2] Nature itself was seen as a cause, since nature playgrounds would help "children grow up as considerate users of nature and environment" and furthermore that play at nature playgrounds would stimulate children's positive development with positive consequences in terms of health, motor functions, and concentration.[3]

The prominence of sensory experiences and health is repeated in descriptions of the nature playground in Copenhagen's Valby neighborhood, published by VisitCopenhagen, a media brand run by Wonderful Copenhagen, the official tourist organization in the Copenhagen region, which states that "you will find outdoor challenges and playful experiences that can get your heart rate up."[4] In today's Nordic welfare society, playgrounds have become part of city branding and tourism marketing strategies. Yet in comparison with their interwar and postwar counterparts, contemporary playgrounds rely on a slightly more passive engagement with matter. While the welfare society still plays an active role in securing space for children to play, the ideas of what this does to children have changed. This chapter explores the discourse and design of playgrounds as part of Danish welfare measures. It includes

1 Helena Mattsson, *Architecture and Retrenchment: Neoliberalization of the Swedish Model across Aesthetics and Space, 1968–1994* (London: Bloomsbury Visual Arts, 2023); Anna Klingmann, *Brandscapes: Architecture in the Experience Economy* (Cambridge, MA and London: MIT Press, 2007).

2 Original quote in Danish: "Børn bør have naturoplevelser som en naturlig del af deres dagligdag, f.eks. på naturlegepladsen, selvom denne aldrig vil og bør kunne erstatte oplevelsen af den ægte skov, strand og mark!" Friluftsrådet, *Naturlegepladser* [Nature playgrounds] (Copenhagen: Frie Børnehavers Forlag, 1998), 4.

3 Friluftsrådet, *Naturlegepladser*, 3.

4 "Nature Playground," Visit Copenhagen, accessed March 2, 2024, https://www.visitcopenhagen.com/copenhagen/planning/nature-playground-gdk493825.

Nature playground, Valby, designed by landscape architect Helle Nebelong, 1994–2004.

considerations of how ideas of children and the usefulness of playgrounds as enculturating social technologies aided the formation of the ideal citizen of the welfare society, tracing changes to these ideas from the mid-nineteenth century until today.

WELFARE AND PLAY

Securing spaces for children was part of the task of the Nordic welfare society during the interwar and postwar decades, not only as part of the "welfare landscapes" of educational programs, which included schools and kindergartens, but also in the context of housing estates and in urban parks and squares.[5] Children were an important target group of welfare spaces, since they were considered to be particularly malleable and in need of care, and thus covered by society's guarantee to provide settings for "the good life." Indeed, children became symbolic figures in the foundation of the welfare society as such and its specific spatializations.[6] Playgrounds are spaces designed for the activities of children yet designed by adults who often have specific ideas about children and how those spaces will affect children. They are also a means of getting children off the street, for security reasons and to allow traffic to run more smoothly. In the Nordic welfare society, playgrounds became settings for educating children to become productive, cultured, and democratically minded citizens, thereby sustaining the welfare society's foundational ideals of participation and equality. These ideas reflected the modern perception of pedagogies as part of a process of enculturating the child, stimulating development. The child was perceived as being "unfinished"—that is, in the process of becoming an adult and thereby an active, contributing member of society. Concurrently, the child was perceived as being in a more "natural" or "wild" state, ready for enculturation just like other "primitive" human beings. Sometimes, this resulted in Social Darwinist attitudes which viewed the child as developing according to natural laws from a primitive or natural state toward cultured adulthood.

Playgrounds were spaces in which considerations pertaining to productiveness, naturalness, health, and cooperation—key ideological aspects of the welfare society—clearly unfolded; in a Danish context, this was particularly apparent in two specific types of playgrounds: the *sand playground* and the *junk playground*. While the former type was imported from other European countries, the latter was invented by the Danish landscape architect C. Th. Sørensen, an important contributor to the design of Danish welfare landscapes during the mid-twentieth century. The junk playground became an international success, inspiring the construction of similar junk or, as they are sometimes called, *adventure playgrounds* in other European countries and the US.

SAND PLAYGROUNDS

The attention to play as a developing factor was already characteristic of pedagogics during the nineteenth and early twentieth centuries. Play was not valuable as such but was a means to developing useful citizens. This idea of children as being in formation, contrary to

5 Concerning the notion of welfare landscapes, see Ellen Braae, Svava Riesto, Henriette Steiner, and Anne Tietjen, "Welfare Landscapes: Open Spaces of Danish Social Housing Estates Reconfigured," in *Mass Housing of the Scandinavian Welfare States: Exploring Histories and Design Strategies*, ed. Miles Glendinning and Svava Riesto (Edinburgh: University of Edinburgh, 2020), 13–23; and Ellen Braae, *Urban Planning in the Nordic World* (Aarhus: Aarhus University Press; Madison, WI: University of Wisconsin Press, 2022).

6 Martin Søberg, "Children as Symbolic Figures in Welfare Space Photography," in *Architectures of Dismantling and Restructuring*, ed. Kirsten Marie Raahauge et al. (Zurich: Lars Müller Publishers, 2022), 50–71. See also Ning de Coninck-Smith, *Barndom og arkitektur: Rum til danske børn igennem 300 år* [Childhood and architecture: 300 years of spaces for Danish children] (Aarhus: Klim, 2011); Roy Kozlovsky, *The Architectures of Childhood: Children, Modern Architecture and Reconstruction in Postwar England* (London and New York: Routledge, 2013); and Marta Gutman and Ning de Coninck-Smith, "Introduction: Good to Think with—History, Space, and Modern Childhood," in *Designing Modern Childhoods: History, Space, and the Material Culture of Children*, ed. Marta Gutman and Ning de Coninck-Smith (New Brunswick, NJ: Rutgers University Press, 2008), 1–19.

7 J. Lauritsen, *Underholdende og dannende legemsøvelser for unge mennesker, især drenge i hjemmet og paa skolens legeplads* [Entertaining and formative physical exercises for young people, especially boys at home and on the school playground] (Copenhagen: Chr. Steen og Søns Forlag, 1865), 3.

8 Legeplads-Foreningen, *Legeplads-Foreningens anden beretning* [The Playground Association's second report] (Copenhagen: O.C. Olsen, 1896), 3–4. Annette Westermann, "De første offentlige legepladser" [The first public playgrounds], *Legepladsen* 3–4 (2009): 12–13.

9 Original quote in Danish: "Bestyrelsen har opfattet det som sin Opgave ikke blot at tilvejebringe Legepladser, men ogsaa at bidrage til at fremme den ordnede Leg. De store Byers indsnævrede Plads hæmmer den frie Leg, forhindrer Børnene i at lege mange af de bedste og fornøjeligste Lege, som de ældre huske fra deres Børneaar." Legeplads-Foreningen, *Legeplads-Foreningens anden beretning*, 5.

10 The articles were published in 1890 and 1891 and reprinted as a small book; see Rigmor Bendix, *Om legepladser* [On playgrounds] (Copenhagen: Fr. G. Knudtzons Bogtrykkeri, 1891).

11 Original quote in Danish: "Børnene vide slet ikke, hvor de skulle gjøre af deres unge Livslyst. Der er ikke det Sted, hvor de kunne vende sig hen med deres Fantasi, med deres Byggelyst og Undersøgelsestrang.... Lidt Grus og Jord, Pinde, Smaasten kunne gjøre et Barn i Timesvis lykkeligt—og artigt." Bendix, *Om legepladser*, 5–6.

adults, was a significant part of welfare society programs during the interwar and postwar decades. Many of society's institutions—older ones like schools and newer ones like public kindergartens—were aimed at contributing to this development and social construction of useful citizens out of the natural phenomenon that is children.

Playgrounds as urban sites designated for child play had already appeared in Copenhagen during the final decades of the nineteenth century. Previously, children had been playing in the streets or on the terrain of the old city fortifications, which were now partly being demolished to make room for new urban quarters including new public parks. The first rather simple municipal playground was established in one of these parks, Ørstedsparken, and constructed between 1876 and 1879. It consisted of an open space with gravel paving intended for children's ball and song games. Playgrounds could however also be found in connection with schools and were used especially for physical exercise. As the teacher J. Lauritsen had argued in an instructive publication in 1865, such exercising was both entertaining and educational and would contribute to a positive development of people's character and freedom.[7]

The early playgrounds in Copenhagen often came about through collaborations between private philanthropists and public institutions. Legeplads-Foreningen (The Copenhagen playground association) was founded in 1891 and established a playground on Grønningen the same year on a site made available by the Ministry of War. Contrary to the playground in Ørstedsparken, it comprised various kinds of play equipment, including swings and seesaws, and featured activities organized by adults.[8] Rigmor Bendix, chair of the association, stated in 1896: "The board has considered it its task not only to provide playgrounds, but also to contribute to the promotion of ordered play. Large cities' limited space inhibits free play, prevents the children from playing many of the best and most amusing games that older ones remember from the childhood years."[9] Curiously, for Bendix, "ordered" and "free" play did not seem to be in conflict. On the contrary, the spatial and behavioral ordering conducted by adults was presented as a prerequisite for the free play of children. Society rescued children from the streets, where many of them would previously have been playing, and provided a space for children's enjoyment and the development, display, and continuation of cultural practices. This reads as a premonition of later welfare programs which would emphasize well-being and culture.

Prior to the foundation of Legeplads-Foreningen, Rigmor Bendix had published several articles on playgrounds in the Danish newspaper *Berlingske Tidende*, calling for more playgrounds to be established.[10] As she stated: "The children do not at all know what to do with their young lust for life. There is no place to where they can turn their fantasy, their urge to build and examine.... A bit of gravel and dirt, sticks, pebbles, could make a child happy for hours—and well-behaved."[11] Hence, rather than the organized activities that she would refer to a few years later, Bendix pointed to things that would be abundantly available for play to children in the countryside—that is, natural things. Indeed, she stressed how children in the city occasionally would behave just like children in the countryside, when they were building and playing on unoccupied urban sites. Concurrently, emphasis was put on good behavior, and while children should be provided with certain degrees of freedom it was important that this

Temporary sand playground in the City Hall Garden, Copenhagen, 1907.

The landscape form of the beach emulated as a sand playground by landscape architect C. Th. Sørensen in the courtyard of the Klokkergården housing estate, Copenhagen, 1938–39.

did not result in chaos. This points to an ambiguous idea of the child around the turn of the twentieth century, which was seen as being in need of freedom but also of education, not least to secure its development in a direction deemed valuable by society. This view was also connected to certain aesthetic views on the city and to questions of beauty. After all, when playing, children easily end up getting dirty. Bendix quoted art history professor Julius Lange, who stated at a meeting that "the time will come when a place with playing children will not be perceived as the ugliest sight, even if each one of them isn't very nice."[12]

A large heap of sand was placed in Copenhagen's City Hall Garden in 1907; this was the first Danish sand playground. It immediately became very popular yet was only a temporary installation. The year after, sand was part of a playground opening on the Elephant's Bastion in the Christianshavn neighborhood, where the old ramparts were still intact; the idea of sand playgrounds soon spread throughout the country. Usually, the sand would be structured by a wooden frame, as a sandbox, and tables to play at would be placed in the sand. The sand playground or sandbox allowed for a stimulation of the enterprise of children, which was seen as healthy and edifying. Pedagogically, sand playgrounds had roots in the romantic movement of the eighteenth and early nineteenth century, for instance in the ideas of Jean-Jacques Rousseau and the German romantic writer Jean Paul.[13]

The head teacher Hans Dragehjelm published the book *Barnets leg i sandet* (The child's play in the sand) in 1909 and contributed to the introduction of sandboxes in Denmark, based on international inspiration. He wrote enthusiastically about the bodily sensations that children experience when playing with sand, comparing their creativity to that of an artist: "Rightly understood, children don't play in the sand. They work like the artist at his work of art. Pose questions to them when they shape and build, speak to them—they will hardly answer! Thoughts and ideas are born and realized, and that doesn't tolerate interruption. This pursuit is such an utterly selfish satisfaction that something bigger hardly exists."[14] The sand would, so to speak, guide the child in its development, it would have an enculturating effect, contributing to developing the child into an "understanding and useful world citizen" and it furthermore encouraged cooperation.[15]

Dragehjelm claimed that playing with sand would contribute to the development of the child's ability to perceive spatial objects and figures, and three-dimensionality as such through bodily sensation, in particular the sensations of the hands in contact with the sand.[16] These ideas were influenced by the pedagogy of Friedrich Fröbel and others. As mentioned, sand also had creative potential, stimulating the imagination of the child: "To the child, the sand play is a language closely related to sketching and drawing with a lead or a slate pencil. Through it, fantasy acquires air, and it is this silent but visible language that delights the audience hungry for spectacle."[17] In line with the philosophy of object lesson pedagogy, Dragehjelm described the "work" with the sand masses as "practical" physics and mathematics, which would prepare the children for "actual work."[18] Again, play and playgrounds were considered elements in the enculturation of children to being useful citizens, that is, productive workers. This might not necessarily relate to a welfare

12 Original quote in Danish: "den Tid vil komme, hvor man ikke anser det for det styggeste Syn at se en Plads med legende Børn, selv om hvert enkelt af dem ikke er saa fint." Bendix, *Om legepladser*, 28. See also Rodrigo Pérez de Arce, "Sand and Snow," in *City of Play: An Architectural and Urban History of Recreation and Leisure* (London: Bloomsbury, 2018), 83–84.

13 See for instance: Jean Paul Friedrich Richter, *Levana; Or the Doctrine of Education* (London: George Bell and Sons, 1898 [1807]), 156–57.

14 Original quote in Danish: "Ret forstaaet, leger Børn ikke i Sandet. De arbejder som Kunstneren ved sit Værk. Ret Spørgsmaal til dem, naar de former og bygger, tal til dem,—der svares næppe! Indfald og Ideer fødes og virkeliggøres, og dette taaler ingen Forstyrrelse. Denne Syslen er en saa inderlig selvisk Tilfredsstillelse, at der næppe gives nogen større." Hans Dragehjelm, *Barnets leg i sandet: Vejledning og vink for hjem, skole og legeplads* [The child's play in the sand: Guidance and tips for home, school, and playground] (Copenhagen: Tillges Boghandels Forlag, 1909), 10. Decades later, Dragehjem would publish an article with a similar title, yet a different content, describing in detail the history and practices of sand play. Hans Dragehjelm, "Barnets leg i sandet" [The child's play in the sand], in *Lærebog i dansk skolesløjd: Smaasløjdssystemet* [Textbook in school crafts], ed. G. F. Krog Clausen, Th. Rasmussen, and R. C. Rasmussen (Copenhagen: L. A. Jørgensens Bogtrykkeri, 1934), 20–54.

15 Original phrase in Danish: "forstaaende og nyttig Verdensborger" Dragehjelm, *Barnets leg i sandet* (1909), 13.

16 Dragehjelm, *Barnets leg i sandet* (1909), 19–20.

17 Original phrase in Danish: "Sandlegen er for Barnet et Sprog, der er i nærmeste Slægtskab med dets Skitseren og Tegning med Blyant eller Griffel. Igennem det skaffer Fantasien sig Luft, og det er dette tavse, men synlige Sprog, der henrykker det skuelystne Publikum." Dragehjelm, *Barnets leg i sandet* (1909), 23.

18 Dragehjelm, *Barnets leg i sandet* (1909), 64.

society ideology, but indeed to ideas of a close relationship between citizens and society. Dragehjelm displayed a pastoral and vitalist attitude according to which children should develop their skills, but in a natural, entrepreneurial way, getting accustomed to work and gaining empirical knowledge of materials and natural forces. As such, play was free, but also useful as part of the development of the child. In his publication *Børns frie leg og legepladser* (Children's free play and playgrounds) published in 1918, he even metaphorically likened children to animals: "Let the child flutter in its butterfly flight and don't touch the dust on its wings!" [19] Children were somehow less spoiled by culture than perhaps adults and playing with sand would keep them innocent from the vices of modern urban life.

JUNK PLAYGROUNDS

The domesticated nature of the mid-twentieth-century playground designed by C. Th. Sørensen or other landscape architects related inherently to a concept of the child as pure potentiality. The child was a sensible adult in formation, yet still in a state of savageness which was gradually diminishing through processes of enculturation. In this sense, children could be likened to plants, their wildness could indeed be tamed and arranged into the formats of society. It was the task of society to perform this enculturation, a process of care by which the welfare society demonstrated its strengths whilst also sustaining itself as a system which needed a constant influx of new citizens. Sørensen pointed to landscape forms that could be emulated in the design of urban playgrounds. As he stated in 1952: "The sand playground should be like a beach which as a matter of course is a wonderful playground." [20] He used such forms as motifs, for instance, in landscapes that he designed in connection with large housing estates during the interwar and postwar decades such as Hjortekær, Højstrupparken, and Tingbjerg, which contained abstracted versions of the groves and deciduous forests typical of the Danish landscape. Such reference to specific landscape forms, motifs, or even landscape pictures had already been present in the work of Danish landscape architect G. N. Brandt, who preceded Sørensen by a generation, yet Sørensen turned this kind of imitation into a higher level of abstraction and stylization.[21] His designs included hedges, hedgerows, orchards, and groves, which were all part of the Danish agricultural landscape.[22] Questions of naturalness were similarly pertinent to the design of playgrounds, often with reference to images of what was considered a typical Danish landscape.[23] The idea was that this naturalness would help children become *healthy*, i.e., natural, individual beings; the enterprise and ingenuity which characterized rural child life was further seen as foundational to the development of healthy welfare citizens.

Sørensen introduced the idea of the junk playground in his book *Parkpolitik i sogn og købstad* (Park politics in parish and market towns) published in 1931 by Dansk Byplanlaboratorium (The Danish town planning institute).[24] Its expressed intended readers were municipal politicians, amongst whom it aimed to stimulate discussion of, in the institute's terms, "park politics"—that is, planning matters regarding green open spaces. Its chapters were organized typologically, focusing, for instance, on cemeteries, road plantation, and

19 Original phrase in Danish: "Lad Barnet flagre i sin Sommerfugleflugt og rør ikke Støvet paa dets Vinger!" Hans Dragehjelm, *Børns frie leg og legepladser* [Children's free play and playgrounds] (Copenhagen: Jul. Gjellerups Forlag, 1918), 24.

20 Original phrase in Danish: "Sandlegepladsen skal være som en strand, der uden videre er en herlig legeplads." C. Th. Sørensen, "Den store have" [The great garden], *Arkitekten månedshæfte* [The architect monthly] 54, no. 1–2 (1952): 45.

21 Malene Hauxner, *Fantasiens have* [The garden of fantasy] (Copenhagen: Arkitektens Forlag, 1993), 151.

22 Annemarie Lund, *Danmarks havekunst III, 1945–2002* [The art of the Danish garden III, 1945–2002] (Copenhagen: Arkitektens Forlag, 2002), 86–87.

23 These images of the typical Danish landscape were established during the nineteenth century; see Gertrud Oelsner, *En fælles forestillet nation: Dansk landskabsmaleri 1807–1875* [A collectively imagined nation: Danish landscape painting 1807–1875] (Copenhagen: Strandberg Publishing, 2022).

24 C. Th. Sørensen, *Parkpolitik i sogn og købstad* [Park politics in parish and market town] (Copenhagen: Gyldendal, 1931).

Junk playground in Emdrup, as part of landscape designed by C. Th. Sørensen, 1943.

Junk playground in Emdrup, as part of landscape designed by C. Th. Sørensen, 1943.

sports grounds. The chair of the institute, Kai Hendriksen, argued in his foreword that such politics would not only benefit and bring joy to all citizens in a "modern, healthy, and democratic way," but that they might even, consequently, bring down expenses in relation to hospitals and prisons.[25] Children's playgrounds were the "first and chief item on the urban park program," according to Sørensen, especially since more and more children were growing up in apartment buildings without gardens.[26] He was particularly critical toward urban apartment buildings where no play areas were provided, a topic he addressed specifically in an article in *Arkitekten* (The architect) a few years later, in 1935.[27] Sørensen provided concrete details on how playgrounds should be laid out: they should be large, sunny, provide shelter and sand, grass and water should preferably be present.[28] He also mentions how children would often prefer to play on unbuilt plots, "they are used for play by the children who, wherever possible, dig caves, set up tents, create gardens and what else children occupy themselves with." [29] It led him to the idea of the junk playground: "Perhaps here we could try and organize a sort of *junk playground* on appropriate and rather large areas where the children would be allowed to make use of old cars, packing cases, brushwood, and those sorts of things." [30] The idea of an actual junk playground was further developed in Sørensen's 1935 essay on apartment building gardens:

> I imagine an area which shouldn't be too small, closed toward the surroundings by thick and dense plantations; here, to the joy of larger children, all sorts of old junk should be collected which the city children from the apartment blocks could work with, just like the children in the countryside and the suburbs have. There could be branches and rubbish from the pruning of trees and bushes, old cardboard boxes, pieces of wooden boards in general, "dead" cars, scrap tires and other things which would be a joy to lively boys to make something out of. It would naturally look terrible and naturally would have to be kept in some sort of order, but I think that such a thing wouldn't go all wrong.[31]

In 1943, the first junk playground was laid out in Emdrup in Copenhagen in connection with the housing estates Emdrup Vænge and Emdrup Banke, built by Arbejdernes Andels Boligforening (the Workers Cooperative Housing Association) in 1938–43 and designed by the architect Dan Fink. In collaboration with Fink, Sørensen designed the junk playground, consisting of a 60 by 80 meter lawn surrounded by 2-meter-high banks with plantation and a wire fence. It included an open shed, toilet, and drinking fountain. In the beginning, it was only open during the summer season from April 1 until October 31. Here, children were allowed and encouraged to build on their own using scrap materials and the playground soon attracted hundreds of children, although providing enough materials proved rather difficult during the first couple of years of the playground's existence, not least due to the scarcity of materials caused by the Second World War.[32] As Ning de Coninck-Smith has argued, the idea was to transform the children into responsible citizens by training their abilities to act on their own and to provide them with ingenuity and a sense of collaboration and democracy.[33] The junk playground in Emdrup attracted

25 Original phrase in Danish: "*moderne, sund og demokratisk Maade.*" Original italics. Kai Hendriken, "Forord [Foreword]," in Sørensen, *Parkpolitik*, 6.

26 Original phrase in Danish: "det første og vigtigste punkt i byernes parkprogram." Sørensen, *Parkpolitik*, 49.

27 C. Th. Sørensen, "Etagehusets have" [The gardens of multi-story buildings], *Arkitekten maanedshæfte* 37, no. 4 (1935): 49–64.

28 Sørensen, *Parkpolitik*, 52–54.

29 Original phrase in Danish: "de udnyttes til leg af børnene, som hvor de kan komme til, graver huler, opsætter telte, anlægger haver og hvad børn nu ellers beskæftiger sig med." Sørensen, *Parkpolitik*, 54.

30 Original phrase in Danish: "Måske kunde vi her forsøge at indrette en slags skrammellegeplads på passende og ret store arealer, hvor børnene fik love at udnytte gamle biler, pakkasser, kvas og den slags ting." Sørensen, *Parkpolitik*, 54.

31 Original phrase in Danish: "Jeg tænker mig et areal af ikke alt for ringe omfang, vel lukket for omverdenen med tykke og tætte plantninger; her skulde man samle til større børns fornøjelse alt muligt gammelt skrammel, som bybørnene fra etageboligerne kunde få at virke med, som børn på landet og i forstæderne nu har det. Her kunde være grene og affald fra beskæring af træer og buske, gamle papkasser, bræddestumper i det hele taget, 'døde' biler, kasserede dæk o.m.a. som det vilde være en fryd for raske drenge at få noget ud af. Naturligvis vilde der se forfærdeligt ud, og naturligvis måtte der holdes en vis orden, jeg vil dog tro, at det ikke behøvede at gå helt galt med noget sådant." Sørensen, "Etagehusets Have," 61.

32 Agnete Vestereg, "Skrammellegepladsens historie" [The history of the junk playground], in *Skrammellegepladsen i Emdrup 1943–1968* [The junk playground in Emdrup 1943–1968] (Emdrup: Skrammellegepladsen i Emdrup, 1968): 3–25. The programme of the junk playground was described by John Bertelsen as a new kind of empirical science: *skrammologi* ("junkology"). John Bertelsen, "Skrammologi" [Junkology], *Arkitekten månedshæfte* 54, no. 1–2 (1952): 35–43. See also Ole Schultze Henriksen, *Skrammellegepladsen* [The junk playground] (Frederiksberg: Dansk Pædagogisk Historisk Forening og Samling; Videncenter for Pædagogiske og Sociale Studier – CVU København og Nordsjælland, 2006); and Ida Vestergaard, "Skrammellegepladsen i dag" [The junk playground today], *Legepladsen* [The playground] 1–2 (2006): 3–5.

33 Ning de Coninck-Smith, *Skrammellegepladsen* [The junk playground] (Aarhus: Aarhus Universitetsforlag, 2022), 7.

international visitors, including, in 1946, the British landscape architect and philanthropist Lady Allen of Hurtwood, who subsequently introduced the concept in the UK, now renamed "adventure playground." Concurrently, a similar type of playground appeared in Switzerland, where it was called a "Robinson playground" after Robinson Crusoe. It also led to similar playgrounds being laid out in various parts of Denmark.

PRODUCTIVITY AND COOPERATION

The postwar baby boom and the rising number of women engaging in paid work resulted in an increasing demand on institutions and care for children. In the Nordic welfare society, it was seen as the obligation of the state to provide such services. According to de Coninck-Smith, the sand playground took traditional play with whatever materials were available such as dirt, pebbles, and sticks and made it more organized, more hygienic, even stimulating the craftsman or engineer in the children.[34] Hence it was a means of formation itself, even if appearing to be more natural and relaxed. As de Coninck-Smith had pointed to, playgrounds became part of the care of children and not only a question of moral education and of getting children off the streets. Pedagogically, rather than the previous disciplining and instructing attitude, emphasis was increasingly put on the active, creative, and curious child.[35] The junk playground expressed this shift, imitating the sort of play which would previously have taken place in rural areas and on unbuilt urban plots, often without interference from adults. As such, it can be viewed as a critique of education and pedagogical measures, and an attempt to enculturate the child toward becoming a productive, active, and morally healthy citizen.

C. Th. Sørensen recognized that the aesthetics of the junk playground differed from conventions. As he stated in 1950: "Of all the things that I have been part of realizing, the junk playground is the ugliest, however to me it is the loveliest and best of my works." [36] These domesticated, urban landscapes of play were aestheticized emulations of existing landscape forms, although also allowing for cracks of destruction and messiness. In his book *Haver: Tanker og arbejder* (Gardens: Thoughts and works) published in 1975, Sørensen emphasized the junk playgrounds as a way of introducing the qualities of the countryside into the modern city: "The considerations which led to the junk playground were based on experiences from the countryside, although I myself hardly used the good conditions that lakes, meadows, and woods offered.... By now it is very clear to me that for outdoor play we should provide the children with three landscape forms, create such ones for them." [37] Those three main forms were the beach, the meadow, and the grove:

— *The beach*: that should be in connection with sand playgrounds and paddling pools but seems to be a more unsolvable problem than spacecrafts. How can that be?
— *The meadow*: fields of grass to play on, that is rather easy.
— *The grove* (i.e., wooded plantations): that is possible, but one problem is that it takes time before the trees are large and strong enough for play.[38]

34 Ning de Coninck Smith, "Den historiske legeplads" [The playground in history], *Legepladsen* 3–4 (2009): 8.
35 De Coninck-Smith, *Skrammellegepladsen*, 36–40.
36 Original phrase in Danish: "Af alt det, som jeg har været med til at føre ud i livet er Skrammellegepladsen det grimmeste, for mig er den dog det skønneste og det bedste af mine arbejder." C. Th. Sørensen, "Skrammellegepladsen" [The junk playground], *Byplan: Vore byer og deres planlægning* [City plan: Our cities and their planning] 2, no. 1 (1950): 3.
37 Original phrase in Danish: "De overvejelser, som førte til skrammellegepladsen, byggede på erfaringer fra landet, men selv udnyttede jeg kun i ringe grad de gode betingelser, som søer, enge og skove bød. ... Efterhånden står det mig ganske klart, at til udeleg skulle vi kunne give børnene tre landskabsformer, skabe sådanne til dem." C. Th. Sørensen, *Haver: Tanker og arbejder* [Gardens: Thoughts and works] (Copenhagen: Chr. Ejlers, 1975), 133.
38 Original phrase in Danish: "*Stranden*, det må blive en forbindelse af sandlegepladser og soppedamme, men det synes et mere uløseligt problem end rumfartøjer. Kan det virkelig være sandt? *Engen*, græsflader, der kan leges på, det skulle være så temmelig let. *Lunden*, d.v.s. skovlignende plantninger, det lader sig gøre, men et problem er, at det tager tid, inden træplanter er store og stærke nok til leg." Sørensen, *Haver*, 134–36.

The emulation of existing landscape forms not only ensured continuity between nature and culture, and between childhood and adulthood, but also between a premodern rural society and a modern urban society based on the productivity and ingenuity of the citizen, the development of which was stimulated and encouraged in the sandbox and the junk playground. In 1945, architect and urban planner in Copenhagen Max Siegumfeldt published a "playground program." Siegumfeldt argued that children knew just as well as any professional adult how to form their playgrounds. He referred to how children historically would play on the ramparts, and he was critical of play equipment and the "ordered play" instructed by adults—of how adults wanted to teach children how to play through, for instance, ball games and singing games.[39] Playgrounds should contain recreational aspects, Siegumfeldt argued, and not resemble amusement parks. They should look more like gardens: "Trees to climb in, bushes to play between, dirt to mess about in, water to splash in and grass to play on and to throw oneself on are the original elements of children's primitive play."[40] This pastoral view of children and play emphasized the sensorial and experiential aspects rather than the educational aspects of playgrounds. As such, it mirrored the contemporary ideas of Dutch cultural historian Johan Huizinga's ideas of ludic man.[41]

In a densely illustrated essay published in 1952, Siegumfeldt along with the architects Grethe Meyer and Ibi Trier Mørch, garden architect Agnete Petersen and psychologist Jens Sigsgaard pointed to the difference between the urban and rural situation, the former in a poor state regarding spaces for play, while the countryside contained an abundance of spaces of ludic potential: "In the countryside, no playground problem exists, apart from the drawbacks of modern traffic. It is easy to understand, you simply point to the few but each of them richly nuanced areas which frame the play of children: the water—the village—the field—the wood."[42] The purpose of such measures was to "lead the children to a healthy social understanding, to make them familiar with cooperation and consideration for others and thereby to contribute to turning them into valuable members of society."[43] Here, the point of creating playgrounds is extremely explicit: it aids the formation of welfare citizens.

In his book *Børn bygger* (Children build), published in 1958, John Bertelsen, the first instructor at the Emdrup junk playground, emphasized the creative powers of children and their inclination to build as a natural drive. As he stated: "Birds build nests—humans houses."[44] The junk playgrounds might have had an appearance of disorganization and jumble, yet to Bertelsen they emblematized human activity and processes of forming matter. This basic experience would often start in the sandbox, Bertelsen argued: "When the sand pours between the children's fingers they sense matter and building soon commences ... Sand play is a wonderful occupation—the child is a creator who plays with matter."[45] Bertelsen linked these experiences of natural elements and matter to processes of enculturation which could also occur when children were playing in the urban fallow fields and were building dens. In the junk playground, these sorts of play—which were of great educational potential—were provided with ample space and matter. Significantly, Bertelsen even considered destruction an inherent part of these processes: "Destruction with a positive intention is easier to accept than the smaller child's destruction for the sake of destruction, yet something indicates that

39 Max Siegumfeldt, "Et legepladsprogram" [A playground program], *Havekunst* [Garden design] 26 (1945): 28–30.
40 Original phrase in Danish: "For træer til at klatre i, buske til at lege imellem, jord til at rode i, vand til at pjaske i og græs til baade at lege paa og smide sig i udgør jo netop de oprindelige elementer for børns primitive leg." Siegumfeldt, "Et legepladsprogram," 30.
41 Johan Huizinga, *Homo Ludens: A Study of the Play-Element in Culture* (London, Boston and Henley: Routledge and Kegan Paul, 1949).
42 Original phrase in Danish: "På landet eksisterer der, bortset fra de ulemper den moderne trafik har hidført, normalt intet legepladsproblem. Det er let at forstå, man behøver blot at pege på de få, men hver for sig så rigt nuancerede områder, der danner rammen om børnenes leg: vandet – landsbyen – marken – skoven." Grethe Meyer, Ibi Trier Mørch, Max Siegumfeldt, Agnete Petersen, and Jens Sigsgaard, "Analyse af legepladsproblemet – særlig med henblik på København" [Analysis of the playground problem with a view to Copenhagen], *Arkitekten månedshæfte* 54, no. 1–2 (1952): 13.
43 Original phrase in Danish: "at lede børnene frem til en sund social forståelse, gøre dem fortrolige med samarbejde og hensyntagen til andre og derved være med til at gøre dem til værdifulde samfundsmedlemmer." Meyer et al., "Analyse af legepladsproblemet," 18.
44 Original phrase in Danish: "Fugle bygger reder – mennesker huse." John Bertelsen, *Børn bygger* [Children build] (Copenhagen: Aktieselskabet Rockwool, Dansk Gasbeton Aktieselskab, 1958), 4.
45 Original phrase in Danish: "Når sandet siler mellem børnenes fingre fornemmer de stof og snart begynder byggeriet.... Sandlegen er en herlig beskæftigelse – barnet er en skaber som leger med stof." Bertelsen, *Børn bygger*, 12.

the practice and command of the art of destruction is necessary for coping with the different tasks of life. Let us therefore include all joys: of destruction, of building, and of the complete work."[46] Play emulated the natural processes of life and death, of growth and decay. It was situated and materialized in specific spaces, in the basic form of the sandbox, in the urban simulations of the bountiful Danish landscape forms, or in the ambiguous material conditions of the junk playground.

COMPETENCE AND EXPERIENCE

During the second half of the 1960s, the junk playgrounds were to an increasing extent made more institutional, including paid teaching staff and public financial support. Even their name changed, as they were now called *building playgrounds*, thereby emphasizing constructive play and building activities.[47] This development was supported by the 1964 Lov om børne- og ungdomsforsorg (Children and youth welfare act) which allowed playgrounds to be acknowledged as independent institutions.[48] Dansk Legepladsselskab (the Danish Playground Society) had been founded in 1959, chaired by C. Th. Sørensen, and focused on stimulating the creative abilities of children through the design of playgrounds. During the 1970s, junk or building playgrounds also became part of alternative, anti-capitalist urban practices such as Hudegrundens Byggelegeplads in Copenhagen's Vesterbro neighborhood and Byggeren in the Nørrebro neighborhood.

Yet while children's education and play were significant aspects of Danish playgrounds, security and risk became steadily more important aspects. This was, for instance, demonstrated by the attention toward installing impact surfaces preventing accidents caused by children falling and the fact that playground design became part of the Danish building regulations in 1994. The individuality of the child also gained in its significance. As Svend Erik Laursen stated in his book *Legepladsen* (The playground), published in 1985: "Opportunities are created at the playground which will support the child in maintaining and developing herself or himself as the unique personality she or he is."[49] This resonated with ideas of children possessing various competences, including, for instance, emotional and motoric competences, which surfaced during the 1990s. Children's experiences and specific cultures became matters of attention, including their sense of place in relation to playgrounds.[50] As mentioned at the start of this chapter, the concepts of "individual competences" and "experiences" would be allocated increasing importance during subsequent decades, becoming key objectives of contemporary Danish welfare production—not only with respect to children and the design of playgrounds but also in the formation of all welfare citizens.

46 Original phrase in Danish: "Ødelæggelse der har en positiv hensigt er nemmere at acceptere end det mindre barns destruktion for destruktionens skyld, men noget tyder på at indøvelse og beherskelse af ødelæggelsens kunst er nødvendig for at klare livets forskellige opgaver. Lad os derfor tage alle glæder med: ødelæggelsens, opbygningens og det fuldendte værks." Bertelsen, *Børn bygger*, 11.

47 See also the publication on building playgrounds, published by Dansk Legepladsselskab (the Danish Playground Society) in 1981. Max Siegumfeldt, ed., *Byggelegepladser i Danmark* [Construction playgrounds in Denmark] (Copenhagen: Dansk Legeplads Selskab, 1981).

48 Jens Sigsgaard, "The Playground in Modern Danish Housing," *Danish Foreign Office Journal* 54 (1965): 15–20.

49 Original phrase in Danish: "På legepladsen kan der skabes muligheder, der kan støtte barnet i at bevare og udvikle sig som den enestående personlighed det er." Svend Erik Laursen, *Legepladsen: indretning, materialer, sikkerhed* [*The playground: Design, materials, safety*] (Copenhagen: Forlaget Børn & unge, 1985), 13.

50 Trine Agervig Carstensen, "Rum til børn – legepladser som børns steder" [Spaces for children—playgrounds as children's places], *Nordisk arkitekturforskning* [Nordic architectural research] 1 (2004): 11–25. See also Flemming Mouritsen, "Børnekultur – legekultur" [Children's culture—play culture], in *Tekster om leg* [Texts on play], ed. Helle Skovbjerg Karoff and Carsten Jessen (Copenhagen: Akademisk Forlag, 2014), 237–65.

Building playground in Kolding, 1961.

Beata Labuhn

CABIN CONTROVERSIES

Balancing Individual and Collective Welfare in Norwegian Cabin Politics

In the first spring of the COVID-19 pandemic, in 2020, a heated debate flared up in Norway when the government restricted the use of cabins. The aim of prohibiting cabin owners from sleeping in cabins outside their home municipality was less to limit the risk of spreading the coronavirus than to handle the pressure that would be placed on healthcare services in remote natural areas (where most cabins are located) if the pandemic escalated. Despite these good intentions, the legislation caused a national conflict. Bent Høie, Norway's Helse- og omsorgsminister (Minister of Health and Care Services) wrote a public letter addressing the most upset voices in the debate, and *Heimevernet* (the home guard) was put into use to ensure that cabin owners stayed at home in the city. The director of *Norges institusjon for menneskerettigheter* (the Norwegian Human Rights Institution), Adele Matheson Mestad, claimed that the restriction contravened human rights.[1] Limiting the use of cabins obviously touched upon a complex range of deeply felt matters, but how could these have been considered more important than distributing pressure on hospitals? How did the balancing of individual and collective welfare become so heated in this case?

Historically, Scandinavian nations have been known for their consensus politics, balancing individual and collective interests in order to secure welfare for all. The Nordic welfare model—characterized by, amongst other things, high employment rates, social security, free education and healthcare, as well as guaranteed holidays—is believed to be rooted in the common core values of prosperity, security, equality, trust, and freedom, which are "both socialist and capitalist."[2] By extension, Scandinavian industrial, architectural, and urban design is thought to rely on the figure of "the reasonable citizen-consumer," whose individual needs and desires are integrated within the idea of common values through a well-organized and standardized system of planning and production, as well as education and democratic discussion involving various media.[3] Yet, balancing individual and collective welfare can be at times extremely difficult, as is shown in the case of (self-built) huts, holiday cabins, and second homes in Norway. These simple architectural structures became unresolved points of collision between ideas of collective versus individual welfare, as well as between two types of contact with nature, wherein enjoying nature from a private hut clashed with the creation of public national parks.

This chapter focuses on the political turn in Norwegian cabin politics that was launched in 1965. From being a beacon of individual freedom and part of basic welfare, the cabin was then branded an enemy of the collective good. The government initiated a re-education campaign which included a reader, a traveling exhibition, public lectures and debates, as well as pilot projects involving new types of designs of cabins and leisure villages. Despite the

1 Alf Jørgen Schnell and Marianne Skjulhaug, "Hyttedebatten handler om norsk urbanitet" [The cabin debate is about Norwegian urbanity], *Plan,* March 27, 2020, https://plantidsskrift.no/debatt/hyttedebatten-handler-om-norsk-urbanitet/.

2 See, for example various publications popularizing the Scandinavian model such as George Lakey, *Viking Economics. How the Scandinavians Got it Right—And How We Can, Too* (New York: Melville House Publishing, 2016).

3 The figure of the reasonable "citizen-consumer" was conceptualized by Helena Mattsson in the context of the Swedish debates, but the tendency to rely on the "reasonable citizen-consumer" is discernible also in Norway and Denmark. Helena Mattsson, "Designing the Reasonable Consumer. Standardisation and Personalisation in Swedish Functionalism," in *Swedish Modernism. Architecture, Consumption and the Welfare State*, ed. Helena Mattsson and Sven-Olov Wallenstein (London: Black Dog Publishing, 2010), 74–99.

consensus that some type of cabin planning was indeed needed, this turn was met with de facto resistance from municipalities, landowners, and cabin users.

CABIN CULTURE

The ideal of owning one's private primitive hut in the middle of nature has played on the Norwegian imagination from the nineteenth century onwards through a combination of scientific explorations of nature and national-romantic narratives of "the good life" in mountain cabins:[4]

> The Norwegian identity that the nation-builders constructed in literary works did not take place in untouched nature, but rather in a border zone between agriculture and wilderness, most often at a *seter* (mountain pasture farm) or in a hunting lodge. It is remarkable how often the action in Norway's most central and nationalist literary works from the nineteenth century occurs in such places.[5]

From Hansen's short story "Luren" (in English meaning "lure," a type of shepherd's horn) from 1819, Asbjørnsen's *Norske Huldre-Eventyr og Folkesagn* from 1848 (published in English as *The Complete and Original Norwegian Folktales of Asbjørnsen and Moe*), and Ibsen's play *Peer Gynt* from 1867, to Hamsun's *Pan* from 1894 or Bjerke's *De dødes tjern* from 1942 (recently released in English as *The Lake of the Dead*), Norwegian literature highlights the cabin as an important setting, as well as an important metaphor, for storytelling.[6] Such cultural efforts enmeshed the cabin not only with ideas of Norwegianness—to be Norwegian is to enjoy time away in a remote cabin—but most of all with the freedom and knowledge that stems from contact with nature.

The image of the primitive hut in the middle of nature corresponded with ideas of freedom to think and do what you want. As early as in the eighteenth century, being in one's own remote cabin was compared to being a king in his realm.[7] And the Norwegian word for outdoor life, *friluftsliv*, literally "free-air life," was coined by Henrik Ibsen in 1859 in his poem "På vidderne" (On the mountain plateaux) in which he wrote that it was in front of the fireplace in a deserted *seter* house far up in the mountains where his protagonist found "free-air life" for his thoughts.[8] During the Second World War, remote cabins became meeting places for the Norwegian resistance, enmeshing the cabin again with freedom—specifically, with the heroic fight for liberation.[9]

According to the architect Odd Brochmann in 1952, in modern times we often consider leisure as "the key to true knowledge."[10] "I can't imagine that I could have worked anywhere as I do here. It's the quiet and, perhaps, the wonderful scenery; I mean, its quiet seriousness," wrote Ludwig Wittgenstein, in 1936, to his Cambridge colleague G. E. Moore when describing his Norwegian cabin that he started to build around 1914 on a cliff above Eidsvatnet, at the outer end of Lustra fjord, near the village Skjolden. The Norwegian cabin was the philosopher's favorite writing retreat and apparently it was there where he wrote significant parts of his *Philosophical*

4 Rune Slagstad, *Da fjellet ble dannet* [When the mountain was formed/cultured] (Oslo: Dreyer Forlag, 2018); Peder Anker, *The Power of the Periphery: How Norway Became an Environmental Pioneer for the World* (Cambridge: Cambridge University Press, 2020).

5 Original quote in Norwegian: "Den norske identiteten som nasjonsbyggerne konstruerte i sine litterære verk, fant ikke sted i den uberørte naturen, men heller i en grensesone mellom jordbruk og villmark, oftest til seters eller på ei jakthytte. Det er påfallende hvor ofte handlingen i Norges mest sentrale og nasjonalistiske litterære verk fra 1800-tallet foregår på slike steder." Ellen Rees, "'Det egentlige Norge' – hytter i norsk litteratur, ca. 1814–2005" ['The real Norway': Cabins in Norwegian literature ca. 1814–2005], in *Norske hytter i endring. Om bærekraft og behag* [Changing Norwegian cabins: about sustainability and comfort], ed. Helen Jøsok Gansmo, Thomas Berker, and Finn Arne Jørgensen (Trondheim: Tapir akademisk forlag, 2011), 23.

6 Rees, "'Det egentlige Norge'…," 23.

7 Povel Juel, *Et lycksaligt liv eftertænct da indbildning og forfarenhed derom disputerede. Af den som søger efter sandhed paa jorden* [A happy life followed when imagination and experience disputed it. Of the one who searches for truth on earth] (Copenhagen: Nørwigs Bogtryckerie II, 1721).

8 Henrik Ibsen, "På vidderne" [On the mountain plateaux], in *Samlede verker 1866–1873* [Collected works 1866–1873], vol. 2 (Oslo: Kagge Forlag, 2005), 495.

9 Randi Skjerstad, "Der landet ble samlet. Friluftsliv som norgeshistorie 1940–1970" [Where the country gathered. Outdoor recreation as Norwegian history 1940–1970] (master's thesis, Oslo University, 2021).

10 Odd Brochmann, "Arkitekten og lediggangen" [The architect and the idle time], *Byggekunst* 8 (1952): 121.

The Norwegian cabin of philosopher Ludwig Wittgenstein near Skjolden.

Arne Næss' cabin Skarveredet built in the first half of the 1940s.

The wild growth of mountain cabins at Ustaoset.

Investigations.[11] Between 1937 and 1944, the Norwegian philosopher and skilled technical climber Arne Næss—who would later become known as one of the fathers of deep ecology and who next to Henry David Thoreau and Aldo Leopold would be celebrated as one of the key thinkers in the history of environmental ethics—built not one but two philosopher huts, both located in the mountain area of Hallingskarvet. The cabin called Tvergastein was built under a tall cliff and was larger and more comfortable than the other—a tiny, box-like shed that Næss called Skarveredet (the cormorant's nest) and that was dubbed "the coffin" by locals. Skarveredet sits almost at the top of the cliff above Tvergastein, and was dangerous to build. It was placed on a narrow mountain shelf and Boss Walther, one of the climber-friends of Næss, died in the process of building it. Both cabins were located above the valley and the tourist resort of Ustaoset, where one could find a large hotel and hundreds of weekend cottages.[12]

Spending free time in nature was typically enjoyed mostly by the better-off families. Yet, after the Second World War, Arbeiderpartiet (The Norwegian Labor Party) governments actively promoted outdoor life for all. Party leaders like Martin Tranmæl and Einar Gerhardsen were themselves enthusiastic hikers and the cabin was their second home and political meeting place.[13] In 1953, in an article titled "Plass for oss alle!" (Room for all of us!) which was published in the yearbook of *Den Norske Turistforening* (The Norwegian Trekking Association), Tranmæl wrote:

> Norway is spacious. There is space and elbow room for all of us. In work and play. In the mountains and the countryside. For a long time, only the few went to the mountains for holidays, to seek change and relaxation and to experience what the mountains can offer. But having obtained three weeks of statutory holidays and a higher standard of living, the many are now seeking the outdoors.[14]

Arbeiderpartiet indeed contributed to making the outdoors accessible for workers. After the Second World War, many people enjoyed increasing amounts of state-regulated free time, mobility, and wealth. The dream of owning one's own primitive hut in the midst of Norwegian nature not only came within reach for many Norwegians, but was sometimes also considered a part of citizens' welfare as it provided necessary respite from the negative sides of industrialization and urbanization. The 1952 Norwegian translation of Henry David Thoreau's *Walden: Or, Life in the Woods* was followed in 1962 by an award-winning essay by Ole Christian Grimnes about the relevance of Thoreau's *Walden* for the building of cabins in Norway, which portrayed them as a necessary counterweight to the standardizing and uniform postwar world.[15]

THE HARMONIOUS VERSUS THE SCREAMING CABIN

Beyond common sense, temporary restrictions, and *allemannsretten* (the ancient right to the commons, allowing all to safely traverse the Norwegian landscape, including across private property),[16] huts, cabins, and second homes were uninhibited by excessive laws and

11 Knut Olav Åmås and Rolf Larsen, "Ludwig Wittgenstein in Norway 1913–50," in *Wittgenstein and Norway*, ed. Kjell S. Johannessen, Rolf Larsen, and Knut Olav Åmås (Oslo: Solum, 1994), 10.

12 Peder Anker, "The Philosopher's Cabin and the Household of Nature," in *Ethics, Place and Environment* 6, 2 (2003): 136–39; Arne Næss, *Det gode lange livs far: Hallingskarvet sett fra Tvergastein* (Oslo: Damm, 1995).

13 Peder Anker, *Livet er best ute. Friluftslivets historie og filosofi* [Life is best outside. The history and philosophy of outdoor life] (Oslo: Kagge Forlag, 2022), 48.

14 Original quote in Norwegian: "Norge er romslig. Det er plass og albueslag for oss alle. I arbeid som til fest. Til fjells som til lands. Lenge var det slik at det var de få som dro til fjells for å feriere, for å søke avveksling og avspenning og for å oppleve det fjellet kan gi. Men etter at vi fikk 3 ukers lovfestet ferie og levestandarden ble hevet, søker de mange ut." Martin Tranmæl, "Plass for oss alle!" [Room for all of us!], *Den Norske Turistforenings årbok 1953. Fjellfolk* [The Norwegian Tourism Association Yearbook 1953. Mountain People] (1953): 58.

15 This essay won the first prize in the essay competition that was organized by the *Norge-Amerika Foreningen* (Norway-America Association) and U.S. Information Service in connection with the 100th anniversary of Thoreau's death. Ole Kristian Grimnes, *Thoreau og vår egen tid* [Thoreau and our own time] (Oslo: De Forente Staters Informasjonstjeneste & Den Amerikanske ambassade, 1962).

16 This customary law was first recorded as an official law for a larger area by king Magnus Haakonsson Lagabøte in his land law from 1274 and in his building law from 1276. In modern Norway, *allemannsretten* was recorded in a somewhat limited, but at the same time more sharply defined way, through the Open Air Act from 1957 (*Lov om frilufslivet* §2 *Ferdsel i utmark*). Marianne Reusch, "Allemannsretten. Friluftslivets rettsgrunnlag" [The common law. The legal basis of outdoor activities] (PhD diss., Oslo University, 2011); republished as Marianne Reusch, *Allemannsretten. Friluftslivets rettsgrunnlag* (Oslo: Flux forlag, 2011), 40–41.

became thus beacons of relative freedom in Norway. With practical tips from various do-it-yourself handbooks,[17] Norwegian cabins were often self-built as remotely and as primitively as possible, often without fences or electricity, and with self-engineered running water and an outside toilet. During the postwar years, many Norwegian architects exercised their freedom to design and build their own dream cabin—many of the most iconic and oft-referenced cabins in Norwegian architectural history stem from the period 1945–65. Knut Knutsen's design for his own cabin in Portør from 1949 was driven by "the search for freedom" from "masks," "straitjackets," "unnaturalness," and "uniformity," as well as a desire to respect nature and achieve harmony between architecture and nature without camouflage.[18] The building transgressed both the modernist and the traditional canons and blended harmoniously with the terrain and surrounding vegetation.[19] Postwar scarcity led to a temporary prohibition on building holiday homes from new materials and Knutsen's cabin in Portør was as a result "built from old materials, mostly from used formwork boards."[20] It became a major reference project for generations of Norwegian architects and arguably "Norway's most published cabin."[21] Wenche and Jens Selmer's holiday cottages—for example, in Ringkollen from 1953 and their own cabin on Beltesholmen from 1957—were also formed to fit to the landscapes they inhabited. Even though comfortably modern, with wall insulation, insulating glass, and floor heating, the Selmers' holiday homes were most praised for their restraint, naturalness, and lack of pretention.[22] Next to these quite well-known cottages, many other less-written-about but nonetheless interesting architectural experiments were drawn, and sometimes built, in those years—for example, the plan for a half buried in the ground and snow-adapted "contemporary cabin where the original primitive concepts have been taken care of"[23] by P. A. M. Mellbye (Peter Andreas Munch Mellbye), the elementary cabins by Vilhelm Reinhardt,[24] or the primitive hut in the form of a hovering roof over the ruins of a Second-World-War Atlantic Wall casemate designed by Robert Clarke Esdaile, who was also an early advocate of connecting architecture and urbanism with ecology.[25] What these architect-designed cabins had in common was that they all respectfully and fittingly added to the landscapes they inhabited.

Many other self-built cabins from the 1940s, 1950s, and 1960s displayed the rather personal tastes of their owners without fitting in within the landscape. Knut Knutsen commented on this development, noting that "the results do their part to destroy the land, destroy the dimensions of the landscape and flatten variations in the moors. The summer houses lie there and scream without integration with their environment."[26] Knutsen advocated an immediate temporary cabin construction prohibition followed by the introduction of adequate laws and regulations specifying how a weekend cottage should relate to its natural environment:

> That way, greater emphasis can be placed on harmony when it comes to this building type. It is therefore reasonable that all construction of such houses be stopped immediately, until we get regulations that do not make it possible to destroy the landscape and to get someone to ensure that the regulations are implemented.[27]

17 For example: N. Peder Nielsen, *Bygging av hytter og småhus: en veiledning for bygningshåndverkere og selvbyggere* [Building cabins and detached houses: a guide for builders and self-builders] (Trondheim: F. Bruns Bokhandels Forlag, 1941–62); Tønseth Roar, *Hytter og strandstuer* [Cottages and beach shacks] (Trondheim: F. Bruns bokhandels forlag, 1955); *Vi bygger en hytte. De beste utkast fra Arbeider-avisen arkitektkonkurranse* [We are building a cabin. The best drafts from the Workers' Newspaper's architectural competition] (Trondheim: F. Bruns bokhandels forlag, 1940–47).

18 Knut Knutsen, "Et fritidshus" [A holiday house], *Byggekunst* 8 (1952): 127.

19 Maria Csaszni Rygh, "Tekst, natur og arkitektur. Knut Knutsens villa Natvig og sommerhus i Portør" [Text, nature, and architecture: Knut Knutsen's villa Natvig and summer house in Portør], in *Brytninger. Norsk arkitektur 1945–65* [Refractions. Norwegian architecture 1945–65], ed. Espen Johnsen (Oslo: Nasjonal museet for kunst, arkitektur og design, 2010), 186–97.

20 Original quote in Norwegian: "bygd av gamle materialer, for det meste av brukte forskallingsbord." Helge Abrahamsen and Hans Grinde, "Fritidshus i Portør" [Holiday house in Portør], in *Bonytts hyttebok* [*Bonytt*'s book of cabins] (Oslo: Bonytts forlag, 1956): 34.

21 Helge Abrahamsen, "Samspillet med naturen" [The interaction with nature], in *På hytta – vårt andre hjem* [At the cabin—our second home], ed. Helge Abrahamsen et al. (Boksenteret, 1996), 57.

22 Elisabeth Tostrup, "Modifikasjoner i landskap" [Modifications in landscape], in *Brytninger. Norsk arkitektur 1945–65*, 198–205. Even though it forms a part of their joint portfolio, the cabin in Ringkollen was designed only by Wenche Selmer, who at the time was known as Wenche Collett.

23 P. A. M. Mellbye, "'Kåk' i Fjellet" ["Shack" in the mountains], *Bonytt* 11–12 (1956): 242–43 (243).

24 V. Reinhardt, "To sjøbuer" [Two sea cabins], in *Byggekunst* 8 (1952): 144–45.

25 Robert C. Esdaile, "Jansholet. Hytte ved Jøssingfjord" [Jansholet: Cabin by Jøssingfjord], *Byggekunst* 1 (1976): cover, 6, 7; Kjetil Fallan, *Ecological by Design: A History from Scandinavia* (Cambridge, Massachusetts: MIT Press, 2022), 61–78.

26 Original quote in Norwegian: "resultatene gjør sitt til å ødelegge landet, ødelegge landskapets dimensjoner og flate ut variasjoner i heiene. Sommerhusene ligger der og skriker uten miljøsammenheng." Knutsen, "Et fritidshus": 126.

27 Original quote in Norwegian: "På den måten kan det legges større vekt på harmoni når det gjelder denne bebyggelse. Det er derfor rimelig at all bygging av slike hus blir stanset straks, inntil vi får bestemmelser som ikke gjør det mulig å ødelegge landskapet og å få noen til å passe på at bestemmelsene blir gjennomført." Knutsen, "Et fritidshus": 129.

The cabin in Portør by Knut Knutsen,
built in 1949.

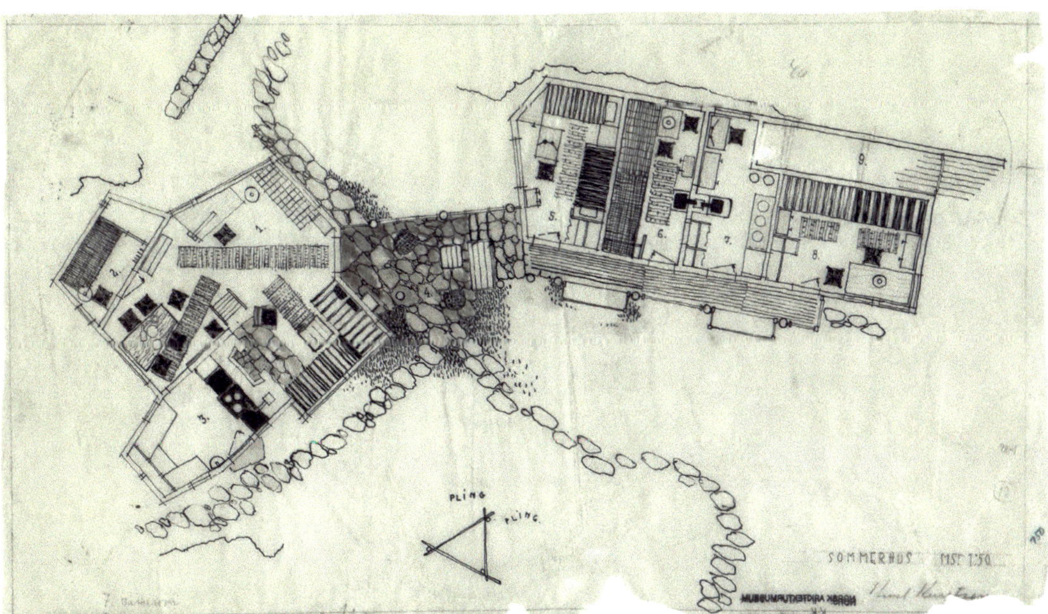

Knut Knutsen, Portør cabin,
furnishing plan, probably 1949.

Jens Andreas Selmer and Wenche Selmer, own cabin on Beltesholmen, built in 1957.

The drawing for the snow-adapted stony cabin by P. A. M. Mellbye, published on the cover of *Bonytt* no. 11–12 (1956).

While Knutsen wanted to develop regulations that would help to fit buildings better into the landscape, Eyvind Alnæs, an architect and the secretary of Oslofjordens friluftsråd (the Oslo fjord outdoor council), did not want any buildings at all—ugly or beautiful—on Norwegian coasts. Already in 1949, Alnæs observed how the Norwegian coast was "being eaten up by buildings year after year" and warned that a conflict would soon arise "between the individual's highly legitimate urge to have land and a house by the sea and the growing general need for free nature to roam in."[28] Alnæs advocated sharper national regulations including a temporary building prohibition specifically for the coastal zones.

THE TURN TO COLLECTIVE WELFARE IN CABIN POLITICS

Even though Alnæs and Knutsen pleaded for cabin regulations as early as 1949 and 1952, the Norwegian government hesitated to intervene for another decade until the liberal approach led to an alarming situation: a rapidly increasing number of cabins with differing qualities were being built on the best spots at the seaside, by fjords and lakes, in forests, and near mountain peaks. Whilst the exact number of cabins in Norway was not known in 1965 (in contrast to Sweden and Denmark, where various surveys were performed), it was estimated that between 150,000 and 160,000 holiday homes existed in Norway around the mid-1960s, with 10,000 new homes being added each year. Cabin construction was thus accelerating—by comparison, during the 1950s, "only" 5,000 new holiday homes per year were added to the landscape. If things were to continue at this speed, it was predicted that there would be half a million cabins in Norway by the year 1990, statistically already one cabin per ten residents.[29] This intensification of the wild growth in leisure cottages, as well as their increasing commercialization,[30] coincided with a growing interest in nature conservation. Taking as an example American nature reserves, Norway also introduced nature protection laws in 1954 and from that year on started preparations for defining national parks. Norway's first national park, Rondane, was formally established in December 1962.

In March 1962, the Minister of Local Governments, Andreas Cappelen (from Arbeiderpartiet) asked the geographer, economist, and educator Axel Sømme—who became a member of the same party in 1926–27 after he left the communist organization Mot Dag—to compose a *fjellplanteam* (mountain planning team) that could propose a draft for regulatory plans for holiday homes in important leisure and holiday destinations bordering some of the nature areas, many of which were soon to become national parks. Firstly, around Rondane, the areas of Venabygdfjellet, Langbakken, Høvringen, Ljosmyra, and Mysusæter were chosen. Secondly, in the Ål municipality between the nature areas of Valdres and Hallingskarvet, places such as Ål, Gol, Vats, Bergsjø, Kamben, and Golsfjellet were examined. Finally, between Røros and Brekken, various areas around the waterways of Aursunden, Brekkefjorden, and Botnen were studied. The idea was to work in such a way as to distill from these specific development plans general planning principles that could be applied all over Norway.

Axel Sømme put together a mountain planning team that brought together complementary expertise, through agriculturist

28 Original quotes in Norwegian: "den spises nå opp av bebyggelse år for år" and "mellom den enkeltes høyst legitime trang til å ha tomt og hus ved sjøen og det økende almene behov for fri natur til å ferdes i." Eyvind Alnæs, "Friarealer ved sjøen" [Open spaces by the sea], *Byggekunst* 3 (1949): 73–83.

29 The exact number of cabins in Norway had not been surveyed until the 1970s when Kommunal- og arbeidsdepartementet [The Department of Municipalities and Employment] estimated that 150,000–160,000 holiday cabins existed in Norway in 1968, with 10,000 new cabins being added every year. See Yngvar Johnsen, ed., *Planlegging. Hvordan planlegger vi arealbruk og utbygging* [Planning: How do we plan land use and development?] (Oslo: Kommunal- og arbeids-departementet, 1968), 164, quoted as "mid-1960s" in Terje Skjeggedal, Kjell Overvåg, Tor Arnesen, and Birgitta Ericsson, "Hytteliv i endring" [Cabin life in transformation], *Plan* (January 25, 2010): 42–43.

30 Many people started to see their cottage as a form of investment and a chance to earn money by renting it to Swedish, Danish, German, and Dutch tourists. Klo, "Veldig vekst i hytteleien. Planer viktigere enn troen på mirakler" [High growth in cabin rentals. Plans are more important than believing in miracles], *Nationen*, November 15, 1965.

Ola Einevoll; architect and consultant in urban and regional planning Erik Langdalen; geographers Arne Thormodsæter and Asbjørn Aase; civil engineer, surveyor, and photogrammetrician Reidar Helming; landscape architect Olav R. Skage; the geographer with tourism industry training Helge A. Sundt; and Sverre Øvstedal, assistant professor at the Department of land transfer and property development.

At first, the idea was to shed light on the extent to which it would be possible to establish good regulatory plans for the mountain areas within the legislative and administrative practices already in place in Norway. Studies started in the fall of 1963 with the help of smaller local committees. In the summer of 1964, the whole mountain planning team surveyed study locations between Ål and Brekken. From September 1964, the team's commission was renewed by the Minister of Social Affairs, Olav Gjærevoll, who became its leader. In parallel, Gjærevoll also led a parliamentary mountain planning committee, which Sømme was also part of, that focused on how to turn the recommendations from the mountain planning team into attachments to or parts of the new building law.[31]

The outcome of the studies was a report that was more or less ready around June 1965 and publicly launched on November 8, 1965 in the presence of journalists from Norwegian television and a plethora of newspapers.[32] The 200-page-long report *Fjellbygd og feriefjell* (Mountain village and vacation mountain) included texts by all members of the mountain planning team and contained a general analysis of current trends, an analysis of the existing situation in each area, and possible scenarios for the planning of future cabins in the specific study areas through regional plans, general plans, disposition plans, and detail plans. From the scenarios that were developed for specific locations, the team extracted general principles according to which one could also plan for holiday homes in other places in Norway.

MOUNTAIN PLANNING PRINCIPLES

The team noticed that in general the typology of the primitive hut in the mountains was transforming into a second home with almost the same level of comfort as the first home. Various technical infrastructures were laid privately, and many car owners made roads all the way up to the cabin. Sømme's team discovered the car garage as a surprising and terrifying mountain planning problem: "The car, as a luxury item and a status symbol, requires protection against the weather and the intrusive curiosity of humans and animals ... there are examples of detached garage buildings that mar the landscape more than any cabin."[33] The roads themselves were also considered a problem. Compared to, for example, the United States, in Norway there were too many roads of too low a standard. The team therefore recommended avoiding creating more roads, recommending improving existing ones instead.[34]

Most of all, the team criticized the disastrous scattering and visual expression of the holiday homes that colonized beautiful recreational areas: "the worst thing is all the houses that city people scatter randomly across the mountains or gather in cottage villages with far too many ugly houses, painted in garish colors."[35]

31 Later, in 1972, Olav Gjærevoll would become Norway's first Minister of Environment.

32 Axel Sømme, Erik Langdalen, Ola Einevoll, Asbjørn Aase, Arne Thormodsæter, Sverre Øvstedal, Olav R. Skage, and Helge A. Sundt, *Fjellbygd og feriefjell* [Mountain village and vacation mountain] (Oslo: J. W. Cappelens Forlag, 1965).

33 Original quote in Norwegian: "... bilen, som luksusartikkel og statussymbol, krever beskyttelse mot vær og vind og nærgående interesse fra mennesker og dyr ... I fjellplanteamets modellområder er det eksempler på frittliggende garasjebygg som skjemmer landskapet met enn noen hytte" in Erik Langdalen, "Natur og menneskeverk i fjellet" [Nature and the man-made in the mountains], in *Fjellbygd og feriefjell* [Mountain village and vacation mountain], ed. Axel Sømme et al. (Oslo: J. W. Cappelens Forlag, 1965), 28.

34 Erik Langdalen, "Norge utenfor bygrensene" [Norway outside of the city limits], in *Byen og samfunnet* [The city and the society] (Oslo: Pax Forlag, 1966), 102–21 (114–16). The same text was also published under the same title in *Byggekunst* 2 (1966): 37–44.

35 Original quote in Norwegian: "det verste er likevel alle husene som byfolkene sprer tilfeldig utover fjellet, eller som de samler i hyttebyer med altfor mange stygge hus, malt i grelle farger..." Axel Sømme, "Regulering i fjellet" [Regulation in the mountains], *Norsk Tidsskrift for jordskifte og landmåling* [Norwegian journal of land change and land surveying] 26 (1963): 185.

Sea shed in Gamle Hellesund by Vilhelm Reinhardt, 1952.

728.72(481)

Arkitekt m.n.a.l. V. REINHARDT: SJØBU VED GAMLE HELLESUND

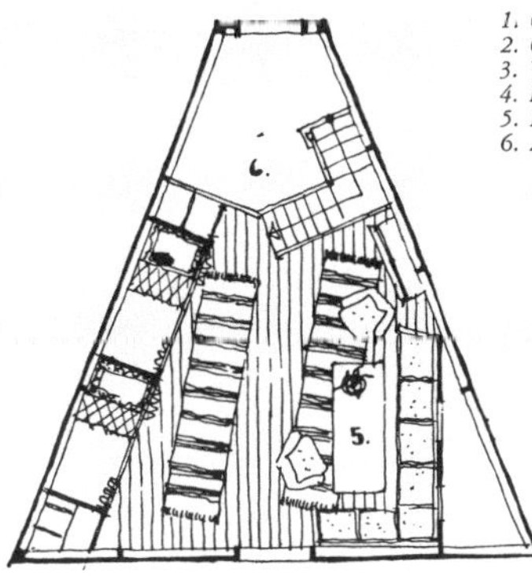

1. Oppholdsrom med kjøkken.
2. Overdekket sitteplass.
3. Vaskeplass.
4. Brygge.
5. Komb. stue og soverom.
6. Åpent rom.

Planer, 1 : 100.

Stedet kaldes Perlevigen. Det udmerker sig ved landskapelig gratie. Sjøen er krystallgrønn og havbunnen hvit sand med østers-avleiringer. Havnen åpner med en storslagen utsikt mot syd og mot horisonten. Sjø-bua er skjøvet inn i en fjellkløft for å virke minst mulig forstyrrende i landskapet. Stedets hummer, østers, sjøørret og flyndre serveres gjerne på bryggen — og rettene får en særlig velsmak på måneskinnsaftener.

V. R.

Plan of the ground floor and the first floor of Reinhardt's sea shed at Gamle Hellesund, 1952.

A hovering roof, a panoramic window, and a fireplace over the ruins of an Atlantic Wall casemate at Jøssingfjord. Designed by Robert C. Esdaile and built in 1964–65.

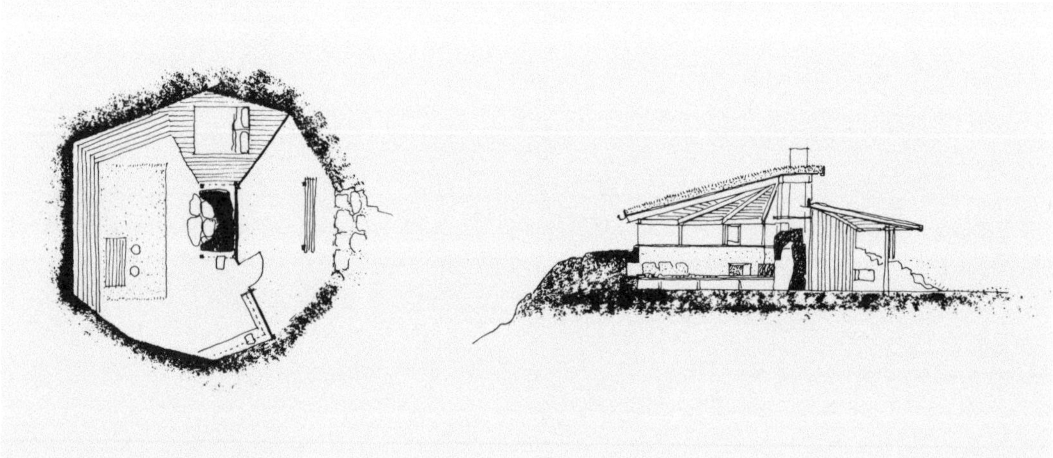

Plan and section of Robert C. Esdaile's cabin at Jøssingfjord that was built in 1964–65.

As a positive counterexample the team pointed to the positioning, the composition, the use of materials, and the color setting of traditional Norwegian wooden architecture which could be found in old *gårdsanlegg* (farms) and *setergrender* (clusters of mountain pasture farms). The team imagined that the restrained aesthetics of these traditional buildings could inspire the design of new individual cabins or groups of cottages. The landscape positioning, the composition and the color schemes of the traditional (groups of) buildings should be carefully studied and turned into principles for the new cabins in the form of *typetegninger* (type drawings) that could possibly be developed as cabin systems, or used as basis for more traditional construction of cabins and do-it-yourself cottages. This could allow for adaptation to individual tastes yet guarantee a calm and coherent overall image.[36] Additionally, the team also proposed to reuse old farms in depopulating rural areas for agrotourism.[37]

When it comes to the problem of the positioning of the houses, cabin planning strategies were developed for roughly three different types of landscapes: coastal zones, mountain areas above the tree line—the altitude at which trees are no longer capable of growing—and unproductive forest areas. The coastal landscapes were the ones to be most strictly protected from new holiday cabins. The updated Strandloven (Beach law),[38] a temporary law that was part of the new Building Law from June 1965 onwards, determined that holiday homes should be built at least 100 meters away from fjords, lakes, rivers, and other waters. The mountain areas above the tree line were also considered to be very vulnerable as sites for new cabins. Without trees, the mountainous terrain above the tree line lies bare and anything that is located there tends to punctuate the landscape in a striking manner: "In particularly exposed terrain, it is often a few meters of displacement of the house which is the difference between adaptation to nature and disruption of the landscape. Both immediate and distant effects must be assessed, and one must take into account the changing seasons."[39]

The team advocated that cabin planning in general should be ideally designated foremost to the unproductive forest areas between the tree line and the lower timber line, below which trees are of good enough quality for timber production. In unproductive forests, the cabins—individually or in a group—could enjoy the greatest freedom when it comes to the spread or clustering of cabins as well as the individual design of each cabin.[40]

Hidden from sight in the unproductive forest areas, the cabin clusters could be designed to be grouped in different ways, preferably as concentrations of buildings very close to each other or in multiple groups, or—even though less ideally—scattered all over the forested terrain.[41] The densification through the grouping of multiple cabins, was the team's strongest recommendation in any case. Holiday home clusters had been successful in Sweden for some time and the committee hoped that this typology eventually would also be embraced by the Norwegians.[42] At the same time, these concentrations of cabins could easily fulfill growing demand for comfort with better facilities and infrastructures.[43]

The previous freedom in choosing one's own spot and design for one's own cabin would not be possible anymore, unless one would give up comforts of the modern life. Freestanding and freely

36 Langdalen, "Natur og menneskeverk i fjellet," 30.
37 Langdalen, "Natur og menneskeverk i fjellet," 34–35.
38 The original Beach Law from 1937 gave the municipalities the right to expropriate use rights or owner rights based on general considerations like necessity for public swimming and other outdoor activities.
39 Original quote in Norwegian: "I særlig utsatt terreng er det ofte noen få meters forskyvning av huset som er skillet mellom naturtilpassing og landskapsbrudd. Både nær- og fjernvirkninger må vurderes og en må ta hensyn til de skiftende årstider." Langdalen, "Natur og menneskeverk i fjellet," 27.
40 Langdalen, "Natur og menneskeverk i fjellet," 27.
41 Langdalen, "Natur og menneskeverk i fjellet," 42–43.
42 For an introduction to the differences in cabin habits between Norway, Sweden, and Denmark see Einar Odden, "Om Svenskene" [About the Swedes], in *Den norske hytta – en biografi* [The Norwegian cabin—a biography] (Kolofon Forlag, 2022), 108–27.
43 Langdalen, "Natur og menneskeverk i fjellet," 35–38.

designed cabins on a self-chosen spot in nature should only be allowed on the condition that they compose themselves discretely into the landscape they inhabit and stay primitive: "Anyone who wants to build their holiday home in solitude must, if we are to let him do so at all, come to terms with using particularly discreet means and renouncing road, power, telephone and similar services."[44]

In short, with the help of these planning principles, large areas could be prevented from being colonized by the cabins and thus kept pristine for the mountain tourist, while the cabins and roads would be sited where they could do least harm to the eye.

RE-EDUCATING THE NORWEGIAN CITIZEN: "ENOUGH SPACE, BUT PLANNING IS NEEDED!"

The *Fjellbygd og feriefjell* report was aptly dubbed a "textbook on the development of Norwegian mountains" by the newspapers *Aftenposten* and *Hamar Arbeiderblad*.[45] The report was indeed also a type of educational textbook as the mountain planning team felt that for the new plans to succeed it was necessary to first re-educate the Norwegian citizen.

The mountain planning team as well as other planners and politicians understood that the changes they envisioned when it comes to cabins were at odds with the established cultural traditions as well as with the previous governmental efforts to popularize cabin ownership among the entire population. "Norwegians still have a somewhat special attitude toward outdoor life and cabin use, a mentality that differs from other European nations," wrote Erik Anker, further specifying this mentality in terms of "the romantic notion of the escape from civilization to solitude."[46] In the cabin, "we want, like the farmer, to be king in our own realm," wrote Axel Sømme, going on to note that "we do not like that the society will regulate the mountains."[47]

Even though the mountain planning team was thus aware that their proposals were extremely challenging toward the longstanding Norwegian cabin traditions and dreams, they had to replace the ideal of the private remote cabin with that of collective welfare. They set up an entire campaign during which they employed a range of methods to stimulate a mentality change and stem people positively toward the new plans.

First of all, the mountain planning team felt it necessary to appeal to the Norwegian citizen's social responsibility and morality in a way which preceded Garret Hardin's "tragedy of the commons":[48] "Building a house is a distinctly selfish act, whether it is a year-round home or a holiday home," wrote Erik Langdalen, adding that when it comes to the holiday home especially, one is "seeking to protect one's own interests and keep other people at a distance."[49] These individual interests are often being executed at the cost of common interests: "The cabin builder has, as can reasonably be expected, thought of his own interests, and the lack of a plan, bylaws and control has given him the freedom to do so, at the expense of his neighbors and the public."[50] Asbjørn Aase warned that if the common good in the form of the beautiful natural landscape will be violated by individual interests long enough and at a large scale, the whole *raison d'être* of recreation in Norway will be destroyed for everyone.[51]

44 Original quote in Norwegian: "Den som vil bygge sitt fritidshus i ensomhet, må, om vi i det hele tatt skal slippe ham til, finne seg i å bruke særlig diskrete virkemidler og gi avkall på veg, kraft, telefon o.l. service." Erik Langdalen, "Norge utenfor bygrensene," 111.

45 "Fjellet kan utnyttes til beste for oss alle. Sommeteamets rapport klar efter 3 års arbeide" [The mountains can be used for the benefit of us all: The team's report ready after 3 years of work], *Aftenposten: Aften*, November 8, 1965, 1, 7; Sverre Østhagen, "Imponerende materiale framlagt av professor Sømmes fjellplan-team" [Impressive material presented by professor Sømme's mountain plan team], *Hamar Arbeiderblad*, November 9, 1965, 6.

46 Original quote in Norwegian: "Nordmenn har ennå en noe spesielt holding til friluftsliv og hyttebruk, en mentalitet som adskiller seg fra øverige europeiske nasjoner," and "den romantiske forestilling om flukten fra sivilisasjonen til ensomheten." Erik Anker, "Fritidsliv og arealbruk" [Leisure and land use], *Byggekunst* 4 (1967): 86–94 (90).

47 Axel Sømme, "Fjellbygd og feriefjell" [Mountain village and vacation mountain], in Sømme et al., *Fjellbygd og Feriefjell*, 9.

48 The "tragedy of the commons" is also the term used by both Reusch and Jørgensen in relation to Norwegian cabin politics. The term was first coined by Garret Hardin in his article from 1968 with the same name: Garrett Hardin, "The Tragedy of the Commons," *Science* 162, no. 3859 (1968): 1243–48. Quoted in: Finn Arne Jørgensen, "Den første hyttekrisa. Samfunnsplanlegging, naturbilder og allmenningens tragedie" [The first cottage crisis. Community planning, natural images and the tragedy of the commons], in *Norske hytter i endring. Om bærekraft og behag* [Norwegian cabins in transformation. On sustainability and pleasure], ed. Helen Jøsok Gansmo, Thomas Berker, and Finn Arne Jørgensen (Trondheim: Tapir akademisk forlag, 2011): 44; Reusch, *Allemannsretten. Friluftslivets rettsgrunnlag*, 15.

49 Original quote in Norwegian: "Å bygge seg hus er en utpreget egoistisk handling, enten det nå dreier seg om helårsbolig eller fritidshus. … søker å beskytte sine egne interesser og holde andre folk på avstand." Langdalen, "Natur og menneskeverk i fjellet," 27.

50 Original quote in Norwegian: "Hyttebyggeren har, som rimelig kan være, tenkt på sine egne interesser, og mangelen på plan, vedtekter og kontroll har gitt ham frihet til å gjøre det, på naboens og allmennhetens bekostning." Langdalen, "Natur og menneskeverk i fjellet," 29.

51 See Asbjørn Aase, "Ål" [Ål municipality], in Sømme et al., *Fjellbygd og Feriefjell*, 119–48

Drawing by architect and regional planner Erik Langdalen ca. 1965. The caption reads: “Each man [is] king on his own hill. Is this how we should dress the mountain?”

Hver mann konge på hver sin haug. Er det slik vi skal kle fjellet?

Drawing by Erik Langdalen ca. 1965 to support the idea of planning cabin clusters. The caption reads “Setergrenda’s dense cluster of houses constitutes a characterful human work in the mountains and enriches the natural landscape. Good landscape anchoring, fixed grouping of houses and uniform house shapes characterize Verkenseter in Grimsdalen. ‘Cultural monuments,’ such as these, are in severe disrepair and will probably be lost to posterity.”

Setergrendas tette husklynge utgjør et karakterfullt menneskeverk i fjellet og beriker naturlandskapet. God landskapsmessig forankring, fast husgruppering og ensartete husformer preger Verkenseter i Grimsdalen. «Kulturmonumenter» som dette er i sterkt forfall og vil trolig gå tapt for etterslekten.

Secondly, the team tried to cater to the Norwegian sensibilities and soften the impact of the proposed changes accordingly. For example, members of the mountain planning team were aware of the Norwegian dream of a remote cabin and that the grouping of cabins was unpopular and therefore probably an unrealistic idea for the moment. The team hoped to get the cabin groups at least started by selling the concept as something perhaps for (international) tourists: "If one cannot count on a strong concentration of built-up areas being realistic as a planning principle for general recreational buildings in the mountains today, it still seems to be a relevant solution for the construction of rental cabins."[52] Understanding the need for isolation from others when in a cabin, the team proposed that planners and designers of cabin clusters "must aim for a certain near zone around the individual holiday home and a utilization of terrain and vegetation to shield against neighbors."[53] Still, the team hoped that eventually the whole idea of an isolated cabin could become a relic from the past—not appropriate of the new Norwegian generation.[54]

Thirdly, in collaboration with the Norwegian government, the team launched an extensive public information campaign that included various publications and an exhibition. In 1966, the report was followed by a series of short, richly illustrated handbooks for the wider public: *Hytteområder. En veiledning i planlegging* (Cabin areas. A guide to planning) by Erik Anker, *Hvordan bygge vakker hytte? Hus og landskap* (How to build a beautiful cabin? House and landscape) by Steinar Skåden, and *Plan i fjellet. Hytta på fjellet* (Plan in the mountains. Cabin in the mountains) by Erik Langdalen and Karl Erikstad.[55] The latter was part of an educational traveling exhibition, *Fjellbygd og feriefjell* (Mountain village and vacation mountain), that distilled the report's main points.[56]

The exhibition contained a total of 39 posters, which were to be set up solo, in pairs, and as tripartitions, in two zigzagged rows. One row of posters explained why cabin planning was needed, the other row explained how the planning could be executed in practice, taking the study areas as examples. In the first poster row, after highlighting the attractiveness of Norway's mountains, fjords, and northern lights for mountain tourists in Europe, the team addressed the main point: namely, the ugly cabins disfiguring the mountain slopes versus the beautiful mountain landscape without buildings. The second row of posters explained the types of planning instruments that existed, how planning processes worked, and how landowners could work together through co-ownership. The specific plans for the study areas were shown at the end. From these plans, the more general mountain planning principles were derived.

The last poster of the first row announced that if the next generation—depicted as children playing—shall "enjoy the mountains," then "planning is needed!"[57] The last phrase was creatively mixed together with the previous Tranmæl narrative of "enough space in the mountains" by Sverre Østhagen to create the slogan "Enough space, but planning is needed!"[58] While this insinuated a certain continuity with the previous cabin politics, this was certainly not the case, as the proposed planning principles meant a drastic confinement of the relative freedom that came before them.

Even though the aforementioned updated Beach Law was already adopted as temporary law from June 18, 1965, as part of

52 Original quote in Norwegian: "Om en ikke kan regne med at sterk bebyggelseskonsentrasjon i dag er realistisk som planleggingsprinsipp ved alminnelig fritidsbebyggelse i fjellet, synes det likevel å være en aktuell løsning ved oppføring av utleiehytter." Langdalen, "Natur og menneskeverk i fjellet," 30.

53 Original quote in Norwegian: "vi må ta sikte på en viss nærsone omkring det enkelte fritidshus og en utnyttelse av terrengformer og vegetasjon til skjerming mot nabo." Erik Langdalen, "Norge utenfor bygrensene," 111.

54 See Langdalen, "Natur og menneskeverk i fjellet," 40.

55 Erik Anker, *Hytteområder. En veiledning i planlegging* [Cabin areas: A guide to planning] (Oslo: Kommunal- og arbeidsdepartementet og utvalg for byplanforskning, 1967 (1966)); Steinar Skåden, *Hvordan bygge vakker hytte? Hus og landskap* [How to build a beautiful cabin? House and landscape] (Grunna Forlag, 1966); Erik Langdalen and Karl Erikstad, *Plan i fjellet. Hytta på fjellet* [Plan in the mountains, cabin in the mountains] (Oslo: A/S Byggtjeneste, 1966); Erik Langdalen, "Plan i fjellet" [Plan in the mountains], in *Den norske turistforenings årbok* (1966): 106–15; Karl Erikstad, "Hytta på fjellet" [Cabin in the mountains], *Den norske turistforenings årbok* (1966): 116–30. A short version of Erik Langdalen's article was published again years later in the magazine *Hytteliv*: Erik Langdalen, "Plan i fjellet 15 år etter" [Plan in the mountains 15 years later], *Hytteliv* 3 (1980): 78–81.

56 The exhibition premiered during Agricultural Week at Sjølyst in Oslo and was thereafter shown in places such as Lillehammer, Otta, Dokka, and Fagernes. Statens informasjonstjeneste, "Pressemelding *Fjellbygd og feriefjell*" [Press release *Mountain village and vacation mountain*] April 15, 1966. Da-0329/ Kommunal- og arbeidsdepartementet, Distriktsplanavdelingen/ Riksarkivet, Oslo.

57 Poster no. 18 features "Skal de få glede av fjellet? – planlegging må til" [Shall they [children] be able to enjoy the mountains? Planning is needed] in Da-0329.

58 Original quote in Norwegian: "Plass nok, men plan må til!" Østhagen, "Imponerende materiale framlagt av professor Sømmes fjellplan-team," 6.

Norway's renewed Building Law, it (together with the other ideas of the mountain planning team) was intended to be first subjected to the scrutiny of the general public, landowners, municipal and provincial governments, professional planners, tourists, and (future) cabin owners before its adoption: "The team themselves say that they have not had time to get to the bottom of the problems, and that more material will eventually come.... It is also important that the investigations become the subject of public debate."[59]

RESISTANCE DURING DISCUSSIONS AND PILOT PROJECTS

The awareness campaign started at the end of 1965 and heated up during 1966 in the discussions that were organized as part of the touring exhibition and public presentations given by members of the mountain planning team. Various pilot projects were launched in the studied municipalities and beyond in 1965 and 1966, many of which were not evaluated until after 1970.

The biggest concern during the discussions was the tension between the plan—to build cabins only in the unproductive forest and to prohibit cabin building in the coastal zones and open plains—and the interests of the landowners. Even before the launch of the report in November 1965, during the meeting between landowners and one of the local mountain planning teams in Sirdal, the landowners—although in general in favor of the common approach to mountain planning—expressed concerns. The most skeptical position was expressed by Knut Suleskard, who, whilst he did not mind that the environment would be developed into a more accessible tourist area, wanted to decide for himself about whether cabins would be built on his own land. Andreas Thu, on the other hand, was inclined to accept the new regulations but only on the condition that everything would be guaranteed to be equal and evenly fair for everybody: "landowners should use uniform contracts and get index-regulated agreements."[60] These two reservations, one against the limiting of the freedom of the owner, the other against possible inequalities, were typical of the feedback given on the plans.

When it came to the proposed clustering and aesthetic disciplining of the cabins, there was little enthusiasm, with the exception of planners and architects. The idea of prefabricated cabins that could be adapted to individual needs of the users was something that architects had been thinking about for some time by then. For example, as early as 1952, P. A. M. Mellbye proposed a modular cabin with a triangular A-section,[61] while Hans Østerhaug and Edvin Helseth connected to the office Arkitim developed from 1963 on the *Trysil-hytte/ Trybo-hytte* (Trysil-cabin/Trybo-cabin) that was launched in 1965 and also included an entire *Trybo* furniture system designed by Helseth.[62] A similar adaptable, prefabricated cabin assignment was launched as a pilot project under the new mountain plan recommendations in 1965. The Ål municipality, which had been one of the study areas for the mountain planning team, launched a competition for the *Ålhytta* (Ål cabin). The main question of the competition was: "What type of cabin is best suited for use in the mountain villages in Hallingdal?"[63] The architecture of the cabin was to be inspired by old *seter* buildings and to be flexible

59 Original quote in Norwegian: "Teamet sier selv at man ikke har rekket å trenge til bunns i problemene, og det vil etter hvert komme mer materiale.... Det er også viktig at utredningene blir gjenstand for offentlig debatt." "Store utviklingsmuligheter i Rondane-regionen" [Great development opportunities in the Rondane region], *Dagningen*, November 9, 1965, 4.

60 "Flertall blant grunneierne for fjellplan i Sirdalen" [Majority of landowners for mountain plan in Sirdalen], *Rogalands avis*, October 14, 1965, 1; "Helårsvei i Hunnedalen" [All-year road in Hunnedalen], *Rogalands avis*, October 14, 1965, 4.

61 P.A. Mellbye, "Monterbar hytte" [Modular cabin], *Byggekunst* 8 (1952): 142–43.

62 Harriet Clayhills, "Hytter med system" [Cabins with system], Bonytt 9 (1965): 240–43; Fallan, *Ecological by Design*, 92–96.

63 Lars Nilssen, *Ålhytta gjennom 50 år* [50 years of the Ålhytta] (Oslo: Kurér forlag, 2016), 11.

View of the exhibition *Fjellbygd og feriefjell* (Mountain village and vacation mountain) in Messehallen (The exhibition hall), Sjølyst, Oslo, 1966.

on many levels and easily customized in order to accommodate the individual's wishes; it had to be suitable for ready-made production, traditional construction, and for self-builders; it had to be adaptable to different plot conditions and to function well both as a detached house and in closer groupings; and it had to be able to be expanded.[64] More than 160 architects participated in this competition. The project that won the first prize, by Turid Haaland, did not make it beyond the prototype. The second prize winners, Kjell Lund and Nils Slaatto, saw their cabins—after some initial start-up problems—put into production. The design started to be developed for production, under the name *Ålhytta*, by Ål hyttebygg, in 1966 and has been commercially produced from 1969 until the present day.[65] The *Ålhytta* system became a private holiday cabin for many all over the world, while in Norway, it was widely used for all kinds of common purposes such as schools or community houses. It was also used as rental cabins, but it was not that popular as a private cabin. Jon Haug, who made drawings for most of the customized adaptations of the *Ålhytta* claimed: "The *Ålhytta* did not seem convincing to the Norwegian cabin buyers, who, disappointingly enough, almost always don't care about appearance and functional design."[66]

A similar rejection awaited the idea of cabin groupings. Therein, the public was joined by some Norwegian architects, who expressed reservations about designing whole groups of cottages. P. A. M. Mellbye—who at the time of the release of the mountain planning team's report in 1965 was the vice president of the Norske arkitekters landsforbund (National Association of Norwegian Architects)—feared that the grouping of cabins would mean a destruction of the solitary cabin-in-nature typology and the de facto imposition of a villa neighborhood typology instead:

> We approach the sight of concentrations of holiday homes—so many and with such a rising standard, that they approach the character of the residential town. Thus, the city's rules begin to apply once again, and we are faced not only with building single cities, but double cities: one for work, one for leisure, for the same people![67]

Other architects like Willy Sveen found the idea of cabin groupings necessary and some even criticized the large minimum distances of 50 to 200 meters between cabins that were prescribed in some areas.[68] Yet, two years after the release of the mountain planning team's report, in 1967, *Byggekunst* still reported that "it is not yet possible to publish Norwegian examples of a successful dense vacation development."[69] A similar picture was reported by the Norwegian Public Investigation committee in 1981.[70] Even though various pilot projects were launched, local municipalities struggled to get the idea to work, even later on. Either the municipalities could not find people interested in investing and in buying cabin clusters, or if they did, the final results received critique.

The mountain planning team's ideas for co-ownership, grouping, and the aesthetic disciplining of the cabins were thus met with resistance. Norwegians, who were used to building their cabins in relative freedom, found the new regulations excessive. As the editor-in-chief of the magazine *Hytteliv* (Cabin life), Tor Trosterud retrospectively summarized the general sentiment around the new

64 Nilssen, *Ålhytta gjennom 50 år*, 13.
65 Nilssen, *Ålhytta gjennom 50 år*, 13–33.
66 Original quote in Norwegian: "Ålhytta virket heller ikke overbevisende på de norske hyttkjøperne, som skuffende nok, stort sett hele tiden har gitt blaffen i utseendet og funksjonell utforming …" Jon Haug, "Ålhytta 30 år" [30 years of the *Ålhytta*], *Byggekunst* 3 (1997): 58–59.
67 Original quote in Norwegian: "… [vi] nærmer oss synet av konsentrerte plasseringer av feriehus – så mange og med en slik stigende standard, at de nærmer seg villabyens karakter. Dermed begynner byens regler å gjelde nok en gang, og vi står overfor *ikke bare å skulle bygge enkle byer, men doble byer: en for arbeide – en for fritid – for de samme menneskene!*" P. A. M. Mellbye, "Tett eller spredt?" [Dense or scattered?], *Byggekunst* 2 (1966): 54.
68 Willy Sveen, "Tett eller spredt nok en gang" [Dense or scattered, again], *Byggekunst* 4 (1967): 96.
69 Original quote in Norwegian: "Det er foreløpig ikke mulig å publisere norske eksempler på en vellykket tett feriebebyggelse." "Ferie?" [Vacation?], *Byggekunst* 4 (1967): 85.
70 Norges Offentlige Utredninger [Norwegian official reports], *Hytter og fritidshus* [Cabins and holiday homes] (Oslo, Bergen and Tromsø: Universitetsforlaget, 1981), 29.

cabin regulations in 1965: "The new law opened up regulatory zeal which eventually became a pure wonderland for the many who knew better and wanted to think for us." [71]

IMPASSE AND A HALF RE-TURN FROM "NO POLITICS" TO "YES POLITICS"

In 1965, the idea was to freeze all cabin development until the government produced zoning plans and guidelines, which were to initially be based on the discussions and pilot projects and then further refined and implemented by the counties and municipalities. Yet, the work at the national level did not progress. The aforementioned resistance toward the new co-ownership principles and the aesthetic controls hampered the already quite slow development of governmental plans. While the production of new holiday homes was halted, the demand for holiday cabins grew.[72] As a result, the prices of the existing cabins rose exponentially. Because of this standstill and inflation, people who dreamt about owning their own cabin or wanted to sell their land to someone who wanted to build one became exponentially frustrated. The situation became unsustainable and dangerous when many owners of coastal land zones started to demand compensation from governments for the loss that they suffered in terms of land value, as they could not sell their land for real estate development anymore.[73]

The ten-year long period of dissent and stagnation which followed after the publication of the mountain plan report and the adoption of the Building Law in 1965 was finally put to an end by the then Minister of Environment Gro Harlem Brundtland. Against the backdrop of a public controversy involving her father's cabin, in 1975, Brundtland unclogged the situation with holiday homes by changing the "no politics" to a "yes politics." [74] The no-to-yes change meant that many original intentions were abandoned, and various regulations were softened. For example, the government waived their involvement in the actual mapping, zoning, and planning. From then on, the national rules could be directly translated by the provinces and municipalities into area-specific policies and plans. The application of exception-stipulations in the Beach Law became a very profitable privilege which many local municipalities eagerly executed (and continue to do so). The municipality or landowner who wants to sell land within 100 meters of the coastline for cabin development can exert or ask for the application of the exception rule. For example, Sarpsborg, a municipality on the eastern bank of the Oslo fjord applies the 100-meter rule without any exceptions, while Sandefjord, a municipality at the western bank of Oslo fjord allows for various dispensations from the 100-meter rule with the result that many leisure cabins occupy the coast.[75]

Municipalities have many reasons for supporting cabin development, which include enabling local landowners to profit from the cabin construction, generating work for local construction firms and maintenance staff, and ensuring a customer base for local shops and services, some of which cater almost exclusively to cabin dwellers. Beyond these regular financial motives for cabin developments for the municipalities and landowners, especially the application of the dispensations, is also entangled with far less

71 Original quote in Norwegian: "... åpnet den loven reguleringsiver som etter hvert ble det rene eventyrland for de mange som visste bedre og ville tenke for oss." Tor Trosterud, "Med lov skal landet bygges" [The country must be built legally], *Hytteliv* 1 (1985): 5.

72 Sveen, "Tett eller spredt nok en gang," 95.

73 John Parr, *Det offentliges erstatningsplikt ved innskrenkninger i eiendomsrådigheten (Bygningsloven, Strandloven, Friluftsloven, Veiloven m.v.)* [The public's obligation to compensate in the event of restrictions on ownership (The building act, the beach act, the outdoors act, etc.)] (Oslo: Den Norske Advokatforening, 1969), 37–40.

74 Harald Ellefsen, "Hytte og båt er ikke lenger urimelig luksus" [Cabins and boats are no longer unreasonable luxuries], *Adresseavisa*, August 18, 1975; "Hyttebygging og valgflesk" [Cabin construction and selection], *Sørlandet Tiden*, August 13, 1975.

75 Sigrun Gjølberg, "Håndtering av byggeforbundet i 100-metersbeltet langs sjøen og bruk av 'annen byggegrense' som virkemiddel i Sarpsborg- og Sandefjord Kommune i lys av regionale føringer" [Handling of the building association in the 100-meter belt along the sea and use of "other building boundary" as a tool in Sarpsborg- and Sandefjord municipality in light of regional guidelines] (master's thesis, Ås, Norges miljø- og biovitenskapelige universitet, 2017).

legal transactions involving personal connections and gains. Corruption cases have been investigated in Færder and Tjøme municipalities, drawing significant attention from the Norwegian media: "Building is prohibited in the beach zone, but larger cabins, new stalls, new tennis courts, or swimming pools are constantly appearing. … The cottages of several of Norway's richest families have been drawn into an extensive investigation."[76] The public is indignant at these special cabins, which have appeared where nobody else was allowed to build. However, there is also an unknown number of other types of illegal construction: the secret primitive huts that have been self-built in remote places all over Norway.[77] These cabins are difficult to find and exist without any type of infrastructure, exerting a relatively low impact on the environment. Even though these cabins are truly illegal, they enjoy some sympathy among the Norwegian population, in contrast to the comfortable holiday homes that have been built on the best spots by way of the corrupt exemptions.[78]

What the Norwegian government and the mountain planning team feared would happen in 1990, finally happened in 2021. That year, there were half a million holiday homes officially registered in Norway, making Norway the world's top country when it comes to private cabins.[79] Growing demand will push these numbers further in coming years, with an estimated 5,000 legal cabins being built per year, despite lasting complains from landscape planners about the cabins' poor positioning and aesthetics, and despite growing moral guilt stemming from the knowledge of the cabins' negative climate effects.[80]

CONCLUDING CABIN CONTROVERSIES

Cabin planning is often described in international discourses as "troubled" or even "cursed."[81] Norwegian cabin politics is no exception. In 1980, when Erik Langdalen was evaluating the then last fifteen years of Norwegian cabin politics, the word that he used remarkably often in his report was "conflict(s)."[82] The many historical and contemporary controversies that appeared to surround the subject matter reveal an ongoing negotiation between collective and individual interests. At stake in the debate are fundamental issues. On one side, there are the rights to individual freedom, possession, and welfare, as well as cultivation of local cultural traditions. On the other side there are values such as protection of nature, egalitarianism, and welfare of the entire community. The past and present cabin controversies worked as catalysators that revealed these competing core values in the Norwegian society, as well as the dilemmas concerning the responsibilities and the limits of the Norwegian welfare state.

In 1965, when the unregulated cabin phenomenon was growing out of proportion, Axel Sømme's team composed mountain planning principles, inspired pilot projects for new types of cabin systems and cabin clusters, and put the co-ownership model on the table for public discussion. However, these ideas never seemed to be accepted by the Norwegian population, even though the majority of citizens rationally grasped the need for a turn from individual freedom to collective welfare when it came to cabin politics.

76 Original quote in Norwegian: "I strandsonen er det forbudt å bygge, men stadig dukker det opp nye større hytter, nye boder, nye tennisbaner eller et svømmebasseng … Hyttene til flere av Norges rikeste familier er trukket inn i en omfattende etterforskning." Marie Olausen, "Strandkongene. På Sommerøya blir det umulige mulig" [The beach kings: On Sommerøya, the impossible becomes possible], *Tønsberg Blad*, accessed January 11, 2023, https://www.tb.no/strandkongene-hor-alle-episodene-her/1/5-76-1483170.

77 Marius Nergård Pettersen, *Hemmelige hytter* [Secret cabins] (Dal Forlag, 2018); Marius Nergård Pettersen, *Hemmelige Norge – det skjulte friluftslivet* [Secret Norway—the hidden outdoor life] (Dal forlag, 2021).

78 Eli Støa, "Drømmen om det enkle liv – et grunnlag for en mer bærekraftig hyttekultur?" [The dream of the simple life—a basis for a more sustainable cottage culture?], in *Norske hytter i endring. Om bærekraft og behag* [Norwegian cabins in transformation. On sustainability and comfort], ed. Helen Jøsok Gansmo, Thomas Berker, and Finn Arne Jørgensen (Trondheim: Tapir Akademisk Forlag, 2011): 53–74; Carlo Aall, "Hyttebruk og miljø: en arena for nøysomhet eller overforbruk?" [Cabin use and the environment: an arena for frugality or overconsumption?], in Jøsok Gansmo et al., "Hyttebruk og miljø," 107–23.

79 Anders Moen Kaste, "Norwegians Have Built a Half-Million Cabins as Holiday Homes: Is That Too Many?" *Sciencenorway* 17, September 2021, https://sciencenorway.no/climate-forestry-nature-conservation/norwegians-have-built-a-half-million-cabins-as-holiday-homes-is-that-too-many/1911180.

80 Jin Xue et al., "The Hidden Side of the Norwegian Cabin Fairytale: Climate Implications of Multi-Dwelling Lifestyle," *Scandinavian Journal of Hospitality and Tourism* 5 (2020): 459–584.

81 Terry Coppock, ed., *Second Homes: Curse or Blessing?* (Oxford: Pergamon, 1977); Dieter K. Müller and Gijsbert Hoogendoorn, "Second Homes: Curse or Blessing? A Review 36 Years Later," *Scandinavian Journal of Hospitality and Tourism* 13, no. 4 (2013): 353–69; Dieter K. Müller, "Second Homes in Rural Areas: Reflections on a Troubled History," *Norsk Geografisk Tidsskrift* [*Norwegian Journal of Geography*] 65 (2011): 137–43.

82 Erik Langdalen, "Second Homes in Norway: A Controversial Planning Problem," *Norsk Geografisk Tidsskrift* [*Norwegian Journal of Geography*] 34, 3 (1980): 139–44.

83 Original quote in Norwegian: "Hva om myndighetene sa ok, vær på hytta, men du må greie deg selv om du blir syk?" Schnell and Skjulhaug, "Hyttedebatten handler om norsk urbanitet."

Possibly too many changes were proposed all at once and especially land ownership appeared to be a core value that almost nobody wanted to compromise. Many continued also to adhere to the idea of a solitary cabin (instead of one placed in a grouping of cabins), and the freedom to design the aesthetics of their own cabin themselves. When the government partially re-liberalized cabin politics in 1975, it opened the door to privileges for some but not for the others when it comes to the opportunity to own a private cabin at a scenic spot in Norway. Such violation of the egalitarian principle can be considered an unwelcome and undermining phenomenon in the welfare state. With the most recent coronavirus cabin crisis, it appeared that staying at the cabin is not only an individual welfare right, but that it has acquired the status of a fundamental human right—even if the visit to the cabin would come at the cost of people's lives, as was the case in 2020 when the hospitals warned that they would break under the burden of a disproportionate number of coronavirus admissions. In the context of the latter debate Schnell and Skjulhaug asked: "What if the authorities said ok, stay in the cabin, but you're on your own if you get sick?"[83] This question is interesting as it touches upon the fundamental issue that runs as a red thread through all the cabin struggles, namely the deep-seated and unresolved clash in opinions about the position of the cabin phenomenon in the welfare state.

The cabin persistently seems to occupy a mental place outside of the Nordic consensus society, conceptually aligning with nineteenth-century ideas of freedom from society in a cabin in the wilderness. Knowing that these ideas have been entangled with each other from the nineteenth century onwards, thanks to various efforts of national (and international) painters, poets, philosophers, as well as previous social democratic politicians, doesn't diminish these sentiments in any way.

One can be a "reasonable citizen-consumer" when it comes to complying with state-organized planning, design regulations for public spaces, and regular homes. At the same time, when it comes to second homes—cabins and self-built huts in nature, one can have a difficult time letting go of one's desire for freedom, despite society's focus on the negative environmental impact of cabins, and on ensuring collective and egalitarian access to (and state-protection of) Norwegian nature. The Norwegian cabin controversies reveal the tendency to celebrate two types of freedom. In the daily life, there is the cultivation of the consensus freedom characteristic of Scandinavia, whereby freedom is not understood one-sidedly as the socialist "freedom from want" or as the liberal "freedom to pursue one's own desires" but as an integration and negotiation of both. However, when it comes to cabin life, there seems to exist a desire for a more individual kind of freedom and welfare.

FRAGMENTS, WHISPERS, AND MATERIALS IN SPRING

Aysha Amin

In my attempt to seek stillness and closure, I start wandering and sensing my surroundings. I visit the still pockets behind buildings in transition. Buildings, previously functioning as non-profit social housing, undergoing demolition, entering a state of metamorphosis.

On these sites, whispers, stories, and material remains become a collection of witnesses nesting in the soil. An organic archive.

In my wandering, I smell notes of mineral dust, engine, moist soil, green leaves, eggs, and canned tomatoes; in the distance, incense for prayer and protection.

With my camera, I see how nature embraces these concrete skeletons in limbo, housing remnants of wallpaper on the concrete walls, now strange objects in their own neighborhood. Loud heavy cracks of concrete, the engines in the distance, the sirens and signals, birds flying by in groups.

I am taking in a monumental change in the architectural landscape. I'm next to the endless summer breeze, caressing the treetops, while I am wondering about how long these moments will last. How much can I remember from when these sites were daily routes to school and adventure? Will the paths miss the sound of kids running home as the streetlamps come on? Will the gardens miss the grandparents caring for the soil?

50-year-old structures housing families wanting space, light, and access to nature. Warm meals, news on the television, kids on the playground, tea and coffee brewing all day, walks and conversations. The modernist planning of housing areas was not perfect. According to some researchers, living a good life in those buildings would be impossible. I believe that the grandparents, gardens, and kids would disagree with this. I know I would. There is a softness in the rough edges of cracked concrete. I am documenting what I see. Wondering.

*

Photos taken in Gellerup, Aarhus

Kingo

2 NETWORKS AND ACTORS

Espen Johnsen

LOCAL AGENCY AND TRANSNATIONAL COLLABORATIONS

Stockholm During the Second World War

The architects, artists, and designers who fled from Nazi Germany and fascist Europe, particularly to the United States, and the ways in which they used their experiences and networks, have been the subject of much scholarship.[1] The situation in Scandinavia remains less scrutinized. As a neutral country, Sweden was affected relatively little by the Second World War, leaving Stockholm in a special position in the postwar period. Certain architects from Germany, Italy, and the Czech Republic had, before the war, emigrated to countries like Norway and Sweden. Sweden attracted both established and radical, young, and talented architects in the period 1942–45, including architects and urban planners from Norway who had held public positions and felt threatened, or were deposed by the German authorities, of which some were part of Nordic avant-garde architectural culture networks during the 1920s and 1930s. Besides the Swedish architects responsible for *acceptera*,[2] Edvard Heiberg and Poul Henningsen from the Danish journal *Kritisk Revy* and Johs. Borchsenius from the Norwegian Sosialistiske Arkitekters Forening (SAF, the Socialist architects association), which was associated with the PLAN Group, plus architects like Arne Korsmo and Jørn Utzon, were all working in Stockholm toward the end of the war.[3] Examination of the formal and informal networks and associations that were established in this period help to explain similarities and differences in the various ideals that informed Nordic postwar architecture. Some of these architects had been involved in resistance struggles in their home countries and several were active in left-wing politics; some with a Jewish background also fled to Stockholm, while others, like a group of young Danish architects, came for work.

Architects from at least nine different nations—Germany, Switzerland, Poland, Hungary, and the Netherlands, alongside the other Scandinavian countries—worked and lived in Stockholm during the war.[4] Many Swedish architects, it is important to note, were positive about hiring Nordic and international colleagues. In Stockholm, these foreign architects experienced buildings from the interwar period by Ragnar Östberg, Gunnar Asplund, and Sven Markelius, and visited exhibitions, museums, and libraries, as well as new development schemes. Uno Åhrén emerged as the most important network agent during the war, helping refugees and Jews escape Nazism, and helping Danish and Norwegian architects, for example Edvard Heiberg, flee.[5] Among the architects in Heiberg's circle in Stockholm was his friend from *Kritisk Revy*, Poul Henningsen, as well as the Dane Arne Jacobsen and the Norwegian Harald Hals. Some of these groupings gathered not only architects but also politicians, engineers, and artists, and other intellectuals engaged in discussing current societal issues.

Between 1935 and 1950, the search for new ideals within urban planning and architecture seems to have led to both a consolidation

1 See, for instance, Stephanie Barron, ed., *Exiles + Emigrés. The Flight of European Artists from Hitler* (Los Angeles: Los Angeles County Museum of Art, 1997), and Elana Shapira and Alison J. Clarke, eds., *Émigré Cultures in Design and Architecture* (London: Bloomsbury Academic, 2017).
2 Gunnar Asplund et al., *acceptera* (Stockholm: Tiden, 1931).
3 This section is partly based on: Espen Johnsen, "Korsmo and Utzon in Stockholm," in *PAGON: Scandinavian Avant-Garde Architecture, 1945–1956* (London: Bloomsbury Publishing 2023), 26–38.
4 Lisa Gjessing, "Planlegging" [Planning], in *Boliger og samfunnsbygg* [Housing and community buildings], ed. Harald Hals (Oslo: Johan Grundt Forlag, 1946), 17.
5 Eva Rudberg, "Uno Åhrén: en föregångsman inom 1900-talets arkitektur och samhällsplanering" [Uno Åhrén: a pioneer of 20th century architecture and civic planning] (PhD diss., KTH, Stockholm, 1981), 154.

of various actors and networks and the formation of new groupings in Scandinavia. The history of Nordic, and especially Norwegian architecture during the Second World War has large gaps, which include the planning work that was done by Norwegian architects in England and Sweden during the war. Following the Nazi occupation of Norway in 1940, Norwegian architects operated as "agents," working through hidden and personal networks; in this text, I address the role of one such architect: Harald Hals. By considering how Hals operated in Stockholm (1944–45), partly via his correspondence with Erik Rolfsen in London, I consider how information flows within the Scandinavian architectural culture during the Second World War contributed to the development, differentiation, and physical manifestation of Scandinavian welfare architecture.

In Stockholm, Danish and Norwegian architects soon became well-informed about developments in Swedish urban planning and domestic architecture; after the war, this gave them an advantage. In practice, all private building activity stopped completely in Norway during the war, and architects had neither assignments nor access to architectural developments in other countries. In 1943, the war took a new turn, in that the Allies began to believe in victory, developing as a result a series of new plans. In Stockholm, architects became aware of Patrick Abercrombie and John Henry Forshaw's *County of London Plan* (1944); Lewis Mumford's *Culture of Cities* (1938) was published in Swedish in 1942. Émigré Norwegian architects may have played a role in linking Swedish planning to what was happening in Britain: Harald Hals, who was working for Sven Markelius in 1944–45, served as a connection to London via his fellow Norwegian, Erik Rolfsen. One of Markelius' first acts in 1944 as Stockholm's Chief City Planner, was in fact to ask for updated information about British planning.[6] The idea of dividing city suburbs into neighborhood units with community centers was promoted in a simple and convincing manner and quickly made an impact in Sweden. Foreign architects in Stockholm also became familiar with the development of various Swedish housing typologies: *smalhus* (shallow houses), *punkthus* (point houses), *stjärnhus* (star houses), *kollektivhus* (collective houses), and *radhus* (terrace houses).[7] Institutions such as the Swedish Society of Architects (SAR) and the Swedish Society of Arts and Crafts (SSF) had great faith in the value of housing research, and their opinions informed the work of the Building Section of the Swedish Standard Association.

AGREEMENT, FRICTIONS, AND TURNS IN NORDIC ARCHITECTURE

International surveys like Alan Colquhoun's *Modern Architecture* often very superficially link the Modern Movement's breakthrough in Scandinavia (1930) to the development of social reforms in Sweden beginning in 1932 with the Social Democrats' assumption of power under the banner of *folkhemmet* (the people's home).[8] Furthermore, the ideas behind the 1940s housing estates in Sweden, often described under the umbrella of New Empiricism, is also often highlighted, and illustrated with examples of buildings in Stockholm that were planned and built during the war, for instance

6 Eva Rudberg, *Sven Markelius, Architect* (Stockholm: Arkitektur Förlag, 1989), 156. See also Peter Carolin, "Sense, Sensibility and Tower Blocks," *Twentieth Century Architecture*, no. 9 (2008), 102.

7 Nils Ahrbom, "Notes on the Planning of Dwellings," in *Swedish Housing of the Forties*, ed. Sven Backström and Stig Ålund (Stockholm: Tidsskriften Byggmästaren, 1950), 33–42.

8 Alan Colquhoun, *Modern Architecture* (Oxford: Oxford University Press, 2002), 195–97. This is also in accordance with contemporary Nordic publications, for example the introduction of Gustav Lettström, *Nordisk Arkitektur 1946–1949* (Stockholm: Byggmästarens förlag, 1950).

the nine "point houses" at Danviksklippan by the architects Backström & Reinius (1940–45) or their "star houses" and residential units at Kv. Akterspegeln in Gröndal (1944–46). A few years after the war, the new ideas from Sweden within urban developments and welfare architecture were spread internationally through journals and G. E. Kidder Smith's well-illustrated book *Sweden Builds* (1950, and second revised edition 1957). This type of publication probably contributed to the strong position Swedish architecture gained early on in the history of postwar architecture.

However, one can ask whether the historical narrative of the Nordic welfare architecture demands further investigation in order to reveal the various factions, frictions, and turns that characterized these very interesting years. Considering the exchanges between architects of different nationalities during the war might contribute to a more nuanced understanding.

Giving a precise overall description of Nordic architecture in the 1940s quickly appears to be an impossible task. Kay Fisker probably succeeds best when he, in 1945, claimed that a common characteristic of Nordic architecture was:

> not pretentious and extravagant as in the Latin countries; monumentality is not the goal in itself; we strive for an art of building that serves life and man, that submits to nature, that does not intrude, but on the contrary, wants to be anonymous.[9]

Fisker's quote synthesizes an overall presentation of Nordic architecture but does not bring out the nuances, contradictions, parallels, intersecting directions, and—most important—the significant differences present within Nordic architectural culture. Most obviously, it ignores the fact that Sweden maintained a close connection between politics and architecture, while this in Norway was more hidden.[10]

Architecture and social housing in Sweden, Denmark, and Norway between 1935 and 1940 can partly be read as being led by an internal self-criticism against modernism. This is relevant to understanding both the background and the significance of the Norwegian and Danish architects' stay in Stockholm. Some Norwegian architects, like Hals and Rolfsen, began to pay more attention to creating continuity with regional and local traditions. Others, like Arne Korsmo and Knut Knutsen, began to move modernism in other directions, concerned with the landscape, natural materials, and non-geometric, partly figurative forms. Within residential architecture, an overarching idea of a green city inspired by Le Corbusier's book *Ville Radieuse* (1935), was in the mid-1930s highlighted in Oslo in the avant-garde environment around Ove Bang. But Bang and members of the Norwegian CIAM group like Blakstad and Munthe-Kaas were not allocated assignments in the country's social housing and the housing cooperative OBOS. The radical SAF milieu (which included Rolfsen) joined Arbeiderpartiet (the Labour Party) in 1936, no longer promoting a progressive architecture. So, in general, there was little experimentation within Norwegian housing in the years leading up to 1940.

9 Original quote in Danish: "Den er ikke pretentiøs og prangende som i de latinske lande, monumentaliteten er ikke maalet i seg selv, vi stræber efter en bygningskunst, der tjener livet og menneske, som indordner sig naturen, som ikke trænger paa, men tvertimod ønsker at være anonym." Quoted in: Nils-Ole Lund, *Nordisk Arkitektur* (Copenhagen: Arkitektens forlag, 1991), 109. See Kay Fisker, "Svensk Bygningskunst," *Arkitektens Ugehæfte* (1945): 30–32.

10 Anne-Kristine Kronborg, "Å reise noe nytt og bedre. Om arkitektur og politikk 1935–1940" [To raise something new and better: On architecture and politics, 1935–1940] (PhD diss., AHO, 2022).

Sven Backström and Leif Reinius, "Star houses" and residential units (1944–46) at Kv. Akterspegeln in Gröndal, Södermalm, Stockholm.

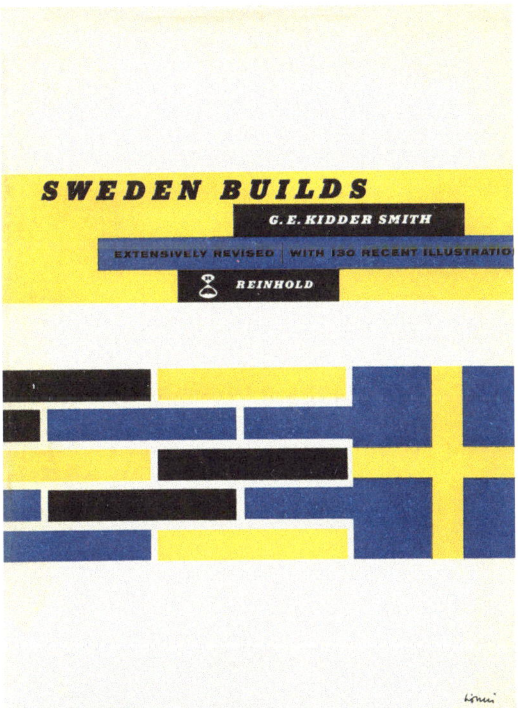

G. E. Kidder Smith: *Sweden Builds.*

Backström & Reinius: “Star Houses,” Gröndal Apartments (1944–46), Stockholm. Photo from Kidder Smith *Sweden Builds*, 33.

11 "Harald Hals: Obituary," *Morgenbladet*, February 23, 1959, 2.

12 Espen Johnsen, "Arkitektur, kultur og kollektivhus. Sovjetiske impulser på norsk funksjonalisme" [Architecture, culture and collective housing: Soviet impulses within Norwegian functionalism], in *Norge-Russland. Naboer gjennom 1000 år* [Norway-Russia: Neighbors for 1,000 years], ed. Daniela Büchten, Tatjana Dzakson, and Jens Petter Nielsen (Oslo: Spartacus Academic Press, 2004), 691.

13 Original quote in Norwegian: "Det er en drabelig kulturell oppgave i den tiden som kommer å føre byggekunsten inn i et riktig spor og opp til det nivå, hvor den etter våre tradisjoner hører hjemme. I denne mørke tiden må vi se det som et stort lyspunkt, at vi får høve til å gjøre det. Og – *arkitektene har ansvaret for at det skjer.*" Harald Hals, "Gjenoppbyggingen" [The reconstruction], *Byggekunst* 3 (1940): 33.

14 Erik Rolfsen, "En ny by – En bedre by. Småprat foran en stor oppgave" [A new city—A better city. Small talk before a big task], *Byggekunst* 3 (1940): 60–63.

HALS AND ROLFSEN'S RESPONSE TO THE OUTBREAK OF THE WAR

The Norwegian architects Harald Hals and Erik Rolfsen represented very different urban planning ideals, and were even in conflict occasionally, but with the outbreak of the war, both showed an immediate willingness to cooperate with each other. Harald Hals (1876–1959), who was educated in Berlin and Stockholm and had studied and practiced in the US, had since 1926 served as Oslo's *reguleringssjef* (Chief planning officer). Recognized for his role as *boligdirektør* (Housing director) in the early 1920s, the plans and housing developments he had worked on in Oslo, including Ullevål Hageby (Ullevål Garden City) 1916–22, combined the formal ideals of Nordic neoclassicism with a modern urban planning approach. After his death, he was both referred to as "the creator of Modern Oslo" and criticized for acting as a dictator.[11] In "Fra Christiania til Stor-Oslo. Forslag til generalplan for Oslo" (From Christiania to Greater Oslo: Proposal for a general plan for Oslo) from 1929, he began to develop plans outside the city core, with green connections and corridors between the city center toward the landscapes of the periphery.

His work in the 1930s maintained a social profile, as seen in the "Stor-Oslo: forslag til generalplan" (Greater Oslo: proposal for general plan) of 1934 and his 1934 book and exhibition *Byen lever* (The city is alive), where he pointed out that Oslo risked being closed in as the result of surrounding islands being seized and privatized by a small number of people. In 1935, he visited and studied urban planning and social housing in Russia, including collective housing, and in 1937 participated (together with Edvard Heiberg, Sven Markelius, and Frank Lloyd Wright) in the Congress of the Soviet Architectural Association, publishing *Moskva i går, i dag, i morgen* (Moscow yesterday, today, tomorrow) in 1937.[12] Unlike other foreign colleagues, Hals was not as critical of the Stalinist neoclassicism that now had taken over after constructivism. In 1940, shortly after Germany's invasion of Norway and the bombing of several Norwegian cities, Harald Hals, as president of Norske Arkitekters Landsforbund (NAL, the Norwegian National Association of Architects), published a text on the first page of the periodical *Byggekunst* urging Norwegian architects to take responsibility for and participate in the reconstruction of the bombed cities. Hals wrote:

> It is a formidable cultural task to set the future of the art of building on the right track and bring it up to that level where, according to our traditions, it belongs. In these dark times, we must see this chance as a great possibility. Architects are responsible for making this happen.[13]

New plans for cities and countrysides were needed and, as Hals clarified, nothing should be allowed to be built until those plans were ready. Through the article, published at a time when the architectural press in Norway was still free of German censorship, he appealed for the help, skill, and insights of his colleagues in tackling this task.

In the same issue, architect Erik Rolfsen (1905–92) also published the article "En ny by – en bedre by" (A new city—a better city).[14] When the war broke out on April 9, 1940, Rolfsen had been employed at the Oslo municipality's urban planning office for two years, under Harald Hals' leadership. While the bombing by the Germans was described as a tragedy, Rolfsen argued that the consequences also represented an opportunity for rethinking how future residential areas should be characterized. In this task, he advocated for the importance of openness and proper dimensioning:

> No endless and disconsolate length either in tenements or terraced houses ... No colossal blocks that create an inhumane scale and difficult traffic and hygienic conditions. The house is *not* a machine to live in. A vitamin pill is not as satisfying as a plate of well-cooked food. It is for this reason that we don't like mechanically ordered *lameller* (slab blocks) and rows of detached houses.[15]

Rolfsen continued:

> What we need is small groupings of tenement blocks by green open spaces and orderly gatherings of small detached houses, adjacent to a *stortun* (a large yard) like our old farmstead buildings, or grouped around a grassy plain like a *setergrend* (a cluster of mountain pasture farms), or like a village formed around a square. We must find a form of housing that is geared toward manageable social interactions and digestible scales. By placing organic groups of houses, neighborhoods, within the framework of a larger society, the intimacy and humanity of the small unit is saved, while isolation and narrowmindedness are avoided. The small town must influence the big city.[16]

Such ideals differed wildly from his own radical proposal from 1936, which was presented in the journal *PLAN*, which envisaged the reshaping of the whole of Oslo through the construction of a vast residential belt, formed like an amphitheater. One plan consisted of 2,000 high-rise buildings, each twelve floors tall, in a sloping terrain that was oriented toward the city's historical center.[17]

By emphasizing that "our tradition" should also be incorporated in contemporary architecture, they both implicitly criticized the Modern Movement, at the same time aligning themselves with ideals popular amongst leading architects in Sweden and England. Hals expressed a clear call for architects to contribute to the community, while Rolfsen signaled that in the future architecture should accept parts of the critique of modernism in order to adjust and renew modern planning. His 1940 essay in *Byggekunst* might be seen as a turning point that both marks the pursuit of a critique of, and a distance from, aspects of modern architecture and urban planning—in particular functionalist housing ideals as they had recently been built and planned in Norway, including in Oslo and other large and small cities in the Nordic region.

These statements from Hals and Rolfsen, both from 1940, are interesting on several levels; they reflect and hint at the complex transition period that preceded Scandinavia's postwar development, especially within the Norwegian architecture and planning discourse. On a general level, Rolfsen's 1940 comments point toward a number of planning and housing ideals that subsequently came to be popularized by the American Lewis Mumford, including

15 Original quote in Norwegian: "Ingen uendelig og trøsteløs lengde hverken på leiegård eller rekkehus ... Ingen kolossalblokker som gjør målestokken umenneskelig og de trafikale og hygieniske forhold vanskelige. Hjemmet er *ikke* en maskin til å bo i. Jeg er ikke likeglad om mitt måltid er en saftig rett mat eller en vitaminpastill. Derfor liker vi heller ikke lameller i mekanisk rekkefølge eller opplinjerte villakolonner." Rolfsen, "En ny by – en bedre by," 63.

16 Original quote in Norwegian: "Det vi må fram til er de små grupper, leiegårder ved en grønn, åpen plass eller små eneboliger i ordnet samling, avsluttede partier omkring et stortun, slik som vår gamle gårdsbebyggelse, setergrenda rundt vollen eller landsbyen omkring torget. Vi må få en boligform som er innrettet på et overkommelig sosialt samkvem og en fordøyelig målestokk. Ved å plassere slike organiske boliggrupper, naboskap, innenfor et større samfunns ramme, reddes den lille enhets hygge og menneskelighet, mens en unngår dens isolasjon og sneverhet. Småbyen må inn i storbyen." Rolfsen, "En ny by – en bedre by," 63.

17 Erik Rolfsen, "Generalreguleringsplanen for Stor Oslo" [The general regulation plan for Greater Oslo], *PLAN* (1936): 42–50.

18 Sven Backström, "A Swede Looks at Sweden," in "Sweden: Outpost of Peace in War," special issue, *Architectural Review* (September 1943): 80.

19 Original quote in Norwegian: "… medlemsskap i N.S. eller innstiling overfor Quisling, N.S. og okkupasjons-myndighetene skulle tillegges avgjørende vekt ved ansettelser, forfremmelser og fortsatt arbeid i det offentliges tjeneste." "Norske Arkitekters Landsforbund 1941–1945," *Byggekunst* 1 (1945): 2.

20 "Norske Arkitekters Landsforbund 1941–1945."

the ideas of new towns and neighborhood units, which were highly influential in British and Swedish town planning. In some sense, the text has a lot in common with Sven Backström's article "A Swede Looks at Sweden," which was published in *Architectural Review* in 1943.[18] Here, we see ideals being formulated that would characterize the early phase of postwar Nordic welfare architecture, but which were present in some form even by the end of the 1930s. Hals' and Rolfsen's respective articles in *Byggekunst* (1940) serve as a reminder to the reader that the years during the Second World War remain under-researched and under-communicated in terms of the history of Nordic architecture in the period 1935–50. While this fifteen-year intermezzo has not yet been clearly defined by scholars, it was, I argue, also characterized by a lack of clarity with respect to the aesthetic strategies and architectural approaches being advanced at the time. This can be linked to the political upheaval of the period: not only did social democratic governments in Sweden and Norway come to power with the aim of attending to the housing question and strengthening housing standards, but Germany's occupation of Norway and Denmark during the Second World War completely changed architectural culture, architecture policy, and reduced the possibility to produce experimental designs.

THE CHALLENGING YEARS 1940–42

For both Hals and Rolfsen, the early phase of the war was professionally very challenging. Shortly after the outbreak of the war, Rolfsen was given responsibility for the reconstruction of the small town of Kristiansund, under the Brente Steders Regulering (Burned places regulation, BSR), which was established under the leadership of Professor Sverre Pedersen, an internationally well-known urban planner and architect, mostly practicing neoclassicism. Pedersen was criticized in the 1930s by a younger generation, including those involved in Socialistiske Arkitekters Forening (SAF)—of which Erik Rolfsen was a member—for not being more updated on modern urban planning. A small avant-garde architectural team was, in 1940, assembled in Kristiansund, including Rolfsen, Øivind Grimsgaard, and Arne Korsmo. A perspective by Rolfsen (1941) shows his now far more traditional attitude.

However, if one was not willing to cooperate with the Germans, it was difficult for Norwegian architects interested in renewing modern urban planning to practice. The German *Reichskommissariat* was early on given responsibility for much of the planning and building activity in Norway. In the spring and summer of 1941, German interference increased. NAL, with Hals as president, was among the organizations that reacted against the memorandum that was circulated, informing that "membership in NS [Nasjonal Samling (National unification)], and attitudes toward Vidkun Quisling of the NS and the occupation authorities are to be given decisive weight in hiring, promotions, and continued work in the public service."[19] On June 18, 1941, the Nazi Reichskommissar Josef Terboven forced NAL to close, and Hals resigned as president.[20] Later in 1941, Hals asked Pedersen to resign from his leadership in BSR. Hals' role as *reguleringssjef* for Oslo was taken over by the Nazi sympathizer F. W. Rode, who also became head of the newly formed Norges Arkitektforbund

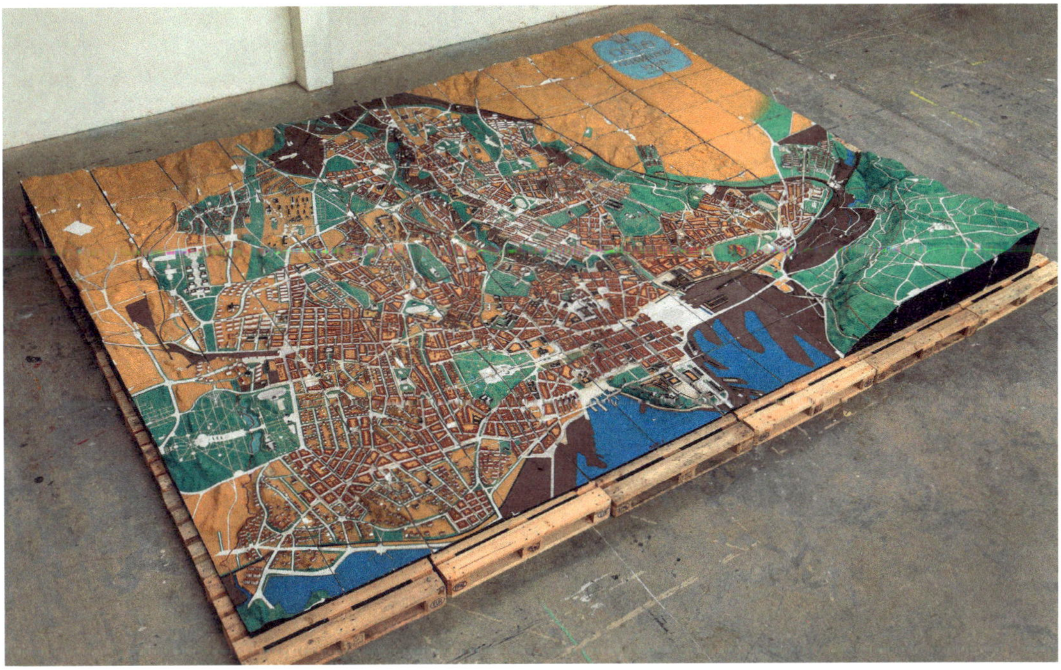

Harald Hals, Generalplan for Oslo (General plan for Oslo), model, (1930, revised 1940).

Erik Rolfsen, sketch for an ideal plan of Oslo, with 2,000 high-rise buildings. *Plan* (1936).

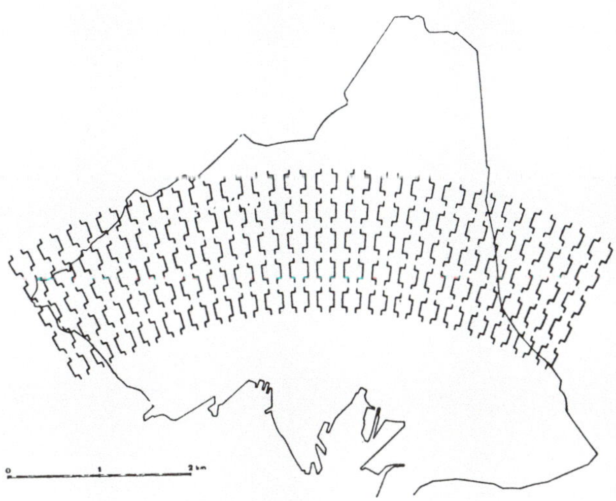

(the Norwegian Architect's Association). Rolfsen left Kristiansund and BSR and fled first to Sweden (in January 1943)[21] and then to England. In London, he worked for the in-exile Norwegian Government's Forsynings og Gjenreisningsdepartmentet (Supply and reconstruction department), acting as an important consultant in regional and urban planning, and planning for reconstruction. In the winter of 1944–45, Rolfsen came in contact with London town planner Patrick Abercrombie, an encounter that may have informed Rolfsen's later reference to the discussions of "urban development, regional plans, green belts, new towns, local centers, enclaves and decentralized services" in the London environment.[22] Sources suggest that Hals did not flee to Sweden until February 1944.[23]

HALS ESTABLISHES A COMMITTEE IN STOCKHOLM

One of Hals' first initiatives was to map and create a network of Norwegian architects working in Stockholm. In his mapping, he included not only those who came as refugees, but also Norwegian architects already living in Stockholm. According to Hals, there were, in the spring of 1944, twenty Norwegian architects in the Swedish capital,[24] including Johs. Borchsenius from the SAF Group, and others like Fredrik Winsnes, Helge Thiis, Arne Korsmo, and the Danish-Norwegian Edvard Heiberg. In a letter to Hals in April 1944, Rolfsen observed that some of the Norwegian architects working in Sweden had jointly expressed a desire to carry out "studies and preparations for the reconstruction at home."[25] Hals informed Rolfsen a few weeks later that an architectural committee with a council had already been formed in Stockholm, with himself as a chairman and secretary. He hoped the committee could assist the Department in London and that they could be of mutual benefit to one another, enclosing a short bibliography on Norwegian urban planning, which Rolfsen had requested.[26] A meeting in May was to take place at Hakon Ahlberg's office.[27] In Stockholm, Hals became a focal point for Norwegian architects, forming a Norwegian architectural committee to prepare for reconstruction after the war. While in London Rolfsen was formulating plans for the reconstruction and rebuilding of Norway through the exiled national government, Hals' agency in Stockholm specifically targeted particular "architectural arenas," work that saw Stockholm attain importance for Danish and Norwegian architects in the postwar years. In the summer of 1944, Den Norske Bygningstekniske Komite (D. B. K., the Norwegian Building Technology Committee) was formally established in Stockholm, under the leadership of Harald Hals.[28] Other members were Lisa Gjessing, Edvard Heiberg, Ole Rolfsen, and Fredrik Størmer. Both Hals' preserved correspondence, which is archived in Riksarkivet in Oslo and his account which is published in *Byggekunst* show a commitment to current topics. The Committee's first objective was to gather information and write reports that could contribute to the reconstruction. This included obtaining information about: (1) ready-to-assemble wooden houses; (2) the economic and technical advantages of standardized house types and building parts; (3) new building materials; (4) community facilities such as kindergartens and kitchens; (5) city and community centers; (6) Swedish housing and housing policy; (7) the interior design and furnishing

21 Den Kgl. Norske Legasjons Flyktningskontor, RA/S-6753/V/Va/L0022; 733. Riksarkivet.
22 Original quote in Norwegian: "byutvikling, regionplaner, grønne belter, nye byer, lokalsentra, enklaver og desentralisert service." Erik Rolfsen, *Underveis i Oslo* [En route in Oslo] (Oslo: Aschehoug, 1975), 126.
23 Den Kgl. Norske Legasjons Flyktningskontor, RA/S-6753/V/Va/L0022; 255. Riksarkivet.
24 Harald Hals, letter to Arne Korsmo, Hals' private archive, PA-0311, Riksarkivet, Oslo.
25 Original quote in Norwegian: "studier og forarbeider til beste for gjenreisningen hjemme." Erik Rolfsen, unpublished letter from London to Harald Hals, Stockholm, April 3, 1944, Harald Hals' private archive, PA-0311, Riksarkivet, Oslo.
26 Harald Hals, unpublished letter to Erik Rolfsen in London, April 22, 1944. Hals' private archive, PA-0311, Riksarkivet, Oslo.
27 Arne Korsmo, letter to Harald Hals, April 23, 1944. Hals' private archive, PA-0311, Riksarkivet, Oslo.
28 The committee was in Stockholm also affiliated with *Den norske legasjons forsyningskontor* [*The Norwegian Legation's supply office*].

of ordinary homes and small apartments.[29] All these seven themes were worked on in Sweden and were all highly topical in rebuilding efforts in the early postwar years. Hals described the correspondence with Rolfsen in London as "fairly secure, but terribly slow" and a possible explanation for the lack of information flow with London could be the role reversal witnessed between Hals and Rolfsen during the war: Rolfsen, who was previously Hals' junior, now represented the future, and the 68-year-old Hals, previously Rolfsen's boss, the past. However, communications indicate that a functioning collaboration nonetheless continued, in which Hals also received manuscripts by Rolfsen about the postwar development of Norway.

EXPERIENCES FROM STOCKHOLM COLLECTED AND PUBLISHED

Early in his correspondence with Rolfsen, Hals saw the need to publish on certain topics. In August 1944, Rolfsen argued that it was in Stockholm that people had the time and opportunity to produce professional studies with sketches and illustrations. Preparing publications would be of great value for professionals, administrative institutions, and the public.[30] Rolfsen singled out community centers, neighborhood units, and industrial planning as important areas to focus on. An editorial committee was established by Hals, and some members of the network, including Rolfsen, were asked to contribute.[31]

In 1946, the D. B. K., with Harald Hals as editor, published *Boliger og samfunnsbygg. Erfaringer fra Sverige* (Housing and community buildings: Experiences from Sweden).[32] As it appeared in the editorial committee's introduction, the composition of refugees was relatively random and the book featured forays by its contributors into a variety of themes, more than solid and targeted presentations. The book was divided into five booklets (A-E). In Booklet A, Lisa Gjessing's article "Planlegging" briefly explained terms like "regional plan," "general plan," and "city plan," highlighting the value of regular discussion evenings with foreign colleagues, for example on building laws, and shared solutions from England, Denmark, and Hungary. In "Retten til jorden" (The right to the land), Edvard Heiberg argued that "the only truly effective and logical solution is for society to take over all land—that the land is nationalized," referring to the fact that the Labour Party in England was in favor of such a solution. Erik Rolfsen wrote about regional planning. In Booklet B, Christian. Fr. Størmer explained economic aspects of housing in Sweden, and E. Heiberg wrote about Swedish kitchens. In Booklet C, Thekla Bruff discussed collective houses in Stockholm, and in Booklet D, E. Heiberg contributed with (another) article about community centers in England and Sweden, while Harald Hals II (Hals' son) wrote about Swedish public parks.[33]

Hals himself published the book *Plan og Planlegging* (Booklet F). In the introduction, he clarified that the text was written in 1944–45 in connection with the preparation of a new general plan for Stockholm City, and thanked *stadsplanchefene* (the chief urban planners) Albert Lilienberg and Sven Markelius and his free access to the library of the *stadsplanekontoret* (the city planning office).[34] The first part of the book explained concepts such as "regional plan," "city plan," "general

29 Harald Hals, "Den Norske Bygningstekniske Komite i Stockholm 1944–1945," *Byggekunst* no. 2 (1945): 36.

30 Erik Rolfsen, unpublished letter to Harald Hals, August 21, 1944, Harald Hals' private archive, PA-0311, Riksarkivet, Oslo.

31 With Lisa Gjessing, Edvard Heiberg, Ole Rolfsen, Fredrik Størmer, and Harald Hals.

32 Harald Hals, ed., *Boliger og Samfunnsbygg. Erfaringer fra Sverige* [Housing and community buildings: Experiences from Sweden] (Oslo: Johan Grundt Tanum, 1946).

33 Original quote in Norwegian: "den eneste virkelig effektive og logiske løsning er at samfunnet overtar all jord – at jorden nasjonaliseres." Hals, *Boliger og Samfunnsbygg*, 21.

34 Yngve Larsson and Erland von Hafsten were also mentioned. Harald Hals, "Foreword," *Hefte F. Plan og Planlegging* [Booklet F: The plan and planning], *Den Bygningstekniske Komités hefter* [Booklets of the Building Engineering Committee] (Oslo: Johan Grundt Tanum, 1946).

The front cover of the book *Boliger og samfunnsbygg. Erfaringer fra Sverige* (Oslo: Johan Grundt Tanum, 1946), edited by Harald Hals.

The front cover of Harald Hals' *Plan og Planlegging* (Oslo: Johan Grundt Tanum, 1946). The illustration shows a Swedish community center, by the architect Nils Einar Eriksson.

35 Harald Hals, *Plan og planlegging* [Plan and planning] (Oslo: Johan Grundt Tanum, 1946), 32–34.
36 Hals, "Den Norske Bygningstekniske Komite," 36.
37 Harald Hals, unpublished notes, Harald Hals' private archive, PA-0311, L0008, Riksarkivet, Oslo.

plan," and "zone plan," with the main body of the text addressing modern planning as it was practiced in western countries (including the Soviet Union, which were given more space than the US). Most attention was given to England, referring to regional reports and Abercrombie's systematic work with London's green belt.[35] In the Nordic section, Sweden was, not surprisingly, addressed at length. Current themes such as neighborhoods, *medborgersentrer* (civic centers) and collective housing forms were discussed. Except for the cover, which featured a perspective drawing of a *svensk borger sentrum* (Swedish community center) by Hans Einar Eriksson, Hals' "Prosjekt for Etterstad ved Oslo" (Project for Etterstad in Oslo) was the book's only illustration. The latter was presented as a *moderne boligkoloni* (modern residential community) within a park, with different housing typologies and a *folkesentrum* (neighborhood center) for approximately 4,000 inhabitants. While all modern planning increasingly involved sociological and scientific findings, Hals concluded that aesthetics still had a substantial impact on design.

NORWEGIAN ARCHITECTS SCATTERED IN VARIOUS OFFICES.

During the war, as is well known, the Swedish authorities undertook significant research within the fields of planning and architecture, collecting data of a social, statistical, and technical nature and working on related planning projects. Hals has pointed out that Norwegian architects and engineers were involved in these efforts, through their work in private, public, and municipal offices, and larger semipublic institutions, including Kungl. Byggnadsstyrelsen (KBS, the National Board of Public Buildings), Stockholms Stadsplanekontor (the City of Stockholm's City Planning Office), Statens Byggnadslånebyrå (the state office for building loans), and the housing developers HSB, Svenska Riksbyggen, and Svenska Trähus.[36]

Hals himself worked in Stockholm at the architectural office of the high-profile modernist and Swedish CIAM delegate Sven Markelius (1889–1972); in 1944, Markelius was appointed Stockholm's Chief City Planner, which helps to some extent explain Hals' motivation for writing his own book. *Boliger og Samfunnsbygg*'s contributors and its five different themes (A-E) were related to Hals' network in Stockholm and were in accordance with the committee's first objectives of gathering information. While some Norwegian architects worked in offices associated with Stockholm's general plan, others worked at institutions that worked on the planning of the Swedish postwar period.

According to Hals, the architect Lisa Gjessing (educated at NTH) had practiced both at Stockholms Stadsplanekontor and Kungl. Byggnadsstyrelsen; Christian Fredrik Störmer (educated at KTH) was employed at Statens Byggnadslånebyrå; and Thekla Bruff (educated at SHKS and KTH) worked, in 1944, at Kooperative Förbundets Arkitektkontor (the architecture office of the cooperative union, KF).[37] Some, such as Vilhelm Brodtkorb Reinhardt (1899–1968), had their own small office. Others worked for renowned Swedish architects such as the Norwegian-Danish architect Edvard Heiberg (1897–1958) and the Hungarian and Jewish architect Fred Forbát who were among the foreign architects that worked for

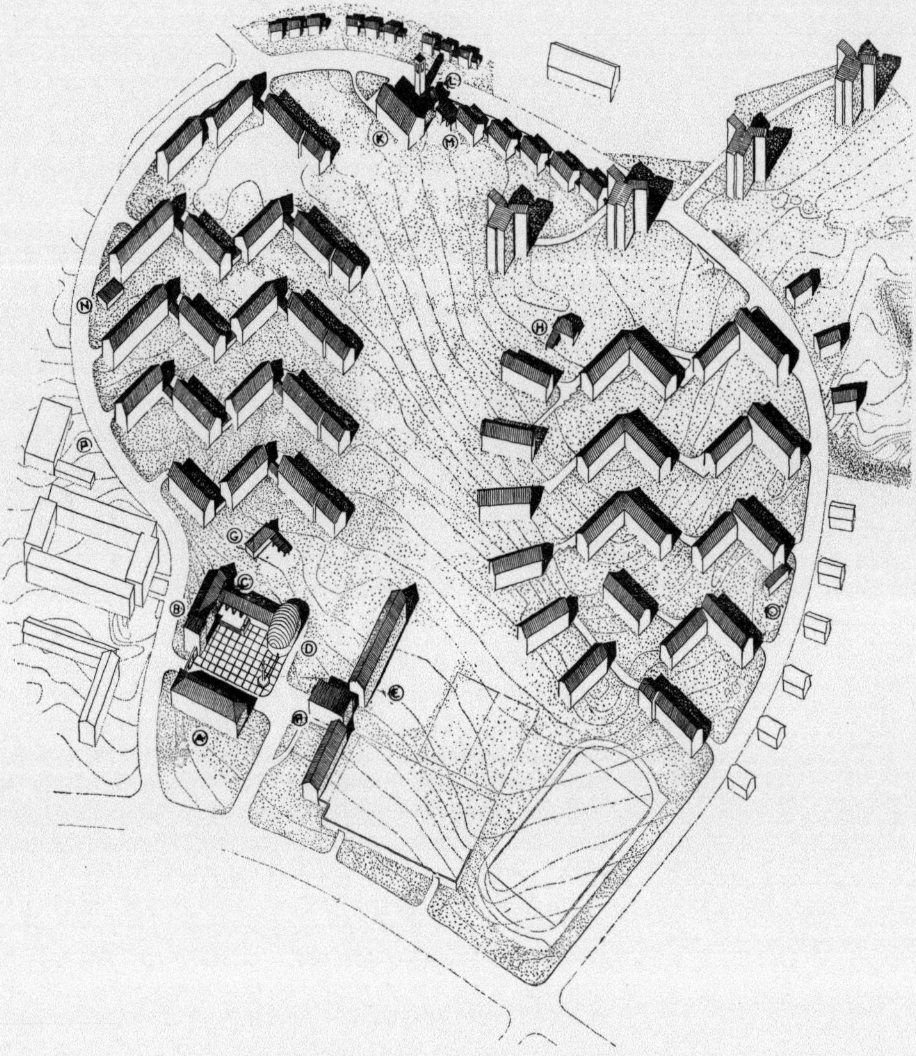

MODERNE BOLIGKOLONI

Gaten som danner adkomsten til kolonien er lagt i sløyfe rundt bebyggelsen, og denne er spredt fritt utover i et åpent parkområde. Fra sløyfen er det stikkveier inn til hvert hus, fra husene igjen slipper beboerne direkte ut i parkområdet uten å krysse noen kjørebane. (Projekt for Etterstad ved Oslo.)

A, B, C, D = Folkesentrum. A = Forretningsgård. B = Møte- og forsamlingslokaler, studierom, bibliotek o. l. C = Konditori, kafé. D = Kino. E = Folkeskole. F = Aula. G, H, og M = Barnehage. K = Småkirke. L = Menighetshus. N og O = Fellesvaskeri. P = Fellesgarasje. I nedre hjørne idretts- og øvelsesplasser.

Harald Hals: *Moderne boligkoloni* (A modern residential community), *project for Etterstad in Oslo* (ca. 1945–46). From the booklet *Plan og Planlegging,* 8.

Uno Åhrén and engaged in Svenska Riksbyggens Arkitekt- och Stadsbyggeavdelning (the architecture and planning devision at the developer Svenska Riksbyggen). Åhrén's efforts during the war are significant, both through his texts, his practical urban planning, and his collaboration with researchers from other fields, like the sociologist Alva Myrdal.[38] In *Arkitektur och Demokrati* (Architecture and democracy, 1942), Åhrén formulated an early internal critique of Swedish functionalism, arguing that it focused too little on peoples' earlier habits and ways of living, and social interaction.[39] In 1940, he wrote about society and urban planning and launched his first ideas for a community center. In Stockholm, Hals and Heiberg had contact through the committee.

NETWORKING ON SEVERAL FRONTS

From the end of 1944, Hals, in correspondence with Johs. Borchsenius, engaged several high-profile Nordic urban planners and architects to comment on BSR's urban plans.[40] Both among architects in Norway and abroad, there was a frustration that in several plans for the city centers, Pedersen had adopted a largely traditional and monumental neoclassical style in accordance with the German occupation authority's ideals. Some of these very critical papers, for instance by Edvard Heiberg and Tage William Olsson, chief planners in Gothenburg, were published in *Byggekunst* shortly after the peace in 1945.[41] In the introduction, Hals called on the Norwegian Government to revise BSR's city plans, which were created under German supervision, overemphasized architectural aspects, and placed too little emphasis on analysis and the development of plans in other democratic countries.[42] Statements to Hals from Albert Lilienberg and Uno Åhrén were also received, but not published. The latter was sharp in his criticism and argued for the need for both sociological research and technical solutions: "The ease with which professor Pedersen seems to assess this questionable relationship stands in clear contrast to the importance he seems to attach to external architectural effects, for example site facilities with a representational character."[43] For Åhrén, the emphasis on aesthetics (through "external architectural effects") represented an outdated methodology. When peace came, Hals addressed the Norwegian government about the need to reconsider BSR's plans developed during the war, in *Byggekunst*'s first issue.[44] Shortly after, Rolfsen became the new leader of BSR (1945–47), and Pedersen's plans for the city centers were processed.

Reconstruction was also clearly a relevant issue for neighboring Finland as a result of the Winter War (1939–40), and with his pavilions in Paris (1937) and New York (1939), Finnish architect Alvar Aalto became an international star-architect. In the period 1941–42, Aalto worked within several arenas, engaging American students at MIT to design an "American Town" which could be realized in Finland, and giving lectures in Copenhagen in 1942, and probably also in Stockholm, about the reconstruction of the Finnish cities.[45] Hals' archive contains letters to Aalto requesting to send Norwegian specialists to Finland to study the reconstruction work.[46] In a reply from the Ministry of Foreign Affairs in Helsinki, Aalto announced that "Norwegian specialists, regardless of the number,

38 Rudberg, "Uno Åhren," 162.
39 Rudberg, "Uno Åhren," 165–66.
40 As chairman of the building council in Porsgrunn, in 1943 Johs. (Johannes Laurentius) Borchsenius refused to accept a regulation plan. He received threats and fled in August 1943 to Stockholm.
41 The statements by Edvard Heiberg and Tage William-Olsson were published in: "B.S.R.: Utenlandske fagfolks mening" [BSR: The opinion of foreign professionals], *Byggekunst* no. 1 (1945): 25–29.
42 Harald Hals, "Henvendelse til Regjeringen" [Application to the Government], *Byggekunst* 1 (1945): 13.
43 Original quote in Swedish: "Den lätthet med vilken professor Pedersen synas bedöma detta betänkliga förhållande står i en tydlig motsats till den vikt han synes lägga vid yttre arkitektoniska effekter, exempelvis platsanläggningar med representationskaraktär." Uno Åhren, unpublished letter to Harald Hals, February 19, 1945, Harald Hals' private archive, PA-0311, L0009, Riksarkivet, Oslo.
44 Harald Hals, "Henvendelse til regjeringen," *Byggekunst*, no. 1 (1945): 12–13.
45 Lisbet Balslev Jørgensen, *Den sidste guldalder. Danmark i 1950'erne* [The last golden age: Denmark in the 1950s] (Copenhagen: Arkitektens Forlag, 2004), 35.
46 There are letters from Hals, as well as the as well as from Den Kgl. Norske Legasjon i Stockholm. When he didn't receive a reply from Alvar Aalto, Hals sent him another letter in January 1945. See Harald Hals, unpublished letter to Alvar Aalto, January 20, 1945, Harald Hals' private archive, PA-0311, L0009, Riksarkivet, Oslo.

47 Harald Hals, unpublished letters addressed to Den Norske Legasjonen in Stockholm, November, 1944, Harald Hals' private archive, PA-0311, L0009, Riksarkivet, Oslo. There are also letters from Hals to Aalto in the same period.

48 Later, Borchsenius got the job for the reconstruction of Vadsø By. Christine Bredegg Hermansen, "En godhjerta raddis" ["A radical with a good heart"] (Master's thesis in art history, University of Oslo, 2005), 34.

49 Herman Munthe-Kaas, unpublished letter to Harald Hals, February 13, 1945, Harald Hals Archive, PA-0311, Riksarkivet, Oslo.

50 Original quote in Norwegian: "Gode naboer er godt å ha. Danmark og Sverige har hver på sitt vis gjort hva det stod i deres makt for å hjelpe oss gjennom tunge krigsår ... Vi takker også for gjestfri mottagelse av norske arkitekter som måtte ta seg over grensen for å unngå Gestapos klør. Våre svenske yrkesbrødre ga støtte og hjelp, ga arbeid og åpnet dørene til sine organisasjoner, biblioteker og arkiver, slik at det ble mulig å forberede det store gjenreisningsarbeid som nå ligger foran oss." Herman Munthe-Kaas, "TAKK, til våre danske og svenske yrkesbrødre" [THANK YOU to our Danish and Swedish professional brothers], *Byggekunst* 1 (1945): 2.

will be received *con amore* and can count on all desired assistance from the state."[47] Through correspondence with Rolfsen, Hals also was involved in the immediate reconstruction of Northern Norway, which in part borders Finland, after the war, including preparing, motivating, and selecting key architects in Stockholm to attend to this task, including Johs. Borchsenius and others. Borchsenius had already traveled north in the spring of 1945 at the behest of the exiled Norwegian Government in London, and took on the job as head of regulation in Øst-Finnmark.[48]

In addition to establishing ties with Norwegian architects in Stockholm, Hals also corresponded confidentially and anonymously with architects in Oslo, including Georg Eliassen and Herman Munthe-Kaas. Both sent him letters toward the end of the war, updating him on the situation in Oslo. Hals also engaged in exchanging publications, sending current Swedish architecture-related books both to London and Oslo. Munthe-Kaas thanked him in February 1945 for *Industriens arbetarbostäder* (Industrial worker's housing) which he deemed a thorough study of great importance, "not only in Sweden, but also to a great extent for the reconstruction in Norway."[49]

EXPERIENCES THAT GAINED IMPORTANCE

In the first issue of *Byggekunst* after the war, Herman Munthe-Kaas stated the following in his opening article:

> Good neighbors are good to have. Denmark and Sweden have each in their way done what was in their power to help us through the difficult war years ... We are also grateful for the hospitable reception of Norwegian architects who had to cross the border to avoid the clutches of Gestapo. Our Swedish professional brothers gave support and help, provided work, and opened the doors of their organizations, libraries, and archives, so that it became possible to prepare for the great reconstruction that now lies before us.[50]

Both Norwegian and Danish architects have expressed a gratitude toward the Swedish architects' hospitality during their stay in Stockholm. In Munthe-Kaas' thanks there is an implicit reference to Hals' network. For both Harald Hals and Erik Rolfsen, their foreign experiences during the war helped them to delve deeper into the projects suggested by the articles that they wrote in 1940. As shown here, Hals operated on several fronts, and had contact with different architects from Norway (Rolfsen, Herman Munthe-Kaas, Arne Korsmo), Sweden (Sven Markelius, Uno Åhrén, Tage William Olsson, Albert Lilienberg), Denmark (Edvard Heiberg), and Finland (Alvar Aalto). His two publications from Stockholm showed both an international and Nordic orientation, which characterized the first years of peace. At the same time, many Norwegian architects were engaged in restoring a connection to Norwegian building traditions. Both Hals and the committee's work seems to have strengthened the new orientation in urban planning, especially in Oslo. Hals was immediately reinstated as president of NAL and as *reguleringssjef* (Chief planning officer) when peace came.

Lisa Gjessing and Th. Johnsen, "Plan for a park system," Oslo (1949), prepared under Rolfsen's Generalplan for Oslo (1950).

Lambertseter, photo of Gråsteinveien (1963) in Blåfjellet borettslag, built 1953–56, with housing blocks by the architect Knut Knutsen.

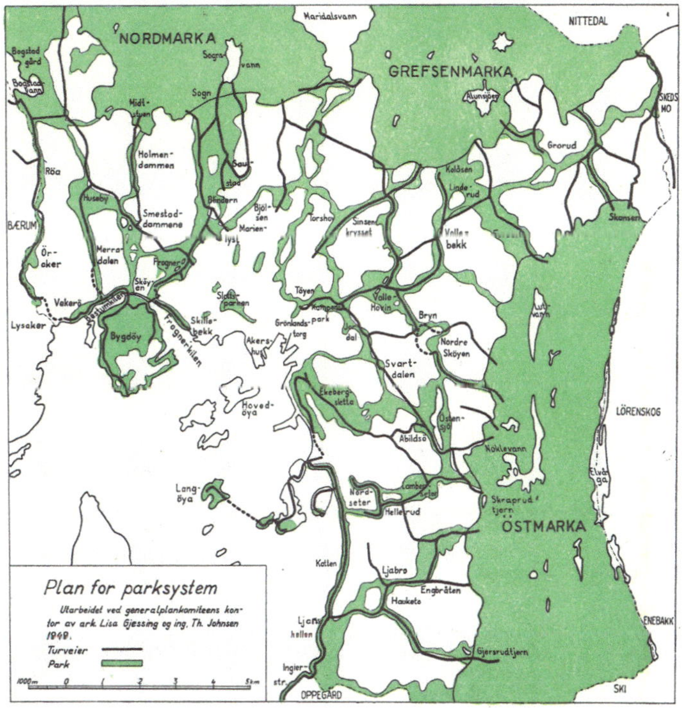

51 Original quote in Norwegian: "Det som skjer i Stockholm kan gi et forbilde, om ikke til direkte efterligning, så til belæring." "Generalplanen for Stor-Oslo trenger revisjon" [The general plan for Greater Oslo needs revising], *Arbeiderbladet*, February 13, 1946, 1.

52 Leonardo Zuccaro Marchi, "Sigtuna inbetween. Report on the small CIAM congress," unpublished report, 2016.

53 Johnsen, *PAGON*, 177.

54 PAGON/Korsmo and Norberg-Schulz, "Bolig?", *Byggekunst,* no. 6–7 (1952): 109.

55 Johnsen, *PAGON*, 173–200.

In 1946, he advocated for the merger of Oslo and Aker through a general plan revision by arguing that "What is happening in Stockholm can provide a role model, if not for direct imitation, then for learning."[51] Hals urged sending professionals to the Swedish capital, who over time could study the plan within geographically limited districts and in detail. Hals was now 70 years old, and served in the position until his successor was in place. The following year, Erik Rolfsen took over, and Oslo was developed with ideas from both London and Stockholm. Stockholm's ABC plans and the close link between transportation planning and the new towns in the suburbs received attention. The committee member Lisa Gjessing, after working as regulation architect in Finnmark, was given an important role in Oslo's park plan, developed from 1948. Both Hals and Rolfsen's foreign experiences and studies helped them to shape the immediate urban planning after the war, especially in Oslo, to which they brought ideas from the English new towns; Stockholm's suburban development with *medborgersentra* (community centers), the New Empiricism, and various housing typologies; and the American focus on traffic, transport, and park plans.

There is little doubt that the Swedish welfare architecture from the 1940s had a great impact on the social democrats in Norway. Especially Stockholm's new town Årsta, planned by Uno Åhrén (and with E. Heiberg as one of the assistants), resembling one of the models of the new town Lambertseter in Oslo, planned by (former SAF member) Frode Rinnan (1949–51), and built with neighborhood units designed by different architects. But it was also something to be resisted. It was that resistance that pulled Norwegian modernism in other directions, and disagreements about Swedish welfare architecture became apparent at and after CIAM's Sigtuna meeting in 1952,[52] and the criticism was particularly expressed by Christian Norberg-Schulz and Arne Korsmo in PAGON's manifesto in *Byggekunst* (1952). During his stay in Stockholm (1944–45), Korsmo became well informed about the new tendencies in Swedish architecture, but reacted with skepticism. At the Sigtuna meeting, Norberg-Schulz criticized Nils Ahrbom's lecture on "Housing Research" and felt modern architecture had lost its cause.[53] PAGON's article "Bolig?" (The Dwelling?) can be read as a commentary to Ahrbom's lecture and the Swedish methodological procedures with the use of collected statistical material as the basis of an ideal type of an apartment plan. "To build a residential district with fixed dwellings, as a whole, is in itself fundamentally and glaringly inorganic and thus inhuman," argued PAGON.[54] They believed in empowering the individual to choose the opportunity for interaction and creating their own well-being. Architects should no longer act as "specialists," but more like "agents," offering a flexible framework of choices.[55] The article was illustrated with Jørn Utzon, Sverre Fehn, and Geir Grung's project *Boliger* på *Arnebråten* (*Housing complex on Arnebråten*, 1951), planned as a continuous row of single-story houses, well-adapted to the sloping terrain. At CIAM 10 in Dubrovnik, Grung and Korsmo presented their alternative *Building and Nature. Flexibility of the Habitat* (1956) with four different types of dwellings to satisfy both old and young, single and larger families in a layout of the buildings combining high and low sections.

Jean-Louis Cohen described, in 2011, the years between 1939 and 1945 as “a blank space in historical accounts” and his study reminds us that the Second World War is too often omitted from the history of architecture.[56] Related to Norwegian architectural history during the war, Despina Stratigakos book *Hitler's Northern Utopia: Building the New Order in Occupied Norway* (2020) contained some new interesting information.[57] There is ongoing research into Norwegian architecture during and just after the war, including perspectives on welfare. It will probably take a few years before we get a greater overview. On that occasion, it is worth remembering that parts of this planning also took place outside Norway. Stockholm's greatest value during the war appears, in this brief overview, to have been in its role as an arena for architectural exchange for Scandinavian and international architects, which opened up for impulses from different countries and cultures, and emphasized the importance of transnational cooperation during a world war.

56 Jean-Louis Cohen, *Architecture in Uniform: Designing and Building for World War II* (Montréal: Canadian Centre for Architecture, 2011).
57 Despina Stratigakos, *Hitler's Northern Utopia: Building the New Order in Occupied Norway* (Princeton and Oxford: Princeton University Press, 2020).

Geir Grung and Arne Korsmo, *Building and Nature. Flexibility of the Habitat* (1956), model.

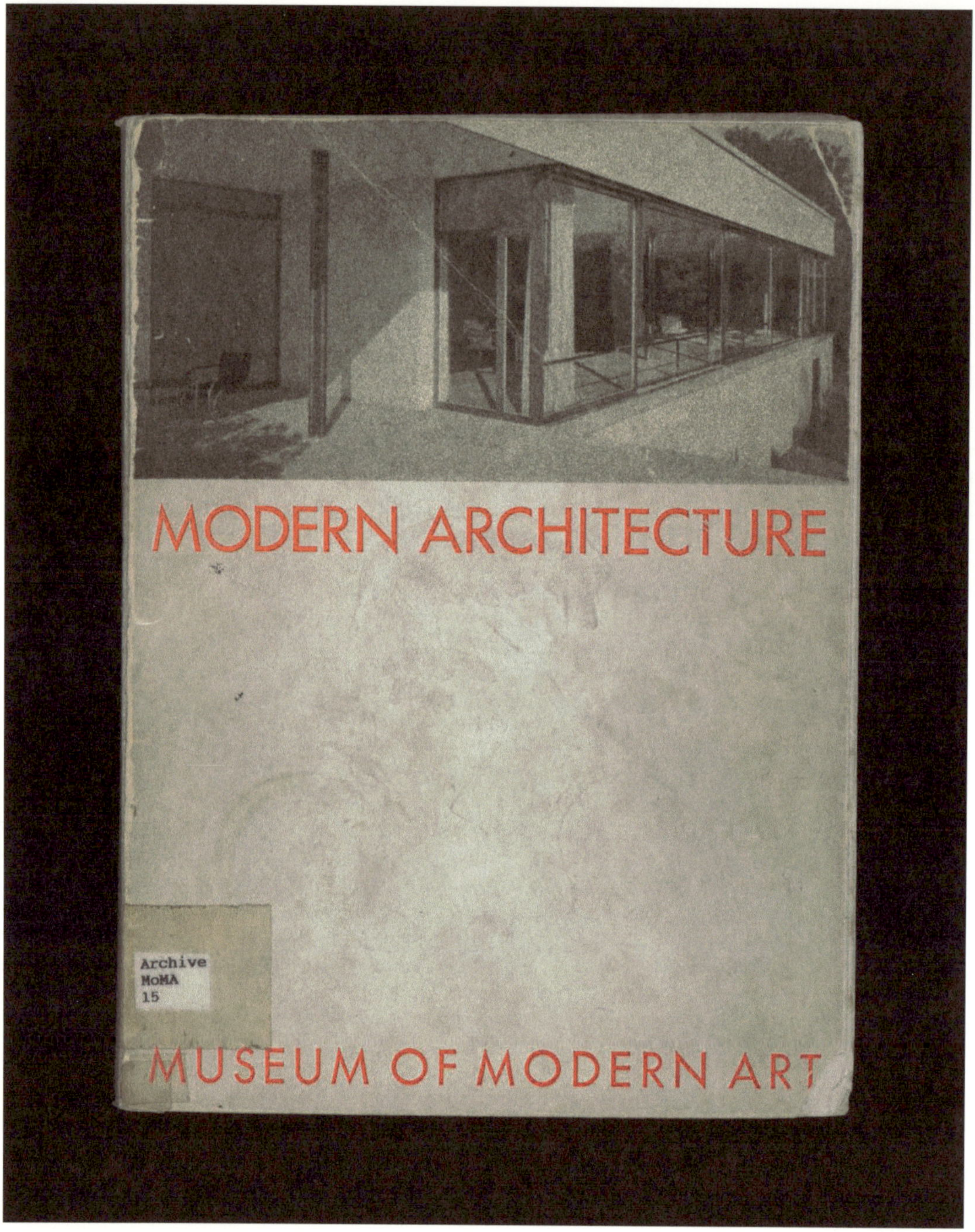

Catalogue cover of the quintessential exhibition *Modern Architecture: International Exhibition*, Museum of Modern Art, 1932.

Frida Rosenberg

CATHERINE BAUER

International Exchanges and Swedish Housing Policy

The American housing activist Catherine Bauer was important in establishing an American perspective on Sweden and Scandinavia. In her work to improve housing in the United States from the 1930s and throughout the postwar years, she contributed to shaping a particular idea of the Swedish Model as it functioned regarding housing.[1] As a well-known advocate of public housing she persistently steered postwar social housing in the direction of community planning in the United States. Bauer believed that housing should become a matter for the state in the United States, kept out of the hands of private stakeholders to enable its broader social significance, and that it should include town planning, zoning, regional planning, and land use. Much of her research and understanding of housing as such came from several research travels to Europe and Scandinavia.

Around 2015, Sweden and the other Nordic countries again found themselves on the agenda when it was suggested, on the cover of *The Economist* under the heading "The Next Supermodel," that the United States could again learn from the Nordic countries, this time in terms of how they had stripped down their welfare states during the preceding three decades and reformed their public sectors, combining capitalism and social advantages with greater efficiency.[2] This ideological transformation from "The Swedish Model" to "the next supermodel" prompts inquiries into the significant shifts in the role of architecture, which transitioned from being considered a public good to becoming a tool to be utilized for financial speculation.[3] At the core of this understanding of how architecture—and in this case, housing—is either for the public good or financial investment, important historical aspects of the relations between Sweden and America have been overlooked.[4] It is therefore valuable to revisit housing, one of the most important armatures in constructing the Swedish Model, to explore this transatlantic exchange. A central figure in this exchange was Catherine Bauer, who persistently affected the outlook on housing for the public in the United States through numerous writings, lectures, and engagement in various organizations effectively becoming a cultural carrier of the Swedish Model.

AN EXHIBITION EMERGING AS A PLATFORM

In the spring of 1932, an event was hosted at the Museum of Modern Art in New York, MoMA, that would turn out to exert profound influence for decades to follow. The exhibition *Modern Architecture: International Exhibition* was a two-part exhibition introducing an emerging canon of modern architecture.[5] The exhibition toured the US for the following two years promoting the modern movement. MoMA proved to be a powerful tool in launching and promoting

1 The postwar Swedish economy was characterized by three key elements, commonly referred to as making up "The Swedish Model." Firstly, it emphasized the establishment of well-functioning relations in the labor market, which were formalized through Saltsjöbadsavtalet (an agreement between various actors in the labor market) in 1938. Secondly, it features a substantial tax-financed welfare state created during the 1930s to 1950s under the concept of *folkhemmet* (the people's home). Thirdly, the model includes a corporatist political system known as Harpsundsandan, a culture of regular consultations between government, trade unions and businesses. See, for example, Hannes Eder, *The Swedish Model* (Stockholm: Publit Förlag, 2010) and Per Thullberg and Kjell Östberg, eds., *Den svenska modellen* (Lund: Studentlitteratur, 1994).

2 Melody E. Valdini, "The Nordic Countries: The Next Supermodel." *The Economist*, February 2, 2013.

3 In a recent critical historiography, Helena Mattsson argues that this "supermodel" image was shaped by architecture, which played a crucial role in advancing the logics of financial speculation in a period of market deregulations. The model fully took shape after the 1990s, when Sweden's property market collapse triggered economic turmoil. See Helena Mattsson, *Architecture and Retrenchment: Neoliberalization of the Swedish Model Across Aesthetics and Space, 1968–1994* (London: Bloomsbury Visual Arts, 2023).

4 See Frida Rosenberg, "The Role of Design in a Swedish-American Landscape," in *Swedish-American Borderlands: New Histories of Transatlantic Relations*, ed. Dag Blanck and Adam Hjortén (Minneapolis: University of Minnesota Press, 2021).

5 Philip Johnson and Henry-Russell Hitchcock, *Modern Architecture: International Exhibition*, Museum of Modern Art, New York, February 10–March 23, 1932.

what was to become known as the "International Style" by presenting various forms of the exhibition at 32 different locations—including art galleries, museums, and even department stores.[6] Part one of the exhibition, curated by architect Philip Johnson and architectural historian Henry-Russell Hitchcock, showcased designs by European and American modernist architects; drawing on work by the European Bauhaus movement and the architecture of Le Corbusier, the curators advocated simple, unembellished forms with an emphasis on open surfaces, large glass partitions, and rational construction techniques.[7] This part of the exhibition—the part that received by far the most attention—established a narrative dominated by well-known architects, forever inscribing them as carriers of modernism, and imparted a somewhat mythical ethos to the event as a whole. The second part of the exhibition, curated by housing activist Catherine Bauer, along with urban planner Clarence Stein and architect Henry Wright (all of whom were part of the Regional Planning Association of America, RPAA) focused on housing.[8] While this part of the exhibition received less attention than the all-star lineup of part one, and has since been somewhat relegated to the margins of history, it did have a profound influence on the production of knowledge and transfer of ideas around modern housing in America and abroad. It was also a significant event in Bauer's work on developing American housing policies and, at the same time, contributing to an American perspective which saw the Nordics as a model society; as such, the exhibition is part of a (still ongoing) history of looking to the social democratic countries—and their combination of capitalism and social well-being—for solutions.

Catherine Bauer, an emerging housing expert in her late twenties, had been appointed as executive secretary at the RPAA, which at the time was actively lobbying for low-cost homes for the general population, during and immediately following the Great Depression.[9] She was a recent graduate from Vassar College and had already formed a position that synthesized the role of housing with that of society. As one of the three curators, and someone who understood the European model for public housing and the particular policies, politics, and institutions that underpinned the success of large housing estates developed after the First World War,[10] Bauer took a leading role in organizing the housing exhibition and introducing modern European housing and Garden City planning ideals to the American public.[11] The housing exhibition at MoMA gave Bauer an opportunity to combine architecture and planning with emerging political and social ideals. The exhibition presented a variety of urban and suburban apartment houses, college dormitories and private houses, and importantly, included a critical reflection upon low-rent housing. An array of visual illustrations and descriptions presented a selection of European models of low-rent social housing from places such as Germany, Switzerland, Holland, and France. The exhibition offered a critique of contemporary urban planning ideals and models of mass housing, based primarily on private initiatives, and suggested that the provision of housing was in fact an urgent social, economic, and political issue.

In contrast to the first part of the exhibition, where Philip Johnson and Henry-Russell Hitchcock argued about who, and what, encompassed "the modern architect" (and who conversely did not),

6 Raffaella Russo Spena. "Museum Exhibitions as Mass Media Spreading Architectural Ideas from Europe to USA in 20th Century," *Histories of Postwar Architecture* 2, no. 4 (2020): 261.

7 The exhibition on architecture included work by the architects Frank Lloyd Wright, Walter Gropius, Le Corbusier, J. J. P. Oud, Mies van der Rohe, Raymond M. Hood, Howe & Lescaze, Richard J. Neutra, Bowman Brothers. See "Modern Architecture: International exhibition, New York, Feb. 10 to March 23, 1932, The Museum of Modern Art," accessed May 17, 2024, https://assets.moma.org/documents/moma_catalogue_2044_300061855.pdf?_ga=2.40799207.476049404.1650309036-914240224.1650309036.

8 See Richard Pommer, "The Architecture of Urban Housing in the United States During the Early 1930s," *Journal of the Society of Architectural Historians* 37, no. 4 (1978): 235.

9 Peter Oberlander and Eva Newbrun, *Houser: The Life and Work of Catherine Bauer* (Vancouver: University of British Columbia Press, 1999), 69.

10 Architecture historian Richard Pommer has argued that Catherine Bauer and Lewis Mumford were the first "to understand the new housing in both its social and aesthetic aspect." Richard Pommer, "The Architecture of Urban Housing in the United States during the early 1930s," *Journal of the Society of Architectural Historians* 37, no. 4 (1978): 261n61.

11 Pommer, "The Architecture of Urban Housing in the United States," 261n61.

Nursery School/Daycare center in Fredhäll, Stockholm, built by HSB in early 1930s. Architect Sven Wallander.

Kitchen interior at housing estate, Maltesholmsvägen 154–92, Hässelby strand, built by HSB. Architects Stig Ancker, Bengt Gate, and Sten Lindegren.

Bandhagen, suburban center developed according to the ABC model, south of Stockholm built by HSB and inaugurated along with the new subway station in 1954. Architect Fred Forbat.

12 Lewis Mumford, "Modern Architecture: International Exhibition," exhibition statement, Museum of Modern Art, New York, February 10 to March 23, 1932, 181.
13 Mumford, "Modern Architecture: International Exhibition," 183.
14 Bauer's European travel lasted from June through November in 1930. See Oberlander and Newbrun, *Houser*, 56–67.

the housing exhibition made a call for modern architecture (and modern architects) to engage with the domestic environment and provide adequate and affordable housing for the entire population in the United States, an attitude summarized in the foreword to the exhibition's statement: "The present century confronted us with this paradox: as the individual house improved, housing in the mass deteriorated."[12] According to the curators, mass housing in the United States needed to take an alternative course to its European counterpart, and first be conceived as "a new community": "The reason for our social backwardness in housing has," it was argued, "been due to the fact that we have habitually confused the real issue of good housing with the very limited and abstract matter of ownership."[13] The foreword can be read as a manifesto—a call to action—offering architects and planners a seven-point plan toward better residential communities, as well as providing practical examples of housing designs where considerations for costs, social issues, light, air, gardens, and recreational spaces aligned with a concern for modern aesthetics. The foreword promoted the benefits of comprehensive planning, large-scale operations, mass production, and efficient designs, and put forth an argument for state involvement through subsidies. The housing exhibition, although clearly overshadowed by Johnson and Hitchcock's show, presented a radical quest for a new domestic environment.

Before launching the *Modern Architecture* exhibition, Catherine Bauer had spent six months traveling throughout Europe, meeting and interviewing architects, and visiting and photographing housing estates.[14] This was her second trip overseas; together with her earlier trip and a subsequent one in 1932, these travels formed a lifelong interest in European models for housing, from which she persistently argued that the United States had a lot to learn. Her two trips in 1930 and 1932 were explicitly research studies, where her notebooks, photographs, and writings express a dedicated inventory, cataloging, and interest in understanding housing estates from several perspectives such as design, plan layouts, community planning, and in particular ownership and tenant structures. In this regard, Sweden stands out as a special case where a humanist and community-oriented architecture elevated the idea of sharing facilities in order to ease everyday life. Beyond the multiple European postwar housing developments that may fall in this category, the Swedish cooperative housing models formed a reference that remains in Bauer's personal research collection. Her photo archive includes multiple images of the early housing developments by Hyresgästernas sparkasse- och byggnadsförening (HSB, the savings and construction association of the tenants). She was intrigued by how HSB actively worked toward improving Swedish housing standards.

HSB functioned as a combination of a company and a cooperative apartment organization and was very much integrated within the political discourse of the Swedish welfare state, receiving state-supported grants and loans for housing construction. HSB was founded in 1923, originating in Stockholms Kooperativa Bostadförening (SKB, Stockholm's cooperative housing association) by people from workers' unions, corporations, state appointees, and the city board. Only a few years after the HSB's initiation, the organization bought a carpentry factory in Sparreholm, which it used to produce kitchen interiors. These were the first standardized kitchen units made in Sweden, which turned HSB into a leading business associated with high-quality housing.[15] As such, they were the first on the market to provide public laundry facilities for their tenants. Within the next fifteen years, HSB bought a mortar factory, a marble quarry, and began to produce prefabricated housing elements, *barnrikehus* (housing for families with many children) and *barnstugor* (orphanages) as well as homes for the elderly.[16]

Bauer was interested in the organizational structure of HSB, as evidenced in her personal notebooks that list acquaintances, addresses, important facts, and other details from her travels in the 1930s. From her perspective as an outsider, she noted how HSB and similar organizations transformed housing into one of Sweden's strongest political and social tools, capable of resisting the market forces which held such a dominant position in American society.

Bauer became particularly interested in this organizational structure as an exemplar of the Swedish Model, which included state-supported grants and loans for housing construction. The organization relied on tenants "buying in," or making an economic contribution in order to become a member and rent an apartment. Essentially, HSB functioned as a bank, borrowing money from its members in order to fund new developments.[17] As such, HSB was part of the cooperative movement, a strong force that aligned with the Folkhem ideology and spanned from institutional to practice-based efforts through architecture offices such as Kooperativa förbundets arkitektkontor (KF, the architecture office of the Swedish Cooperative Union and Wholesale Society) to housing agencies like HSB, which used a variety of methods to resolve the housing issue.[18] In constituting a type of political organ, these cooperative organizations which functioned under the auspices of the welfare state, were "the most important counterbalances to the privately owned housing companies."[19] Advocating for low-cost housing with efficient housing plans, their apartment blocks and houses were often configured in clusters around playgrounds, emphasizing community and childcare.

HSB was not the single actor in this regard but stood out in its capacity to expand its organization during the 1930s and 1940s as well as equip all dwellings with a shower or a bathroom.[20] HSB was also one of the first housing organizations that introduced garbage disposals, balconies, landscaped courtyards, and playgrounds, thereby improving both interior and exterior living conditions. An additional aspect was the social agenda, typified by the introduction of day nurseries and play schools run by the housing cooperatives. This dimension of the significant investment and power that lay in the hands of housing organizations in Sweden intrigued Catherine Bauer, who sought to better understand the politics and financial circumstances, city planning and the underlying armatures that paved the way for mass housing in Sweden.[21]

One can only speculate about the connection between Catherine Bauer's second trip to Europe in June 1930 and the "Modern Architecture" show that was mounted in February 1932. It is, however, well-known that the director at MoMA, Alfred Barr, had made plans for such an exhibition in the early 1930s.[22] The trip deepened Bauer's interest in architecture and regional planning, and it was prolonged by two additional months with financial assistance

15 In 1930, HSB had 12,000 members and built 6,200 apartments. Ten years later, these numbers had almost tripled: it had built 23,500 apartments and had 23,600 members. In the late 1940s, the collaboration between the HSB and the municipalities increased.

16 As a result of a government-supported investigation in 1933 looking at social living conditions, a state-sponsored borrowing fund was instituted to support housing developers that would build for the lower classes. Using this fund, municipalities could build for families with many children through public utility or municipal housing companies, which initiated the formulation "barnrikehusen" (housing for families with many children) or "Myrdalshusen" (Myrdal housing). See Ulrika Sax, *Stockholm nittonhundra* (Stockholm: Stockholms stadsmuseum, 1998), 23–24; and Eva Rudberg, *Folkhemmets byggande: under mellan- och efterkrigstiden* (Stockholm: Svenska turistföreningen, 1992), 25.

17 Sven Wallander, "What Is HSB and How Does It Work," in *Ten Lectures on Swedish Architecture* (Stockholm: Svenska Arkitekters Riksförbund, 1949), 65.

18 KF designed some of the highlights of Swedish functionalist architecture. As the largest architecture office in Scandinavia, KF also influenced many of the period's key architects, many of whom worked in the organization for several years. KF, HSB, and KBS designed buildings and then also administered and managed the completed buildings. See Frida Rosenberg, "Science for Architecture: Designing Architectural Research in Post-War Sweden," *Footprint: Delft School of Design Journal* 6, no. 10/11 (2012): 97–112.

19 Ola Wedebrunn, ed., *Modern Movement in Scandinavia: Vision and Reality* (Århus: Fonden til udgivelse af Arkitekturtidsskrift B, 1998), 180.

20 HSB:s riksförbund, *HSB Sweden* (Stockholm: HSB:s riksförbund, 1971), 17.

21 Her lantern slides indicate an interest for Swedish housing in general but also diagrams and calculations of living standards comparing Sweden and the United States. See Wurster (Catherine Bauer) photograph collection, BANC PIC 1974.029, Carton 1:23. The Bancroft Library, University of California, Berkeley)

22 Raffaella Russo Spena, "Museum Exhibitions as Mass Media Spreading Architectural Ideas from Europe to USA in 20th Century," *Histories of Postwar Architecture* 2, no. 4 (2020): 262.

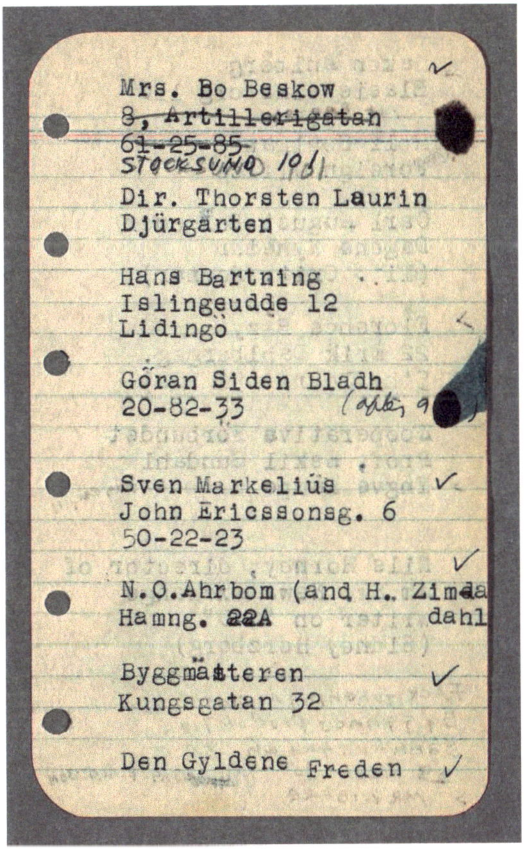
Mrs. Bo Beskow
~~8, Artillerigatan~~
~~61-25-85~~
STOCKSUND 101
Dir. Thorsten Laurin
Djürgarten
Hans Bartning
Islingeudde 12
Lidingö
Göran Siden Bladh
20-82-33
Sven Markeliüs
John Ericssonsg. 6
50-22-23
N.O.Ahrbom (and H. Zimdahl
Hamng. 22A
Byggmästeren
Kungsgatan 32
Den Gyldene Freden

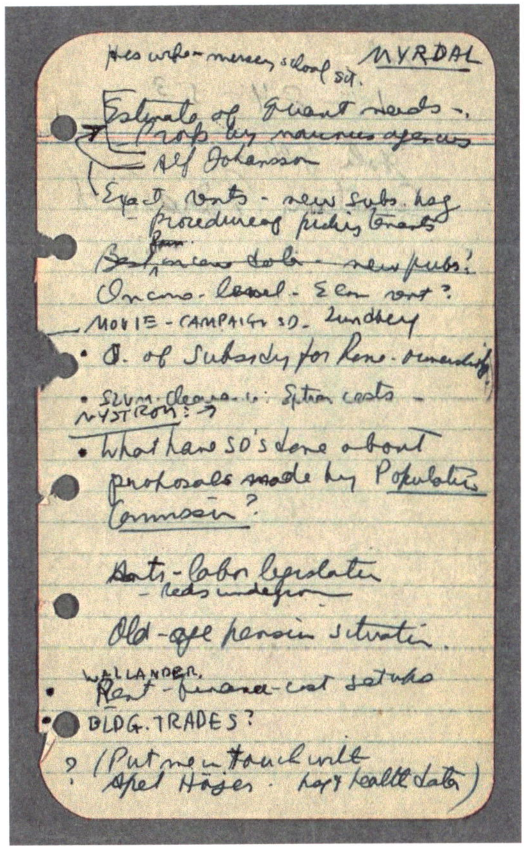
MYRDAL
Alf Johansson
MOVIE - CAMPAIGN SD. Lundberg
What have SD's done about proposals made by Population Commission?
Old-age pension situation
WALLANDER
BLDG. TRADES?

Catherine Bauer's notebook, ca 1930.

23 Oberlander and Newbrun, *Houser,* 56.
24 Oberlander and Newbrun, *Houser,* 67. See also Taina Marjatta Rikala, "Catherine Bauer and Six Riddles of Modernism," *Journal of Architecture* 7, no. 2 (2002): 191–203, in particular 196.
25 Announcement in *The New York Times,* May 7, 1932, 17.
26 Barbara Penner, "Foreword: Housing Is More than Houses," in Catherine Bauer, *Modern Housing* (Minneapolis: Minnesota Press, 2020), xxi.

from Lewis Mumford, a companion with whom she shared a close professional and romantic relationship. Bauer's friendship with Mumford introduced her to his architectural network of European acquaintances.

While in Sweden, she made friends with the architect and urban planner Sven Markelius as well as with the young, versatile architect Uno Åhrén, who showed her around in Stockholm.[23] Both Sven Markelius and Uno Åhrén were prominent figures in Swedish architecture and played a significant role in shaping the modernist movement in Sweden. They were both involved in various urban, institutional, and housing projects, including the Stockholm Exhibition of 1930, where modernist design principles were showcased, and the Student Union building at KTH Royal Institute of Technology in Stockholm, a photograph of which was included in the *Modern Architecture* exhibition.

These newfound, like-minded connections between Bauer and figures such as Sven Markelius and Uno Åhrén would inform her professional life and her knowledge of European housing projects and urban planning models. They would also shift the terms of her relationship with Mumford, who asked her for guidance on publishing matters: "Lewis increasingly turned to her for advice. Often, he sent her first drafts of manuscripts, and she took the responsibility very seriously, sending the draft back with several typed pages charting annotations, paragraph by paragraph."[24] As such, Bauer's contributions (to housing), based on her shared interest with Mumford, her assistance in supplying knowledge both through her research travels and Mumford's written drafts, and her authorship with respect to the *Modern Architecture* exhibition on housing at MoMA are most likely much greater than has been previously acknowledged.

In April of 1932—the same year as the exhibition at MoMA—Bauer made another tour of Europe, again under the direction of Lewis Mumford. Bauer had received a fellowship fund from the Women's Club, which provided for a year's advanced study abroad.[25] Her aim was to collect material, including photographs, for a series of articles for *Fortune* magazine, with the first one to be published in November that same year. The article highlighted a social agenda for architecture exemplifying housing in Frankfurt, Germany, while also daring to assess both flaws as well as strengths of canonical European modernist architecture. Catherine Bauer called upon architects, urban planners, and politicians to redefine architecture in order to meet the urban challenge of the twentieth century—to house the poor, the homeless, and the displaced, as well as unionized workers and working women—and in this her work was finally acknowledged.

BAUER'S BOOK ON MODERN HOUSING

In her canonical 1934 book *Modern Housing* (re-published in 2020 with a foreword by Barbara Penner), Bauer problematized the housing situation in America, observing that there was very little housing for average citizens that met minimum standards regarding cross-ventilation, sunlight, adequate privacy, space, sanitary facilities, and adjacent spaces for children's play.[26] According to

Student Union building designed by architects Sven Markelius and Uno Åhrén, 1928–30.

HSB cooperative housing estate Marmorn, Skinnarviksringen 19–21 and Lundagatan 36–40, in Stockholm constructed 1930–42. Architect Sven Wallander. This photograph is also published in the book *Modern Housing*. Some of the apartment plans for this building were presented at the Stockholm Exhibition in 1930.

Row housing for workers at the cooperative union's flour-mill at Kvarnholmen, 1930. This photograph is almost identical to the one published in the book *Modern Housing*. Designed and developed by Kooperativa Förbundets Arkitekt- och Ingeniörsbyrå (KFAI, The architectural and engineering office of the cooperative union), Architect Olof Thunström and Eskil Sundahl.

27 The book was well-received when it was published. Major newspapers and journals paid attention to Catherine Bauer and her book had an advocate role in the American contemporary housing policy debate. For the original edition, see Catherine Bauer, *Modern Housing* (Boston: Houghton Mifflin Company, 1934).

28 A collection of photographs on HSB housing environments confirms this interest filed under "Research Housing in Sweden," Wurster (Catherine Bauer) photograph collection, BANC PIC 1974.029, The Bancroft Library, University of California, Berkeley.

29 Bauer, *Modern Housing*, 18–19.

30 Bauer, *Modern Housing*.

31 The drawing of four different variations of the kitchens for the housing designs at the Stockholm Exhibition forms part of the Uno Åhren Collection, ArkDes Archive. There were few female architects involved in the exhibition. One of them was Ingrid Wallberg, who investigated social housing issues in collaboration with HSB. She represented HSB together with Alfred Roth at the 1930 Stockholm Exhibition. Anne Brügge, *Ingrid Wallberg: Arkitekt och funktionalist* [Ingrid Wallberg: Architect and functionalist] (Stockholm: Balkong, 2020).

32 Wurster (Catherine Bauer) photograph collection, BANC PIC 1974.029, Carton 1:23. The Bancroft Library, University of California, Berkeley.

33 Wurster (Catherine Bauer) photograph collection, BANC PIC 1974.029, Carton 1:23. The Bancroft Library, University of California, Berkeley.

34 Wurster (Catherine Bauer) photograph collection, BANC PIC 1974.029, Carton 1:23. The Bancroft Library, University of California, Berkeley.

Bauer, while America enjoyed a period of prosperity before the Great Depression, Europe had experienced economic depletion, and political conflicts had made it necessary to embrace a new kind of housing norm.[27] The examples of Swedish housing referenced in the book, while limited, are pivotal, indicating what would become a lifelong interest for Bauer—as well as other American housing proponents—in cooperative housing initiatives.[28]

Bauer references three different cooperative housing projects which are shown in photographs and short descriptions: Kv. Marmorn in Stockholm by architect Sven Wallander built in 1930–42; small houses and apartments for workers at Kvarnholmen in Stockholm by architect Olof Thunström; and a drawing illustrating "open-row planning for a Gothenburg development." [29] Bauer was particularly interested in the apartment block Marmorn. Many of Marmorn's apartments have one of the layouts that Sven Wallander presented at the Stockholm Exhibition in 1930 with experimental mini-kitchens designed by architects Ingrid Wallberg and Alfred Roth.[30] This modern kitchen design was first displayed and based on research studies toward the kitchen designs at the Stockholm Exhibition in 1930.[31] Ingrid Wallberg argued that although the preference was for larger kitchens, space could be used more efficiently in small apartments. Sven Markelius and Gunnar Asplund had also displayed different versions of small, functional kitchens at the Stockholm Exhibition, which had room for no more than two people—reinforcing the contemporary view that the modern and efficient woman of the future only needed a rational workspace. This emerging idea that architecture could give form to living conditions in the home environment that supported women—both in the domestic sphere, as well as enabling them to participate in the workforce—was particularly exciting for Bauer.

The sheer number of photographs that Bauer took which documented the HSB organization and the approach to improving the built environment—through housing, implementing standards, both in the plan layout of an apartment as well as amenities such as a standard kitchen sink or access to garbage disposal in every apartment stairwell—attests to her fascination with HSB as an important factor in improving housing in Sweden. In several cases, she annotated the back of these photographs: for instance, on the back of a photograph picturing a woman doing the dishes, she noted "Standard kitchen equipment in Sweden. For public and coop as well as private housing, includes stainless steel sinks and built-in manufactured cabinets." [32] On another photograph picturing children around a small table: "Nurseries are maided [attended by maids] both in cooperative apartments and in municipal apartments for many children." [33] Also, on the back of a photograph picturing a construction site: "The biggest apartment block put up by the union for the HSB cooperative housing society. This project is part of a slum clearance plan in Stockholm." [34] The extensive research, high levels of government support, and construction know-how concerning mass housing were all elements of Swedish welfare-state design that Bauer later disseminated to architects and planners in the United States. In Catherine Bauer's lantern slide archive, one can further trace moments of revealing Sweden as an example in portraying housing. Finally, the concluding section of the fourth part of Bauer's book *Modern Housing* aims to extend

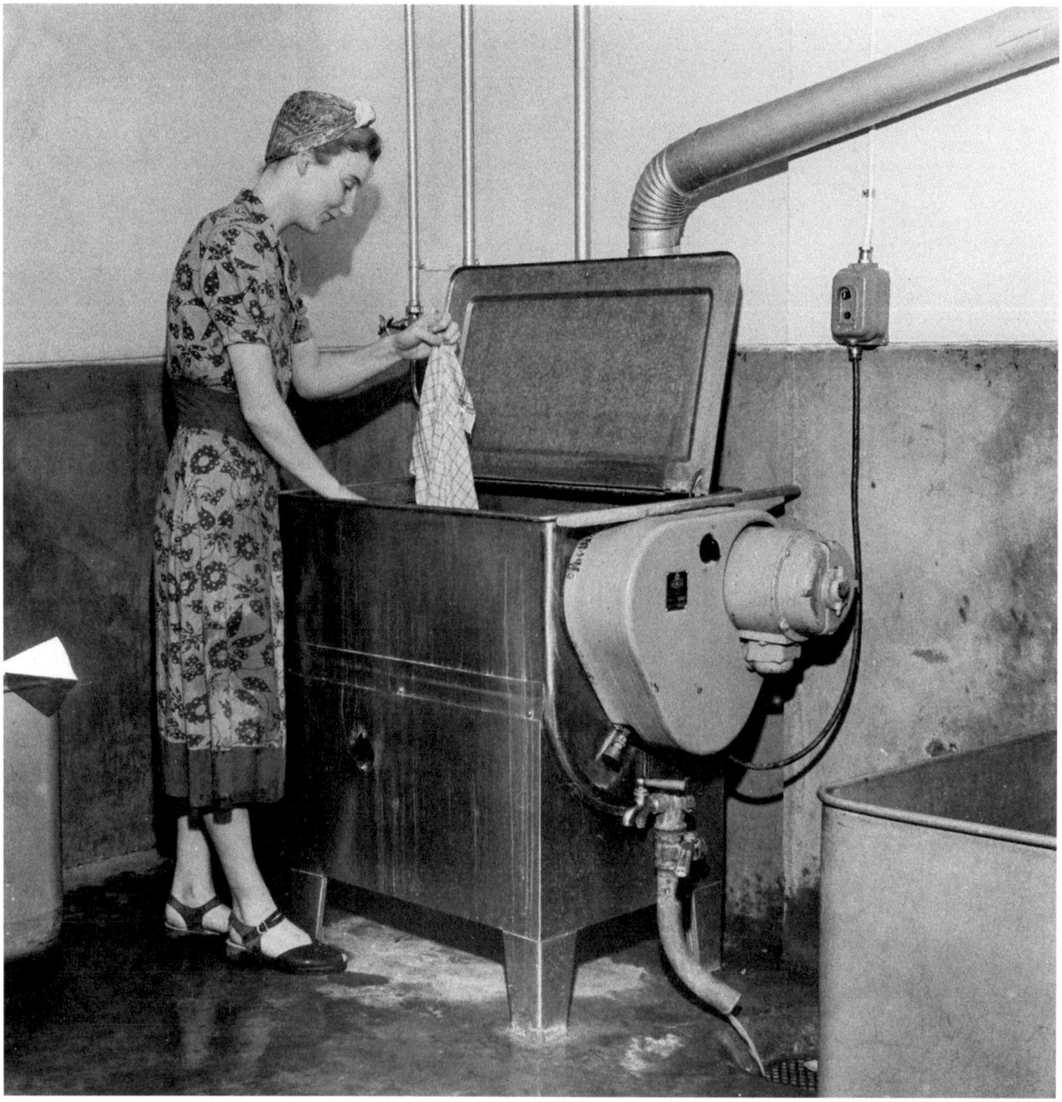

Communal laundry facility at municipal housing built by HSB in Stockholm mainly for large families at Slalomvägen, Västertorp. Several photos distributed by HSB are found in Catherine Bauer Wurster Papers, which includes notes on the backside. One comment she makes is: "Annual subsidies are paid by the state, to keep rents down, similar to the USHA program."

HSB was first to develop this kind of garbage disposal on every floor of their mass housing estates from 1928 and onwards. Sven Wallander received a Swedish patent for the garbage chute in 1934. Catherine Bauer collected the photograph of the garbage chute in her personal research archive on housing in Sweden.

her examination of European socialized housing experiments to the American context, offering recommendations to the American public. Bauer supplements her analysis with a comprehensive appendix, detailing national housing measures in Europe from 1850 to 1934. Additionally, she includes forty-eight pages of photographs capturing housing and architecture gathered during her research expeditions across Europe, where Sweden is represented by three HSB projects.

THE AMERICAN HOUSING PROBLEM

When Franklin D. Roosevelt became President of the United States in 1933, the Democratic Party recognized housing as one of the most acute problems of the time. This led to the creation of a national housing act in 1934 and the establishment of the Federal Housing Administration.[35] However, the focus on housing was relatively limited and President Roosevelt's New Deal politics primarily addressed various other aspects of economic recovery, such as public works projects. Many housing advocates argued that these measures were not even remotely sufficient; among these voices was Catherine Bauer. Through her service as an executive secretary to the RPAA and the Labor Housing Conference, she co-authored the housing bill in 1934, which sought to direct more substantial funding to public housing. This was different from the mortgage insurance legislation, which focused on insuring the existing market, rather than subsidizing new construction.[36] While the bill did not pass in 1934, it acted as a base for what became the Housing Act of 1937.[37]

The implementation of the 1937 Housing Act was accompanied by the establishment of the United States Housing Authority, USHA, which headed one of the USA's few large-scale public housing projects. Within the program, 500 million USD were spent on public housing subsidies, mainly distributed as bonds and loans for public housing construction. In this way, the initial housing interventions in the USA can be seen as more preventive than remedial. The purpose of the FHA was insurance, not subsidization, meaning that people without income or lacking sufficient means to be approved for a loan still were not benefiting from this program.[38] Essentially, while USHA's ambitions were good (to address slum clearance and to provide public housing), the scope was not as extensive as in many other countries.

In Sweden, the social democratic government (1932–76) supported rapid urbanization and widespread social reforms centered on housing. Both undoubtedly had a strong impact on twentieth-century Swedish domestic architecture, urban planning, and development. Housing for all citizens, regardless of income, was a core tenet in the social democratic ideology of the 1930s and 1940s, which emphasized social equality and welfare. An important politician in Socialdemokraterna (the Swedish Social Democratic Party) at the time was Alva Myrdal, a social activist, "radical" author, and later Nobel Peace Prize recipient. In 1936, she published her book *Kris i befolkningsfrågan* (*Crisis in the population question*).[39] Following a brief period of studies in America, from 1929 through 1931, on a fellowship granted by the Laura Spelman Rockefeller Memorial, Alva Myrdal and her politician husband Gunnar Myrdal

35 The Federal Housing Administration aimed to provide state-subsidized lender mortgage insurance, meant to incentivize lender organizations to offer more mortgages to lower income families and allow people to enter the housing market. This was deemed a necessity given the poor economic circumstances with which many individuals and families were faced during the Great Depression. Ruth G. Weintraub and Rosalind Tough, "Federal Housing and World War II," *The Journal of Land & Public Utility Economics* 18, no. 2 (1942): 155–62.
36 Weintraub and Tough, "Federal Housing and World War II."
37 Barbara Penner, "The (Still) Dreary Deadlock of Public Housing," *Places Journal*, October (2018).
38 Catherine Bauer Wurster, "The Dreary Deadlock of Public Housing," *Architectural Forum* 106, no. 5 (1957): 140–42, 219–21.
39 See Sondra R. Herman, "Children, Feminism, and Power: Alva Myrdal and Swedish Reform, 1929–1956," *Journal of Women's History* 4, no. 2 (1992): 82–112.

returned to Sweden invigorated with grand new ideas on feminism, parenthood, and childcare. As a social democratic politician and activist, Alva Myrdal fought for a stronger welfare state and available low-cost housing.[40]

The realization of Myrdal's vision of affordable housing for financially constrained families with many children, a housing type called *barnrikehusen*, had a lasting impact on Sweden's built environment and its population. The children living in this housing type were colloquially called "Myrdalingarna," associating them with Alva and Gunnar Myrdal's ideas. Alva Myrdal's advocacy for universal public housing played a pivotal role in Sweden. The successes achieved by placing housing at the core of the Swedish welfare state is important in "the Swedish Model," which in the context of housing is a term used to describe state support for, and extensive collaborations with, industries, housing actors, and housing reformers. A major point on the agenda in Sweden's state-supported structure was to develop standards for the built environment. One research institute that directly informed architecture was Hemmens forskningsinstitut (HFI, the Home [Domestic] research institute), which was established in 1944. The Institute's aim was to take a holistic approach in researching the actual circumstances of housewives, it sought to find out how they themselves wanted to change their situation and thus sought to develop better tools and equipment for housework and more practical kitchens and homes.

This stands in stark contrast to the United States, where the Housing Act of 1937 remains one of the nation's few significant forays into public housing. In America, housing initiatives were a modest component of the New Deal, lacking widespread party support. Conversely, in Sweden, the provision of affordable housing for all was a central tenet of the social democratic ideology.

In an interview from 1939 published in the Swedish daily paper *Göteborgs-Posten*, Catherine Bauer expressed that "it is difficult to find a really bad house in Sweden." Referring to building construction, she declared, "Sweden is better than any other country." As a housing expert for Roosevelt's subsidized building program which saw 160,000 apartment units constructed for low-income families, she was impressed by the speed with which houses had been constructed in Sweden since her previous visit in 1932. She was fascinated by how the radical architects of the time—the "crazy architects with new ideas"—were now "the best ones!"[41] Presumably, she was referring to some of the architects responsible for the housing section at the Stockholm Exhibition, which included architects Sven Markelius, Paul Hedqvist, Kurt von Schmalensee, Nils Ahrbom, Helge Zimdahl, Uno Åhrén, and Sigurd Lewerentz, concluding : "We have a lot to learn from you."[42]

BAUER'S INTEREST IN THE COOPERATIVE HOUSING MODEL

The Scandinavian models of cooperative housing were a recurring interest throughout Bauer's career, and something she tried to advocate for in the United States. In 1949, in an article in *The New Republic*, Bauer argued that cooperative housing could potentially "fill the gap" between social housing and the middle class,[43] stating that "the families that are ineligible for subsidized public housing

40 These measures to counteract the population decline in Sweden in the early 1930s (47 percent more children were born in 1920 than in 1930 in Sweden) were the subject matter of *Kris i Befolkningsfrågan*. Alva Myrdal and Gunnar Myrdal, *Kris i Befolkningsfrågan* (Stockholm: Albert Bonniers Förlag, 1934).
41 "'Crazy-arkitekterna' år 1930 äro bäst nu!" *Göteborgs-Posten*, September 28, 1939.
42 "'Crazy-arkitekterna' år 1930 äro bäst nu!"
43 Catherine Bauer, "The Middle Class Needs Houses Too," *The New Republic*, August 29, 1949, 17–20.

:r 262 GÖTEBORGS-POSTEN Torsdagen den 28 sept. 1939

”Crazy-arkitekterna” år 1930 äro bäst nu!

Svårt att leta upp ett riktigt dåligt hus i Sverige, säger miss Bauer.

Lilla miss Catherine Bauer, Washington, U. S. A. — konsultativ byggnadsexpertis i det stora Rooseveltska byggnadsprogrammet — har varit i Sverige för tredje gången och är nu i Göteborg ett par dagar. När Kungsholm går, reser hon vidare.

Åren 1930, 1936 och 1939 har hon besökt oss och sett på hus. Denna gången dock i mindre omfattning än tidigare. Sverigevisiterna började i år med en cykeltur i Bohuslän.

— Allt för vacker cykeltur, för att jag ens skulle tänka på byggen, säger miss Bauer.

Efter den bar det iväg till Ryssland för att se på byggnadsverksamheten, men så kom kriget, och det blev att huvudstupa ge sig iväg till Sverige igen. Krig är något förskräckligt! Det var så svårt att få passvisum till Sverige! Rysslandsvisiten räckte bara en vecka, och miss Bauer han knappt se mera än att det bygges mycket, stort och bra — stora, ljusa, luftiga rum, väl inredda, utmärkta kök. På hemvägen har hon så sett på byggen i Stockholm och Göteborg.

— Det har blivit många nya hus här i Göteborg, sedan jag var här sist, säger miss Bauer. Under de senaste fem åren ha ni gjort bättre byggnadskonstruktioner än något annat land. Det är nog inte lätt att leta upp ett

Miss CATHERINE BAUER.

verksamhet avser mest barnrika familjer. För mig som utlänning tycks det, som om ni skulle bli nödsakade att ge det en vidsträcktare omfattning, så att den kommer att avse även tvåbarnsfamiljer.

— I Amerika räknar vi med tre kategorier. För den mellersta av ha vi ej byggt något alls. I Sverige har ni gjort mycket för den kategorien. Jag tänker på edra H. S. B.-hus. Där ha vi mycket att lära av er. För den lägsta kategorien har vi däremot gjort mycket mera än ni. Omkring tjugo gånger så mycket! Myrdal tyckte, att

Newspaper clipping from the Swedish daily newspaper Göteborgs-Posten in 1939, featuring Catherine Bauer stating “Hard to find bad housing in Sweden.”

but cannot afford the speculative home as currently produced" constitute "a gap" in the current legislation, forming a major group interested in cooperatives. Furthermore, she argued:

> There has been, in fact, a spontaneous burst of interest in cooperative housing all over the country ever since the war. The National Cooperative Mutual Housing Association lists about a hundred such groups, of whom it has some direct knowledge. Nothing could be more important for the future of housing and community life in America than to implement this movement.[44]

This "spontaneous burst of interest" that Bauer mentions refers to an extensive report on Swedish cooperative housing, as well as a series of articles, that had been published in the United States after the Second World War following a survey of successful examples of cooperative housing in Europe.[45] The comprehensive report included Norway, Sweden, Denmark, the Netherlands, France, Switzerland, and Great Britain. In a review of the report, architect Donald Monson expressed that it put particular emphasis on Sweden and the Netherlands, "which have had the longest experience with cooperative housing and whose experience has been, to a large extent, the basis for much of the legislation adopted more recently in the other countries."[46]

To the Americans, Sweden offered a variety of novel and innovative housing models, which could potentially be imitated across the Atlantic. The long-sightedness of organizations such as HSB and KF inspired Catherine Bauer and the other authors of the various reports and it was seen as a way of not only providing housing, but also of building resilient neighborhoods for long-term communities. While the housing cooperative model, exemplified by HSB, offered one solution, another program offering affordable housing for the general population was the *egnahem* (own home) initiative, which provided single-family homes, combining the economy of mass production with realization through self-build construction. The report's conclusion emphasized the carefulness with which Sweden had implemented nation-wide planning for community development in relation to other factors such as industry and regional growth. Catherine Bauer's interest in housing and knowledge of the European context gave her an undisputable foundation to argue for how the United States could translate European examples into legislation. Her persistent calls to improve housing conditions were tireless. In the Swedish cooperative housing examples, Bauer could both demonstrate the inadequacy of current housing legislation in the USA and find examples from which to argue for alternative solutions.[47]

The holistic approach to housing advocated in the seven points of the second part of the *Modern Architecture* exhibition at MoMA in 1932 found its answer in Sweden's cooperative housing agencies. Cooperative housing agencies in Sweden had been able to implement and build large-scale housing estates using test-case scenarios that eventually gave shape to building standards in the home environment, as well as scenarios such as communal settings of welfare state housing. Catherine Bauer's particular interest in the HSB cooperative movement and the effects it had on other European nations as well as the United States was understood as a model for long-term communities.

44 Bauer, "The Middle Class Needs Houses Too," 19.
45 Catherine Bauer refers to a series of articles in *The American City* by architectural planner Donald Monson and economist Astrid Monson, two young Detroit city planners who helped to organize the United Auto Workers in that city. See Donald Monson and Astrid Monson, "Ideas from Sweden for an American Cooperative Housing Program," Donald Monson and Astrid Monson, *The American City* 64, no. 3 (1949): 84–86, "Ideas from Sweden (Conclusion)," *The American City* 64, no. 5 (1949): 140–42, and *Cooperative Housing in Europe: A Report of the Banking and Currency Subcommittee Investigating and Studying European Housing Programs*, Senate document (United States. Congress. Senate), 81st Congress, no. 148 (Washington: U.S. Govt. Print. Off., 1950)
46 Donald Monson, "Review," *Land Economics* 27, no. 1 (1951): 87–89.
47 Catherine Bauer concludes the article in *The New Republic* by explaining the prerequisites for cooperative housing to become successful in the interest of the tenant. See Bauer, "The Middle Class Needs Houses Too," 20.

What is remarkable about Bauer's studies of Swedish housing policy is how she was able to covey and overcome the political xenostereotypes concerning the Swedish Model in the US, while transferring the detailed knowledge on housing plans, housing planning, and policy development. The description of Sweden following a political "middle way" was a xenostereotype created by Marquis Childs in the US through the book *Sweden: The Middle Way* published in 1936.[48] Politically attractive representations of Sweden—the "Swedish Model"—were developed through the constant interplay between xenostereotypes developed abroad and autostereotypes formulated by domestic actors.[49] Catherine Bauer's role as a housing advocate demonstrates how ideological content of Swedish housing policy could be reinterpreted, even for North American politics.

Exhibitions emerge here as platforms on which to present new ideas for housing, with new housing plans acting both functionally and aesthetically but also being used to advocate for certain political positions. The *Modern Architecture* exhibition, like the Stockholm Exhibition of 1930 were crucial sites for these trans-Atlantic connections. Catherine Bauer exerted influence and inhabited a particular space of action that had long-lasting consequences for urban development. Her documentation and empirical research became not only the foundation for political decision-making, but ultimately played a central role and became visible through exhibitions at MoMA as well as through her book *Modern Housing*.[50]

Bauer's dream of producing public housing in the US was never quite fulfilled; this was largely due to the income requirements and other barriers that prohibited many people from living in the buildings that were constructed. Only the poorest individuals could access public housing.[51] In comparing the cooperative ownership structure that existed in Scandinavia and the limiting model that was implemented in the United States in the late 1930s, it is, however, premature to invoke "the failure of public housing" in the US, as the country at the time had not really acted upon public housing ideals as they were developed in Scandinavia.[52] Nevertheless, Catherine Bauer helped inform the Housing Act of 1937 that established the U.S. Housing Authority (USHA) and provided federal funding for the construction of low-income housing projects. This marked the beginning of a significant federal role in providing housing for low-income individuals and families and enabled the construction of thousands of public housing units across the country, which may be seen as a small-scale American version of the Swedish Model.

48 See Marquis William Childs, *Sweden: The Middle Way*, New Haven: Yale University Press, 1936.

49 Kazimierz Musiał, "Roots of the Scandinavian Model: Images of Progress in the Era of Modernisation" (PhD diss., Humboldt University, Berlin and Baden Baden, 2002), 196, 225.

50 In 1934, MoMA showed an exhibition on housing in New York titled "America Can't Have Housing." Catherine Bauer wrote an essay called "Housing: Paper Plans or a Workers Movement" for the catalog. See Catherine Bauer, "Housing: Paper Plans, or a Workers' Movement," in *America Can't Have Housing*, ed. Carol Aronovici (New York: Committee on the Housing Exhibition by the Museum of Modern Art, 1934), 20–23.

51 Penner, "The (Still) Dreary Deadlock of Public Housing."

52 Roger Biles, "Nathan Straus and the Failure of U.S. Public Housing, 1937–1942," *The Historian* 53, no. 1 (1990): 33–46.

nummer

3. 1935

Innhold:

Familien og boligen.
Byregulering eller konditorkunst?
Hvor meget koster lys og luft?
Sven Markelius: Olika husbredder och deras byggnadskostnader.
Ned med boligstandarden?
Oslo kommunes Arkitektkonkurranse.
Veien til lavere husleier.
Boligkooperasjonen og Brødrene Johnsen.
Boligundersøkelsen i Gøteborg.
Boligsituasjonen i Oslo i virkeligheten og i den officielle statistikk.
Aker. Vestkantens villaer og østkantensskrammelbebyggelse.
Rådmann Bassøes mening om Plan.
Husleiestreik i kommunens gårder.
Framhuset skal bygges!
Nye bøker. —

PLAN

Tidsskrift for bolig- og byggespørsmål
Utgitt av Socialistiske Arkitekters Forening

The magazine *PLAN*, issue 3, 1935.

Anne-Kristine Kronborg A WELFARE STATE ON THE DRAWING BOARD

Socialist Architects in the Norwegian Labor Movement

In 1935, Arbeiderpartiet (the Norwegian Labor Party) formed its first government. This is considered the beginning of a new era in the country's political and social history—the prelude to the welfare state. Shortly after, a group of young architects joined Arbeiderpartiet. Among them were Erik Rolfsen, Frode Rinnan, Carsten Boysen, Gunnar Øvergaard Jørgen, Eyvind Alnæs, and Gunvor Eliassen.[1] They were all educated at NTH (Norges tekniske høgskole, the Norwegian University of Technology) in Trondheim around 1930 and belonged to a generation of architects who experienced significant professional changes during their studies. The professional reorientation went hand-in-hand with a political awakening.[2] The students believed that the education was outdated. Inspired by Bauhaus, they wanted to focus on housing conditions, urban planning, psychology, and sociology. Ultimately, this was a question about the architect's role in society. The students rejected the traditional role of the architect as an artist and believed that architects had to see themselves as planners and builders of society instead.

After their studies, the architects joined the organization Mot Dag (Toward Day), which was a gathering place for socialist intellectuals. The members organized themselves into different professional groups: the Socialist Doctors' Association, the Socialist Philologists and Scientists' Association, the Socialist Technicians and Engineers' Association, and the Socialist Lawyers and Economists' Association. The architects followed the same pattern and founded the Sosialistiske Arkitekters Forening (SAF, the Association of Socialist Architects) in 1932. SAF published the magazine *PLAN*, which was published in four issues in the period 1933–36. In the magazine, the architects formulated a harsh critique of social conditions in general, and especially of the current housing policy. In the summer of 1936, Mot Dag was dissolved, and most of its members joined Arbeiderpartiet. Several of the professional groups from Mot Dag were incorporated into the party organization, including SAF. This means that a group of professionally and politically engaged architects joined the party exactly at a time when it was consolidating itself as the country's center of political power. The architects' involvement in the Mot Dag movement is well documented in architectural history. The same applies to their significance in postwar housing construction and urban planning. However, the architects' professional and political engagement in the Arbeiderpartiet and the broader labor movement between 1935 and 1940 was crucial for the postwar developments, and there is a rich source material from these years, in the form of texts produced by socialist architects, which include newspaper and journal articles, reports, and other study materials.[3] The source material includes two booklets titled "Bo bedre" (Better living) and "Boligbygging i Norge" (Housing construction in Norway), thirty articles

1 The first three in particular made their mark in architectural history: Erik Rolfsen became the city planning director in Oslo after the Second World War, Frode Rinnan established an architectural firm that grew to become one of the largest in the country in the postwar period, and Carsten Boysen played a key role in the development of the housing cooperative movement in Norway and in housing research.

2 Jon Guttu, *Carsten Boysen* (Oslo: Kolofon forlag, 2019), 79.

3 This essay builds on my PhD dissertation: Anne-Kristine Kronborg, "Å reise noe nytt og bedre… Om arkitektur og politikk 1935–1940" (PhD-diss., Oslo School of Architecture and Design, 2022), and portions of the text have been previously published (in Norwegian) in Anne-Kristine Kronborg, "Arkitektene som kom inn fra kulda: Socialistiske Arkitekters Forening fra Mot Dag til Arbeiderpartiet," ed. Erlend Hanssen Sjåvik and Kim Pløhn, *Ny boligplan: tidsskrift for boligpolitikk*, no. 1 (2024): 115–27.

in the journal *Bygningsarbeideren* (The construction worker), and a collection of articles titled "Vi snakker om hus" (Talking about houses). The architects also gave lectures and campaigned. The source material clearly shows that the new political situation represented a new space for action for the architects, and that they assumed the role of experts in their field.

THE TECHNICAL ASSOCIATION OF THE NORWEGIAN LABOR PARTY

When the architects joined Arbeiderpartiet, SAF became a part of the party's Teknisk Forening (Technical Association), its own association for engineers and other technical professionals. The Technical Association became an important arena for professional and political work for the socialist architects.

The Technical Association was founded in 1934, and among the initiators was one of the party's most important strategists in the 1930s, journalist Ole Colbjørnsen. One of the other leaders of the association, engineer H. C. Sandbeck, presented the association in the party's journal *Det 20de Århundre* (The twentieth century) shortly after it was founded in 1934. He explained that the purpose of the association was to contribute to analyzing the conditions for the production industry and to design a planned economy; it was also supposed to function as a sort of interest group for technical professionals, and would educate both the technical profession and the general public. Sandbeck concluded: "What can and should be done will be decided by the working people themselves. Technical professionals with fresh intellectual abilities can greatly contribute to clarifying how it best can be done."[4]

In an academic article about the Technical Association in the journal *Arbeiderhistorie* (Labor history), the historian Rolv Petter Amdam describes the Technical Association as a planning apparatus for Arbeiderpartiet, which developed plans and studies, thus contributing to shaping the party's policies.[5] Significant knowledge production took place within the association, and according to Amdam, it was the members' ability to integrate technology and planned economy that allowed them to have their key issues included in the party's program.[6] Amdam points out that many issues were discussed and explored within the Technical Association *before* they were presented to the party's governing bodies and incorporated into the party's programs. This means that the members of the Technical Association had significant power in defining the party's agenda. According to Rolv Petter Amdam, the reason that the Technical Association gained such importance in shaping politics during the second half of the 1930s lay in its founder, Ole Colbjørnsen, being one of the party's chief ideologists. Amdam describes Colbjørnsen's characteristic way of shaping political agendas:

> He must have had a burning desire to shape the party's policy, and he chose partly unconventional but effective means to succeed. ... And through the Technical Association, he took the initiative to start concrete planning before it was addressed by the party otherwise. ... Colbjørnsen's commitment thus expressed a willingness to translate politics into action.[7]

4 H. C. Sandbeck, "Teknikk og socialisme" [Technology and socialism], *Det 20de århundre* 10 (1934): 317.

5 Rolv Petter Amdam., "Teknologi og planøkonomi" [Technology and the planned economy], *Arbeiderhistorie* (1988): 107–23.

6 Amdam. "Teknologi og planøkonomi," 107–23.

7 Original quote in Norwegian: "Han må ha hatt ein brinnande trong til å forme partiet sin politikk, og han valde til dels ukonvensjonelle, men effektive middel for å vinne fram. ... Og gjennom Teknisk Forening tok han initiativ til å få sett i gang konkret planarbeid før dette blei tatt opp av partiet elles. ... Engasjementet til Colbjørnsen uttrykte dermed vilje til å omsette politikk til handling." Rolv Petter Amdam, "Teknologi og planøkonomi," 112.

When the socialist architects became part of this association, they became part of a professional-political environment that demanded their knowledge and allowed it to be used to shape political plans and programs. The Technical Association published its own series of writings, called *Teknisk-økonomiske småskrifter* (Technical-economic pamphlets), which addressed some of the most important political issues of the time, particularly those related to business and labor. The pamphlets in the series were written by members of the various specialized groups within the Technical Association and were used as a knowledge base within the party organization.

BETTER LIVING

As early as 1936, architects contributed to this series with a booklet. It was called "Bo bedre: bolignøden og boligbehovet, bygger vi for mange boliger, retningslinjer for norsk boligproduksjon" (Better living: The housing shortage and housing need, are we building too many homes? Guidelines for Norwegian housing production) and was written by Gunnar Øvergaard Jørgen. The booklet was only sixteen pages long, but it was extensive in terms of content. The text covered the following topics: *bolignøden i den offisielle statistikk* (housing shortage in official statistics), *overbefolkede leiligheter* (overcrowded apartments), *en ny by av Oslos størrelse* (a new city of Oslo's size), and *hvor meget må det bygges* (how much needs to be built)?[8]

Gunnar Øvergaard Jørgen started with a definition of the poor housing conditions: "Partly, there is the condition of the houses, which is not always as it should be.... The other side of the housing shortage becomes apparent when we look at how many people live in each housing unit."[9] The housing problem was thus expressed in two ways: the physical condition of the houses and overcrowding. The architect pointed out that although there were no statistics on the percentage of the country's housing that had a poor technical standard, it was likely to be quite high. Overcrowding, on the other hand, was well documented. Øvergaard Jørgen claimed that although the data from the last census was quite alarming, the official statistics still did not provide an accurate picture of the real housing shortage: while according to the official criteria, there were 160,000 people living in severely overcrowded housing (the same amount as the entire population of Bergen and Trondheim combined), he argued that the official statistics were too theoretical in their definition of overcrowding and didn't for instance consider the fact that overcrowding was unevenly distributed among the population.[10] This overcrowding in turn had significant negative consequences for the population, particularly in terms of their mental health: Øvergaard Jørgen described the family life that it supported as both difficult and exhausting—particularly problematic was the fact that both the kitchen and living room had to serve as bedrooms: "Individuals cannot avoid disturbing each other; they go to bed and wake up at different times; schoolchildren have to do homework while the adults come in and out; someone in the family might have night work and try to sleep while others are awake."[11] He concluded his diagnosis of the housing problems with the demand

8 Gunnar Øvergaard Jørgen, "Bo bedre: bolignøden og boligbehovet, bygger vi for mange boliger, retningslinjer for norsk boligproduksjon," *Teknisk-økonomiske småskrifter* 4 (Oslo: Det Norske Arbeiderpartis forlag, 1936).

9 Original quote in Norwegian: "Dels er det husenes tilstand som ikke altid er som den bør være.... Den annen side ved bolignøden viser sig, når vi ser efter hvor mange mennesker det bor i hver enkelt bolig." Jørgen, "Bo bedre," 3.

10 Original quote in Norwegian: "like mange som hele befolkningen i Bergen og Oslo tilsammen." Øvergaard Jørgen, "Bo bedre," 4.

11 Original quote in Norwegian: "De enkelte kan ikke undgå å forstyrre hverande; de går til sengs og står op til forskjellig tid; skolebarn skal lese lekser mens de voksne går ut og inn: en av familien har kanskje nattarbeide og skal forsøke å sove mens de andre er i virksomhet." Øvergaard Jørgen, "Bo bedre," 5.

In the years after Arbeiderpartiet (the Norwegian Labor Party) came to power, Teknisk Forening (Technical Association) contributed to the party's policy development through a series of publications. The booklet "Bo bedre" (Better living) was published in 1936 and contained an analysis of the housing situation.

12 Øvergaard Jørgen, "Bo bedre," 7.
13 Øvergaard Jørgen, "Bo bedre," 7.
14 Original quote in Norwegian: "Det dreier seg om å utbygge bygningsindustrien, å hindre den spekulasjon som allerede nu er påferde og som er blitt hovedårsaken til de stigende byggepriser; og det dreier seg om å ordne kredittvesenet og gjøre det til et hensiktsmessig redskap for byggevirksomheten. Til slutt blir det for de for de laveste inntekters vedkommende nødvendig å øke betalingsevnen ved offentlig støtte i en eller annen form." Øvergaard Jørgen, "Bo bedre," 11.
15 Øvergaard Jørgen, "Bo bedre," 10.
16 Original quote in Norwegian: "Vi har i byggevirksomheten et særlig tydelig eksempel på, at det er ulønnsomt å la være å sette arbeide igang." Øvergaard Jørgen, "Bo bedre," 10–11.
17 Original quote in Norwegian: "Det forutsetter blandt annet en arbeiderregjering som har støtte i et sterkt stortingsflertall, og som kan samarbeide med arbeiderstyrte kommuner." Øvergaard Jørgen, "Bo bedre," 13.

for a completely different housing standard, both in terms of quality and size.

Having identified the problem, Øvergaard Jørgen then moved on to outlining proposed solutions. First of all, new criteria for overcrowding had to be developed. The architect's main requirement was that the kitchen should not be considered a living space, as it was in the official statistics, and that the minimum size of a dwelling should not be calculated on the basis of more than two people per room, meaning that a household of four people needed at least two rooms *and* a kitchen. By applying this criterion, an even greater housing shortage was revealed. According to Øvergaard Jørgen, this could only be met through systematic new construction, at a scale commensurate with a new city the size of Oslo.[12] This meant that the intensity of construction activity had to be doubled. The socialist architect dismissed the conservatives' claim that the housing shortage would disappear if left to market forces for a few years.[13] To combat overcrowding and eliminate substandard housing, a systematic transformation of the entire housing sector was required:

> It is about expanding the construction industry, preventing the speculation that is already underway and has become the main cause of rising construction prices; and it is about organizing the credit system and making it an appropriate tool for construction activity. Finally, for those with the lowest incomes, it will be necessary to increase their ability to pay through public support in some form or another.[14]

Gunnar Øvergaard Jørgen did not describe in detail how the transformation should take place in practice, but he emphasized an important basic principle: namely, that such a transformation would yield significant socioeconomic benefits, particularly in terms of the general labor market.[15] Increased housing production would mean increased employment and production in the construction industry, transportation sector, and among material producers. It would also mean increased investments and increased national income. "In the construction industry," Øvergaard Jørgen concluded, "we have a particularly clear example of the fact that it is unprofitable to refrain from initiating work."[16] This represented a new approach to the housing issue, reframing housing construction as a form of value creation that the whole society would benefit from. This would become the focal point of the socialist architects' and Arbeiderpartiet's housing policy program, and the small booklet represented a breakthrough in this way of addressing the housing question.

In this key text on housing policy, Gunnar Øvergaard Jørgen argued along three lines: a technical and functional line (addressing the homes themselves), an organizational line (addressing housing production), and a political line (addressing governance): a plan that could guarantee individuals and families a dignified existence in the future required, in his words, "among other things, a Labor government with support from a strong majority in parliament and the ability to collaborate with worker-controlled municipalities."[17] The sentence becomes particularly interesting when considering the timing of the booklet's release. "Bo bedre" was published just a few weeks before a parliamentary election in October 1936, a period of great anticipation. While Arbeiderpartiet was indeed in government, their position was far from secure. The party campaigned on a program focused on action and change and needed strong issues for the election campaign. The housing issue was one such matter. And *this* is where "Bo bedre" came into the picture and likely had far greater significance than its modest format would suggest. The booklet was actively used in the election campaign and in the party's education and information activities. For example, in September 1936, a whole range of newspapers within the labor movement's press published an abbreviated version of the text, spread across two articles. These articles were prominently featured in newspapers such as *Sarpsborg Arbeiderblad* (on Saturday, September 12) and *Tidens Krav* (on September 18, 1936) and authored by Gunnar Øvergaard Jørgen. In this way, both the housing issue and the young architect became known to newspaper readers across the country just before the parliamentary election.

The booklet was also utilized in the educational activities of the labor movement. The movement placed a strong emphasis on education within its own ranks, particularly through the so-called Arbeidernes Oplysningsforbund (AOF, or the Workers' Enlightenment Association). In 1936, AOF offered a correspondence course on "Current Politics." One of the topics covered in the course was housing policy, and "Bo bedre" was listed as required reading. In the autumn of 1936, the socialist architects also delivered a series of radio lectures that were broadcast nationally including a lecture by Gunnar Øvergaard Jørgen, "Hvordan bor folk i Norge? – Hvad trenges det av hus?" (How do people in Norway live? What kind of houses are needed?), an adapted version of "Bo bedre."[18]

The way the small booklet "Bo bedre" was distributed, discussed, and used illustrates how the socialist architects operated and spread their knowledge and viewpoints. The booklet is a prime example of how the architects in the Technical Association contributed to exploring the housing issue and proposing solutions at the intersection of technology and the planned economy. Through this seemingly modest publication, the architects helped outline the contours of a new housing policy. At the same time, the extensive publicity that the booklet received must have contributed to establishing the socialist architects as experts and giving them credibility within the labor movement.

NEW GUIDELINES FOR HOUSING POLICY

The following year, in 1937, the architects in the Technical Association released a new booklet on housing policy, this time titled "Boligbygging i Norge" (Housing construction in Norway).[19] The title page indicates that the booklet was written by the Technical Association at the request of Arbeiderpartiet's labor planning committee. While "Bo bedre" can be seen as a fresh approach to the housing issue, "Boligbygging i Norge" appears more as a study and a draft of a housing policy program.

The text began by stating, "Housing conditions are one of the most crucial factors for the overall living conditions of the people" and "Housing construction plays a vital role in the country's economic life."[20] With these two sentences, the socialist architects

18 Gunnar Øvergaard Jørgen, "Hvordan bor folk i Norge? – Hvad trenges det av hus?," in *Vi snakker om hus* [Talking about houses], Eyvind Alnæs (Oslo: Stenersen 1937), 14–15.
19 Teknisk Forening av D.N.A, "Boligbygging i Norge" [Housing construction in Norway], *Teknisk-økonomiske småskrifter* (Oslo: Det Norske Arbeiderpartis forlag, 1937).
20 Teknisk Forening av D.N.A, "Boligbygging i Norge," 5.

The 1937 booklet "Boligbygging i Norge" (Housing construction in Norway) was Teknisk Forening's second publication on housing policy. Here, the architects proposed a number of measures to solve the housing problem. Their analysis formed the basis for a completely new national plan for housing construction.

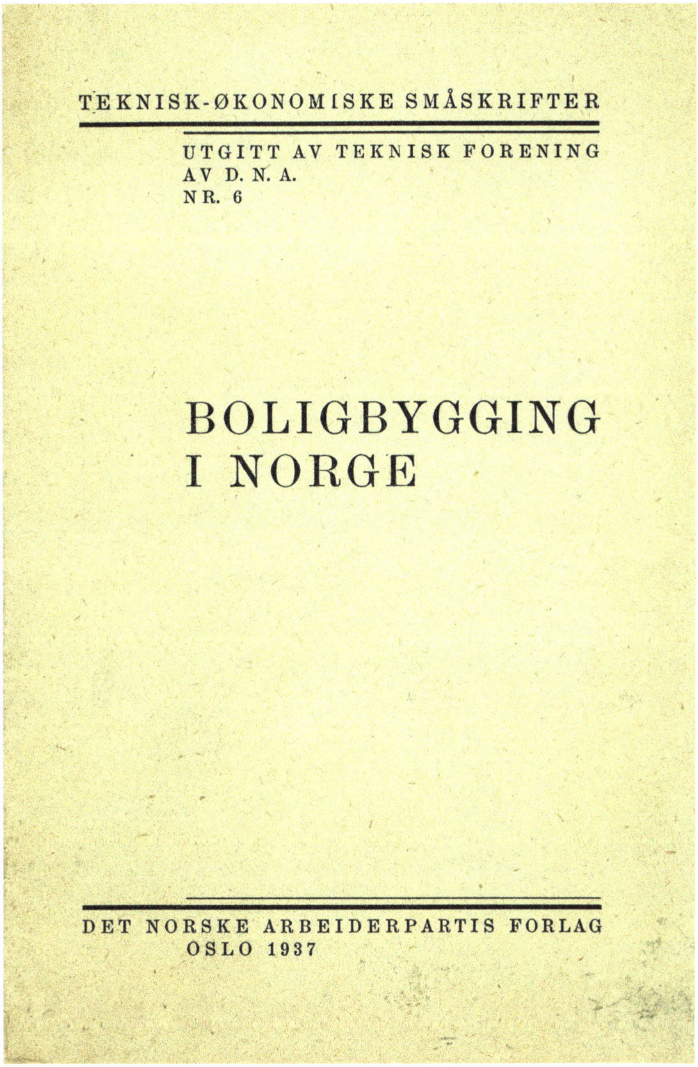

21 Original quote in Norwegian: "stor betyding for samfundet om boligbyggingen holdes oppe eller om den ligger nede." Teknisk Forening av D.N.A, "Boligbygging i Norge," 5.

22 Original quote in Norwegian: "Over hundre års erfaring har vist at det kapitalistiske samfunds boligbygging på privat initiativ ikke kan løse boligspørsmålet slik som befolkningens behov krever det." Teknisk Forening av D. N. A., "Boligbygging i Norge" 7.

23 Teknisk Forening av D. N. A., "Boligbygging i Norge," 8.

24 Teknisk Forening av D. N. A., "Boligbygging i Norge," 12.

25 Teknisk Forening av D. N. A., "Boligbygging i Norge," 12.

placed the housing issue where they believed it belonged, namely at the intersection of the people's living conditions and the country's economy. The following paradox was thereby presented: half of the country's population lived in unsatisfactory housing conditions, while a significant portion of the country's construction workers were unemployed. The argument was that doubling housing construction would meet the housing needs while simultaneously creating full employment in the construction industry. Therefore, it was deemed "of great importance to society whether housing construction is maintained or halted."[21] In the text, the housing issue was thus portrayed as a source of increased employment, production, and value creation, but not as an area for regular business activities. In a capitalist society, it was the availability of land and capital that governed housing construction, and these assets were controlled by a few. Therefore, it was also the prospect of maximizing profits that directed housing construction, rather than the actual housing needs. "Over a hundred years of experience has shown," wrote the booklet's authors, "that housing construction in a capitalist society based on private initiative cannot solve the housing question as required by the needs of the population."[22]

The solution lay in a systematic planning of the housing construction industry that would place housing production and the housing stock under public control and management, and raise the average income level to enable rent to be paid without public subsidies.[23] In other words, housing construction had to be significantly expanded, while the population simultaneously had to be enabled to afford the new homes. This required a rationalization of construction activities, a new organization of housing credit and public support, and a general increase in income. Doubling housing construction would lead to a significant increase in employment and production in the construction industry. Increasing employment in the construction industry was an important point in itself, and it went hand-in-hand with the general demand within the labor movement for modernization and rationalization. The construction industry, which was disparaged for not having properly utilized the progressive potentials of modern technology, included not only construction workers but also those involved in producing, supplying, and importing building materials, as well as other industries such as the transportation sector. In other words, it was an industry of great socioeconomic significance.

Furthermore, it was necessary to establish a "technical apparatus that can gather experiences and disseminate them to all the thousands of construction sites."[24] Cooperative building societies should be responsible for construction activities, and a central consulting office for cooperative building societies should be established. The tasks of the consulting office would include "developing building designs, conveying technical expertise, assisting with loan acquisitions, and providing advice when organizing cooperative building societies."[25] A similar central office, the Building Industry's Material Office, would handle material distribution. The Material Office was intended to play a key role in construction activities, and it would be organized as a joint-stock company with the state, municipalities, cooperative building societies, construction worker unions, material factories, and material dealers as shareholders. The office would contribute to rationalizing the production,

26 Teknisk Forening av D. N. A., "Boligbygging i Norge," 14.

distribution, storage, and transportation of building materials, as well as keeping track of the building industry's material needs and the production capacity of companies producing building materials. The central office would allocate orders, make purchases, control prices, and help initiate domestic production of building materials. And, importantly, prevent speculation.

The construction workers' trade unions were assigned an important role in the new housing system described by the socialist architects in the booklet. The construction workers possessed valuable knowledge, already had an effective, nationwide organization, and represented a significant power factor within the labor movement. However, the architects would also play a role in the new system, amongst other things in formalizing urban and regional planning work in the face of higher densities.[26] A State Urban Planning and Building Directorate had to be established, and county architects had to be appointed. The county architects would assist the cooperative building societies and serve as a link between the local building societies and the central office. The booklet also discussed new ways of financing the housing construction. Commercial housing credit had to be better organized, and effective public financial organizations needed to be established. The architects suggested that a state bank for housing should be established as well as systems for rental support. The municipalities were also allocated an important role, primarily in facilitating cooperative housing construction. This involved assessing housing conditions, housing needs, and affordability, as well as providing land areas and necessary infrastructure.

In "Boligbygging i Norge," the architects outlined a series of measures that can be understood as constituting a comprehensive plan to solve the housing problem. To achieve a new systematic approach in housing construction, a new organizational and technical apparatus had to be established, along with the creation of new financing schemes and institutions. The starting point was the significant social and socioeconomic importance of housing construction, and the argument that increased housing construction would not only eliminate the housing shortage, but also boost employment and production across all aspects of the construction industry runs as a common thread throughout the entire text.

A NATIONAL PLAN FOR HOUSING CONSTRUCTION

It was Arbeiderpartiet's program committee that had commissioned the architects of the Technical Association to develop a national plan for housing construction, and in the spring of 1937, Minister of Social Affairs Oscar Torp announced that such a plan was underway. In June 1937, Arbeiderpartiet's national executive committee held a meeting. Here, a new plan for the party's economic and social policies was adopted, including new guidelines for its housing policy.

The new guidelines were published in the form of a small pamphlet titled "Aktuelle Arbeidsopgaver for Det Norske Arbeiderparti" (Current tasks for the Norwegian Labor Party), which gave housing issues its own chapter and began by stating that "Good housing is necessary to create a healthy and happy generation; poor housing

27 Original quote in Norwegian: "Gode boliger er nødvendige for å skape en sund og lykkelig slekt, slette boligforhold er en av de fremste årsaker til dårlige levekår, sykdom og nedsatt arbeidsevne." An excerpt of "Aktuelle Arbeidsopgaver for Det Norske Arbeiderparti" (Current tasks for the Norwegian Labor Party) was included in the booklet "Boligbygging i Norge," from which the following quotes are taken. See Teknisk Forening av D. N. A., "Boligbygging i Norge," 30.

28 Teknisk Forening av D. N. A., "Boligbygging i Norge," 30.

29 Teknisk Forening av D. N. A., "Boligbygging i Norge," 30.

30 Gunnar Øvergaard Jørgen, "En landsplan for boligbygging" [A national plan for housing construction], *Det 20de århundre* 4 (1937): 161; Gunnar Øvergaard Jørgen, "Boligplanen i praksis" [The housing plan in practice], *Det 20de århundre* 8 (1937): 304.

31 Gunnar Øvergaard Jørgen also published two articles about the plan for housing in the architect's journal *Byggekunst*. See Gunnar Øvergaard Jørgen, "Landsplan for boligbygging" [National plan for housing construction], *Byggekunst* (1937): 207; and Gunnar Øvergaard Jørgen, "Boligsaken på landsbygden" [The housing issue in the countryside], *Byggekunst* (1938): 87.

32 Teknisk Forening av DNA. D. Saksarkiv. Mappe Boligkonferanse 18. september 1937. Arbeiderbevegelsens arkiv og bibliotek. [Archive of the Technical Association, archive series D, Housing Conference September 18th 1937, The Norwegian Labor Movement archives and Library].

33 Gunnar Øvergaard Jørgen, "Hvad trenger Oslo av boliger?" [What does Oslo need in terms of housing?], *Arbeiderbladet*, October 12, 1937.

conditions are one of the leading causes of poor living conditions, illness, and reduced work capacity."[27] It further emphasized that the housing issue could not be solved by the market; in this field, the state and municipalities had to take the lead. It stated: "To provide homes for the growing population, to reduce the existing housing shortage, and to create sustainable employment in the construction industry and related industries, there must be a significant expansion of housing construction."[28] These are the same viewpoints expressed by the socialist architects in "Bo bedre" and "Boligbygging i Norge," and the pamphlet advocated alleviating the housing shortage, providing employment for construction workers, and stimulating growth in related industries. Continuing in the same vein, it repeated the ideas and arguments from the architects' texts point by point, culminating in the following proposal: "A national plan for housing construction should be developed, which integrates the measures to be promoted regarding technology, credit, and budgetary matters."[29] The socialist architects' writings formed the basis for this national plan, and the new guidelines emerged as a summary and concise formulation of the knowledge base that the architects had developed during their first year as party members and members of the Technical Association.

The national plan was made known through the party press in 1937. Gunnar Øvergaard Jørgen presented the plan in two extensive articles, published in the journal *Det 20de århundre*[30] and the members' magazine of the Building Workers' Union, *Bygningsarbeideren*.[31] The national plan for housing construction was also the topic for a preparatory meeting organized by the Technical Association in collaboration with Arbeiderpartiet and the Norwegian Building Workers' Union in Oslo on September 18, 1937. This meeting took the form of a major housing conference with participants from across the country, including some of the top politicians from within the party, with the purpose of gaining an overview of housing conditions in different parts of the country and discussing how the national plan should be implemented in practice.[32]

Just under a month after the housing conference, on October 11, 1937, the architect group within the Technical Association organized an open housing meeting in collaboration with the Oslo branch of Arbeiderpartiet. The program featured lectures by Gunnar Øvergaard Jørgen and Frode Rinnan. Øvergaard Jørgen's lecture was titled "Good Housing for the Whole People" and focused on the national plan for housing construction. Following the lectures, the party's election film *By og land, hand i hand* (City and countryside, hand in hand) was shown. While the housing conference in September had gathered professionals and party members for discussions on the housing plan, this was an election meeting open to everyone. There were elections in 1937 as well—specifically, municipal elections. Housing became one of the main issues for Arbeiderpartiet, granting the socialist architects, led by Gunnar Øvergaard Jørgen, both speaking time and media coverage.

The day after the election meeting, *Arbeiderbladet* (The workers' newspaper) featured a prominent article by Øvergaard Jørgen on its front page. The title was "Hvad trenger Oslo av boliger?" (What does Oslo need in terms of housing?).[33] In the article—the first in a series of newspaper articles that the architect wrote in *Arbeiderbladet* leading up to the election—he wrote about the

Det 20de århundre

HEFTE 4
MAI 1937

MOT-DAG

Innhold:

Utenrikskronikk.

—

1ste mai 1937.

—

Dagfin Juel:
Den kapitalistiske opgangstid.

Ole Colbjørnsen:
Krisefast folke-økonomi.

Johan Vogt:
Lønn, pris og profitt.

Gunnar Øvergård Jørgen:
En landsplan for boligbygging.

Olav Storstein:
Nordahl Grieg.

Ingrid Gaustad:
Lærebøkene i historie.

—

Kronologi.

Redaksjon:
Finn Moe.
Arne Ording.

50 ØRE

The journal *Det 20de Århundre* (*The 20th Century*) was published by the labor party and featured articles of a more academic-ideological nature as well as articles on culture. The journal was important for policy development within the party, and in 1937, architect Gunnar Øvergaard Jørgen introduced housing policy into its pages.

overcrowding and the poor condition of many dwellings in the city, ultimately concluding that a new housing policy was needed.

One of Øvergaard Jørgen's articles stood out from the rest. Published in the magazine *Arbeiderkvinnen* (The working woman), he presented the housing issue as a particularly important matter for women. Food, clothing, and shelter were stated as the most essential needs for families, and it was the responsibility of women to take care of the home—and, most importantly, to make ends meet: "But those who have little to spend must soon lower their housing demands," he stated.[34] Far too many people lived in housing that was inconvenient, expensive, and a threat to both their physical and the mental health. The architect wrote that new and larger homes needed to be built, and "it must be done in a way so that most people can afford to live there."[35] Furthermore, working-class women should also be entitled to "some of the technical improvements that greatly facilitate housework" and in cities, "residential areas should have childcare facilities and playgrounds where children can be safe while their mothers are at work."[36]

In the article "'Et dobbelt ansvar' – kvinner og menn i norsk arbeiderbevegelse 1918–1940" ("A dual responsibility": Women and men in the Norwegian labor movement, 1918–1940) from 1998,[37] historian Ida Blom describes *Arbeiderkvinnen* as a political magazine for working-class housewives, noting that throughout the interwar period, the magazine specifically appealed to working-class women to fight for those of the party's core issues that concerned families: "Housing policy, free school materials, better wages for male workers, support for strikers were seen as important measures to protect the family from capitalist exploitation."[38] According to Blom, women's particular understanding of social policy issues made welfare a suitable arena for them, which could be used to garner their vote: for this reason, Arbeiderpartiet appealed to women to "work for the best housing policy, the best childcare, and support for mothers, the disabled, and the elderly."[39] Gunnar Øvergaard Jørgen's article fits well within this framework. The article addressed an important social policy issue, and the author specifically appealed to women as managers of the household and as holders of a special understanding and interest in housing policy. Arbeiderpartiet represented those who suffered the most from the housing shortage and was therefore the only party that could create "order, fairness, and security in the housing market," wrote Gunnar Øvergaard Jørgen in the last paragraph, before concluding with a spirited appeal: "Working women! Rally for the 1937 municipal elections and support the housing construction campaign!"[40]

The national housing construction plan was also the subject of study, education, and discussion in various parts of the labor movement. For example, the Building Workers' Union made the national plan a key issue at its national convention. The Tenants' Association in Oslo formed its own study circle, where all the points in the plan were "thoroughly debated," according to *Arbeiderbladet* on February 12, 1938.[41]

Housing had been on Arbeiderpartiet's agenda since the late nineteenth century, but the national plan of 1937 represented something new. Previously, the party had primarily advocated for rent regulation and increased public support for housing construction, without delving deeper into the questions of housing production

34 Original quote in Norwegian: "Men den som har lite å rutte med, må snart slå av på kravene til boligen." Gunnar Øvergaard Jørgen, "Riv rønnene. Bygg vakre hjem" [Tear down the derelict houses. Build beautiful homes], *Arbeiderkvinnen* 10 (1937): 7.

35 Øvergaard Jørgen, "Riv rønnene. Bygg vakre hjem," 7.

36 Øvergaard Jørgen, "Riv rønnene. Bygg vakre hjem," 7.

37 Ida Blom, "'Et dobbelt ansvar' – kvinner og menn i norsk arbeiderbevegelse 1918–1940" ["A dual responsibility": Women and men in the Norwegian labor movement, 1918–1940], *Arbeiderhistorie* (1998): 5–33.

38 Original quote in Norwegian: "Boligpolitikk, gratis skolemateriell, bedre lønninger for den mannlige arbeider, støtte til streikende ble sett som viktige tiltak for å beskytte familien mot kapitalistisk utbytting." Blom, "'Et dobbelt ansvar,'" 9.

39 Original quote in Norwegian: "arbeide for den beste boligpolitikken, den beste barneomsorgen og støtte til mødre, handikappede og eldre." Blom, "'Et dobbelt ansvar,'" 29.

40 Original quote in Norwegian: "Arbeiderkvinner! Frem til kommunevalget 1937 med boligbyggingen som merkesak!" Øvergaard Jørgen, "Riv rønnene. Bygg vakre hjem," 7. The election went very well for the Labor Party. The party received 43 percent support nationwide and 52 percent in Oslo.

41 "Boligplanen studeres" [The housing plan is being studied], *Arbeiderbladet*, February 12, 1938.

42 Øvergaard Jørgen, "Boligplanen i praksis," 304.
43 Berge Furre, *Norsk Historie 1914–2000: Industrisamfunnet – Frå vokstervisse til framtidstvil* [Norwegian history, 1914–2000: Industrial society, from certain growth to future doubt] (Oslo: Det Norske Samlaget, 2000), 86.
44 Øvergaard Jørgen, "Boligplanen i praksis," 305.
45 Furre, *Norsk Historie 1914–2000,* 71.

itself. The housing construction proposed by the socialist architects was not to be seen as yet another expense on a crisis-ridden social budget, but as an engine for production, employment, and economic growth. The architects were particularly concerned with this socio-economic argument and repeatedly emphasized that "Among social economists, there is practically unanimity that greatly expanded housing construction is the most effective measure that states can deploy against the crisis that is expected."[42] This was a new way of looking at, and arguing for, large-scale housing construction. When the party rallied around this new approach, it was likely because the architects managed to incorporate housing into the current political discussion. The keyword here is *crisis policy*.

HOUSING CONSTRUCTION AS *CRISIS POLICY*

The political project of the labor movement during the second half of the 1930s can be summarized in one term: *crisis policy*. Arbeiderpartiet came to power in a period of crisis. The party campaigned on a crisis policy and gained support because of it. The state of crisis stimulated new thinking, particularly in the economic field. An important feature of the crisis policy was the new role assigned to the state, which was to create growth through active economic policies. The belief that it was possible to steer the economy and actively shape society created new space for the action of professionals in various areas of society. In short, crisis policy meant a new way of understanding and shaping politics, and several historians argued that this laid the foundation for the postwar era of the planned economy. According to historian Berge Furre, the Arbeiderpartiet government appeared exceptionally active in the years after 1935:

> Particularly, the government managed to create an image of itself as proactive and industrious. It displayed significant activity, especially in the economic field, and announced numerous "measures" and initiatives. ...There were constant discussions about new plans: both short-term and long-term. There was a flurry of reports, committees, proposals on social security, housing construction, industrial development, new roads, railways, power plants, schools, and so on.[43]

The crisis politics were all about issues, measures, and plans. The main focus was *to get the wheels turning*: namely, to boost production, employment, and economic growth. This was how the crisis could be overcome, and this is what Gunnar Øvergaard Jørgen referred to when he wrote that economists believed housing construction could be used as a form of crisis management.[44] The fact that architects used arguments from economics is a sign of the paradigm shift that took place in economic thinking in the 1930s, which was characterized by the belief that change was possible through implementing new economic policies—referred to by Berge Furre as "the Keynesian revolution."[45] The architects had evidently embraced this line of thinking and now applied it to their own field. Ole Colbjørnsen, one of the party's key strategists and the one who first formulated *crisis politics*, also emphasized this in an

Det 20de århundre

HEFTE 8
OKT. 1937
38. ÅRGANG

MOT·DAG

Innhold:

Utenrikskronikk.

—

Nye opgaver.

Karl Evang:
Ernæringspolitikk.

Fredrik Haslund:
Elektrisitetspolitikk.

Øvergård Jørgen:
Boligplanen
i praksis.

Åke Ording:
Budgettet.

Innenrikskronikk

—

Redaksjon:
Finn Moe.
Arne Ording.

(Illustrasjon fra La Turquie Kamaliste.)

MOT NYE OPGAVER

50 ØRE

Gunnar Øvergaard Jørgen continued with an explanation of the new housing plan in a later issue of the journal *Det 20de Århundre* in 1937. There were municipal elections in Norway at the time, and the Labor Party made the housing issue into one of its main topics.

article in 1937, wherein he described housing, alongside nutrition, as "the nearly perfect synthesis between social progress policy and active economic expansion policy."[46] This is a good example of how the socialist architects worked at the intersection of their profession and politics. It can be assumed that they gained support for their ideas about housing and housing policy exactly because they anchored their housing policy in crisis politics and argued credibly that housing construction could contribute to pulling the country out of that (economic) crisis.

THE ARCHITECTS AND THE CONSTRUCTION OF THE WELFARE STATE

In his book on the theory of history, historian Jan Eivind Myhre uses the term "windows of opportunity" to characterize situations where new possibilities arise; according to Myhre, we encounter such windows "when the possibility for a new type of action emerges at a specific point in history, where a structural change has taken place or where the relationships between individuals and specific structures have changed."[47] It was precisely such a window of opportunity that opened up in 1935 when Arbeiderpartiet formed the government. The years between 1935 and 1940 can be seen as a period in which ideas, viewpoints, solutions, and perspectives were introduced, debated, and further developed. 1935 thus represents a moment in history where it became possible to act in new ways, and the socialist architects seized this opportunity.

During this period, the labor movement attracted professionals from various fields of society. This was related to the fact that social planning lacked a tradition and had not yet been experienced. The very idea of actively planning for the future was new, and there was a need for knowledgeable and creative individuals who could contribute to the development of the plans and programs that the party needed. The socialist architects took on this role, and their primary contribution lay in their ability to formulate and concretize important social tasks and develop professional solutions to political problems. The national plan for housing construction is a good example of this. The architects succeeded in integrating the housing issue into the current political discourse and making it relevant and manageable. And although they did not offer architectural solutions in a strict sense—they wrote more about the financing of housing than the physical design of them, to put it simply—there was no doubt that they acted and saw themselves as architects, and that they believed that the organizational aspect of shaping the environment also was a question of architecture.

The formation of the government in 1935 has thus remained a pivotal moment in history. 1935 is regarded as the beginning of the so-called "social democratic era" in Norwegian history, and among historians, there is consensus that it was between 1935 and 1940 that the outlines of the postwar welfare state were drawn. The epoch-making aspect of the power shift in 1935 was that politics changed its character and came to be understood as a form of active societal transformation. Historian May-Brith Ohman Nielsen particularly emphasizes the new and modern way in which Arbeiderpartiet formulated and implemented their policies. According

46 Ole Colbjørnsen, "De aktuelle arbeidsopgaver" [The relevant tasks], *Det 20de århundre* 6 (1937): 224.
47 Jan Eivind Myhre, *Historie. En introduksjon til grunnlagsproblemer* [History: An introduction to fundamental problems] (Oslo: Pax Forlag, 2014), 175–76.

48 May-Brith Ohman Nielsen, *Etter 1914* [After 1914] (Oslo: Aschehoug, 2011), 84.
49 May-Brith Ohman Nielsen, *Etter 1914*, 84.

to Ohman Nielsen, a new type of politician and a new political language emerged: "From around 1930, the 'objective' expert who was a 'specialist' and 'expert' in a particular area of politics became the new type of politician. Especially in times of crisis, politicians needed specialized knowledge and often education."[48] Regarding the changes in language, Nielsen writes: "The old politicians quoted famous poets, 'great men,' and historical events. The new ones presented tables and charts and discussed future solutions."[49] The socialist architects thrived in this new political environment. They represented a new type of professionals, who were both politically engaged and capable of presenting tables and charts and planning the future.

Arbeiderpartiet developed a program for systematic and far-reaching societal transformation while also focusing on solving practical and concrete tasks in the present. This means that the overarching political objectives needed to be concretized and linked to practical, feasible measures as a response to the current situation. In order to formulate constructive policies, the labor movement needed experts with knowledge in various fields, such as doctors and economists, engineers—and architects. The socialist architects established themselves as actors in a complex network of organizations, unions, and associations. Through their new role as experts, they also contributed to expanding the space for political action. Through their work in the Technical Association of Arbeiderpartiet and the Building Workers' Union, with the formulation of the national plan for housing construction, campaigning during elections, and extensive writing and lecturing activities, the socialist architects unfolded themselves in the architect role they had fought for since their student days, namely as planners and builders of society.

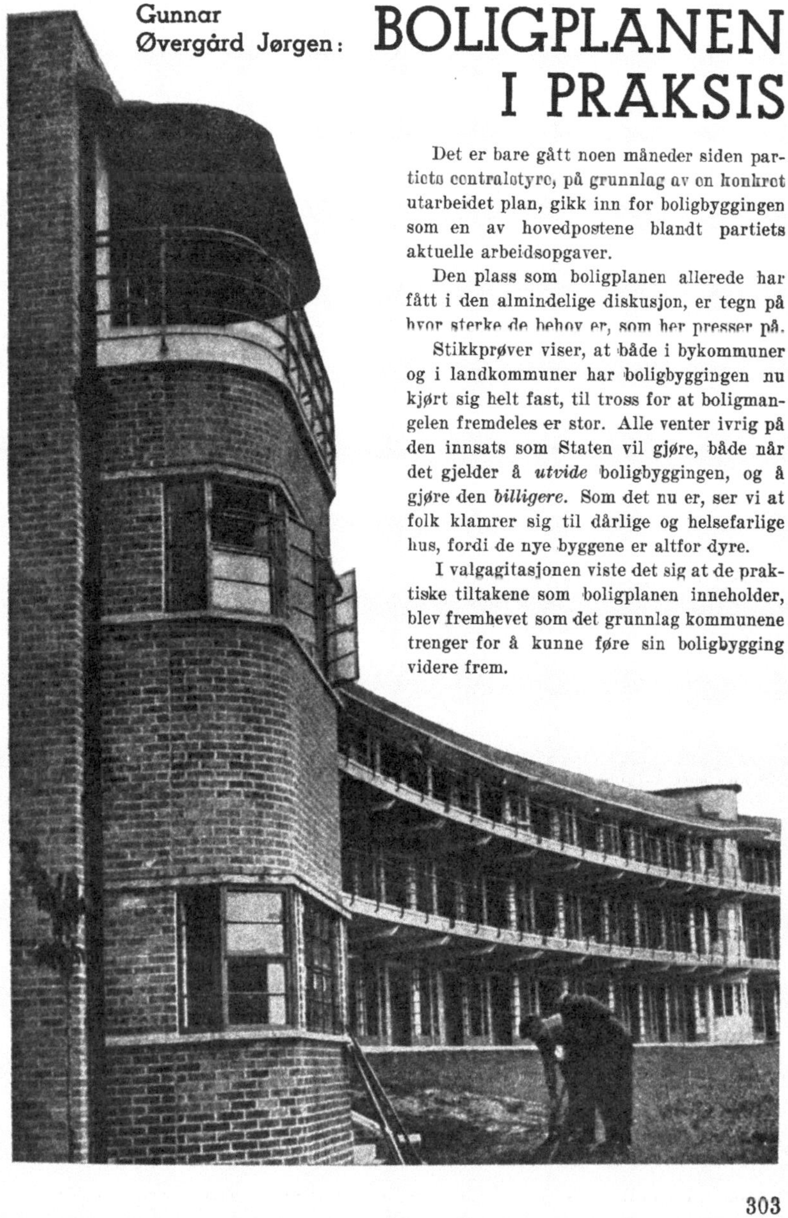

Gunnar Øvergård Jørgen:

BOLIGPLANEN I PRAKSIS

Det er bare gått noen måneder siden partiets centralstyre, på grunnlag av en konkret utarbeidet plan, gikk inn for boligbyggingen som en av hovedpostene blandt partiets aktuelle arbeidsopgaver.

Den plass som boligplanen allerede har fått i den almindelige diskusjon, er tegn på hvor sterke de behov er, som her presser på.

Stikkprøver viser, at både i bykommuner og i landkommuner har boligbyggingen nu kjørt sig helt fast, til tross for at boligmangelen fremdeles er stor. Alle venter ivrig på den innsats som Staten vil gjøre, både når det gjelder å *utvide* boligbyggingen, og å gjøre den *billigere*. Som det nu er, ser vi at folk klamrer sig til dårlige og helsefarlige hus, fordi de nye byggene er altfor dyre.

I valgagitasjonen viste det sig at de praktiske tiltakene som boligplanen inneholder, blev fremhevet som det grunnlag kommunene trenger for å kunne føre sin boligbygging videre frem.

303

"Boligplanen i praksis" (The housing plan in practice) was the title of Gunnar Øvergaard Jørgen's second major article in *Det 20de Århundre* in 1937. Through his numerous articles in the various organs of the labor movement, the architect established himself as the Labor Party's expert on housing.

Matthew Ashton and Erik Stenberg

MATERIAL NETWORKS

Art in Concrete and the Swedish Building Industry

In Scandinavia, the concrete neighborhoods constructed during the 1960s and 1970s are often framed—in a revisionist manner—as a historical anomaly: a material and urban artifact that sits uncomfortably with the perceived image that the Nordics have of themselves and wish to project outwards, as smart, cosmopolitan, and environmentally conscious. Large-scale prefabricated housing estates are viewed as something that must be remedied, at the extreme through demolition, but otherwise through different forms of integration, transformation, discipline, and intervention. This is a trend clearly observable in Denmark and Sweden, where many such neighborhoods are listed on official lists as "ghettos" or "vulnerable areas" and slated for different forms of redevelopment, often reconfigured according to more traditional urban ideals, under the thin guise of "sustainability."[1] It could be argued that today we are observing the slow dismantling of the welfare state, empowered through alternative narratives transmitted through the medium of concrete. While current political, economic, and cultural forces seem more intent on tearing things apart, previous constellations were more interested in building something new.

Concrete played a pivotal role in materializing the Nordic model of welfare, giving it an architectural form and aesthetic sensibility, and embodying the ideals of democracy and equality. Its historic rise to dominance during the welfare-state era, however, was no mere coincidence, but emerged through the particular socioeconomic circumstances of the period, cultivated by an alignment of shared interests. Through concrete, the economic dream of rationalized construction processes intersected with the artistic desire for aesthetic experimentation. As Norwegian artist Carl Nesjar proclaimed, "concrete is a meeting point for the architect and the artist."[2]

On May 23, 1964, the exhibition *Konst i betong* (Art in concrete) opened at Moderna Museet (Museum of Modern Art) in Stockholm, offering the public a chance to see a selection of artworks by contemporary artists working experimentally with the material of concrete. Pablo Picasso's sculpture *Fågelfisken* (The Bird Fish) was a major drawcard, sandblasted in concrete by Carl Nesjar. Works by Nordic artists such as Siri Derkert, Lars Englund, Einer Höste, Erik Hesselberg, Inger Sitter, as well as individual work by Nesjar, were also on display.[3] The exhibition was a collaboration between the museum and Svenska Väg- och Vattenbyggares Riksförbund (SVR, the Swedish Association of Road and Water Builders), with curatorial credit given equally to the museum's director, Pontus Hultén, and Olle Rinman, the chairman of SVR. Situated on an island in central Stockholm, surrounded by the waters of the Baltic Sea, the museum offered an avant-garde setting for SVR to celebrate their twenty-year jubilee.[4] Some of the biggest names in the Swedish

1 In Denmark the term "ghetto" was officially used in government planning documents to refer to socially and economically disadvantaged neighborhoods with a high proportion of residents from a non-European background.

2 Original quote in Swedish: "Betongen är en mötesplats för arkitekt och konstnär," "(T)ung Konst," *Dagens Nyheter*, May 23, 1964.

3 Pontus Hultén and Olle Rinman, *Konst i betong* [Art in concrete] (Stockholm: Moderna Museet, 1964), 5. Published in conjunction with an exhibition of the same title.

4 "Konst i betong" [Art in concrete], *Dagens Nyheter*, May 21, 1964.

5 "Jubilerande Vägbyggare" [Jubilant road builders], *Dagens Nyheter*, May 17, 1964.

6 Skarne System International, company catalogue, 1967, in the Skarne Family collection of Erik Stenberg's Million Program Archive.

7 Original quote in Swedish: "Klart att rationalisering av byggande kräver rationell planering och det bör ger arkitekterna mer tid att ägna sig åt de verkligt stora uppgifterna – att forma vår inre och yttre bostadsmiljö och att ge den i arbetslivet hårt pressade nutidsmänniskan en fritidsmiljö som skänker både ro och stimulans." Alan Skarne, "Från hantverk till byggnadsindustri, 1965" [From craft to construction industry] in *Med kran och krok* [With crane and hook] (Stockholm: Ohlsson & Skarne Byggförlag, 1987), 23.

8 Press release from the archive of *Svenska Väg- och Vattenbyggares Riksförbund.* SE/RA/730307/10/01/E/E 5/2.

construction industry at the time sponsored the event, including the two largest cement producers, Cementa and Gullhögen, as well as public housing organizations such as Svenska Bostäder and Hyreshus i Stockholm, and half a dozen private builders, including John Mattson, Olle Engkvist, and Ohlsson & Skarne.

The exhibition opening was a gathering that would bring together artists, curators, engineers, architects, planners, builders, landlords, material suppliers, and politicians, staging a broad discussion about concrete as a material, and its place within the future of the Swedish welfare state. In attendance was a powerful yet diverse group of actors with substantial cultural, political, and economic muscle, who could exert substantial influence over governmental policy directions. The opening party was followed by a four-day conference, with Allan Skarne, owner and director of Ohlsson & Skarne, invited as a distinguished keynote speaker.[5] Skarne (1909–98) was a second-generation builder deeply involved in the shift from a craft-based to an industrialized construction sector in Sweden and abroad; starting in 1963, licensees of the Skarne System were located in six European countries, as well as the Middle East.[6] He also shared a close personal relationship with the museum's director Pontus Hultén, who was married to his niece, Anna-Lena Wibom. Skarne was a keen collector of modern art, amassing an enviable collection at his private island residence in Stockholm, and upon the occasional request from Hultén, provided financial support to the budding museum, including the purchase of the large-scale Alexander Calder sculpture *The Four Elements* in 1961, which he gifted to the Museum's permanent collection in 1967.

Skarne was an advocate of the need for rationalization and technological innovation in the construction industry, but he was also a strong supporter of art and architecture. He firmly believed that further mechanization of building processes would give greater freedom to artists and architects, arguing that:

> It is clear that the rationalization of construction requires rational planning, but this should give architects more time to devote themselves to greater undertakings—to shape our interior and exterior residential environments and to give the hard-pressed modern working citizens an environment of leisure that provides both peace and stimulation.[7]

The exhibition *Konst i betong* aimed to highlight the artistic and aesthetic possibilities of concrete. By building with rational construction techniques and processes, in close collaboration with architects and artists, a new architectural aesthetic was to be produced that was representative of the ideals of the welfare state. This point of view was emphasized at the exhibition conference, where Skarne, together with architect Johannes Olivegren and artist Bertil Gottsén partook in a discussion concerning art in construction, with a particular focus on the 1 percent rule—a principle applied in Sweden, Denmark, and Norway, which stipulates that 1 percent of a building's construction costs should be spent on commissioning artistic work for the project.[8]

Between June 7 and June 13, 1964, Socialdemokraterna (the Swedish Social Democratic Party) held their twenty-second congress at the recently built Folkets Hus (People's House), a civic

Carl Nesjar in his studio in Oslo with the finished Picasso sculpture *Fågelfisken* (formerly titled *Figure Découpée*) which was exhibited at the exhibition *Konst i betong* (Art in concrete) at Moderna Museet in Stockholm in 1964.

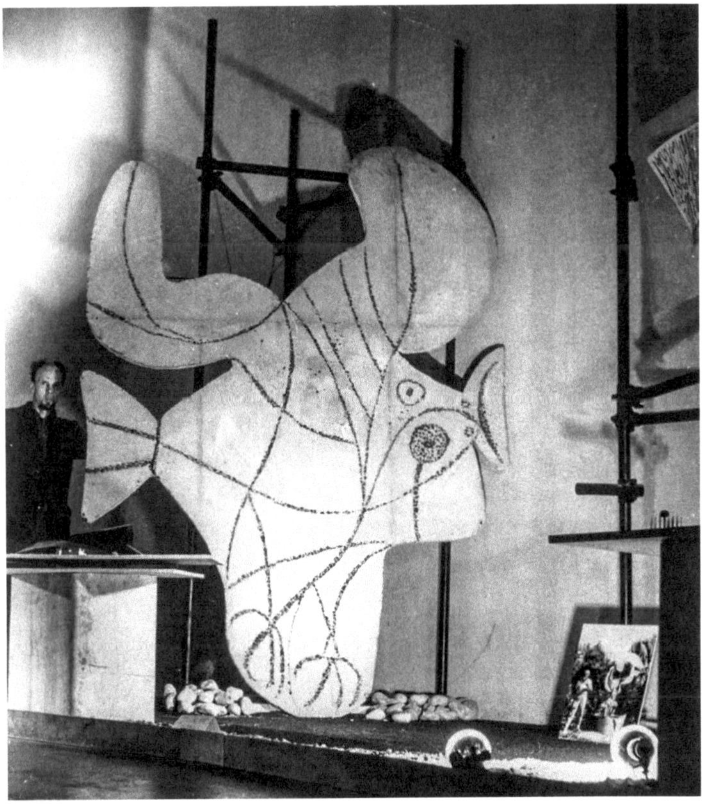

Allan Skarne assisting in the mounting of a prefabricated interior wall element in the project Kv. Diset in Uppsala, the prototype for the S66 System.

9 "Statens bostadspolitik får kritik i SAP-debatt" [State housing policy critiqued in SAP debate], *Dagens Nyheter*, June 10, 1964.
10 Statens offentliga utredningar (SOU), *Höjd bostadsstandard* [Raised building standards] (Stockholm: SOU, 1965), 32.
11 "Rationalisering Strängs lösen" [Rationalization is Sträng's answer], *Dagens Nyheter*, April 21, 1964.
12 "Rationalisering," 10.

center designed by the celebrated Swedish modernist architect Sven Markelius. On Tuesday June 9, the party held a heated debate on housing and land policy—a critical issue at the time, as the country was still suffering from a substantial housing deficit, combined with rising construction costs and acute labor shortages. The debate was led by the Minister of the Interior, Rune Johansson, and addressed the many factors hindering the production of new housing, such as the difficulty that builders had in securing financing, and the obstructions faced by municipalities in attempting to purchase land for development. Johansson emphasized the necessity for municipalities to engage in long-term urban planning to ensure that builders received plots in good time and highlighted the need to pursue "rational" construction processes.[9] The debate ended with party members voting to establish a working group that would put together a report on the housing situation and present proposed solutions. The resulting government white paper *Höjd Bostadstandard* (Raised housing standards) laid the foundations for the housing policy of the Million Program, an ambitious government-led plan to construct one million new dwellings within a ten-year period across Sweden (1965–74).[10]

The housing shortage combined with rising building costs was a thorny political issue for the government at the time, emphasized by Finance Minister Gunner Sträng at a public debate organized by SVR in the spring of 1964, arguing "one must invest in standardization. Everything to keep price increases at bay."[11] Present at the same debate, and representing the interests of private builders, was Alan Skarne, who presented his view that: "The construction industry should learn from the shipbuilders and the auto industry ... both single family houses and rental apartments 'in packages' should and could be delivered, similar to Volvo's car packages. A few models that have the essentials in common."[12] It was the emphasis on "rationality" in both construction processes and urban planning principles that paved the way for concrete to emerge as the preeminent material from which the Million Program would be constructed, and perpetually reinforce its association with the architecture of the welfare state. Concrete was cheap, plentiful, durable, and above all, suited to industrial production methods; this combination made it especially attractive as a political solution to the housing deficit, which would not put too much inflationary pressure on the economy.

STATE OF THE ART IN CONCRETE

As a material, concrete is plastic, malleable, and shapeable; it is capable of expressing a diversity of colors, textures, finishes, surfaces, and, thus, atmospheres. While industrialists and politicians were praising the technological and economic potential of the material, the exhibition *Konst i betong* put its aesthetic qualities on display, demonstrating a multitude of ways combinations of sand, water, stone, and cement could be crafted competently by artists and architects. The future city of concrete would be rational, but also beautiful, sensuous, and demonstrative of human creativity. 1964 can be seen as a watershed year for concrete in Sweden, when political, economic, and cultural forces momentarily converged, setting the conditions for the unprecedented large-scale era of construction that was to follow. The rise of concrete did not, as such, emerge out of a vacuum, just as its eventual dominance within the Swedish construction industry was neither inevitable nor guaranteed. Sweden had strong domestic timber and steel industries, equally capable of producing rational housing solutions on a large scale, yet it was concrete that took the early initiative, a development in no small part due to technological innovations in prefabricated concrete panel construction developed by a pioneering group of builders, in which Ohlsson & Skarne played a decisive role.

One of the main factors driving an increased interest in prefabricated concrete construction methods in the early 1960s were acute labor shortages, and the sky-rocketing building costs that followed. Real economic growth was achieved through the export-orientated manufacturing industry, not the local construction industry, so with a limited supply of workers it was preferable to automate building processes as much as possible to increase the supply of labor available to manufacturers. Once the prefabrication technology had been implemented in residential construction, the following step was to develop integrated building systems where the elements were part of an interconnected chain from design and project planning, to factory production and implementation.[13] Rationalized construction methods dramatically improved productivity—in 1950, it took approximately eight hours of work to complete a cubic meter of housing with traditional craft-based construction, while by the start of the 1970s the same amount of work could be completed in two and a half hours.

The construction firm Ohlsson & Skarne were pioneers of prefabricated concrete building systems, optimizing and rationalizing construction processes, and implementing and developing technical innovations within the construction industry. In 1963, they were ranked the seventh largest producer of concrete construction elements in Sweden, with production spread across four factories.[14] Allan Skarne had a long interest in transforming and modernizing the Swedish construction industry, often using his own building firm to experiment with new technological innovations, explore more efficient, cost-effective construction methods and streamline organizational structures. Concrete was at the core of Skarne's construction business—it was the material which could dramatically revolutionize the Swedish construction industry, through rationalization, standardization, and prefabrication. By the mid-1960s, early prefabrication methods and prototypes had now also shifted to building systems, with the prefabricated concrete elements provided in "packages" of project planning, production, and delivery of whole precast structures comprising of floor slab elements and interior and exterior load-bearing wall units. By 1967, these building systems were being used to produce more than 8,000 flats in Sweden, with a capacity estimated to increase to 30,000 flats by 1970.[15]

In 1955, Allan Skarne was influential in establishing a network of like-minded individuals interested in developing, improving, and sharing knowledge about prefabricated concrete panel construction. The group, known as "D4 Gruppen" (the D4 Group), consisted of builders Allan Skarne, Ernst Sundh, Sven Gendt, and Bo Bouvin, with Kurt Månsson serving as secretary. All had senior roles in

13 Kurt Månsson, "Integrated Housing Construction," *Byggnadsindustrin* 10 (1960): 571–75.

14 B. Isaksson, *Statens Pris- och Kartellnämnd, Byggnadsutredning, Bilaga 2* [The Swedish Competition Authority, Construction Report, Appendix 2] (Stockholm: SPK, 1964).

15 Gösta Andersson, "Flerfamiljshus med stommelement av betong" [Multi-family house with frame element in concrete], *Byggmästaren* 6 (1968): 24–35; and Gösta Andersson, "Svenska element byggsystem för flerfamiljshus 1" [Swedish element-based construction system for multi-family housing 1], in *Byggforskningen informerar* 7, Statens institut för byggnadsforskning (1968).

The construction site of the project Kv. Söderby, built by Ohlsson & Skarne using the Heavyweight System.

Allan Skarne, Ernst Sundh, Sven Gendt, secretary Kurt Månsson and Bo Bouvin, known as D4-gruppen, gathered for a meeting in 1957.

16 Parts of this chapter builds on Erik Stenberg, "D4 Gruppen 1955–1961: Pioneers of the Swedish Post-War Panel Era," in *Flying Panels: How Concrete Panels Changed the World* (Stockholm and Berlin: ArkDes and DOM Publishers, 2019).

17 Skarne, *Med kran och krok*, 9.

18 R. M. E. Diamant, "The Bollmora System – 10," *Architect and Building News*, May 16, 1962, 720–22.

companies and organizations pursuing technical innovation and rationalization within the construction industry. Over the course of forty documented meetings, everything from safety at work during prefabrication to pricing for assembly work was discussed, and in 1960 they even founded the company Sprutteknik AB together—to circumvent the painting trade union—and built forty-two houses in Jakobsberg.[16] D4 Gruppen formed a hub for element-based construction, primarily through collection and dissemination of know-how, as well as the development of new financial and technological models. The members were in touch with all parallel developments in industrial construction in Sweden—architects, government initiatives and investigations, as well as with other element builders. The group and its members thus played a critical role in innovating, expanding, and disseminating knowledge about prefabricated concrete panel construction methods in the period directly preceding the Million Program, and set the conditions for the unprecedented large-scale housing construction necessary for its implementation.

Allan Skarne describes the role of the builder changing in the early 1950s in line with the shift from craft to industry, foreseeing the potential of both increasing the quantity and quality of housing built using prefabricated building elements.[17] The Östberga project, built between 1950 and 1954, in collaboration with architect Lars-Magnus Giertz and Sven Wallander of HSB, became a fundamental testing ground for implementing new construction methods and techniques, such as flexible floor plans, battery casting of elements, a heat-exchange ventilation system, and attempts to reduce labor costs through total prefabrication. These early experiments in the on-site casting of room-sized elements faced several challenges. The measurements and tolerances of the elements were not sufficiently precise to be repeated in larger quantities, and working unprotected during the harsh Swedish winter months made it even harder to ensure that consistent quality was maintained. As a response to these shortcomings, temporary field factories that could produce, store, and deliver elements to the site in greater quantities were built on-site specifically for larger developments. For the Bollmora project, built by Ohlsson & Skarne between 1959 and 1961, a field factory was set up with a capacity to produce precast elements for up to 500 units per year. The project also utilized a French Pingon tower crane with a lifting capacity of 16 metric tonnes to construct almost 1,000 units in twelve blocks, at 6–8 stories each.[18] In less than fifteen years the technology and capacity needed to shift the Swedish housing sector into a large-scale adaption of prefabrication had thus been established.

Throughout the 1950s and 1960s, Ohlsson & Skarne developed three prefabricated concrete panel systems: the Lightweight System, the Heavy System, and System S66. The Lightweight System was developed following Ernst Sundh's method of building with room-sized elements mounted on a gantry crane, and first implemented by Ohlsson & Skarne in Stabby Gärde in Uppsala, which was built between 1952 and 1953. The Heavy System, which was developed specifically for the Östberga project in Stockholm, used fewer yet larger concrete elements with a maximum weight of up to 12 metric tonnes, and could be assembled using a small number of large cranes. Kv. Diset in Uppsala, which was built in just twenty-eight days in the spring of 1966, became the prototype building for

19 Ohlsson & Skarne, "Typ Skarne 66: Typhus med flexibla och elastiska lägenheter konstruerad enl. System S-66" [Type Skarne 66: A type house with flexible and elastic apartments constructed using System S66], an unpublished drawing set from the Janne Lundquist collection of Erik Stenberg's Million Program Archive.

20 Skarne, *Med kran och krok*, 130.

21 The Swedish Council for Building Research and Skarne Systemutveckling, "The Convertible Building" (Uddevalla: The Swedish Council for Building Research and Skarne Systemutveckling, 1988).

22 Original quote in Swedish: "system S85 är en beteckning med teknisk klang. i själva verket gäller det en bebyggelse som har starka beröringspunkter med den gamla svenska småstaden, en tät låg, enhetlig men rikt varierade bebyggelse som bildar ramen kring stadens boende och verksamhet." Skarne, *Med kran och krok*, 132.

23 Skarne, *Med kran och krok*, 111.

what came to be known as System S66. This system is perhaps the most advanced industrialized element system made of concrete ever built, combining a very high degree of spatial flexibility with prefabricated concrete panel construction. System S66 used slab structures that rested on load-bearing external and apartment-separating walls, with a centrally positioned column ensuring that the slab sizes were manageable, rendering the remaining interior walls flexible or movable. This allowed residents to easily reconfigure the spatial layout of their homes to cater for their diverse and changing needs, or as a brochure for the system writes, "System Skarne 66 will instead give house consumers the utmost freedom to shape their own dwelling—and more than that, their home."[19]

The final concrete panel system developed by Allan Skarne was System S85 (the Convertible Building), which was produced in the mid-1980s in collaboration with Lennart Adolfsson and Curt Hunhammer, with support from Skanska and the Swedish National Council for Building Research.[20] Like the preceding System S66, System S85 was also designed to maximize "flexibility" for residents and "convertibility" over time, with the possibility of joining smaller and larger apartments together to create multi-generational homes, as well as the foresight to adapt apartments to other activities and functions—such as an office, school, or kindergarten—if need be.[21] The major point of difference between System S66 and System S85 was that the latter was conceived following the Million Program, in an era where the ideals of the welfare state were radically shifting. As Skarne himself describes it, "The name 'System S85' has a technical sound, but it actually concerns buildings that have a strong association with the historic Swedish small town—a dense, uniform but richly varied urban form that creates the framework for the city's inhabitants and activities."[22] The system was never an economic success in Sweden, nor as widely implemented as previous systems, yet it presents a fascinating example of an innovative attempt to adapt standardized prefabricated panel systems to the changing aesthetic, social, economic, and political realities of the time.

On the precipice of the Million Program, Allan Skarne, alongside other members of D4 Gruppen, could effectively demonstrate the merits of concrete as a rational, cost-effective, and robust building material. A material particularly well-suited to industrial production processes and the demands required of such a large, and unprecedented housing policy. Acquiring essential knowledge on rationalized production processes and effective organizational structures from the likes of the carmakers Volvo, the shipbuilders Kockum, and the electrical manufacturers ASEA, Ohlsson & Skarne developed what promised to be the most rational concrete panel system yet, System S66. The building system for multi-story residential construction was to accommodate the entire building process—from land acquisition and planning through to the finished residential neighborhood—as well as covering building operation, management, maintenance, and eventual renovation requirements.[23] System S66 had ambitions to become, in essence, the standard Volvo model of the construction industry—a building system that could easily be implemented on a large scale throughout Sweden, and even beyond. In 1967, Skarne sold Ohlsson & Skarne to Skånska Cementgjuteriet (today known as Skanska), transferring the company's rich knowledge and experience in prefabricated concrete

Ohlsson & Skarne heavy panel system field factory at Bollmora, Stockholm, 1965.

Råslätt structural frame construction in progress, Jönköping, 1968.

panel construction to the dominant construction firm in the Nordic region. While Ohlsson & Skarne were certainly trailblazers, the other major construction firms soon followed, and knowhow about prefabricated concrete construction rapidly spread throughout the industry and is still the prevailing technology in contemporary housing construction.

ART IN CONCRETE

While the technological innovations in concrete construction methods appealed most to builders and politicians, aesthetic considerations were equally significant. As a construction material, concrete was nothing new in the Nordic countries and had been readily used for decades, yet it was normally concealed in the load-bearing structure, hidden behind a façade of stucco or masonry. The shift to prefabricated panel construction integrated the façade and the load-bearing structure at the factory, reducing the need for expensive on-site scaffolding and labor to add surface cladding, which would have increased building costs and undermined the rational logic behind the construction technique. Thus, in order to gain widespread acceptance of prefabricated concrete construction, it was necessary to elevate the status of the material—to present it not only as something modern and rational, but also elegant, respectable, and cool. It was important to make it socially acceptable, even desirable, to live in a modern concrete home. The *Konst i betong* exhibition at the Museum of Modern Art in Stockholm could be viewed as one such effort to shift perceptions on concrete—among both building professionals and the general public—and present it as the material that would unite structural efficiency with artistic expression. As Carl Nejsar writes in the catalogue accompanying the exhibition:

> Concrete is the most important building material of our time. It has broken the hegemony of stone and wood. But this does not mean that we have yet fully mastered concrete, or that we have consistently let its special properties have free play in the design of our architecture, or that we have fully utilized its possibilities constructively and aesthetically.[24]

Concrete offered the possibility of a new synthesis between art and architecture, where artistic ornamentation of buildings would not come as an afterthought, but would instead be integrated into the architectural design from the beginning, or as Nesjar writes "that the art both conceptually and materially is part of the architecture."[25] This view was reiterated by the exhibition's curators, Hultén and Rinman, writing in the introduction, "traditionally, artists have beautified our communities and neighborhoods afterwards—when the architects and builders have done their part. Concrete has given them opportunities to participate in creation from the beginning."[26] The exhibition displayed a selection of large-scale concrete sculptures and reliefs, many of which were based on public art commissions carried out in new subway stations, housing estates, and public spaces. A series of photographs were also exhibited, illustrating creative collaborations between artists and

24 Original quote in Norwegian: "Betongen er vår tids viktigste byggemateriale. Den har brutt steinens og treets hegemoni. Men dermed er ikke sagt at vi ennå fullt ut behersker betongen, eller at vi konsekvent har latt dens spesielle egenskaper få fritt spill i var arkitekturs formgivning, eller at vi helt har utnyttet dens muligheter konstruktivt og estetisk." Carl Nesjar, *Konst i betong*, 7.

25 Original quote in Norwegian: "at kunsten både idemessig og materialmessig er en del av arkitekturen." Nesjar, *Konst i Betong*, 7.

26 Original quote in Swedish: "Traditionellt har konstnärerna förskönat våra samhällen och stadsdelar i efterhand—när arkitekterna och byggarna gjort sitt. Betongen har givit dem möjligheter att deltaga i skapandet från början." Hultén and Rinman, *Konst i betong*, 4.

A housing project in Stuttgart Germany is featured on the cover of an Ohlsson & Skarne brochure describing the Heavyweigh System, ca. 1967/1968.

System 85 from the mid-1980s, also known as The Convertible Building, was the last of the four building systems that Allan Skarne developed.

SKARNE SYSTEM INTERNATIONAL

HEAVY SYSTEM

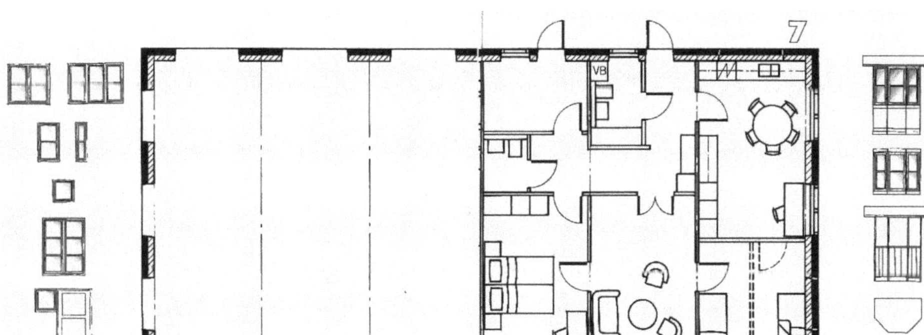

Entrance doors, windows and French windows are all interchangeable.

The use of a bay-window or special window for flowers means that a whole cladding panel has to be exchanged. The access balcony rests on cantilevered supports.

A shell to do what you want with

A building which is built using the Skarne 85 system is primarily a shell. What then happens inside the shell is up to you. The plans at the top of this page illustrate some of the many internal planning alternatives and combinations.

1 To begin with the building is simply a single large area enclosed by external walls. The "shell" which is waiting to be filled.

2 A day-nursery with three all-purpose rooms, kitchen, workshop, room where the children can play with water, rest room, entrance hall and staff room. Suitable for 15–20 children and staff (subject to local regulations).

3 "Group-housing" for disabled people. 4 single rooms, "group" living room, kitchen, large hygiene room with WC, wash-basin and shower, and staff room.

4 Office with about 15 work places, meeting room, lunch room, rest room, etc.

5 Dwelling for a family consisting of several different generations. 2 two and a half room and kitchen apartments, and 2 one room and kitchen apartments. There are connecting doors between the larger apartments and the smaller ones.

6 Shop accommodation and workshop accommodation. Each with storeroom, staff room, bathroom, and toilet with WC, wash-basin and shower.

7 Apartments. 1 one-module apartment, 1 two-module apartment, and 1 three-module apartment. The dividing walls are moveable and therefore plan solutions are possible where the dividing walls do not strictly follow the modules.

So that the buildings can be used for as many different functions as possible the ceiling height which we have chosen for our system is 2.50–2.55 m. The hollow-core floor slabs can take heavy loads and the buildings can therefore be used by light-industry.

Buildings using the system are also suitable for self-build projects once the basic structural frame has been completed. For example, a co-operative can hire a completed structural frame and then carry out the remaining internal work themselves.

Because of the flexibility which the use of our system entails, the actual function of a building does not really have to be decided on until a very late stage in a project – and the fact that a building may be put to a completely different use at some time in the future is no longer a problem.

There are three basic types of alterations which can be carried out in a building which has been built using the Skarne 85 system:

I **Partition walls**
The moveable partition walls make it possible to alter the size, shape, and number of rooms. Drains and special ventilation, such as kitchen extract fans, are left as they are.

II **Rooms with water**
It is also easy to alter and convert rooms even where this will mean that the drainage system must be altered. The drains must be kept within the drainage zone, that is to say a 5 m deep zone within a building along its entrance side.

III **Choice of facade treatment**
Entrance doors, windows and French windows are all interchangeable, and this does not need to have any effect on the cladding panels. On the other hand, a bay-window or a special window for flowers means that a whole cladding panel has to be removed. Alterations of this type require expert help.

We have compiled a manual which describes in detail how to carry out alterations of this type. Wall panels and doors etc. can be ordered from a building component terminal.

The great flexibility and convertibility of a building using our system guarantees that the tenants will be able to get exactly the apartment or other type of premises that they want—and when they want it. The tenant only pays for what he himself has chosen. This concept stretches further than to internal planning and the standard of fitments and finishes. Every apartment or other type of premises has individual heating and ventilation, and the amount of mains water used is measured individually for each tenant. Also, each tenant pays his own water heating costs.

LIMITATIONS: The most rational solution is to locate all of the drainage services in a zone within a building along one of its entrance sides, even if the depth of the zone is only 5 metres. However, if you particularly wish to be able to cover the entire floor area then there is no reason why there should not be a drainage zone along both long sides of a building.

Front cover of the exhibition catalog for *Konst i betong* (Art in concrete), which was held at Moderna Museet in Stockholm, May 23–June 17, 1964.

A spread from the exhibition catalog *Konst i betong* (Art in concrete) with artworks by Inger Sitter and Christer Sjögren demonstrating how art and architecture can be integrated through the material of concrete.

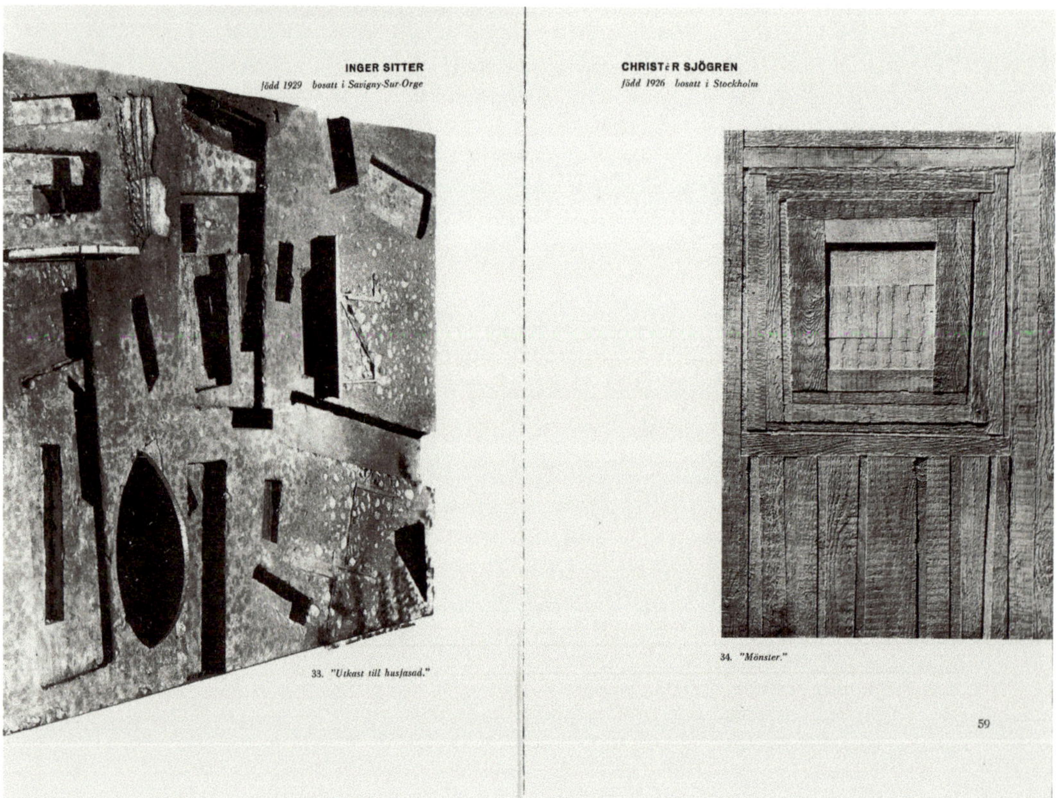
INGER SITTER
född 1929 bosatt i Savigny-Sur-Orge

33. *"Utkast till husfasad."*

CHRISTER SJÖGREN
född 1926 bosatt i Stockholm

34. *"Mönster."*

59

Carl Nesjar sandblasting his own artwork onto an interior wall of Erling Viksjø's Government Building in Oslo, 1957.

27 Hultén and Rinman, *Konst i betong*, 63.
28 Sally Fairweather, *Picasso's Concrete Sculptures* (New York: Hudson Hills Press, 1982), 31.
29 Erling Viksjø, "Et nyt byggemateriale med mange muligheder" [A new building material with many possibilities], *Ingeniørens Ugeblad* (December 1958): 6.
30 Viksjø, "Et nyt byggemateriale," 6.
31 Viksjø, "Et nyt byggemateriale," 6.
32 Karin Hermerén and Henrik Orrje, *Offentlig Konst: Ett Kulturarv* [Public art: a cultural inheritance] (Stockholm: Statens konstråd, 2014), 249–55.
33 Original quote in Swedish: "Och, som sagt, diskussionerna med den stora gamla på Rivieran, om skulpturer stora som hus, och hus. Vem vet, nog kan det finnas plats för ett på Skeppsholmen ..." Guat, "Picasso i Naturbetong" [Picasso in natural concrete], *Dagens Nyheter*, October 10, 1962.

architects, including Carl Nesjar and Inger Sitter's work with Erling Viksjø on the new government quarter in Oslo, as well as Odd Tandberg and Bengt Olson's contributions to new courthouses in Borås and Kristinehamn, respectively.[27]

Carl Nesjar was undoubtedly a central figure behind the exhibition, as one of the leading Nordic artists working with concrete at the time. He had become one of the preeminent experts in the technique of sandblasting concrete—a method of engraving a concrete surface by exposing it to a flow of sand pumped under immense pressure, which he likened to painting with a firehose.[28] He perfected this technique through years of close collaboration with the Norwegian architect Erling Viksjø on the government quarter in Oslo, which was constructed entirely of *naturbetong* (natural concrete). *Naturbetong* is a particular concrete process and technique developed through experimentation by Viksjø, and later perfected, and patented, with the help of the civil engineer Sverre Jystad.[29] The process involved first tightly packing a formwork with clean, washed aggregates of a similar grade, before injecting a fine liquid cement mixture, which filled in the voids between the stones. Before the concrete hardened completely, the formwork was removed and the surface sandblasted, revealing an even layer of tightly packed stones.[30] *Naturbetong* accentuated the intrinsic aesthetic qualities of the material itself, transforming the composite character of concrete into a creative palette that offered endless opportunities for artists and architects. As Erling Viksjø reflected, "concrete is in the process of finding its own architectural and constructive language, and we can no longer accept cladding with stone or clay. The concrete—the building material itself—must have its own expression of architectural value."[31] *Naturbetong* transformed concrete into a luxurious material, worthy of adorning important public buildings traditionally clad in stone or masonry, and as with prefabricated concrete panel construction, the façade and the structure are one and the same. While the technique employed in the construction of *naturbetong* differed significantly to that developed by Ohlsson & Skarne in their building systems, they both supported each other in elevating the status of the material, both technically and aesthetically. The use of unadorned concrete in these high-profile architectural projects would no doubt lend some legitimacy to its usage in more everyday situations—schools, offices, and apartment blocks.

In October 1962, Nesjar visited Stockholm to meet the Swedish artist Siri Derkert, who had recently won the public art commission for the new subway station of Östermalmstorg. Derkert planned to decorate the station with two 145-meter-long panels of *naturbetong* stretching the length of the platform, sandblasted with her expressionist motifs.[32] The artwork took inspiration from the women's rights, peace, and environmental movements, with figures including Rachel Carson, Simone de Beauvoir, Albert Einstein, and Jean-Paul Sartre etched into the concrete surface. Nesjar was to assist the then 77-year-old Derkert with the technical aspects of the project and provide consultation on the sandblasting process. It was here while in Stockholm that Nesjar met with Pontus Hultén at the Moderna Museet, and the initial idea to host an exhibition on art in concrete began to develop.[33] Nesjar had a close friendship, and productive working relationship with Pablo Picasso, with

Artist Siri Derkert working on her public artwork *Ristningar i betong* (Carvings in concrete, 1961–65) for the subway station at Östermalmstorg in Stockholm.

Artist Erik Hesselberg (to the right) working on Siri Derkert's public artwork for the subway station at Östermalmstorg in Stockholm, 1964.

34 Fairweather, *Picasso's Concrete Sculptures*, 31.
35 Fairweather, *Picasso's Concrete Sculptures*, 71.
36 Adrian Forty, *Concrete and Culture: A Material History* (London: Reaktion Books, 2012), 10.

the two artists collaborating on a series of large-scale concrete sculptures. Picasso would provide sketches or small models, which Nesjar then transcribed into full size concrete forms.[34] This collaboration led him to work on projects all over Europe, including several private commissions in France, as well as a wall frieze for the College of Architects in Barcelona. Pontus Hultén, as director of the Museum of Modern Art, was tasked with building up the young institution's permanent collection and regarded a Picasso/Nejsar sculpture as a self-evident addition to the sculpture garden. In 1963, Hultén approached Nesjar with a more formal proposal, inviting him to construct a Picasso sculpture for the forthcoming exhibition *Konst i betong*—with the explicit aim of later purchasing the sculpture for the museum's permanent collection. The sculpture, originally titled *Figure Découpée*, but renamed *Fågelfisken* (The Bird Fish) for the exhibition, was based on a design previously executed by Picasso and Nesjar for the *Mur Vivant* exhibition at the Grand Palais in Paris in 1963—an exhibition visited by Hultén, which also showcased possibilities for collaboration between art and architecture. Following *Konst i betong*, however, the board of the museum did not grant permission to acquire *Fågelfisken* for their permanent collection and the sculpture was sold to the City of Helsingborg in southern Sweden, where it was installed on a wall in the new municipal housing estate of Norlunda.[35]

THE MATERIAL LEGACY OF CONCRETE

The mid-1960s offers a fascinating vantage point from which to explore the entangled aesthetic, political, and industrial dimensions of concrete at a critical juncture point in the historical development of the Swedish welfare state. As architectural historian Adrian Forty has remarked, it's "more productive to think of concrete as a medium than as a material … a medium through which all sorts of ideas, some of them architectural, have been communicated."[36] The era in Sweden could be considered that of "peak concrete" as production of the material surged to keep apace the booming construction industry. When a political consensus concerning housing policy was achieved within Socialdemokraterna in the summer of 1964, the material of concrete was strategically placed to rise to the task. Through a concerted, but by no means formally organized, effort by political, economic, and cultural forces, concrete became the hegemonic material of the expanding welfare state. Innovative builders such as Ohlsson & Skarne and other members of the D4 group had already proven the structural and economic case for prefabricated concrete panel construction through extensive built work, utilizing a variety of methods, machines, and models. Simultaneously, artistic and architectural experimentation using unadorned concrete, illustrated by work put on display at *Konst i betong*, nurtured a social and cultural acceptance of the material. Large-scale public artworks in concrete by the likes of Pablo Picasso, Carl Nesjar, and Siri Derkert, gave the material extra legitimacy, as well as increased media coverage.

In the 1960s, concrete became a medium through which the hopes and ideals of the welfare state received a tangible form—where the promise of progress, prosperity, and the good life could be grasped and experienced. For a brief moment in time, the material presented new possibilities to politicians, builders, architects, engineers, curators, and artists alike. The plastic, malleable, moldable properties of concrete left it wide open to multiple interpretations, dreams, and ambitions. In concrete, each could imagine their own version of a better future, and as such, it was perfectly suited to the task of constructing the welfare state—a "people's home" for all, to quote Socialdemokraterna's oft-repeated *folkhemmet* adage. Yet as the contested legacy of welfare-state era architecture reveals, narratives can easily shift, political ideologies change, and new economic regimes emerge. If concrete was once a medium associated with positive images of progress and prosperity, today the material carries the collective burden of society's perceived failures. However it's important to emphasize that industrialized and prefabricated concrete element construction still provides affordable housing to thousands of Nordic residents, often those with the least means. The promise is somewhat kept, albeit in a radically reduced scope. Maybe it's time to rethink the material legacy of the welfare state and see its concrete built form as a gift—a collective inheritance bequeathed to society—rather than a burden we must rid ourselves of at once.

CONCRETE SUBURB

John Håkansson

Skarpnäck, Stockholm

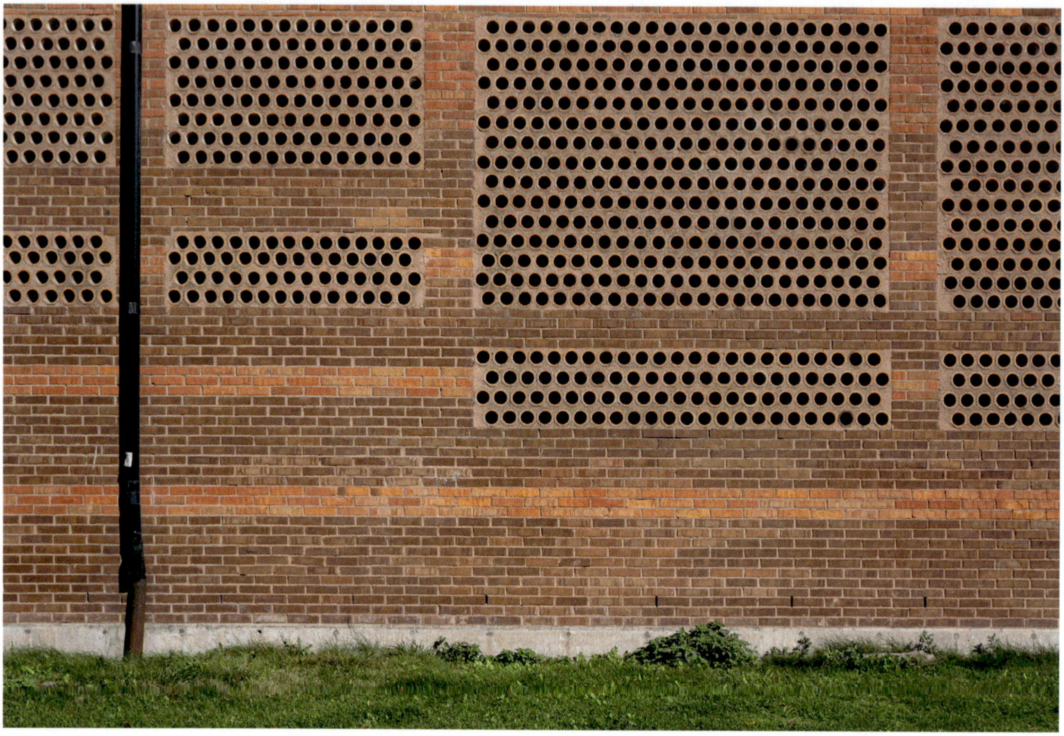

Husby, Stockholm

Hjulsta, Stockholm

Biskopsgården, Göteborg

Rinkeby, Stockholm

Dalen, Stockholm

Skärholmen, Stockholm

Bredäng, Stockholm

Lindängen, Malmö

Jordbro, Haninge

Rosengård, Malmö

Henriksdal, Nacka

Navestad, Norrköping

Akalla, Stockholm

This photographic project is about searching and collecting. I go to a suburb and photograph for a whole day, and from all the pictures I take, I choose a few that work. It might be just one: a picture of a corner with a bush. I live in a Stockholm suburb, so most of the photos are taken around Stockholm, but my ambition is to travel to other parts of the country. The work is in progress.

The title "Concrete Suburb" is a play on the concept of *concrete art*. This term was coined by the Dutch artist Theo van Doesburg in 1930 when he founded the group Art Concret. In their manifesto, the group argued for "concrete painting": painting which should not refer to any reality or meaning beyond itself, and be entirely about its own plastic elements, its own surfaces and colors. One of the artists who signed the manifesto was the Swede Otto G. Carlsund, who introduced concrete art to Sweden with a large international group exhibition at the Stockholm Exhibition in 1930. The exhibition was an economic disaster for Carlsund, but concrete art eventually gained a significant place in the history of Swedish modern art, its golden age paralleling the building of modern suburbs on the outskirts of Swedish cities.

3 DISCOURSES AND CRITIQUES

Guttorm Ruud

CHILDREN IN CRISIS

Community, Activism and Norwegian Satellite Town Stigma

Children hold an important position in Scandinavian societies today, just as they did in the postwar welfare states policies and planning, when they were, quite literally, considered to constitute the future. This is probably why stories of "children in danger" have such a startling effect: they invert the image of the child in the welfare state—no longer the welfare state's primary subject and protagonist, the child becomes its helpless victim. The alleged crisis of children and young people is currently a ubiquitous topic in Scandinavian discussions of the postwar urban developments connected to the expansive period of the welfare state. In mass media, socioeconomic and cultural challenges concerning juveniles are treated as defining features of these urban areas. In the present-day Norwegian discourse on Oslo's satellite towns, there is a contrast between a negative media portrayal, which focuses on problematic events, and accounts by inhabitants, who defend the satellite towns as non-exceptional, ordinary urban areas—which are lovely places to live.[1] The inhabitants thus present positive perspectives, but even their stories are told as reactions to and in the context of enduring problem narratives. The positive qualities and problems of the satellite town are thus addressed in such a way that they become locked together, bringing into being a dichotomy that contributes to the construction of territorial stigma.

Territorial stigma, building on the sociologist Erving Goffman's model of stigma as "the management of spoiled identity," is a key term that denotes a collective representation of space that, according to Loïc Wacquant, is "equated with social disintegration, racialized through selective accentuation, and it elicits revulsion often leading to punitive corrective measures."[2] The satellite towns' challenges are, as a consequence, often addressed by defending and safeguarding the area's reputation through place branding, brand management, and design measures taken to improve aesthetic attractiveness, as well as the explicit or implicit instruction of inhabitants to speak highly of the area and its facilities (in particular, the school).[3] This plays into the present-day focus on managing public image and reputation, where businesses and institutions expect employees to avoid expressing critique and doubts, which potentially may place the business, the company, or, as is the case for the development of territorial stigma, the place, in a bad light. When based on notions of children in crisis, territorial stigmatization has been used to motivate various social and physical transformations of specific areas to improve their reputation and valuation—in cultural and economic terms. Such discourses work across Scandinavia: the area-based policies for problematic urban areas in Oslo (satellite towns) refer to Danish and Swedish examples of what should be avoided.

1 See Kjersti Gakkestad, "Romsås – en stigmatisert bydel? En studie av territoriell stigmatisering: medias rolle og konsekvenser for beboerne" [Romsås—a stigmatized district? A study of territorial stigmatization: the role of the media and consequences for residents] (Master's thesis, University of Oslo, Oslo, 2003); Ingar Brattbakk and Thorbjørn Hansen, "Post-War Large Housing Estates in Norway – Well-Kept Residential Areas Still Stigmatised?" *Journal of Housing and the Built Environment* 19, no. 3 (2004): 311–32; Kirsten Danielsen and Ada Ingrid Engebrigtsen, "Stovner – problemområde eller lutter idyll? Om forholdet mellom statistikk og erfaring" [Stovner—problem area or pure idyll? On the relationship between statistics and experience], *Tidsskrift for velferdsforskning* [Journal for welfare research] 17, no. 3 (2014): 27–40.

2 See Erving Goffman, *Stigma: Notes onthe Management of Spoiled Identity* (Englewood Cliffs, N.J.: Prentice-Hall, 1963); Loïc Wacquant, Tom Slater, and Virgílio Borges Pereira, "Territorial Stigmatization in Action," Environment and Planning A: Economy and Space 46, no. 6 (June 2014): 1270.

3 Examples of aesthetic improvements are the "lamp" at Haugenstua, the "tower" at Stovner, and the underpass at Ammerud. See Per-Øystein Lund, *Innsatser i utsatte byområder: Erfaringer fra Groruddalssatsningen* [Interventions in vulnerable urban areas: Experiences from the Groruddal project] (Oslo: Oslo kommune, 2014), 63.

These discourses of place image, territorial stigma, and the often-debated dichotomy of media critique and inhabitant pride must be challenged. To do this, I turn to the history of Norwegian satellite town stigma. Norwegian satellite towns have received critique since the 1950s. At first, the critique faulted a lack of aesthetic and urban qualities; in the late 1960s and early 1970s, a more severe criticism emerged, which questioned social policies, raised psychological issues, and suggested the failure of planning and the welfare state.[4] Crucially, the notion of "children in danger" was at the center of this critique. In this chapter, I challenge this narrative by examining the story of Stovner, a satellite town of Oslo. In 1975, starting with a publication by the magazine *Sinnets Helse*, it became the epicenter of a nationwide media outcry and critique of children having been let down by society, initiating a stigmatization process that has continued until the present day. However, a closer look at the background and context of this critique reveals other ways of understanding the beginning of this discourse: as a concrete conflict of interest in the satellite town of Stovner, community engagement and political activism. Furthermore, in this analysis, I point to the broader societal problem of a contradiction between the welfare state and the local community and debates on how society should be designed and governed.[5]

THE SATELLITE TOWN OF STOVNER

From 1950 onwards, the urban expansion of Oslo followed the General plan for Oslo, which described a pattern of distributed housing areas and "sub-centers" according to international planning ideas of neighborhood units.[6] The neighborhood unit was a general planning principle for small, close-knit, integrated, and democratic urban communities. Disseminated by Lewis Mumford, this concept initially stems from Clarence Stein and Clarence Perry, the latter of whom emphasized the school's central role in creating well-functioning local communities.[7] This was also the case in the General plan for Oslo, which positioned the school as an essential and central part of the neighborhood unit idea upon which the postwar satellite towns were built.

Located at the northern border of the Oslo Municipality, the satellite town of Stovner was planned for about 30,000 inhabitants and was thus (significantly) more extensive than earlier Oslo satellite towns.[8] The area was laid out in Tokerudplanen, which was approved in 1966.[9] Stovner is divided into several precincts or neighborhoods with several schools; the largest is Vestli, which was planned by the private company Selvaag and built between 1967 and 1974 as the pinnacle of Selvaag's rational housing production effort. A notable feature of this precinct is its signature housing typologies, which consist of terrace blocks and pyramid blocks terraced on two sides, and were allegedly employed to combine the advantages of the housing block and the individual house.[10] The other precincts within Stovner are Forsheimer and Haugenstua, where blocks were built by the cooperative housing company USBL; the areas of Lower Stovner and the Stovner housing cooperative, with terrace housing built by the cooperative housing company OBOS; and the old and new detached houses in the area of old

4 This type of criticism also happened elsewhere, see, for example, the infamous Swedish reports: Olle Bengtzon, Jan Delden, and Jan Lundgren, *Rapport Tensta* [Report on Tensta] (Stockholm: Pan/Norstedts, 1970); Hans Gordon and Peter Molin, eds., *"Man bara anpassar sig helt enkelt": en forskningsrapport om människor i Skärholmen* ["One just adapts, quite simply": A research report on people in Skärholmen] (Stockholm: Pan/Norstedts, 1972); Margareta Schwartz and Suzanne Sjöqvist, *Kvinnoliv, Förortsliv* [Women's life, Suburban life] (Stockholm: Gidlunds, 1978).

5 This chapter is based on my PhD dissertation. See Guttorm Ruud, "Sites of Crisis. Histories of the Satellite Town" (PhD diss., The Oslo School of Architecture and Design, 2021), chap. 5.

6 Erik Rolfsen, *Generalplan for Oslo: et utkast lagt fram som diskusjonsgrunnlag for de kommunale myndigheter og etater og for andre interesserte* [General plan for Oslo: a draft presented as a basis for discussion for the municipal authorities and agencies and for other interested parties] (Oslo: Oslo reguleringsvesen, 1950).

7 See Clarence Perry, "City Planning for Neighborhood Life," *Social Forces* 8, no. 1 (September 1, 1929): 98–100; Lewis Mumford, "The Neighborhood and the Neighborhood Unit," *Town Planning Review* 24, no. 4 (January 1, 1954): 256–70.

8 The size of Oslo satellite towns has generally been around 10,000 inhabitants. See, for example, Frode Rinnan, *Lambertseter: en forstad til Oslo med 10000 innbyggere* [Lambertseter: a suburb of Oslo with 10,000 inhabitants] (Oslo: Cappelen, 1950); Frode Rinnan and Olav Tveten, *Tveita: en forstad til Oslo: 6. km. fra sentrum, 9000 innbyggere* [Tveita: A suburb to Oslo, 6 kilometers from the center, for 9,000 inhabitants] (Oslo kommune ved byplankontoret, 1960); Jon Kojen, "Bort fra sovebyen: Romsås – ny forstad for 8000 mennesker" [Beyond the dormitory town: Romsås, a new suburb for 8,000 people], *Arbeiderbladet*, March 2, 1968.

9 "Tokerud – Reguleringsplan for området mellom Trondheimsveien – kommunegrensen mot Skedsmo og Hovedbanen" [Tokerud: Regulation plan for the area between Trondheimsveien, the municipal border toward Skedsmo, and Hovedbanen], September 9, 1966, S-1352, Saksnummer 190001310 – Reguleringssak, Archive of Plan- og bygningsetaten, Oslo.

10 Jon Skeie, *Bolig for folk flest: Selvaagbygg 1920–1998* [Housing for most people: Selvaagbygg 1920–1998] (Oslo: Tano Aschehoug, 1998), 226.

The Oslo satellite town of Stovner, 1972. The Vestli precinct with its characteristic pyramid blocks on the left, old Stovner on the right, and the Fossumsletta neighborhood in the center.

Housing blocks under construction at Fossumsletta, 1969.

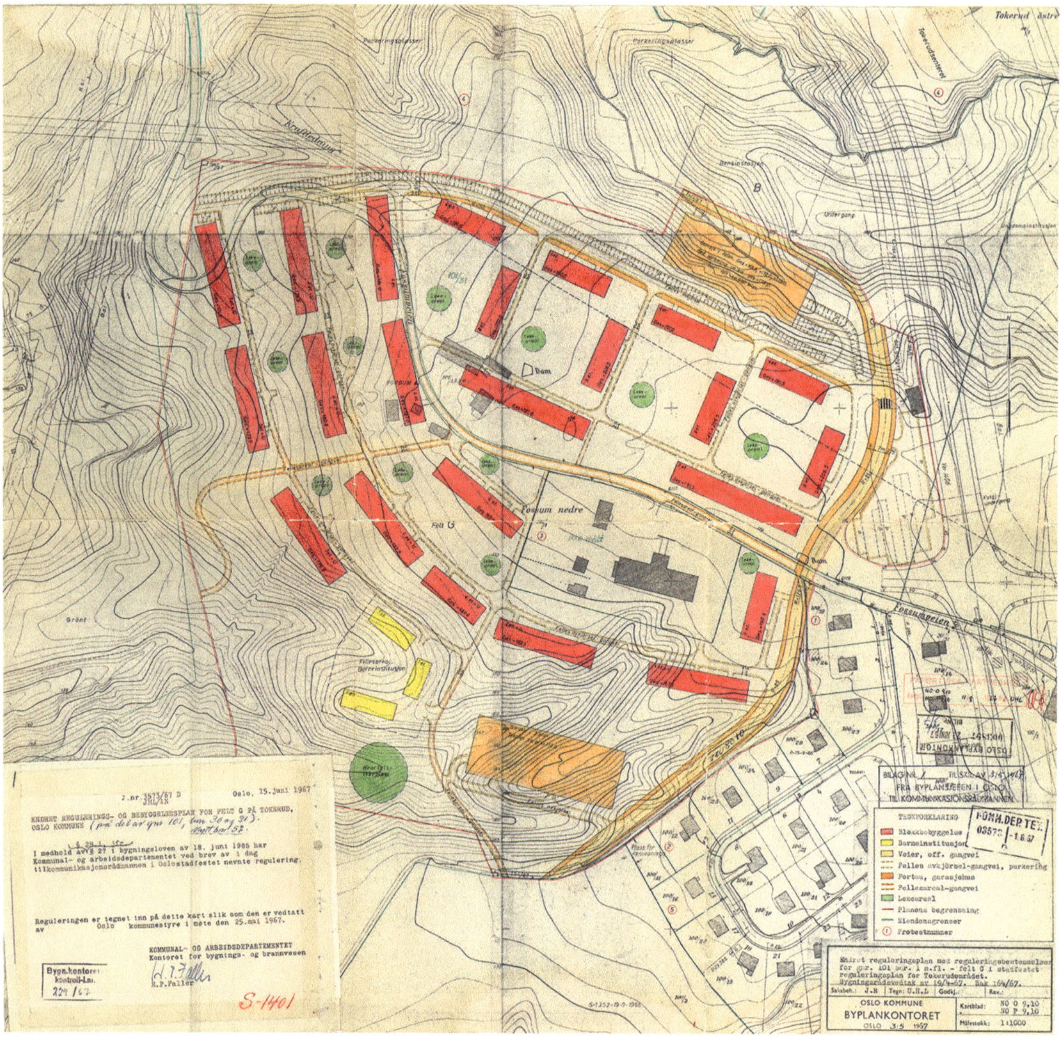

Plan for Tokerud field G (Fossumsletta), adopted by Byplankontoret (the city planning office) in 1967: the planned playgrounds are indicated as green circles.

Stovner, 1972. The Fossumsletta neighborhood on the left and Smedstua primary school on the right played central roles in the 1975 publication on children in crisis by the magazine Sinnets Helse.

Stovner. Finally, the neighborhood of Fossumsletta in Stovner—which would play a central role in the critique of 1975—was built by the private entrepreneur Nils Stiansen. In contrast to Selvaag's terrace and pyramid blocks, the housing blocks at Fossumsletta are simple prismatic volumes. The layout comprises of five three-story blocks, fourteen four-story blocks, and four nine-story blocks. Some blocks are organized to form open courtyards; others have a linear configuration that follows the site's natural contours. In the plan, small circles between the blocks or in the open courtyards denote playgrounds.

The primary school Smedstua, also central in the 1975 critique, was located south of Fossumsletta and is part of Haugenstua skoleanlegg (the Haugenstua school campus) and was designed by Paul Cappelen and Torbjørn Rodahl. According to the City Heritage Authority, Smedstua was one of only nine instances of a new type of school building, called "open schools," which were built in Oslo between 1968 and 1972.[11] It had an open and flexible "learning landscape" in low, one- or two-story buildings organized around atriums to help learning and cooperation.

THE OUTCRY

In 1975, the magazine *Sinnets Helse* (Health of the mind) published a special issue entitled "Barn i krise" (Children in crisis).[12] This seemingly small and insignificant booklet played a crucial role in describing and disseminating what was apparently a failure of Norwegian social policy, by posing a critique of the welfare state and the failures of its physical planning. With articles on the Oslo satellite town of Stovner, the special issue was seen as a harsh satellite town critique. It became known as *Stovnerrapporten* (the Stovner report), a name that smacked of trouble and closely associated the magazine issue with a specific site, at the same time attributing this special issue an official, scientific formal status and importance. Labeling the special issue as a "report" on a specific place forged a conceptual link to *Ammerud 1*, a 1969 research publication from Norges byggforskningsinstitutt (The Norwegian building research institute). Formally a report on satellite town planning in general, *Ammerud 1* was soon seen as a report on the place Ammerud and became known as *Ammerudrapporten* (the Ammerud report). This is often considered the first significant critique of the planning of satellite towns from a social instead of an aesthetic or technical perspective.[13] In it, various social aspects of satellite towns and their planning were scrutinized and judged harshly, and the report is often considered a turning point in Norwegian planning history.[14]

Nevertheless, the later, more journalistic report on Stovner is especially notable for its focus on psychosocial factors and its great impact on the public discourse on Norwegian satellite towns. This is evident in its much-quoted introduction, referenced repeatedly in mass media since 1975. It is part of the history of the territorial stigmatization—the attachment of stigma to a place—of Stovner and other Norwegian satellite towns:

11 Oslo kommune Byantikvaren to Oslo kommune Plan- og bygningsetaten [Oslo Municipality Cultural Heritage Management Office to Oslo Municipality Planning and Building Agency], "102/1123 – Smiuvegen 255 og 257 – Smedstua og Haugenstua skole – uttalelse til riving av skolebygninger," January 15, 2014, Byggesak 201315123, Archive of Plan- og bygningsetaten, Oslo; Kari Funderud, *Åpen skole: blinkskudd eller bomskudd?* (Oslo: Aschehoug, 1975), 44–45.

12 Terje Gummelsrud, ed., "Barn i krise" [Children in crisis], special issue, *Sinnets helse: Tidsskrift for mentalhygiene* [Health of the mind: Magazine for mental hygiene], no. 5 (1975).

13 Anne Sæterdal and Thorbjørn Hansen, *Ammerud 1: planlegging av en ny bydel*, Rapport 58 (Norges byggforskningsinstituttet, 1969).

14 See, for example, Sture Kvarv, "Yrkesroller og fagideologiske brytninger i fysisk planlegging i Norge, 1920–1970" [Professional roles and ideological clashes in spatial planning in Norway 1920–1970] (PhD diss., Arkitekthøgskolen i Oslo, 2003); Thorbjørn Hansen and Jon Guttu, *Oslo kommunes boligpolitikk 1960–1989: fra storskalabygging til frislepp* [Oslo municipality's housing policy 1960–1989: from large-scale construction to liberation] (Oslo: Norsk Institutt for by- og regionforskning, 2000); Erling Annaniassen, *Nå bygger vi den nye tid*, vol. 2, Boligsamvirkets historie i Norge [Now we're building the new era, vol. 2, The history of housing cooperatives in Norway] (Oslo: Gyldendal, 1996); Elsa Reiersen, *De tusen hjem: Den norske stats husbank 1946–96* [The thousand homes: The Norwegian State Housing Bank 1946–96] (Oslo: Ad notam Gyldendal, 1996); Jon Guttu, "Høyhuset i etterkrigstidens boligdebatt" [The tower block in the postwar housing debate], *St. Hallvard*, no. 1 (2001): 4–25; Jon Guttu, "'Den gode boligen': fagfolks oppfatning av boligkvalitet gjennom 50 år" ["The good home": professionals' perception of housing quality through 50 years] (PhD diss., Arkitekthøgskolen i Oslo, 2003); Ane Hjort Guttu, "Å bo i drabantby" [Living in a satellite town], *Byggekunst: The Norwegian Review of Architecture* 87, no. 3 (2005): 20–31; Edgeir Benum, *Byråkratienes by: fra 1948 til våre dager* [The city of bureaucracy: from 1948 to the present day], vol. 5 (Oslo: Cappelen, 1994); Ola Svein Stugu, "Vekst og vendepunkt" [Growth and turning point], in *Norsk byhistorie: urbanisering gjennom 1300 år* [Norwegian urban history: urbanization through 1,300 years], Knut Helle et al. (Pax, 2006), 447–72.

> In Stovner, one of Oslo's newest city districts, there are many children—up to 11–12 years old—who do not know the words for their thumb, the days of the week, or the seasons of the year. They are ignorant of when they are born, and have a poor concept of where they live. Several children seem to have lost the ability to learn to read, write, and do maths, and they will probably become almost illiterate. Their problems often seem inaccessible and impervious to known treatment methods.[15]

This quote describes what psychologist Anne-Marit Duve, in the special issue, argues is a previously unseen "welfare-induced disease" found among the children in this area. The introduction of the special issue thus characteristically linked ominous descriptions of children in crisis with the failures of the welfare state and the satellite town environment by criticizing "the planning of society that allows entire urban areas to be built and put into use without concern for conditions fundamental to the human existence."[16] The following enormous media coverage of the Stovner report attached a stigma to Stovner. With a second special issue of *Sinnets helse* in 1976, entitled "Rapport fra Oslo: Barn i krise 2" (Report from Oslo: Children in crisis 2), which became known as *Romsåsrapporten* (the Romsås report), this stigmatization was extended to encompass the satellite town Romsås.[17] The two issues *of Sinnets helse* are still considered crucial historical events in the development of contemporary satellite town stigma.[18]

The presentation of the special issue on Stovner has a distinct tone of urgency in the face of acute crisis. Even the table of contents constitutes a short, tragic story. Under the title "Theme: Children in crisis," a teacher's testimony ("I cried every day and felt sick on the way to school") leads to "A school's plea for help." Because "most children get inadequate help," the publication witnesses the rise of "illiterates in welfare-Norway," where as many as "40 percent of the pupils were weak readers"; crucially, this seems to be induced by "an environment that promotes passivity, vandalism, and defeat."[19]

These foreboding titles are accompanied by three children's drawings. While these are left unexplained, they allude to the use of child drawings in psychological analysis of mental development.[20] On the cover of the magazine, a child's drawing depicts a person sleeping in a bed, dreaming that a giant is destroying a tall housing block, with the word *drøm* (dream) in the upper left corner. The title of the special issue—"Barn i krise" (Children in crisis)—is strategically positioned next to the sleeping person. An uncaptioned child's drawing of two human figures illustrates the article titled "Jeg gråt hver dag og var kvalm på veien til skolen" (I cried every day and felt sick on the way to school). Next to the article on illiterates is a drawing with the words *hvem er jeg* (who am I) written across it in large letters.[21]

So, why this dramatic tone? The journalist Terje Gammelsrud had recently become editor of *Sinnets helse*. At the same time, the magazine changed ownership, which meant a new focus on children's mental health. As an editor, Gammelsrud aimed to address essential and sometimes controversial topics of everyday life, and among these were *drabantbyproblemer* (satellite town problems). In tackling this issue, he built on some of his earlier work, notably two reports on playgrounds.

15 Original quote in Norwegian: "På Stovner, en av Oslos nyeste bydeler, fins mange barn – opp til 11–12 år gamle – som ikke kjenner navnet på sin tommelfinger, ukedagene eller årstidene. De er uvitende om når de er født, og de har dårlig begrep om hvor de bor. En rekke barn ser ut til å ha mistet evnen til å lære å lese, skrive og regne, og de vil sannsynligvis komme til å bli noe bortimot analfabeter. Deres problemer virker ofte utilgjengelige og upåvirkelige av kjente behandlingsmetoder." The quote appears in the editor's introduction to "Stovnerrapporten" and the first article in "Romsåsrapporten," see Terje Gammelsrud, "Skal vi snakke høyt om det?" [Shall we talk about it out loud?], in "Barn i krise" [Children in crisis], special issue, *Sinnets helse: Tidsskrift for mentalhygiene*, no. 5 (1975): 3; Terje Gammelsrud, "Saken anses som ferdig behandlet" [The matter is considered to have been dealt with], in "Rapport fra Oslo: Barn i krise 2" [Report from Oslo: Children in crisis 2], special issue, *Sinnets helse: Tidsskrift for mentalhygiene*, no. 5 (1976): 4–6.

16 Original quote in Norwegian: "den samfunnsplanlegging som tillater at hele bydeler kan bygges og tas i bruk uten hensyn til elementære betingelser for menneskelig tilværelse." Gammelsrud, "Skal vi snakke høyt om det?"

17 For the extension to Romsås, see Tone B. Jamholt, "Romsås har tiet om sin sosiale nød" [Romsås has been silent about its social distress] in "Rapport fra Oslo: Barn i krise 2" [Report from Oslo: Children in crisis 2], special issue, *Sinnets helse: Tidsskrift for mentalhygiene*, no. 5 (1976): 8–9.

18 See, for example, Øyvind Holen, *Groruddalen: en reiseskildring* [Groruddalen: a travelogue], 2nd ed. (Oslo: Cappelen Damm, 2016); Olav Elgvin, Jon Rogstad, and Sarah Fossen Sinnathamby, "Rurbane møter: deltakelse og samhold blant ungdom og kvinner på Stovner" [Rurbane meetings: participation and solidarity among young people and women at Stovner], Fafo-rapport (Oslo: Fafo, 2013), 15.

19 The original Norwegian titles are: "Jeg gråt hver dag og var kvalm på veien til skolen," "En skoles bønn om hjelp," "De fleste barn får utilstrekkelig hjelp," "Analfabeter i velferds-Norge," "40% av elevene var lesesvake," and "Et miljø som innbyr til passivitet, hærverk og nederlag." Gammelsrud, "Barn i krise," 2.

20 The Norwegian psychologist Helga Eng was a pioneer in the study of mental development using children's drawings, see Helga Eng, *Barnetegning: fra den første streken til farvetegningen* [Children's drawing: from the first line to the color drawing], 2nd ed. (Oslo: Cappelen, 1959).

21 The drawing "Drøm" (Dream) on the front is by a fourth-grade boy, and the drawing "Hvem er jeg" (Who am I) is by an 8-year-old girl. See Gammelsrud, "Barn i krise," cover, 2, 6, 12.

The cover of "Barn i krise" (Children in crisis), a 1975 special issue of *Sinnets helse* (Health of the mind).

"Analfabeter i velferds-Norge" (Illiterates in welfare-Norway) published in "Barn i krise" (Children in crisis).

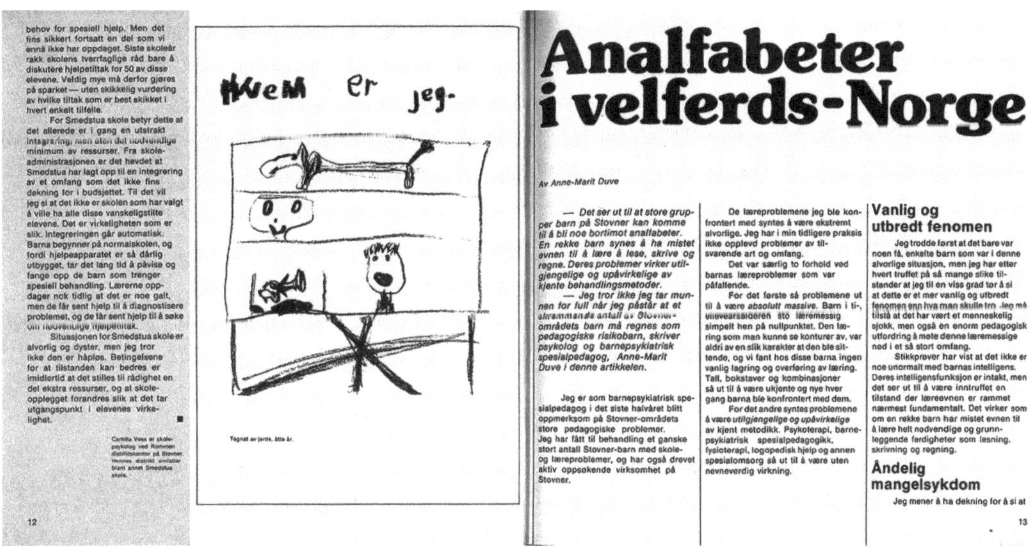

behov for spesiell hjelp. Men det fins sikkert fortsatt en del som vi ennå ikke har oppdaget. Siste skoleår rakk skolens tverrfaglige råd bare å diskutere hjelpetiltak for 50 av disse elevene. Veldig mye må derfor gjøres på sparket — uten skikkelig vurdering av hvilke tiltak som er best skikket i hvert enkelt tilfelle.

For Smedstua skole betyr dette at det allerede er i gang en utstrakt integrering, men uten det nødvendige minimum av ressurser. Fra skoleadministrasjonen er det hevdet at Smedstua har lagt opp til en integrering av et omfang som det ikke fins dekning for i budsjettet. Til det vil jeg si at det ikke er skolen som har valgt å ville ha alle disse vanskeligstilte elevene. Det er virkeligheten som er slik. Integreringen går automatisk. Barna begynner på normalskolen, og fordi hjelpeapparatet er så dårlig utbygget, tar det lang tid å påvise og fange opp de barn som trenger spesiell behandling. Lærerne oppdager nok tidlig at det er noe galt, men de får sent hjelp til å diagnostisere problemet, og de får sent hjelp til å søke om nødvendige hjelpetiltak.

Situasjonen for Smedstua skole er alvorlig og dyster, men jeg tror ikke den er håpløs. Betingelsene for at tilstanden kan bedres er imidlertid at det stilles til rådighet en del ekstra ressurser, og at skoleopplegget forandres slik at det tar utgangspunkt i elevenes virkelighet. ■

Camilla Voss er skolepsykolog ved Rommen distriktskontor på Stovner. Hennes distrikt omfatter blant annet Smedstua skole.

12

Tegnet av jente, åtte år.

Analfabeter i velferds-Norge

Av Anne-Marit Duve

— Det ser ut til at store grupper barn på Stovner kan komme til å bli noe bortimot analfabeter. En rekke barn synes å ha mistet evnen til å lære å lese, skrive og regne. Deres problemer virker utilgjengelige og upåvirkelige av kjente behandlingsmetoder.

— Jeg tror ikke jeg tar munnen for full når jeg påstår at et ekstremt mange antall av Stovner-områdets barn må regnes som pedagogiske risikobarn, skriver psykolog og barnepsykiatrisk spesialpedagog, Anne-Marit Duve i denne artikkelen.

Jeg er som barnepsykiatrisk spesialpedagog i det siste halvåret blitt oppmerksom på Stovner-områdets store pedagogiske problemer. Jeg har fått til behandling et ganske stort antall Stovner-barn med skole- og læreproblemer, og har også drevet aktiv oppsøkende virksomhet på Stovner.

De læreproblemene jeg ble konfrontert med syntes å være ekstremt alvorlige. Jeg har i min tidligere praksis ikke opplevd problemer av tilsvarende art og omfang.

Det var særlig to forhold ved barnas læreproblemer som var påfallende.

For det første så problemene ut til å være *absolutt massive*. Barn i ti-, elleveårsalderen sto læremessig simpelt hen på nullpunktet. Den læring som man kunne se konturer av, var aldri av en slik karakter at den ble sittende, og vi fant hos disse barna ingen vanlig lagring og overføring av læring. Tall, bokstaver og kombinasjoner så ut til å være ukjente og nye hver gang barna ble konfrontert med dem.

For det andre syntes problemene å være *utilgjengelige og upåvirkelige* av kjent metodikk. Psykoterapi, barnepsykiatrisk spesialpedagogikk, fysioterapi, logopedisk hjelp og annen spesialomsorg så ut til å være uten nevneverdig virkning.

Vanlig og utbredt fenomen

Jeg trodde først at det bare var noen få, enkelte barn som var i denne alvorlige situasjon, men jeg har etter hvert truffet på så mange slike tilstander at jeg til en viss grad tør å si at dette er et mer vanlig og utbredt fenomen enn hva man skulle tro. Jeg må tilstå at det har vært et menneskelig sjokk, men også en enorm pedagogisk utfordring å møte denne læremessige nød i et så stort omfang.

Stikkprøver har vist at det ikke er noe unormalt med barnas intelligens. Deres intelligensfunksjon er intakt, men det ser ut til å være inntruffet en tilstand der læreevnen er rammet nærmest fundamentalt. Det virker som om en rekke barn har mistet evnen til å lære helt nødvendige og grunnleggende ferdigheter som lesning, skrivning og regning.

Åndelig mangelsykdom

Jeg mener å ha dekning for å si at

13

The first of these reports, by Gammelsrud and Hanne Frobenius, was published by Forbruker- og administrasjonsdepartementet (the Ministry of Consumer Affairs and Administration) in 1973 and presented to Oslo Municipality as a public demand for better living environments. Crucially, the report comprised of a study of Swedish and Danish playgrounds. It dismissed the park playgrounds introduced in the 1930s as compensation for lost natural playgrounds in urban environments and especially favored the Danish *skrammellegepladser* (junk playgrounds).[22] The second report on playgrounds was initiated by the inhabitants of Stovner and carried out by the authors of the later article in the special issue of *Sinnets Helse*.[23] With Fossumsletta as a test site, the report was used actively to challenge the municipality to act at Stovner.[24]

Gammelsrud's dramatic language was meant to serve as an activist call to action. In mass media, this playground research was used as part of the residents' fight to improve the living environment in the satellite towns, by enhancing the environment for play.[25] This agenda needs to be seen in the context of a 1972 report on the initiatives taken by inhabitants in Stovner, *Stovnerboere spør stovnerboere* (Stovner dwellers ask Stovner dwellers), which described problems but also argued that the community had many resources for dealing with them.[26] Rather than dismissing Stovner and its inhabitants, Gammelsrud aimed to serve as a source for empowerment and community engagement at Stovner and get the municipality and school authorities to take action. Or, at least, this was the idea.

A MIX OF PROFESSIONAL POSITIONS AND AGENDAS

The special issue, however, included other contributions and perspectives. The first two articles came from the staff at Smedstua school. The two anonymous teachers behind the "I cried every day ..." article described disheartening classroom experiences of struggles with discipline and feelings of shortcomings. They claimed that the problems were caused by a shortage of institutional resources, a lack of parental cooperation, and failing support from Nic Waals Institutt (the leading psychiatric clinic) and the school's psychology team. They also suggested that the parents were simultaneously insecure and in denial about the problems, keeping their children from being assessed by the school psychologist or from consulting a psychiatric clinic.[27] The teachers still admitted, however, that social, organizational, and pedagogical adaptations made with school resources had already helped, thereby pointing to possible solutions to the crisis by continuing such efforts. This note was, however, overshadowed by the dramatic descriptions of problems.

Eli Aanjesen's "En skoles bønn om hjelp" (A school's plea for help) was a central contribution to the special issue.[28] Aanjesen was the principal of the open school of Smedstua from 1971. She described the situation as a "tragedy," dramatically warning of a school system that is more likely to create failure than learning and self-respect. This crisis, Aanjesen argued, was a problem that would not diminish if it wasn't spoken about. Nevertheless, she understood the unwillingness to speak out about the issues in the

22 See Hanne Frobenius and Terje Gammelsrud, *Barnet, leken og lekeplassen: en utredning om kommunale lekeplasser for barn fra syv til fjorten år* [The child, play, and the playground: an investigation into municipal playgrounds for children aged seven to fourteen] (Oslo: Forbruker- og administrasjonsdepartementet, 1973).

23 Kåre Tarjem, "Fossumsletta-undersøkelsen: Barnas behov kolliderer med 'voksne' oppfatninger" [The Fossumsletta survey: Children's needs clash with "adult" perceptions], *Dagbladet*, September 26, 1974.

24 "Krav om bedre bo-miljøer: Fossumsletta borettslag utfordrer Oslo kommune" [Demand for better living environments: Fossumsletta housing association challenges Oslo municipality], *Aftenposten*, January 29, 1975.

25 Sissel Benneche Osvold, "Miljø – hva er det?" [Environment: What is it?], *Dagbladet*, January 29, 1975; Sissel Benneche Osvold, "500 barn og fire sandkasser: Forsøk med utvikling av bedre lekemiljø på Stovner" [500 children and four sandboxes: Experiments with the development of a better play environment at Stovner], *Dagbladet*, January 29, 1975; "På Fossumsletta er det få barn som leker ute! Undersøkelser viser nedslående resultater" [At Fossumsletta, there are few children who play outside! Surveys show disappointing results], *Arbeiderbladet*, January 29, 1975; Tone B. Jamholt, "Lekemiljøet sjokkerende dårlig i flere bydeler" [The play environment is shockingly bad in several districts], *Arbeiderbladet*, January 30, 1975.

26 Odd Aksum et al., "Stovnerboere spør stovnerboere: En undersøkelse om res[s]urser, behov og Stovner sentrum" [Stovner residents ask Stovner residents: A survey about resources, needs and central Stovner], *Arbeidsrapport* 1 (April, 1972).

27 "Jeg gråt hver dag og var kvalm på veien til skolen," in "Barn i krise," special issue, *Sinnets helse: Tidsskrift for mentalhygiene*, no. 5 (1975): 4–7.

28 Eli Aanjesen, "En skoles bønn om hjelp," in "Barn i krise," special issue, *Sinnets helse: Tidsskrift for mentalhygiene*, no. 5 (1975): 8–10.

satellite town: professionals feared that drawing attention to social inequality by describing the different social compositions, milieus, housing typologies, and allocation criteria could stigmatize inhabitants, framing them as second-rate humans. Aanjesen nevertheless argued that stigma is created when moralist perspectives are used to blame individuals for their problems; thus, stigma can be avoided by placing responsibility on society instead. In avoiding focusing on parts of the population, she consequently directed her critique at the municipal school administration, society as a whole, and the total environment.

In placing the responsibility on society at large, Aanjesen referred to the report from the inhabitants of Stovner, "Stovnerboere spør stovnerboere."[29] She pointed to larger structural causes, arguing that the situation in the school described in the special issue were "some of the difficulties that have to arise when one pushes so many people together without possibilities for solving their problems."[30] At Stovner, she argued, there was a high concentration of families whose housing allocations were based on social criteria (meaning that most of the population had been struggling economically even before moving in), the average age of mothers was unusually low, there were many small children, and there were many households with two or more working family members. The Fossum neighborhood, Aanjesen added, had the largest share of struggling families and the worst school situation: many children had to change schools several times—a situation which, according to her, was not only causing tremendous strain, considering the many pre-existing problems, but also anxiety and aggression among families and children that was quickly directed against the school.

In contrast to the inhabitants' report, which emphasized their own resources and interests, Aanjesen—possibly inadvertently—depicted the population as passive victims of the welfare state system and the environment. Furthermore, in broadening the issue to avoid stigmatization of the children, she effectively defined it as an environmental problem, thereby allowing for the social construction of a territorial stigma instead of an individualized stigma. Crucially, the system critique from the school institution—represented by Aanjesen and the anonymous teachers—implies that the *total* environment causes the problems they experience in the school.

Two articles in the special issue were written from a psychological perspective. While school psychologist Camilla Voss, writing in the article "De fleste barn får utilstrekkelig hjelp" (Most children get inadequate help), described the severe work overload on her team and lack of resources, psychologist Anne-Marit Duve's article entitled "Analfabeter I velferds-Norge" (Illiterates in welfare-Norway), outlined a more dramatic story, strongly emphasizing the severity of the learning problems encountered, for which psychotherapy, child psychiatry, special needs pedagogy, physiotherapy, speech therapy, and other specialized methods were apparently without effect. Since the children were of normal intelligence, she proposed that there existed a widespread failure in the ability to learn; she referred to this as "a new *spiritual deficiency disease* in the wake of the welfare society."[31] Duve referred to English and American research in order to describe this "disease," which was allegedly caused by a psychologically confusing and unstable environment in which the child cannot organize its mental, emotional, and intellectual life.

29 Aksum et al., "Stovnerboere spør stovnerboere."

30 Original quote in Norwegian: "en del av de vanskelighetene som må oppstå når man presser så mange mennesker sammen uten at de har muligheter til å løse sine egne problemer." Aanjesen, "En skoles bønn om hjelp," 9.

31 Original quote in Norwegian: "en ny *åndelig mangelsykdom* i velferdssamfunnets kjølvann." Anne-Marit Duve, "Analfabeter i velferds-Norge" [Illiterates in welfare-Norway], in "Barn i krise," special issue, *Sinnets helse: Tidsskrift for mentalhygiene*, no. 5 (1975): 13–15.

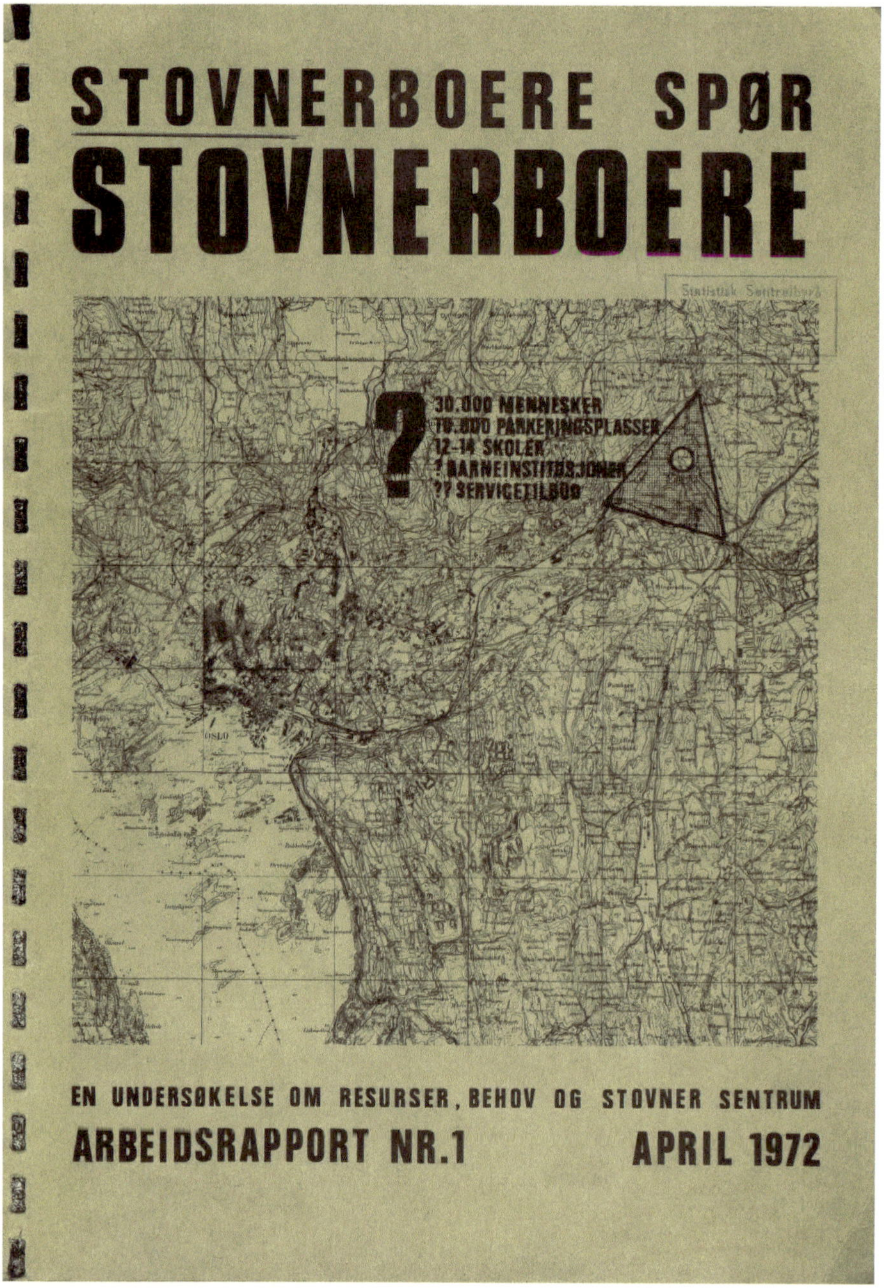

"Stovnerboere spør Stovnerboere," a 1972 report from the inhabitants of Stovner describing problems but also the community's resources, opinions and ideas.

32 Original quote in Norwegian: "vår tids egentlige sykdom er et nær sagt utdødd følelsesliv." Christian Norberg-Schulz, "Fra gjenoppbygging til omverdenskrise" [From reconstruction to environmental crisis], *Byggekunst* [*The Norwegian Review of Architecture*] 6 (1970): 202.

33 See Anne-Marit Duve, "Fremmedgjøring" [Alienation], in *Barn* [Children], ed. Kari Bruun Wyller and Thomas Chr. Wyller, Motforestillinger 4 (Oslo: Gyldendal, 1978), 11–22.

34 Ivar Blomfeldt, Terje Gammelsrud, and Rigmor Vesje, "Et miljø som innbyr til passivitet, hærverk og nederlag" [An environment that promotes passivity, vandalism, and defeat], in "Barn i krise," special issue, *Sinnets helse: Tidsskrift for mentalhygiene*, no. 5 (1975): 16–20.

For Duve, the situation at Stovner was an example of fundamental problems of civilization processes that arose not in developing countries but inside the modern welfare state. Earlier, Duve and her husband had claimed that modern society's distress is not caused by physical and material deficiencies but by the absence of spirituality and consciousness. Duve's arguments thus have affinities with those of the Norwegian architectural theorist Christian Norberg-Schulz, who dismisses politicized discourses of social and economic structures and instead emphasizes that the environment crisis of the 1970s is a mental problem and that "the real disease of our time is an almost extinct emotional life." [32] For Duve, the modern welfare society is especially to blame for an alienating environment for children.[33] In her contribution to the special issue, Duve thus dramatically asserts that the welfare state has a human responsibility to address these problems, regardless of the cost.

The report's final article, "Et miljø som innbyr til passivitet, hærverk og nederlag" (An environment that promotes passivity, vandalism, and defeat) describes several physical factors that allegedly create an inferior environment for children based on Gammelsrud's two earlier reports on playgrounds. Like these two reports, the final article in the special issue on Stovner used the notion of crisis as a call for action, presenting a series of arguments also made in the earlier report from Ammerud. These arguments correlate the problems in the area to physical attributes that result from architecture and physical planning: there are too many children, so playgroups do not form; buildings with more than four floors mean that children have less outdoor time; one-sided flats do not allow for contact between the flat and the playground, so parents and children alike become insecure and nervous. The article describes the outdoor area as monotonous and unchangeable, with building orientations and materials creating adverse local weather conditions and acoustic environments in which children's play is both unsheltered and disturbing to other inhabitants. Other problems include the danger of traffic accidents, a lack of common indoor space for children, a lack of social interaction between adults in the area, and vandalism as a logical consequence of creating a "forgotten youth." In conclusion, the authors warned of a constant risk for physical and mental damage, which called for immediate action.[34]

This article was the part of the report where the claim of a crisis was most explicitly connected to the physical environment. In this way, the final article conflates the complexity of the problems of the school and neighborhood with faults in the physical environment, and this spatial determinism effectively became the conclusion of the special issue.

EDITORIAL ACTIVISM

Gammelsrud's strategy for gaining attention for a seemingly obviously good cause by calling it a "crisis" is characteristic of the special issue as a whole, and it was enabled by the editorial synthesis of the diverse contributions, where the focus was on the most alarming aspects. The editorial work consisted of combining different types of professional criticisms and popularizing them. The first and most obvious example is the combination of statements in the introductory qoute, which synthesizes Duve and Voss' contributions and utilizes Aanjesen's "Should we speak about it out loud?" to create a greater impact.

Another example is that by concluding with the focus on the physical environment, Gammelsrud helped synthesize the school environment, learning environment, mental environment, institutional environment, play environment, and housing environment into one, to pose a critique of the total physical environment of the neighborhood in the satellite town. Gammelsrud strategically used expert voices to support his activist endeavor to improve the physical space on behalf of the inhabitants, with the consequence that the special issue removes nuances to emphasize a general crisis.

While the authors and the editor would be right in suggesting that the problems are interlinked and complex, the links that they all make to the physical environment of the satellite town as a major source of the problems make it hard to grasp the specificity of the problems and how to handle them—the discourse becomes vague and abstract. They argue that one needs to speak openly about problems, yet many aspects remain unclear or merely hinted at in their generalizing descriptions. Aanjesen's attempts to avoid stigmatizing the school and school children added to the confusion: by sidestepping steps that might address the problem at scales other than that of the society as a whole, the article instead contributed to establishing territorial stigma.

The persuasive but somewhat speculative editing of the different contributions also involves the visual presentations in the special issue—for instance, the cover image, a children's drawing used to enforce the psychological "crisis" of children—which were used to affect rather than clarify or illustrate arguments. Furthermore, the concluding analysis of playgrounds at Stovner is built on the premise that the central error, according to Gammelsrud, was thinking that adults could design an environment for children: the children needed to create their environment for themselves. The welfare state efforts for and on behalf of children thus become problematic in a way that essentially finds fault in welfare state architecture.

MASS MEDIA AND TERRITORIAL STIGMA

Gammelsrud's journalistic methods were immensely successful in drawing attention. Under the nickname "Stovnerrapporten," the special issue was debated on national television and in hundreds of articles published in national and regional newspapers across Norway. This mediation displayed different—and contradictory—explanations for the nature and possible causes of the crisis. It introduced additional agendas, such as the critique of the architecture of open schools. Debates and discussions abounded, and the reports did produce new political engagement in Stovner and elsewhere. It also led to political decisions that resulted in the distribution of more resources to Stovner, and were thus at least partly successful in generating the desired change: securing resources for the school.

Nevertheless, the intense mass media exposure was even more efficient in creating lasting stigma, almost completely dismissing the environment and the inhabitants in newspapers, and on television and radio. One example is the vagueness in describing the problems in any straightforward way in the radio interviews in the program *Ekko*—instead, the "satellite town problem" was apparently so well-known that it didn't need analysis, only descriptions of its consequences.[35] Furthermore, in contrast to the focus on the inhabitant's resources in *Stovnerboere spør Stovnerboere*, the repeated use of the word *fattigdom* (poverty) in the television presentation of "Stovnerrapporten" is notable for creating a sense of absolute impoverishment:

> Poverty of impulses, poverty of experiences and the local environment, poverty in the environment in which children should play and develop are the main reasons pointed out in the report. The children bring this poverty with them into school, and then it may be too late.[36]

With this type of melodramatic mediation, it could be easily missed that the special issue of *Sinnets Helse* had at its core a more pragmatic aim, as a particular activist call for action. It concluded with a small note: a demand from the parents and the school, which, beyond more resources for the Smedstua school, comprised of the construction of a new school for the Fossumsletta community.

According to the historian Bernt H. Lund, the goal for schools in satellite towns was that they be constructed at the same speed as housing; this was seldom achieved, however, and provisional solutions were attempted, to which parents protested significantly. Lund saw the situation of Fossumsletta as an example that such strong reactions led the municipality to allocate funds to new schools, even if the problem of local school capacity was temporary.[37] Here, Lund's argument takes on a pragmatic and supposedly objective perspective, seeing the school institution's capacity as a matter for governmental bodies and long-term planning (accepting short-term problems) rather than recognizing it as the source of problems with significant, immediate local implications. The parents, however, were concerned with the essential function of the school in the community.[38] In correspondence with Perry's emphasis on the school's important role in the neighborhood unit, they demanded a school specifically for the Fossum neighborhood.[39] Crucially, Gammelsrud had already presented this demand in the 1974 playground report.[40] With the special issue on Stovner, this playground report was justified anew. Aanjesen and the Smedstua school called for a parent meeting at which they could present the demands to the municipality, and the parents and the school agreed that a strike would ensue if the municipality did not meet their demands.[41] The combined efforts from Stovner were a success: the new school was constructed and opened in the autumn of 1976 as a direct result of the struggles.[42]

This cooperation between parents and the school appears to be a realization of community power in line with the neighborhood unit idea, but in confrontation and struggle rather than in line with the harmonic and orderly system of the satellite town plans. This conflict could easily be seen as a failure of planning, but it could just as well be interpreted as a prerequisite for creating political and social awareness. As the journalist Tone B. Jamholt emphasizes in a newspaper interview with local politicians, the special issue on

35 For the radio interviews, see *EKKO*, "Stovner-rapporten: Intervjuer på bakgrunn av artiklene i tidsskriftet *Sinnets helse*" [The Stovner report: Interviews based on articles in the journal *Sinnets helse*], with Inger Johanne Agerup and Rolf Børke, aired September 11, 1975, on NRK (the Norwegian Broadcasting Corporation).

36 Original quote in Norwegian: "Fattigdom på impulser, fattigdom på opplevelser og nærmiljø, fattigdom i det miljø hvor barn skal leke og utfolde seg, er de hovedårsakene som rapporten peker på. Den fattigdommen tar barna med seg inn i skolen, og da kan det være for sent." *EKKO*, "Stovner-rapporten."

37 Bernt H. Lund, *Beretning om Oslo kommune for årene 1948–1986* [Report on Oslo municipality for the years 1948–1986] (Oslo: ProArk, 2000), 305.

38 "Foreldrene forsvarer skolen: samfunnet har ansvar for barna" [Parents defend the school: society has a responsibility for the children], *Dagbladet*, August 15, 1975.

39 Else-Beth Roalsø, "Usikker framtid for Stovner-barna" [Uncertain future for the Stovner children], *Dagbladet*, August 20, 1975.

40 "Krav om bedre bo-miljøer: Fossumsletta borettslag utfordrer Oslo kommune."

41 "Smedstua skole innkaller til foreldremøte" [Smedstua school invites to a parents' meeting], *Arbeiderbladet*, August 20, 1975.

42 "Smedstua-lærerne utsetter streiken" [Smedstua teachers postpone strike], *Arbeiderbladet*, September 5, 1975; "Smedstua-lærere: Fossum må ha en ny 6-årig skole" [Smedstua teachers: Fossum must have a new 6-year school], *Arbeiderbladet*, September 23, 1975; "Streik blant Smedstua-lærerne" [Smedstua teachers on strike], *Klassekampen*, October 15, 1975; "Fossum bygd på rekordtid – Åpner den med streik?" [Fossum built in record time—Will it open with a strike?], *Arbeiderbladet*, August 11, 1976.

43 Tone B. Jamholt, "Selvoppgivelse er ingen løsning – Vi går løs på problemene" [Self-abandonment is not a solution—We tackle the problems], *Arbeiderbladet*, August 19, 1975.

Stovner should not be a cause for despair but rather a motivation to take up arms and lead to community initiatives.[43]

Thus, the special issue is more than a mere description of errors, mistakes, or failures in planning satellite towns as physical and social environments. Instead, it represents several different facets of a complex discussion: on one side, passive inhabitants and children under the state organization, administration and (architectural) design, and the neighborhoods and playgrounds as compensations for modernity's ills. On the other side, resourceful communities with agencies fighting for their neighborhoods and playgrounds but also creating them. Here, active, creative, autonomous inhabitants and children are presented as ideals. It is, however, unclear if this ideal was part of the development of a new community focus or rather a sign of an emerging neoliberal, individualist ideology: The social and ideological aspects inherent in the planning critique were hardly communicated in the special issue or the mass media. Instead, the critique was simplified and conflated with the physical environment, constructing a stigmatizing image of the satellite town: an image that still lingers.

In the present day, this type of simplified and superficial discourse is deeply embedded in the ideas for improving these areas. In Norway, this is formulated in area-based policies for hindering *utenforskap* (outsiderness), with explicit reference to apparently worse conditions in Denmark and Sweden. In this way, the discourses are connected across Scandinavia, and the Danish "ghetto laws," with their own territorial stigma, become part of Norwegian imaginations and conceptualizations of such places. It is these perceptions that area-based initiatives have sought to change through a focus on rebuilding reputation. From this point of view, the special issue—*Stovnerrapporten*—was an irresponsible, destructive act.

Crucially, however, such discourses tend to avoid a system critique of central topics, including inhabitants' political power and influence, social inclusion, and community autonomy and agency. Instead, they transform the two special issues of *Sinnets Helse* into generalizing "reports" on places and, by extension, specific social issues that require political solutions into horror stories that provoke fear-based reactions. As such, these activist attempts to generate discussion and political action become superficial arguments for urban redevelopment—linking social issues to urban environments through the mechanisms of territorial stigmatization. In this transformation, the child is a central figure, but not in the role of the primary welfare state subject carrying intrinsic value: conceptualized as a victim, the child becomes an instrument for other agendas. Similar stories exist across Scandinavia: The tales of children in crisis in today's satellite towns, instead of becoming starting points for discussing and acting on structural social challenges, all too often become mere devices to propel urban transformation processes.

Stills from the NRK (Norwegian Broadcasting Company) television coverage of "Stovnerrapporten."

The opening of a new school in the Fossumsletta neighborhood, built in 1976 as a result of school strikes and community activism.

Mikkel Høghøj

DANGEROUS YOUTH

Spatial Determinism and the Rejection of Modernist Mass Housing in 1970s Denmark

> Beers and concrete constitute everyday life for the young people in Gellerupplanen. It is this conglomerate of human silos, on the periphery of Aarhus that, according to a new report, was built for the building industry rather than the residents. Teenagers turn to alcohol in order to endure the monotony of living amidst concrete giants.[1]

These words stem from a sensationalist article published by the Danish tabloid newspaper *Ekstra Bladet* in January 1974. Entitled "Unge drikker for at klare sig i betonslum" (Young people are drinking to cope with life in the concrete slum), the article reported widespread alcoholism among children and young people living on the mass housing estate Gellerupplanen (Gellerup Plan, 1967–72), which had been built only a few years earlier on the western periphery of the Danish city of Aarhus. In the article, *Ekstra Bladet* not only condemned Gellerupplanen as a place of social decline, but the newspaper specifically blamed the spatial environment of the estate, and the matter of concrete in particular, as the primary cause of the youth problems it identified. By linking modernist architecture to juvenile alcoholism, the newspaper identified Gellerupplanen as a place of ultimate resignation. The feeling of hopelessness among young people had ostensibly reached a level where violent opposition was no longer seen as a viable solution. Only alcohol could soothe the pain.

In contrast, Gellerupplanen had, only four years earlier, been awarded the title of "the prettiest city of the year" by another Danish tabloid newspaper, *BT*.[2] Here, the estate had been praised for its multi-faceted and diverse environment, and the way in which it brought people of various generations together in a strong and affluent local community. From this perspective, Gellerupplanen materialized the architectural visions for family life in the emerging Danish welfare state.[3] As private and volunteer organizations were increasingly, from the late interwar years onwards, replaced by the state as the main distributor of child welfare, family policy gradually developed into a cornerstone of the Danish welfare model.[4] In many ways, the aim to regulate and facilitate family life became key objectives in the planning and design of modernist mass housing estates. With playgrounds, youth clubs, and a broad range of public institutions for child welfare, including nurseries, kindergartens, and elementary schools, Danish mass housing estates were designed to offer socially and spatially child-friendly environments and prepare a new generation for life in the Danish welfare society.[5] Mass housing, in other words, was not only supposed to house the future generations of the Danish welfare society but also to facilitate happy and healthy childhoods and hence the development of thriving citizens. Already by 1974, however, Gellerupplanen was no

1 Original quote in Danish: "Bajere og beton er hverdag for de unge i Gjellerup-planen. Det er denne samling af menneskesiloer i udkanten af Århus, der ifølge en frisk rapport i højere grad blev bygget af hensyn til betonindustrien end til de personer, som skulle bo i dem. Teenagere må drikke for at udholde den ellers så dræbende ensformighed med cementgiganter på alle sider." "Unge drikker for at klare sig i betonslum" [Young people are drinking to cope with life in the concrete slums], *Ekstra Bladet*, January 7, 1974.

2 Henrik Sten Madsen, "B.T. har valgt Danmarks kønneste by: Gjellerup ved Århus betonby med trivsel" [B.T. has chosen Denmark's most beautiful city: Gellerup near Århus, concrete city with well-being], *BT*, August 14, 1970.

3 For studies of the role of architecture in the shaping of welfare states, see Helena Mattsson and Sven-Olov Wallenstein, *Swedish Modernism: Architecture, Consumption, and the Welfare State* (London: Black Dog Publishing, 2010); Katrine Lotz et al., eds., *Forming Welfare* (Copenhagen: The Danish Architectural Press, 2017); Mark Swenarton, Tom Avermaete, and Dirk Van der Heuvel, *Architecture and the Welfare State* (London: Routledge, 2015).

4 Jørn Henrik Petersen et al., *Dansk Velfærdshistorie – Bd. 3. velfærdsstaten i støbeskeen: 1933–1956* [Danish welfare history vol. 3: The welfare state in the melting pot, 1933–1956], ed. Jørn Henrik. Petersen et al., University of Southern Denmark Studies in History and Social Sciences, vol. 410 (Odense: Syddansk Universitetsforlag, 2012), 549–665.

5 Mikkel Høghøj and Silke Holmqvist, "Da betonen blev belastende. Den emotionelle kamp om Gellerupplanen i 1960'erne Og 1970'erne" [When concrete became a burden: The emotional struggle over the Gellerup Plan in the 1960s and 1970s], *Temp* 16 (2018): 128–32, https://tidsskrift.dk/temp/article/view/109158.

side 6 mandag den 7. januar 1974 — EKSTRA BLADET

UNGE DRIKKER FOR AT KLARE SIG I BETON-SLUM

Beboerne i Gjellerup-planen er end ikke alene i deres egne stuer – de hører naboer på alle sider

– Det kræver tilpasning at bo her i Gjellerupplanen, siger familien Koitzsch.

Fra Ekstra Bladets Jyllandsredaktion

Bajere og beton er hverdag for de unge i Gjellerup-planen. Det er denne samling af menneskesiloer i udkanten af Århus, der ifølge en frisk rapport i højere grad blev bygget af hensyn til betonindustrien end til de personer, som skulle bo i dem. Teenagerne må drikke for at udholde den ellers så dræbende ensformighed med cementgiganter på alle sider.

KRAVLER HJEM

– Her er drikkegilder for skolebørn hver weekend. Det starter tidligt om lørdagen, og de sidste nærmest kravler hjem hen på søndagen, fortæller den 14-årige Leo Koitzsch, en af de tusinder af unge i den århusianske milliardslum. – Næsten alle ryger hash. Der er også mange, der sniffer cellulosefortynder. De gør det bare for at få noget skæg. Vi har ikke andet at give os til.

Ekstra Bladet's article from 1974 portrayed a group of children on a concrete deck in Gellerupplanen. The image was in black and white to emphasize the dismal atmosphere of the housing estate.

Brochure for the modernist mass housing estate Gellerupplanen from 1972. The housing estate was built on the western periphery of Aarhus between 1967 and 1972. Envisioned as an urban totality, it comprised—in addition to housing—a shopping center, a church, schools, and kindergartens as well as several cultural amenities including a swimming bath, a library, football fields and a tennis court.

longer portrayed as a place of well-being in the public discourse. As was the case in many other Northern and Western European countries, the public image of Danish modernist mass housing changed drastically in the 1970s.[6] This change happened swiftly and was entrenched through a broad range of different channels. From architectural debates and social science research to fiction, music, and the mass media, contemporary observers now criticized the spatial environment of modernist housing estates and questioned the livability of these places. As the case of Gellerupplanen suggests, this discursive shift in a Danish context entailed—and was preconditioned by—new representations of the relationship between mass housing estates and the well-being of children and young people. As negative representations of mass housing started to proliferate, one strand of criticism specifically addressed the relationship between mass housing and contemporary problems of juvenile delinquency and violence. Suddenly, modernist mass housing estates were depicted as breeding grounds of an unhealthy and even dangerous youth culture that posed a significant threat to the social order of the Danish welfare society.

Historically and today, the Danish welfare society has been organized around different citizen categories such as the consumer, the patient, the immigrant, the worker, and the unemployed person.[7] In various historical contexts, actors including politicians, unions, intellectuals, and professionals have mobilized such categories to either legitimize or challenge the social order of the welfare society. While some citizen categories have functioned as role models for the pursuit of individual happiness and social prosperity more generally, others have represented danger and threats to the welfare state. In this context, modernist mass housing estates have worked as more than just architectural expressions of welfare politics. After their construction, they have continued to exert influence and work as laboratories for broader negotiations of the Danish welfare city's social order and its citizen categories.

Thus, this chapter explores the public rejection of Danish mass housing through the lens of one particular citizen category: that of "the dangerous youth." In many ways, the category of "the dangerous youth" was modeled on its relationship with architecture and urban space. It emerged in the immediate postwar years, yet in the 1970s it specifically became linked to the public rejection of modernist mass housing. On the one hand, "the dangerous youth" became instrumental in the rejection of mass housing estates in public opinion. On the other hand, mass housing estates became formative in the reappraisal of "the dangerous youth" in popular imagination. This dialectical relationship hints at how Nordic welfare architecture became shaped not only within the realm of planning and design but also through popular representations in the mass media and popular culture.

THE EMERGENCE OF THE DANGEROUS YOUTH

In the immediate postwar years, "the youth question" occupied a prominent position in public debates in Denmark. In 1945, *Ungdomskommissionen* (Youth Commission) was created by the Danish government to improve social conditions and opportunities

6 For studies of the rejection of modernist mass housing in Denmark, see Sidse Martens Gudmand-Høyer et al., *Gellerup* (Copenhagen: Arkitektens Forlag, 2021); Jon Helt Haarder, "The Precariat as Place A Literary History of the Danish Ghetto," *Scandinavica* 59, no. 2 (2020): 29–50; Mikkel Høghøj, "Between Utopia and Dystopia: A Socio-Cultural History of Modernist Mass Housing in Denmark, c. 1945–1985" (PhD diss., Aarhus University, 2019). For Nordic studies, see Laura Falender, "Social Housing in Postwar Oslo and Edinburgh: Modernizing, Decentralizing, and Renewing the Urban Housing Stock, ca. 1945–1985" (PhD diss., University of Oslo, 2013); Per-Markku Ristilammi, "Rosengård och den svarta poesin: En studie av modern annorlundahet" [Rosengård and black poetry: A study of modern difference], *Symposion Bibliotek* (Stockholm: Brutus Östlings Bokförlag, 1994); Guttorm Ruud, "Sites of Crisis: Histories of the Satellite Town" (PhD diss., The Oslo School of Architecture and Design, 2021). For studies with transnational and global perspectives, see Kenny Cupers, "Human Territoriality and the Downfall of Public Housing," *Public Culture* 29, no. 1 (2017): 165–90, https://doi.org/10.1215/08992363-3644445; Kenny Cupers, Catharina Gabrielsson, and Helena Mattsson, *Neoliberalism on the Ground: Architecture and Transformation from the 1960s to the Present* (Pittsburgh: University of Pittsburgh Press, 2020), https://doi.org/10.2307/j.ctvzxxb75; Christopher Klemek, *The Transatlantic Collapse of Urban Renewal: Postwar Urbanism From New York to Berlin* (Chicago: University of Chicago Press, 2012); Florian Urban, *Tower and Slab: Histories of Global Mass Housing* (London: Routledge, 2011).

7 Jesper Vestermark Køber, Niklas Olsen, and Heidi Vad Jønsson, *Citizen Categories in the Danish Welfare State: From the Founding Epoch to the Neoliberal Era*, University of Southern Denmark Studies in History and Social Sciences, vol. 623 (Odense: University Press of Southern Denmark, 2021).

of young people, and in the course of the following seven years, the committee surveyed the general living conditions and behavioral patterns of young people in both rural and urban Denmark.[8] This resulted in several reports focusing on topics such as leisure, social problems, education and residential patterns, which became formative in the development of Danish youth policy in the subsequent decades. Arguably, the work of the committee reflects the emergence of "the youth" as a distinct citizen category in Danish society. Besides putting the political and social rights of young people on the political agenda, the creation of the committee points to a wider public interest in *the youth* as a social and cultural phenomenon. With the massive increase in societal affluence in the 1950s and 1960s, this interest accelerated even further and led to an increasing individuation of the family into new consuming subjects and the construction of a new kind of citizen, "the citizen-consumer."[9] As the term "teenager" gradually took hold in the public discourse, young people became a new and powerful consumer group absorbing many new types of goods and cultural products, especially from North America.[10]

Indubitably, "the youth" was a contested social category in postwar Danish society. While the Youth Commission refrained from adopting a moralizing view on the behavior of young people and instead pursued a more pragmatic approach drawing on psychological knowledge, more critical voices also populated the debate. In the wider public, the youth spurred concern, fear, and fascination. These emotions were particularly elicited by the notion of *the dangerous youth* that, in addition to the committee's work, found expression in various novels and films.[11] Initially, the category had been used to define booming crime rates among young urbanites during the lawless last phase of the Nazi occupation, i.e., 1944–45. In the postwar years, the category quickly expanded and became coupled with representations of new, problematic youth groups including "rockers" and "leather jackets" who embraced various cultural tendencies from the USA.[12] In this way, "the dangerous youth" emerged as a way of critiquing various aspects of contemporary Danish society. From a conservative standpoint, the dangerous youth was dangerous because it represented a break with traditional cultural values and, ultimately, the dissolution of the family. From another angle, as the work of the Youth Commission illustrates, this category also served as a prism to critique and thereby improve the social conditions and welfare of young people in the early postwar years.

Both in the work of the Youth Commission and in the popular imagination, the notion of the dangerous youth was from the outset intimately connected to urban culture. In the 1940s and 1950s, "the dangerous youth" was predominantly located on street corners and in the bars and coffee shops of Copenhagen, where the amusement districts around the central station in particular constituted an arena for this troubled generation. Thus, two of the commission's reports specifically addressed the unhealthy impact that urban life could have on young people.[13] In this context, newcomers—and particularly those who had moved to Copenhagen from the countryside or villages—were seen as vulnerable to the dangers and temptations of the urban environment. The perceived effects of the big city were highly gendered; while young men were drawn

8 Hans Sode-Madsen, *Farlig ungdom – samfundet, ungdommen og Ungdomskommissionen 1945–1970* [Dangerous youth: Society, youth and the Youth Commission, 1945–1970] (Aarhus: Aarhus Universitetsforlag, 2003).

9 For studies of "the citizen-consumer" in an urban and architectural context, see Janina Gosseye and Tom Avermaete, eds., *Shopping Towns Europe: Commercial Collectivity and the Architecture of the Shopping Centre 1945–1975* (London: Bloomsbury Visual Arts, 2017); and Alistair Kefford, "Housing the Citizen- Consumer in Postwar Britain: The Parker Morris Report, Affluence and the Even Briefer Life of Social Democracy," *Twentieth Century British History* 29, no. 2 (2018): 225–58.

10 For studies of cultural transfers from USA to Denmark in the postwar decades, see Sissel Bjerrum Fossat, *Den lille pige med iskagen: Marshallplan, produktivitet og amerikanisering* [The little girl with the ice cream: The Marshall Plan, productivity, and Americanization], University of Southern Denmark Studies in History and Social Sciences, vol. 505. (Odense: University Press of Southern Denmark, 2015); Dorthe Gert Simonsen and Iben Vyff, eds., *Amerika og det gode liv: Materiel kultur i Skandinavien i 1950'erne og 1960'erne* [America and the good life: Material culture in Scandinavia in the 1950s and 1960s], University of Southern Denmark Studies in History and Social Sciences, vol. 425 (Odense: University Press of Southern Denmark, 2011).

11 Sode-Madsen, *Farlig ungdom*, 94.

12 Original terms in Danish: "Rockere" and "Læderjakker." Bertel Nygaard, "Lyden af farlig ungdom og sort ekstase. Bill Haleys Rock Around the Clock hørt i Danmark – fra 1950'erne til 1970'erne" [The sound of dangerous youth and black ecstasy: Bill Haley's "Rock Around the Clock" heard in Denmark, from the 1950s to the 1970s], *Temp* 10, no. 19 (2019): 156–78; Sode-Madsen, *Farlig ungdom*.

13 Ungdomskommissionen, "Betænkning om den tilflyttede ungdoms særlige problemer" [Report on the special problems of displaced youth] (Copenhagen: Ungdomskommissionen, 1948); Ungdomskommissionen, "Ungdommen og fritiden" [The youth and leisure] (Copenhagen: Ungdomskommissionen, 1952).

The official posters for the movies *Farlig Ungdom* (Dangerous youth) from 1953 and *Bundfald* (Sediment) from 1957. Both films starred popular Danish actors Ib Mossin and Birgitte Price as representatives of the social and moral downfall caused by the urban environment of Copenhagen's inner city.

EKSTRA BLADET fredag den 31. december 1976 side 3

VOLD OG TERROR HÆRGER FORSTÆDERNE

Unge bander skaber skræk og rædsel – ingen tør anmelde dem

AF JENS RØGIND

En dreng blev stoppet på sin nyerhvervede knallert. Det var ikke politiet, men seks læderjakker i alderen 16-17 år. De afkrævede ham overtøj, penge og knallerten. Han turde ikke andet. Han fik et par slag og spark, hvorefter bøllerne kørte væk med hans knallert og ejendele.

Det er noget af truslen og volden i forstæderne omkring København som borgerne må leve med. Politiet erkender den er der og frygter den bliver endnu mere omfattende. Kriminalpolitiet i Gladsaxe, der dækker en af de største områder ved København, har netop startet en større efterforskning, hvor godt 36 helt unge læderjakker er implicerede. De er sigtede og afhørt for omkring 90 hårde kriminelle forhold, der alene er begået i oktober og november. Det drejer sig om grove røverier, vold, indbrud og hæleri.

Om dagen er de fredelige unge lærlinge og skoleelever, men om aftenen og natten samles de i flok og terroriserer hele bydele. Skuepladsen for gade-volden er flyttet fra de traditionelle steder omkring Nyhavn og Vesterbro til sovebyerne udenfor storbyen.

Ifølge kriminalpolitiet er der mange af disse kriminelle forhold, som de ikke får kendskab til. Folk er bange for repressalier fra de unge voldsmænd. I stedet for at gå til politiet, lader folk vold og terror gå uanmeldt hen, siger man hos politiet i Gladsaxe.

Politimester Mogens Grau, Gladsaxe, siger til Ekstra Bladet, at han til en vis grad godt kan forstå, at folk er bange for repressalier.

– Men denne frygt er overdrevet. Det er kun såre meget få gange, at en voldsmand har hævnet sig på anmelderen. Vi yder fuld beskyttelse for de mennesker, der er blevet truet af eventuelle voldsmænd. Desuden søger vi at dæmme op for volden gennem en bedre planlægning af politi-patruljernes kørsel. De skal være på de rigtige steder til de rigtige tider, siger Mogens Grau.

SAG MOD 36

– Det er ikke realistisk med den megen tale om, at folk, der griber ind for at hjælpe andre mod voldsmænd, eventuelt selv kan blive sigtet for vold. Det drejer sig om nødværge, og vi ville aldrig tage sådanne skridt, når en fornuftig borger uddeler øretæver til en voldsmand. Det skal være meget groft, eventuelt ved unødig anvendelse af våben, før der kan blive tale om en sigtelse.

I den store sag med 36 læderjakker implicerede i Værløse forsikrer politimesteren, at der vil blive krævet betydelige straffe.

De grove overfald og røverier ligner næsten alle hinanden. De sker i flok.

En ung mand bliver standset på sin knallert og under trusler om tæsk bliver han frarøvet alt af værdi, overtøj, penge og knallerten sammen med forsikringspolicen. Derefter bliver den overfaldne alligevel fulgt på vej med slag og spark. I flere tilfælde er en ung mand kommet hjem, forslået og frarøvet alt. Men hverken han selv eller forældrene har turdet anmelde det af frygt for voldsmændene.

Politiet fik først kendskab til disse hændelser, da man havde de 16-17-årige voldsmænd til afhøring enkeltvis. De var i de fleste tilfælde blevet anholdt efter forsøg på at sælge de stjålne knallerter, som de samtidig havde taget forsikringspolicerne til.

Derudover havde nogle af dem været impliceret i et overfald på en tjener i Værløse. Da de ved en restaurant forsøgte at stjæle øller, blev de overrasket af tjeneren. Han prøvede at stoppe dem, men blev mishandlet og slået med flasker i ansigtet. Han blev blindet og lå på hospitalet i lang tid, inden han fik synet igen.

KLÆDT AF TIL SKINDET

En ung mand på vej hjem på knallert havde en sen aftentime en anden ubehagelig oplevelse med de unge læderjakker. Han blev på sædvanlig facon standset og afkrævet værdier. Han havde syv kroner, dem fik de udleveret. Under trusler om klø beordrede de ham til at tage bukserne af, hvilket han efterkom fuld af angst. De forlangte også, at han skulle afføre sig underbukser, hvorefter den unge mand måtte stå med nøgent underliv i vinterkulden. Han tiggede og bad, om de ikke ville lade ham køre hjem. Han fik tildelt nogle kraftige slag og spark, hvorefter voldsmændene kørte.

Heller ikke dette blev anmeldt af offeret. Han var blevet skrækslagen og tav om episoden.

Mange af de 36 implicerede har været fængslet i flere uger. Ifølge politiet drejer det sig ikke om en bestemt gruppe af de såkaldte knallert-rockere, men af tilfældige unge, der finder sammen. Hele tiden er nye unge impliceret i vold og røveri. Der vil nu i de fleste tilfælde blive rejst tiltale.

'Nomaderne' i klubtøjet. Fra venstre er det Jeppe, Pio, Pelz og Junior. (Foto: Asger Sessingø)

Gladsaxe-gruppen 'Nomaderne':

VI ER IKKE VOLDSMÆND

– Når folk ser en læderjakke, bliver de panikslagne. Det er der ikke grund til, vi slår ikke løs på sagesløse.

Sådan siger nogle medlemmer af en motorcykelklub fra Gladsaxe 'Normaderne', der føler, at de er blevet udlagt som voldsmænd af aviserne. Den stigende voldsmentalitet har skabt en frygt i befolkningen for unge mennesker i læderjakker, men det er ikke dem alle, der overfalder folk på gader og stræder.

– Det er nogle af de mindreårige 'knallert-rockere' eller 'mini-rockere', der skaber al den ballade. Det gør at folk også er bange for os og tror vi er voldsmænd. Men er der ingen grund til. Det vi slås for regår indbyrdes, siger Jeppe fra 'Normaderne'.

VI HJÆLPER

– Det er tværtimod sådan, at hvis vi ser nogle af minirockerne overfalde folk på gaden, skal vi nok komme og hjælpe de overfaldne. Bagefter vil de voldsmænd ikke overfalde nogen mere, forsikrer 'Normaderne'. Gruppen synes det er kedeligt, at der er så meget vold i deres kvarter. De vil gerne have det fredeligt og passe sig selv, men de savner et sted at være.

– Vi har søgt borgmesteren i Gladsaxe om et lokale, men er

As this article from *Ekstra Bladet* from 1976 illustrates, the 1970s witnessed a shift in the imagined geography of urban violence.

into organized crime and violence, young women were invited to indulge in a promiscuous lifestyle that ultimately resulted in prostitution. This narrative was also reproduced through popular films including *Farlig Ungdom* (Dangerous youth) from 1953 and *Bundfald* (Sediment) from 1957, and novels including conservative journalist Kate Fleron's *Afsporet Ungdom* (Derailed youth) from 1942. All portrayed the multiple temptations of the big city that corrupted young people into a life of prostitution, alcoholism, and violence.[14] In these depictions, the big city was more than an arena of troubled behavior: it actively contributed to the social downfall of a new generation.

NEW IMAGINED GEOGRAPHIES OF YOUTH AND VIOLENCE

While Copenhagen's inner-city constituted the main spatial setting for the dangerous youth in the early postwar years, popular representations increasingly linked this troubled group to the concrete suburbs from the early 1970s onward. This move coalesced with a broader shift in the imagined geography of urban violence. In an article entitled "Vold og terror hærger forstæderne" (Violence and terror ravage the suburbs) from 1976, *Ekstra Bladet* specifically pointed to such a shift in contemporary urban Denmark. The article argued that "the scene of street violence has moved from the old, traditional places around Nyhavn and Vesterbro to the new dormitory towns outside the big city."[15] Besides housing the urban working class, the districts of Nyhavn and Vesterbro were places of amusement, drinking, and thus temptation. In contrast, not much amusement was ascribed to the social and spatial environment of Danish modernist mass housing in the 1970s. Rather, these places were depicted through emotional values such as boredom, loneliness, and fear, and were specifically criticized for their lack of social facilities.[16] In this sense, the *Ekstra Bladet* article not only identified a shift in the imagined geography of urban violence, but it also alluded to a shift in the imagined cause of this violence. While urban violence in the inner city had been rooted in the temptations of the big city, the violent behavior in the concrete suburbs ostensibly originated from a feeling of alienation.

Two years later, the left-wing newspaper *Information* linked this shift to contemporary problems of juvenile delinquency. In a series of three articles, the newspaper sought to explain the destructive behavior of certain youth groups in modernist housing estates, consulting both local police forces and criminologist Flemming Balvig.[17] The articles focused mainly on the housing areas Albertslund Syd (1963–68) and Ishøjplanen (1970–73), both located in the western and southern suburbs of Copenhagen, but they also addressed the links between criminal behavior and modernist housing estates more generally. The first article, the title of which translates to "vandalism and violence in the concrete city," addressed the contemporary increase in vandalism, burglary and violence committed by the so-called "rockers" or "leather jackets" on the urban periphery.[18] This was followed by an interview with criminologist Flemming Balvig[19] who reflected upon the linkages between these behavioral patterns and the spatial and

14 Sode-Madsen, *Farlig ungdom – Samfundet, ungdommen og Ungdomskommissionen 1945–1970*, 83–94.

15 Original quote in Danish: "Skuepladsen for gade-volden er flyttet fra de traditionelle steder omkring Nyhavn og Vesterbro til sovebyerne udenfor storbyen." "Vold og terror hærger forstæderne," *Ekstra Bladet*, December 31, 1976.

16 For studies of the emotional history of modernist mass housing, see Høghøj and Holmqvist, "Da betonen blev belastende"; Christiane Reinecke, "Into the Cold: Neighborliness, Class, and the Emotional Landscape of Urban Modernism in France and West Germany," *Journal of Urban History* 48, no. 1 (2022): 163–81, https://doi.org/10.1177/0096144220931197.

17 Povl Høst-Madsen, "Hærværk og vold i betonbyen" [Vandalism and violence in the concrete city], *Information*, May 19, 1978; Povl Høst-Madsen, "Politiets samarbejde med private og kommunale vagtværn giver store problemer for retssikkerheden" [Cooperation between the police and private and municipal security forces causes major problems for the rule of law], *Information*, May 23, 1978; Jørgen Kjærgaard, "Livet i betonbyen. angsten, volden – kedsommeligheden" [Life in the concrete city: Fear, violence—boredom], *Information*, June 9, 1978.

18 Høst-Madsen, "Hærværk og vold i betonbyen."

19 Flemming Balvig later became professor in sociology and criminology at the University of Copenhagen.

social structure of suburban housing developments.[20] In contrast to traditional provincial towns, he argued, the concrete suburbs did not offer many possibilities for diversion for the young people living there. The combination of the lack of social activities and the presence of unsupervised public and semi-public spaces on the estates encouraged acts of vandalism in particular. Thus, although *Information* did not reduce modernist housing estates to the main culprit, the spatial environment of such estates was nonetheless portrayed as complicit in the production of new geographies and patterns of youth crime.

This imagined link between juvenile delinquency and mass housing estates was even more explicitly articulated in other mass media representations. *Ekstra Bladet*'s story about Gellerupplanen from January 1974, for example, specifically blamed the architectural monotony of the housing estate for the social demise of teenagers. In 1978, the television broadcast "En Kirke i beton" (A church in concrete) reiterated this point by arguing that the built environment of Gellerupplanen was producing a new generation of restless and vengeful young people.[21] In the case of Vollsmose (1967–81), a mass housing estate located in the northeastern part of the city of Odense, the local magazine *UGEavisen* in 1979 portrayed the housing estate as a major source of the neglected children that were ending up at a local orphanage. The article argued that "due to their parents' excessive drinking problems, divorces, and corporal punishments, many Vollsmose children approach the social authorities in Odense themselves."[22] In this view, Vollsmose actively contributed to the destabilization of the entire social structure of families living on the estate. To escape the abuse they experienced at home, children saw no other option but to abandon their housing estates altogether. Yet, instead of turning to alcohol or violence, they approached the public authorities, begging to be removed from their homes.

The representation of juvenile delinquency on mass housing estates not only found expression in the Danish mass media. It also featured in a range of novels from the mid-1970s, in which Danish authors addressed the imagined linkage between mass housing estates and the production of "the dangerous youth."[23] In the mock-documentary, multi-protagonist novel *Blokland* from 1975, Marxist author Michael Buchwald portrays everyday life on the fictive housing estate of Blokland, including the stories of a number of maladapted youth groups inhabiting the estate.[24] The most notorious of these groups was the so-called "black leather boys." Repeatedly assaulting innocent groups of people in the multiple pathways and underpasses of the estate, the group encapsulated the ruthlessness and violence of Blokland. Similarly, in the youth novel *Katamaranen* (The catamaran) from 1976, Bent Haller locates the violent and ruthless behavior of young people in the setting of the concrete environment of a modernist housing estate on the periphery of the city of Aalborg.[25] The novel provided a penetrating socialist critique of contemporary Danish society through the lens of two boys, Peter and Thomas, who attempt to escape the brutal reality of their housing estate by sailing to Sweden in a dilapidated catamaran. As in several mass media representations, Haller and Buchwald depict mass housing estates as more than the context of their plots. Instead, the spatial environment of modernist housing works actively to further the demise of the protagonists. On several

20 Høst-Madsen, "Politiets samarbejde med private og kommunale avgtværn giver store problemer for retssikkerheden."
21 *Danmarks Radio*, "*En kirke i beton*," aired October 23, 1978.
22 Original quote in Danish: "På grund af forældres druk, skilsmisser og korporlig afstraffelse, henvender mange Vollsmose-børn sig til socialforvaltningen i Odense." "De skal vokse op på børnehjem – det er en tilværelse, fortvivlede børn i dag selv beder om" [They will grow up at the orphanage—that is a life that despaired children are asking for today], *UGEavisen*, January 17, 1979.
23 For studies of the role of fiction and literary thinking in the shaping of the welfare society, see Haarder, "The Precariat as Place A Literary History of the Danish Ghetto"; and Horne Kjældgaard, *Meningen med velfærdsstaten: Da litteraturen tog ordet – og politikerne lyttede* [The meaning of the welfare state: When literature took the word—and the politicians listened], (Copenhagen: Gyldendal, 2018).
24 Michael Buchwald, *Blokland* (Viborg: Arena, 1975).
25 Bent Haller, *Katamaranen* (Copenhagen: Borgen, 1976).

Aerial photo of the mass housing estate Vollsmose from the late 1970s. Like Gellerupplanen, Vollsmose included public institutions, communal and mercantile facilities as well as significant green spaces.

occasions, Haller specifically identifies the spatial environment of the estate as the main catalyst of youth violence and crime. While Peter, who had only recently moved to the estate, still upholds a childish attitude and exhibits innocent behavior, Thomas and the other characters who have lived on the estate for several years are hardened and without any form of remorse.

As such, it is possible to identify both significant continuities and ruptures in the public representations of the relationship between juvenile delinquency and urban space in postwar Denmark. On the one hand, mass media and literary depictions of juvenile delinquency on mass housing estates echoed notions of the dangerous youth from the 1940s and 1950s. In both cases, the dangerous youth were depicted in leather jackets and portrayed as an unavoidable consequence of the urban environment. What had changed, in this context, was not so much the perceived links between urban space and the depravation of young people, but rather the geographies and architecture in question. On the other hand, notable differences can also be identified. While the social decline of young people in the big city was tied to the many forms of urban temptation, the destructive behavior of youth gangs on the urban periphery was portrayed as the result of alienation and boredom.

SPATIAL DETERMINISM AND THE REJECTION OF MODERNIST HOUSING

Thus, in 1970s Denmark both mass media and literary representations of mass housing were underpinned by a strong belief in spatial determinism.[26] Such representations specifically tied the social decline of children and young people to the spatial environment of the mass housing estates and thus criticized modernist architecture for actively depraving this vulnerable group. Whereas representations of "the dangerous youth" in the immediate postwar years had focused on the urban environment more generally, emphasis was now placed on the social role of specific forms of architecture. Arguably, this had dramatic implications for the popular representation of Danish modernist mass housing and architecture, as the belief in spatial determinism was a powerful discursive tool in changing the public opinion on modernist mass housing and architecture. The idea that mass housing estates actively corrupted children and young people—the future of the welfare society—into maladjusted criminals undoubtedly produced a striking image in conveying the idea of mass housing as places of crisis and stagnation to the broader public.

Yet, the idea that urban space and architecture had the capacity to shape social life was neither a particularly Danish, nor a particularly new, idea. As urban historian Rosemary Wakeman argues, it had underpinned the entire ideological framework of the transnational New Town movement that proliferated in the postwar decades and was central to the urban visions behind Danish mass housing:

> Perhaps the most quixotic aspect of this vision was that physical design could affect human action and standards of conduct. With the correct urban design and configuration, it was believed, neighborhoods, towns, and regions, and ultimately

26 Besides "spatial determinism," scholars and practitioners often refer to "environmental determinism" and "architectural determinism." For studies of spatial determinism in architectural and urban thought in the twentieth century, see Simon Richards, *Architect Knows Best: Environmental Determinism in Architecture Culture from 1956 to the Present* (Farnham: Ashgate Publishing Limited, 2012); Falender, "Social Housing in Postwar Oslo and Edinburgh," 381–446.

the nation, would transmute into a modern way of life. In alliance with the modernization regime, the planning and new towns became a laboratory for this social engineering.[27]

Thus, in its positive form, spatial determinism had justified a belief that better housing would produce better people. But in its negative form, spatial determinism was conceived as a condemnation of mass housing environments as places that prevented social well-being and produced antisocial behavior and crime. Both forms of spatial determinism found expression and travelled internationally in the postwar decades.[28] Notably, the negative depictions of mass housing that proliferated in the Danish mass media and fictional literature in many ways echoed American urbanist Oscar Newman's theory of "defensible spaces."[29] Linking the existence of high crime rates to the territorial indefensibility of modernist architecture and design, Newman's theory came to influence urban policy in various European countries from the late 1970s onwards, with British geographer Alice Coleman's role in legitimizing Margaret Thatcher's infamous right-to-buy scheme of the 1980s as the most notable example.[30] Although the defensible space theory never gained a strong foothold in architectural theory in Denmark or the Nordic countries generally, the representations of Danish mass housing estates as generators of specific social problems in the form of juvenile delinquency and violence allude to the connections between the Danish case and wider transnational tendencies in urban theory.

The neoliberal potential of the defensible space theory points to the capacity of spatial determinism to encompass several ideological positions at the same time. In the case of Denmark, spatial determinism helped to legitimize both conservative and neo-Marxist critiques of the relationship between urban space and the delinquent youth. Whereas the depiction of the big city as a generator of youth problems had, in the 1940s and 1950s, mainly come from a conservative standpoint, the representations of juvenile delinquency on modernist housing estates were in the 1970s often rooted in a Marxist critique of late-capitalist society. From this point of view, mass housing represented the epitome of alienation and a loss of solidarity within the urban working class, and hence the violent behavior of young people was typically interpreted as a desperate attempt to oppose the hegemonic structures of Danish society.[31] Thus, despite their contrasting ideological content, both positions reproduced the notion that urban space and architecture were capable of actively shaping social relations and subjectivities. In this sense, the ideological malleability of spatial determinism to some extent provides an explanation as to why the critique of modernist mass housing could become so powerful in 1970s Denmark: it resonated on both sides of the political spectrum.

CONCLUSION: MASS HOUSING AND THE "CITIZEN CATEGORIES" OF THE WELFARE STATE

In many ways, the evolution of "the dangerous youth" in Danish mass media and popular culture exhibits how modernist mass housing estates worked actively in shaping the citizen categories of the Danish welfare society. From a planning perspective, mass

27 Rosemary Wakeman, *Practicing Utopia: An Intellectual History of the New Town Movement* (Chicago: University of Chicago Press, 2016), 298–99.
28 See, for instance, Klemek, *The Transatlantic Collapse of Urban Renewal: Postwar Urbanism From New York to Berlin*.
29 Oscar Newman, *Defensible Space: Crime Prevention through Urban Design* (New York: Macmillan, 1972).
30 For studies addressing the transnational history of defensible space theory, see Cupers, "Human Territoriality and the Downfall of Public Housing"; Klemek, *The Transatlantic Collapse of Urban Renewal: Postwar Urbanism From New York to Berlin*; and Sam Wetherell, *Foundations: How the Built Environment Made Twentieth-Century Britain* (Princeton, NJ: Princeton University Press, 2020).
31 This argument also found expression in Danish cultural sociology. See, for instance, Birte-Bech Jørgensen and Leif Thomsen, *Hverdagslivet i en forstad: drømme, realiteter og sociale konflikter* [Everyday life in a suburb: Dreams, realities, and social conflicts], Socialpædagogisk Bibliotek (Copenhagen: Munksgaard, 1978); Leif Thomsen, *Den autoritære by: Storbykrise, bykampe, sociale bevægelser og lokal magt* [The authoritarian city: Metropolitan crisis, urban struggles, social movements, and local power], Kultursociologiske Skrifter, vol. 14 (Copenhagen: Akademisk Forlag, 1981).

housing estates had been designed to fit the nuclear family, but already during the 1970s this type of housing became increasingly associated with socially disadvantaged citizen groups including receivers of social benefits, troubled young people, single mothers, and later on immigrants.[32] In this context, the trope of "the dangerous youth" came to, in various ways, influence discussions about welfare in postwar Denmark. As a citizen category, "the dangerous youth" did not merely emerge in political language and legislation but also *through* the spatiality of the modern city. Representing both a threat to and a critique of modern Danish society, it became a powerful tool in entrenching the negative reputation that Danish mass housing estates acquired from the early 1970s onwards.

During the 1970s, Danish modernist mass housing transformed from a viable solution to one of the most urgent societal challenges of the twentieth century, namely the housing question, and into a political problem that needed to be managed.[33] The combination of an increasing housing surplus, the enactment of new housing policies promoting home ownership through favorable state loans, and a disproportionately high rent level compared to the rest of the housing market left many modernist mass housing estates battling severe socioeconomic difficulties.[34] As Danish social housing associations now struggled to rent out dwellings, modernist mass housing estates became key sites for the municipal allocation of socially disadvantaged citizen groups. While the political legitimacy of the social housing sector became increasingly tied to its role as a provider of housing to underprivileged groups, mass housing estates became prime markers of social decline and impoverishment.

In this context, the category of "the dangerous youth" came to work as a vehicle for identifying and understanding broader welfare issues related to urban poverty and social precarity. As literary scholar Jon Helt Haarder argues, Buchwald and Haller's novels represent the reinterpretation of modernist housing estates into places symbolizing the precariat in 1970s Denmark.[35] In other words, these literary depictions of juvenile delinquency on mass housing estates were not, first and foremost, critiques of modernist housing; rather, they used such housing estates as sites for discussing broader issues concerning class and precarity in the Danish welfare society. More broadly, this illustrates how urban architecture can serve as a symbolic battleground over the values of the welfare society. It also invites us to investigate further the welfare history of urban architecture through the citizen categories which have been imagined, produced, and experienced in relation to different architectural forms and typologies. By spatializing the social underbelly of the otherwise increasingly affluent Danish welfare society, mass housing estates came to influence how social problems and marginalized groups were constructed, understood, and visualized in the Danish public sphere.

32 Høghøj, "Between Utopia and Dystopia," 128–226; Claus Bech-Danielsen and Marie Stender, *Fra Ghetto til blandet by: danske og internationale erfaringer med omdannelse af udsatte boligområder* [From ghetto to mixed city: Danish and international experiences with conversion of marginalized residential areas], 1st edition (Copenhagen: Gads Forlag, 2017), 7–25; and Gudmand-Høyer et al., *Gellerup*, 220–306.

33 Lotte Jensen, "Danmark – Lokal boendedemokrati och nationell korporatism" [Denmark: Local resident democracy and national corporatism], in *Varför så olika? Nordisk bostadspolitik i jämförande historisk ljus* [Why so different? Nordic housing politics in a comparative light], ed. Bo Bengtsson (Malmö: Égalité, 2006), 92–93.

34 Jensen, "Danmark – Lokal boendedemokrati och nationell korporatism." See also The Ministry of Housing, "Redegørelse fra udvalget vedrørende den almennyttige sektors fremtidige rolle å boligmarkedet" [Statement from the committee regarding the future role of the non-profit sector in the housing market] (Copenhagen: The Ministry of Housing, 1986).

35 Haarder, "The Precariat as Place A Literary History of the Danish Ghetto."

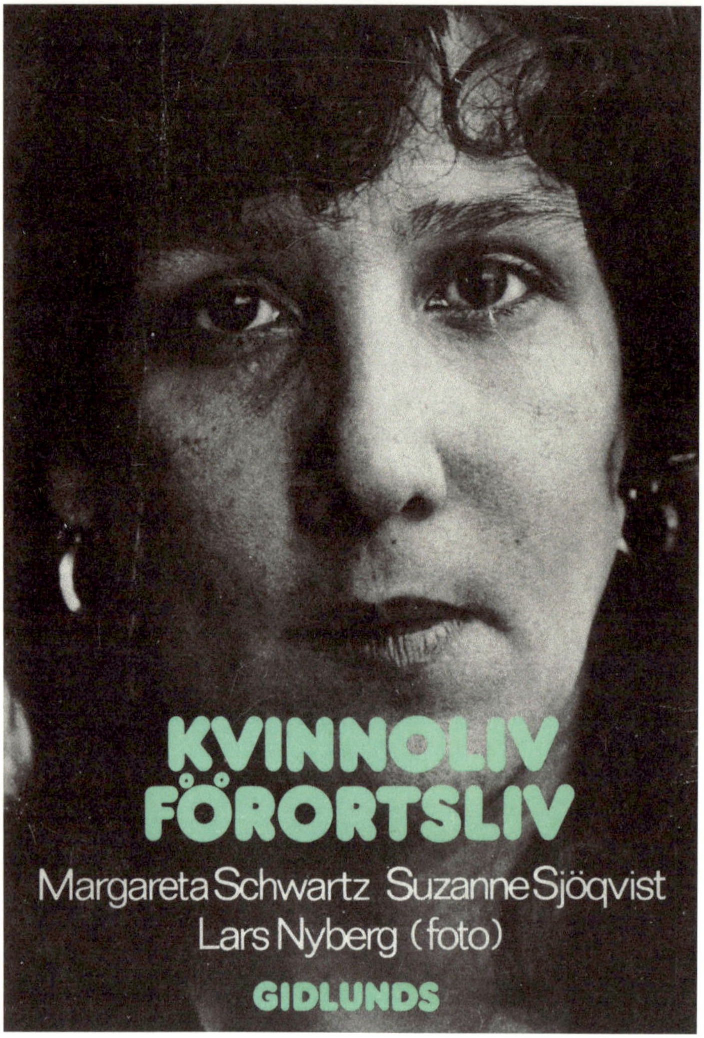

Front cover of the 1978 report *Kvinnoliv, Förortsliv* (Women's life, suburban life) by Margareta Schwartz and Suzanne Sjöqvist, on the town of Norsborg, showing the fictitious character Gun-Britt, an unemployed single mother.

Jennifer Mack

"DADDY IS A COMPUTER"

The Stubborn Story of the Swedish Million Program

In a scathing 1978 report about a modernist Swedish neighborhood located just outside Stockholm, journalists Margareta Schwartz and Suzanne Sjöqvist suggested caustically that "Norsborg's daddy is a computer."[1] There was no other explanation, they contended, for the neighborhood's insensitively designed indoor and outdoor environments. Rather than living architects who would have paid attention to details, materials, and a human-scaled living environment, Schwartz and Sjöqvist attributed the designs to a non-human machine, underscoring how many new Swedish neighborhoods—intended as built utopias to fulfill mid-twentieth-century welfare state promises—had come to symbolize a heartless approach and the failure of postwar design and planning instead.

The report, entitled *Kvinnoliv, Förortsliv* (Women's life, suburban life), appeared as one of many exposés published in the aftermath of the Swedish national housing project popularly known as the "Million Program," which constructed over one million dwelling units across the country between 1965 and 1974. Today, Million Program neighborhoods are still widely presented in the media and in political speech as alienating, unnatural, and unwanted environments. When the areas built during this period are discussed in newspapers or in speeches leading up to national and local elections in the present, the results of architects' designs are portrayed as unequivocal failures. Together with their racialized residents (largely migrants and their descendants), the "ugly" and "inhumane" architecture of the Million Program is blamed for a range of social problems, from unemployment to gang-related crime. This is a far cry from how they were initially envisioned.

From the 1930s, the political agenda to enact a Swedish welfare state—known as *folkhemmet* (the people's home)—had heralded what was supposed to be a new modern era of hygienic, modern housing, and neighborhood infrastructure that would address urban squalor and overcrowding. By the 1960s, this welfare state had turned to ever higher speeds of architectural production to achieve these goals, with its apotheosis in the Million Program and related ideas of "rationalized" (machine-led) construction. Beginning during the period of the Million Program's construction, however, journalists, academics, and the Swedish public alike increasingly conflated its modernist architecture and landscapes with social problems.

In this chapter, I examine several reports commissioned by leading newspapers or carried out as academic studies, and representative of a much larger oeuvre of exposés from the 1970s. All of them include interviews with the inhabitants and descriptions of the physical environment. Here, I look closely at three reports concerning the Stockholm regional suburbs of Tensta, Skärholmen, and Norsborg, all published between 1970 and 1978: during or shortly after the construction of the Million Program.

1 Original quote in Swedish: "Pappa till nya Norsborg är en dator." Margareta Schwartz and Suzanne Sjöqvist, *Kvinnoliv, Förortsliv* [Women's life, suburban life] (Stockholm: Gidlunds, 1978), 31.

2 Åsa Asplid, "Olle Bengtzon hedras med nytt journalistpris," *Expressen*, October 2, 2018, https://www.expressen.se/nyheter/olle-bengtzon-hedras-med-nytt-journalistpris/.

Reports like these entrenched links between modernist designs and resident's apparently miserable lives and, in their repetition and monolithic views, eventually provided a new order of interpretation for Million Program suburbs: a stubborn story. The causal links they made between (bad) architecture and (miserable) social lives entrenched them, a connection that persists into the present day. As Swedish journalists traveled to Million Program neighborhoods in the 1970s to uncover the salacious details of this national mistake, they thus created a new reality: while reporting on residents' unemployment, depression, isolation, and alcoholism, their representations became so powerful that they no longer merely "represented." When the narrative of "failed" Million Program designs took root, there was no longer room for interpretation. These words surpassed mere representation and evolved instead into world-making, a stubborn story that proved unchangeable.

In their book, for example, Schwartz and Sjöqvist explain how their study emerged from their own interests in the plight of women in new suburbs. As they explicitly blamed women's social problems on neighborhood designs, they framed a new reality: suburban women were not living in cities of the future but were trapped in an unfortunate prison made by architects whose hubris had produced unequivocally inhumane, unlivable environments.

Other authors made the revelation of suburban miseries in the Million Program a central feature of their work, such as Olle Bengtzon, a journalist for the newspaper *Expressen*, who wrote the article "Planerad stad eller nybyggd slum" (Planned city or newly built slum) as early as September 1965 and then made it a personal mission to draw attention to shortcomings in contemporary urban design. He became known as "the journalist that the authorities feared the most when he scrutinized their decisions."[2] In his writings, Bengtzon hoped to draw attention to the fact that living conditions for working class Swedes—predicated on earlier ideas of a People's Home offering its "welfare" to all—had not actually improved with the rise of the Million Program.

Notably, even though new neighborhoods were still under construction or had not yet had time for their trees to grow or subways to open, none of the reports' authors treated the neighborhoods as works in progress. Journalists and researchers presented half-finished housing and landscapes instead as final results, producing both immediate and enduring narratives of catastrophe. Bengtzon and his contemporaries often offered subjective descriptions and confirmed their pre-existing biases, yet their words evolved into accepted truths—a stubborn story. Far from being neutral, these initial descriptions continue to shape the way that Million Program neighborhoods are perceived today. Over the decades that followed, these portrayals became not just one version of events but the only story, one from which it was impossible to diverge. Ideas of failure and inhumane living conditions took root culturally, even though trees and bushes were simultaneously growing to leafy complements and shading playgrounds. This single stubborn story remained, despite renovations that added pergolas, pavers, and decorative entrances that began almost as soon as the initial construction projects ended, and despite the reverence for neighborhood designs that past and present residents have often articulated.

BACKGROUND: A PEOPLE'S HOME WITH NO VACANCY

Critiques about the Million Program posited as truths also produced uncomfortable questions about Nordic welfare architecture more generally. During the mid-twentieth century, the Swedish welfare state expanded broadly under continuous Social Democratic leadership, which defined it, as noted, as "the people's home": a catchall term intended to signify the state's promises to care for its citizens and to boost their upward mobility and standards of living.[3] In this spirit, the years before the creation of the Million Program were years of anticipation, defining an era of hope for the future and excitement about new living environments, with the Stockholm Exhibition of 1930 showcasing new designs and collaborations between the state and industry making distribution of these innovations increasingly possible.[4]

During the 1940s and 1950s, government-supported research produced housing and landscape standards that builders taking national loans were required to implement. It was not until the Million Program and its special emphasis on the notion of "rationalized" construction through cranes, however, that spreading these standards on a larger scale became possible. When planned in the 1960s, these scientifically planned neighborhoods represented a welcome departure from the squalor and overcrowding that defined Swedish housing up to that time. Into the mid-twentieth century, urbanization had outpaced the availability of the urban housing stock, which was already woefully low in quality and insufficient in quantity. The Million Program would erase these problems in favor of sanitary outdoor environments and spacious apartments with running water and modern appliances. It would house the new Swedish middle class.

As early as the late 1960s, however, optimism from government officials had already given way to whispers of suspicion in the general public: that the program had been a mistake. The brand-new neighborhoods included lovely new apartments, but the outdoor spaces, infrastructures, and other public and commercial services remained lacking or, in some views, were too prominent. And worse, the architecture might be "ugly." This intensified after the onset of the global economic crisis of the early 1970s, which reduced the need for new housing and made the ongoing construction of the Million Program appear an exercise in waste and illogic.

More information was needed, however, with visits to the neighborhoods needed to gather it. Journalists of the built environment like Bengtzon, feminist journalists like Margareta Schwartz and Suzanne Sjöqvist, and scholars from universities like psychologists Hans Gordon and Peter Molin sought to perform a public service—a warning and a call to action—by offering close descriptions of problems and the unhappiness of residents within individual neighborhoods. These reports represented the Million Program (and its "rationality") as an unequivocal mistake.

3 See, for example, Lars-Erik Borgegård and Jim Kemeny, "Sweden: High-rise housing for a low-density country," in *High-rise housing in Europe: current trends and future prospects*, ed. Richard Turkington, Ronald van Kempen, and Frank Wassenberg, Housing and Urban Policy Studies 28 (Delft: Delft University Press, 2004), 31–48; Claes Caldenby, ed., *Att bygga ett land: 1900-talets svenska arkitektur* (Stockholm: Byggforskningsrådet, 1998); Thomas Hall, ed., *Rekordåren: en epok i svenskt bostadsbyggande* (Karlskrona: Boverket, 1999); Lisbeth Söderqvist, *Att gestalta välfärd. Från idé till byggd miljö* (Stockholm: Formas, 2008).

4 Additional references include Eva Hedman, "A history of the Swedish system of non-profit municipal housing," *Boverket-Swedish Board of Housing, Building and Planning* 1 (2008); Thomas Hall and Sonia Vidén, "The Million Homes Programme: A review of the great Swedish planning project," *Planning Perspectives* 20 (2005): 301–28; Britta Roos and Hanna Gelotte, *Hej Bostad! Om bostadsbyggande i Storstockholm 1961–1975* (Stockholm: Länstyrelsen i Stockholm, 2004).

5 Olle Bengtzon, Jan Delden, and Jan Lundgren, *Rapport Tensta* (Stockholm: Pan/Nordstedts, 1970), 7.
6 Original quote in Swedish: "Till sist tröttnar man på att klaga. Det är kanske det dom väntar på." There is also an outset version of this quote earlier on the page where "sist" is replaced by "slut." Bengtzon, Delden, and Lundgren, 12.
7 Original quote in Swedish: "som hade hållt [sic] på i en timma och bara kommit halvvägs." Bengtzon, Delden, and Lundgren, 18.

1970: MISSING INFRASTRUCTURE —THE SUBURB THAT NEVER WAS

One of the first major accounts of the new towns of the Million Program was published in 1970 under the title *Rapport Tensta*, focusing on residents' struggles and dissatisfaction in the northern Stockholm suburb of Tensta. The suburb was one of several built around Järva Field, a former military training ground, with the master plan finalized in 1965, ground broken in 1966, and the first residents arriving in 1967. When the producers of the report—Olle Bengtzon (author), Jan Delden (photographer), and Jan Lundgren (interviewer)—arrived to the neighborhood, many sections of Tensta remained unfinished, and the subway had not yet been opened. This did not stop them from assessing the new suburb as a living environment, despite referring to this work as a "partial report"—perhaps suggesting that it is only addressing part of the project, an unfinished one—in the opening pages.[5] Certainly, it is difficult to differentiate these objectives or to assess it as a snapshot of a neighborhood not yet finished because the report offers such a scathing critique of the neighborhood.

After a short introduction and a chronology of the neighborhood's construction, past and future, the authors turn to their interviews with Tensta's many dissatisfied residents. Each interview is provided a title taken from the interview material itself, with the very first example as "In the end, you get tired of complaining. Maybe that's what they're waiting for."[6] Opening with such a quote quickly brings the reader into a dysfunctional space, both materially and socially; here, Tensta does not just have problems, but no one listens when you call to complain about them. This frames a discussion of terrible everyday lives in this brand-new suburb.

Most of the interviews in *Rapport Tensta* focus on the lack of "service," especially shops for food and clothing, as well as the lack of public transportation. Daycare serves as an especially controversial topic, given that its apparent absence meant that many women were forced to either stop working or to continue with daycare solutions in other neighborhoods, requiring automobile commutes.

The need for cars also controverted the promises made in the General Plan of Stockholm in 1952: a visionary master plan for the entire region of Stockholm meant to be described in the detailed development plans (*detaljplaner*) that took this vision into real spaces at the local level. A central feature of the 1952 General Plan comprised new suburbs and transit-oriented planning, enabling uncomplicated travel into central Stockholm at a moment's notice. Dissonances between idyllic depictions of modern public transit, copious green spaces, and immaculate new housing with optimal living conditions, along with the timelines for constructing infrastructural projects, ultimately served as sources of disenchantment. In Tensta, for example, some housing was available to residents by the late 1960s, yet the local subway station did not open until 1975.

For example, one 24-year-old teacher with two children, ages one and three, told the authors that she felt sorry for her neighbors who did not own cars, such as when she was walking toward the suburb's only shop and encountered a mother, likely carrying her shopping home, "who had been in progress for an hour and only come halfway."[7] In her nuclear family, she explained, they have two

Front cover of *Rapport Tensta* (Tensta Report, 1970) by Olle Bengtzon, Jan Delden and Jan Lundgren, a reportage on the Stockholm suburb of Tensta, showing a boy playing in a precarious environment.

Woman walking in the Stockholm suburb of Tensta while still under construction, 1970, from *Rapport Tensta*.

People walking on a path in unfinished Tensta, 1970, from *Rapport Tensta*.

Child perched on a post in Tensta, 1970, from *Rapport Tensta*.

cars because both she and her husband work. She noted that the newspaper *Expressen* had asked her and her husband to experiment with leaving their cars at home for a week and taking public transit. She said, "It was a pure test of strength. The poor ones who have to schlep their kids from one bus to another every morning. I was whiny and dull and fell asleep as soon as I came in the door. Some kind of family life wasn't even part of the discussion." [8]

The lack of daycare is portrayed as even more vexing, and the officials responsible for its implementation are described as uncaring or ambivalent to the plight of the residents. For instance, a mother of two working in an office explained that she had thought she might need to quit her job owing to lack of daycare, but then she found a private solution with two women who live close by. She recounted a story of threatening the authorities that she would seek a divorce from her husband because of the impossibility of her situation, suggesting that she could then be "a catastrophic case" (*katastroffall*) instead (meaning a single mother)—a category that guarantees priority for daycare spots. The authorities tried to convince her otherwise, but "one person there thought I should take leave from work. For how many years, one wonders?" [9] This unsustainable situation and its social implications accentuated how life in Tensta simply did not work for many residents.

But in this suburb, according to *Rapport Tensta*, designs do not only create inconveniences and social problems but are actually dangerous to your health—maybe even a risk to your very life. The story is stubborn. Accounts to support it include an interview with a 28-year-old housewife whose three-year-old child, Helene, fell "seven and half meters into blasted stone" when she and her siblings were left alone outside to play.[10] The woman describes Helene's ongoing health issues resulting from this accident, including a recent epileptic seizure and her need to take continuous medication to alleviate the symptoms. Most dramatically, she says, "This summer, they might do a cerebral angiography [a very painful form of neuroradiology that was discontinued in the 1970s]. Then she will have to stay at the hospital for three weeks." [11]

Further evidence of the hazardous conditions for those living in Tensta is provided in a multi-page photo insert in the middle of the report. The photographs shot by Jan Delden depict residents and the state of the project in various guises. One clear theme constitutes images of children in extremely precarious situations: a young child on a bicycle riding on rubble directly in front of a large bulldozer (featured on the cover), a young child balanced much too high on a fence with the weight of a crane perched uncomfortably right over his head, and a group of four young children kicking a ball inside what appears to be a parking garage. The perspectives Delden chooses in arranging these pictures—for example shooting the cycling child from an oblique angle that makes the bulldozer appear to be on a path toward him—accentuate the environmental dangers. The implied culprits are machinery like the bulldozer, as well as unfinished landscapes more generally, and from cars that could back out at any second. Vulnerable children are the implied potential victims of catastrophes (such as that befalling little Helene) that are just about to happen.

To be fair, *Rapport Tensta* does include some residents' voices cautioning that "people should wait until it's finished," and notes that

8 Original quote in Swedish: "Det var rena kraftprovet. Stackars de måste kånka på sina ungar från den ena bussen till den andra varje morgon. Jag blev gnällig och tråkig och somnade så fort jag kom innanför dörren. Något familjeliv blev det ju inte tal om." Bengtzon, Delden, and Lundgren, 18.

9 Original quote in Swedish: "En människa där tyckte jag skulle ta tjänstledigt. I hur många år kan man undra?" Bengtzon, Delden, and Lundgren, 22.

10 Bengtzon, Delden, and Lundgren, 33.

11 Original quote in Swedish: "I sommar skall dom kanske ta en färgskalle på henne. Då får hon ligga inne i tre veckor." Bengtzon, Delden, and Lundgren, 33.

some people believe in Tensta's potential. As in other reports I will describe below, however, these positive assessments are sprinkled throughout a report that highlights the potential for disaster and the inhumanity of it all: the buildings, the machines, the landscapes, the lack of service, and even the missing daycares that prevent mothers from working. Most residents interviewed explain that they plan to remain in Tensta for a few more years at most. Their eyes toward the future are eyes toward other urban and suburban environments where, at least as the authors are concerned, the residents are more in control of their public and private spaces and generally less at risk.

1972: DARING TO COMPLAIN —"ADAPTATION PATTERNS" IN SKÄRHOLMEN

The neighborhood of Skärholmen, built during the early years of the Million Program, was the topic of a report by a group of researchers from Stockholm University published in 1972 under the title, "Man bara anpassar sig helt enkelt" (One just adapts, quite simply!). The report, edited by psychologists Hans Gordon and Peter Molin, investigated living conditions in this regional hub, which was designed in the earlier phases of the Million Program and officially opened in September 1968 with a triumphant ceremony that featured a speech by the Swedish prince. A main focus of Gordon and Molin's text describes how inhabitants of Million Program areas like Skärholmen have been forced to find ways to "adapt" or cope in order to live there, a theme that runs through all three of the reports.

The Skärholmen report grew out of an initiative from a therapist working in an advisory center within Skärholmen who "wanted to know more about the encompassing environment's meaning for human problems, which she was confronted with in ever greater extent in her work."[12] Gordon and Molin, affiliated with Stockholm University, explain that the area had already been critiqued widely, arguing that the only people who ever defended it were the building owners and urban planners.

Departing from the assumption that "adaptation" is necessary for living in a modernist suburb like this, the authors offer a scientific assessment of the various ways residents go about this. They present eight different "coping patterns," which are represented by eight different composite characters, each given a first and last name. The environment is presented as unworthy of human inhabitation.

In carrying out 58 interviews with their research group, Gordon and Molin explain that they have grouped responses into eight different "adaptation patterns." To introduce the eight categories, they begin with "Karin Lindgren," a pseudonym representing, they say, "one of the most common adaptation patterns: An inward material level of calm, low level of contact with people, high sense of isolation and powerlessness, low stimulation in daily activities, resignation, and passivity."[13] It is notable that the number of people in each category diverges widely, with one category represented by one person, another by three people, and another by sixteen (Karin Lindgren's), yet the presentation of the categories on equal footing suggests opinions of equal significance.

The category "Ove Ström" (representing 13 others) has "a strong, open, critical attitude toward Skärholmen as a residential

12 Original quote in Swedish: "Hon som arbetade där ville veta mer om den omgivande miljöns betydelse för de mänskliga problem, vilka hon i allt större utsträckning konfronterades med i sitt arbete." Hans Gordon and Peter Molin, eds., *"Man bara anpassar sig helt enkelt!" En forskningsrapport om människor i Skärholmen* ["One just adapts, quite simply!": A research report on people in Skärholmen] (Stockholm: Pan/Nordstedts, 1972), 8–9.

13 Original quote in Swedish: "stå som representant för ett av de vanligaste anpassningsmönstren: En måttlig materiell anspråksnivå, låg kontaktnivå med andra människor, hög känsla av isolering och maktlöshet, låg stimulans i den dagliga sysselsättningen, resignation och passivitet." Gordon and Molin, 12.

environment."[14] In this group, residents are better off economically than "Karin Lindgren" and express intentions to move away from Skärholmen as soon as possible, especially because of the perceived effects on their children of this "sterile, impersonal, and generally inhibiting environment."[15] These complaining residents are characterized as exhibiting bravery in their candidness, with Gordon and Molin explaining that "Ove Ström" has more liberty to tell the truth because "those who dare to admit this negative attitude also often have economic guarantees and a working situation that makes, in part, compensatory leisure time outside Skärholmen possible, and partially [makes possible] an active scheming to move from there as soon as possible."[16]

Another type, called "Anna Roos," is treated more patronizingly. Gordon and Molin suggest that residents who had lived in urban squalor during the 1930s and 1940s gave themselves tunnel vision about their children having a better environment, forcing them to delude themselves about the quality of their new lives in Skärholmen. This character, "Anna Roos," begins with positive descriptions of Skärholmen and "states that she enjoys it very much" but then explains immediately afterward that "she thinks certain days are so crushing that she doesn't even have the strength to pull up the blinds."[17]

Notably, interviewees with positive view of Skärholmen are sandwiched in between the negative accounts and also depicted as deluding themselves. Their categories of adaptation are defined in one case (representing eight people) as "a let-go mentality" *(låt gå-mentalitet)*, as though these residents are just avoiding the obvious. Another strategy, the researchers note, is defined by "idealizing" and "censorship tendencies." Thus, rather than listening to these residents' testimony and acknowledging the worth of their opinions, the editors provide alternative explanations for their views, such as "Eva Larsson's" description of Skärholmen Centrum as "just like a Roman piazza with playful fountains, and full of life and movement" with a "beautiful view" from her balcony of flowers and water.[18] Gordon and Molin explain that the "Eva Larsson" type is a person who "censors away things that are not in agreement with one's own values and ideas."[19]

In editing *Man bara anpassar sig helt enkelt!* Gordon and Molin appear to have developed their categories prior to arriving on the scene. Their subjective and scientifically suspect "adaptation patterns" lead them to treat interview subjects as not in possession of the facts, "censoring" the truth, or too downtrodden to be able to comment. For them, the positive perspectives—of which there were many—were treated with condescension or skepticism. Presenting the "facts" in a research report thus became a way of solidifying evidence about what were increasingly understood to be wholly dystopian suburbs.

1978: THE STRANGE SOCIETIES OF NORSBORG

In the aftermath of the Million Program, which ended in 1974, the reports of catastrophe continued to flow, and it seemed that the public's appetite for salacious descriptions of suburban wastelands was insatiable. In the 1960s, a new *Botkyrkastaden* (Botkyrka

14 Original quote in Swedish: "en stark, öppen, kritisk inställning mot Skärholmen som boendemiljö." Gordon and Molin, 17.

15 Original quote in Swedish: "steril, opersonlig och allmänt hämmande." Gordon and Molin, 17.

16 Original quote in Swedish: "De som vågar erkänna denna sin negativa inställning har ofta också ekonomiska garantier och en yrkesverksamhet som möjliggör dels ett kompenserande fritidsliv utanför Stockholm, dels en aktiv planering för att snarast flytta därifrån." Gordon and Molin, 17–18.

17 Original quote in Swedish: "Hon uppger sig trivas alldeles utmärkt. Strax efteråt framkommer att hon tycker vissa dagar är så pressande att hon inte ens orkar dra upp persiennerna." Gordon and Molin, 19.

18 Original quote in Swedish: "'Precis som en romersk piazza med spelande fontäner och fullt av liv och rörelse. Vi brukar stå på balkongen på sommarkvällarna och njuta av den vackra vyn, blommorna prunkar i sina trälådor och fontänerna sorlar.'" Gordon and Molin, 20.

19 Original quote in Swedish: "Den finns tendenser till idealiseringar och en viss 'censurbenägenhet': man censurerar bort sådant som inte star I överensstämmelse med de egna värderingarna och föreställningarna." Gordon and Molin, 21.

Front cover of the 1972 report *Man bara anpassar sig helt enkelt* (One just adapts, quite simply) by Hans Gordon and Peter Molin, investigating the Skärholmen neighborhood, built as part of the Swedish Million Program.

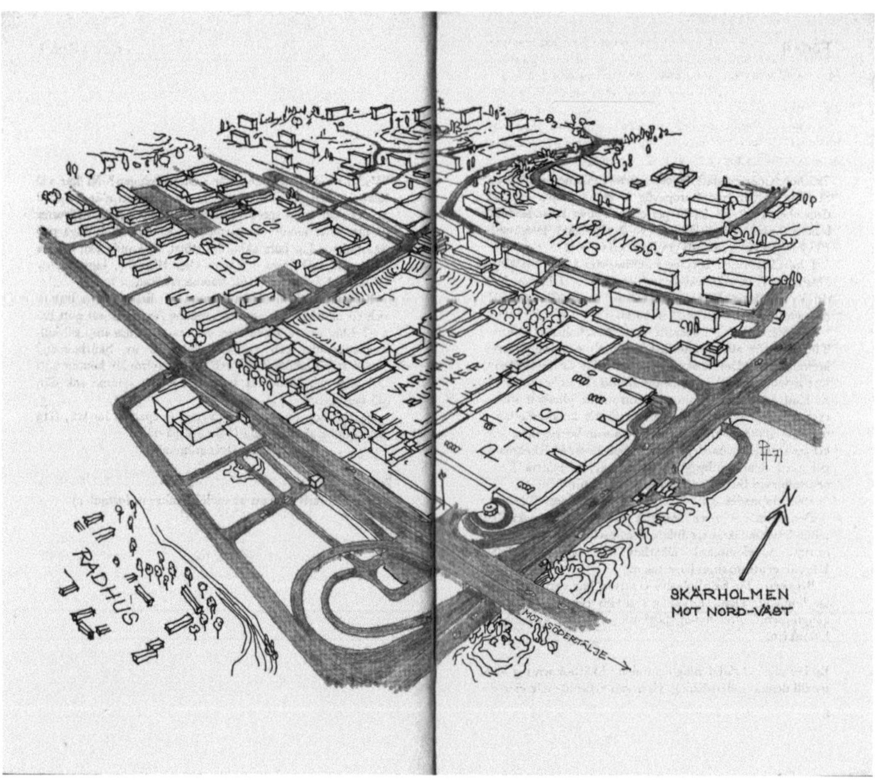

Plan of the town center in Skärholmen, from *Man bara anpassar sig helt enkelt*.

City) was marketed as the wave of the future for the municipality of Botkyrka to the southwest of the capital. Here, the advertisements promised, "every child will have a tree to climb," and a new extension of the subway would connect several new neighborhoods to the center of Stockholm, offering short commuting distances.

By the mid-1970s, however, these dreams of the future had been tempered by a new spirit of pessimism about residents with social problems, unfinished transit, and, especially, the culpability of the modernist architecture and urban designs. The journalists Margareta Schwartz and Suzanne Sjöqvist, together with photographer Lars Nyberg, began to publish a series of articles about the neighborhood of Norsborg in the 1970s. In 1978, these were compiled into the report *Kvinnoliv, Förortsliv* (Women's life, suburban life) and published by Gidlunds, which opened with the line, "The suburb Norsborg 20 km south of Stockholm is a cement slab on top of living soil."[20] For Schwartz and Sjöqvist, a key interest was the plight of women who were left alone all day in suburbs like Norsborg, and how they coped with the spatial and social conditions in which they found themselves. For this reason, they chose a main character: unemployed, 33-year-old single mother Gun-Britt. Her story is central to the text, and, for the authors, her struggles symbolize how the physical environment simply never lets one catch a break.

Norsborg's architectural and urban designs are described as having erased the cultural heritage of those who farmed the land before the project was enacted. Instead, "When the first people came to the new Norsborg, they found no inheritance, no last year's leaves, no weaving begun. They had to start over, it was recently, it was seven years ago."[21] The planning and construction of the environment is thus explained as an obliteration violating both ecology and history, leaving the residents, apparently, hapless in a disorienting, unhospitable environment with nothing left to guide them.

Describing the buildings and landscapes in Norsborg, the authors' sardonic and extended accounts of an imagined architectural design process that repeatedly suggests the absence of a human touch—a lack of care—in its creation. Instead of sentient human architects, we are told, this neighborhood was created by a computer "daddy" who "counted out how everything would be without leaving anything to chance."[22] The speed of construction (five years) is then compared to another Swedish neighborhood of the same size, Halmstad, which, they explain took 500 years to develop. The architects are belittled as having arrived after the computer had finished its work. At this juncture, according to Schwartz and Sjöqvist, they were invited according to the following conditions:

> Did they want to be polite and take care of the finish and add a little spice? If the architects felt humiliated and really first wanted to cry in their mothers' arms and then set fire to the whole project, they at least kept a poker face.[23]

The authors thus portray these architects as both the only characters who could have saved this suburb from itself (if only they had replaced the "daddy" computer) and—at the same time—impotent, cynical fools who go through the motions of supporting the project for a commission that merely allows them to "add a little spice."

20 Original quote in Swedish (and notably the very first line of the book): "Förorten Norsborg 20 km söder om Stockholm är en cementplatta ovanför levande mulla." Schwartz and Sjöqvist, *Kvinnoliv, Förortsliv*, 5.

21 Original quote in Swedish: "När de första människorna kom till nya Norsborg fann de inget arv, inga fjölårslov, ingen påbörjad väv. De fick börja om, det var nyss, det var för sju år sedan." Schwartz and Sjöqvist, 5.

22 Original quote in Swedish: "Pappa till nya Norsborg är en dator. Den räknade ut hur det skulle bli utan att lämna någonting åt slumpen." Schwartz and Sjöqvist, 31.

23 Original quote in Swedish: "Ville de vara hyggliga och ta hand om finishen och sätta lite piff? Om arkitekterna kände sig förnedrade och egentligen först ville gråta i sina mammors famnar och sedan tutta eld på hela projektet, så höll de i alla fall masken." Schwartz and Sjöqvist, 33.

Woman pushing a stroller in Norsborg, 1970s, published in *Kvinnoliv, Förortsliv*.

Construction workers in Norsborg, 1970s, from *Kvinnoliv, Förortsliv*.

The architecture of Norsborg is not merely said to be ugly, however. Over and over again, Schwartz and Sjöqvist tell us, fear of strangers deeply embeds itself in the concrete, with suspicions extending across courtyards and neighborhood boundaries. In fact, Norsborg residents say that the residents of the adjacent Million Program neighborhood of Hallunda are criminals; in Hallunda, they think the same of the Norsborg residents. In fact, the authors continue, "We don't meet anyone who has been subjected to crimes themselves, but everyone has heard about them in some roundabout way."[24] This apparently pervasive fear is represented in the accounts of several residents. For instance, "Mrs A in Norsborg has not been accosted either. But she has of course heard a lot, so for safety's sake she has taped up a photo of her boxer on the front door and a sign with the text: 'Warning, guard dog.'"[25] The authors imply that fear of one's neighbors—especially for women alone—is a universal condition in the Million Program.

These critiques at the scale of urban design also identify the neighborhood as unable to foster neighborly contact and friendship, citing the problems that neighbors have had getting to know each other in a strange society where almost everyone is young and has children. Various residents are described as merely looking out of their windows at others and guessing about their ages or other qualities, of failing to interact with those living in the same building, and of generally being socially isolated. All of these ills are blamed on the design of the neighborhood and the lack of attention paid to the physical and social conditions needed to support such contact. With disdain and irony, they write, "Why would a common registered address create the foundation for a heartfelt friendship?"[26]

But it is not just the outdoor spaces that have failed to become productive of neighborly contact. In their interview with Gun-Britt, Schwartz and Sjöqvist quote her as saying she only feels "at home" when she closes the door of her apartment. They then ask, leading her, "Don't you feel that way on your block and on your street?" The next line in the text reads, "No, it doesn't feel like that."[27] Yet this is not a quote from Gun-Britt. The statement appears without quotation marks, suggesting the authors are paraphrasing their interviewee but not providing direct evidence of her feelings. This is then followed by the statement, "Instead, she feels nervous about living in houses like these."[28] No specific quotations from Gun-Britt herself are provided to support this authorly analysis. To describe how she is "not so relaxed" and "restless" even inside her apartment, Schwartz and Sjöqvist's only quote concerns Gun-Britt's interest in renovating her apartment's interior design and how she would actually like to move to another apartment.[29] These assessments are meant to reflect the problems of Norsborg as a whole but sound, when taken out of context, similar to the dreams of remodeling and upward mobility shared by many people, like Gun-Britt, in their thirties or otherwise.

Again and again, Schwartz and Sjöqvist cherry-pick their quotations and elaborate their descriptions to support claims that seem to have already congealed prior to their arrival to the neighborhood. The tenor of the report seems to have been determined before any interviews were actually conducted, and before any architecture was experienced in person. *Kvinnoliv, Förortsliv*, one could argue, is an exercise in confirmation bias.

24 Original quote in Swedish: "Vi träffar ingen som själv varit utsatt för illadåd, men alla har hört talas om sådana, på omvägar." Schwartz and Sjöqvist, 38.

25 Original quote in Swedish: "Fru A i Norsborg har inte heller blivit antastad. Men hon har ju hört en del, så för säkerhets skull har hon tejpat upp ett foto av sin boxer på ytterdörren och en skylt med texten: 'Varning, hunden vaktar.'" Schwartz and Sjöqvist, 38–39.

26 Original quote in Swedish: "Varför skulle en gemensam mantalsskrivningsadress vara en särskilt god grogrund för innerlig vänskap?" Schwartz and Sjöqvist, 22.

27 Original quote in Swedish: "'Känner du inte att det här är ditt kvarter och din gata?' Nej, så känns det inte." Only the first sentence is presented in quotation marks. Schwartz and Sjöqvist, 26–27.

28 Original quote in Swedish: "I stället känner hon att hon blir nervös att bo i sådana här hus." Schwartz and Sjöqvist, 27.

29 Schwartz and Sjöqvist, 27.

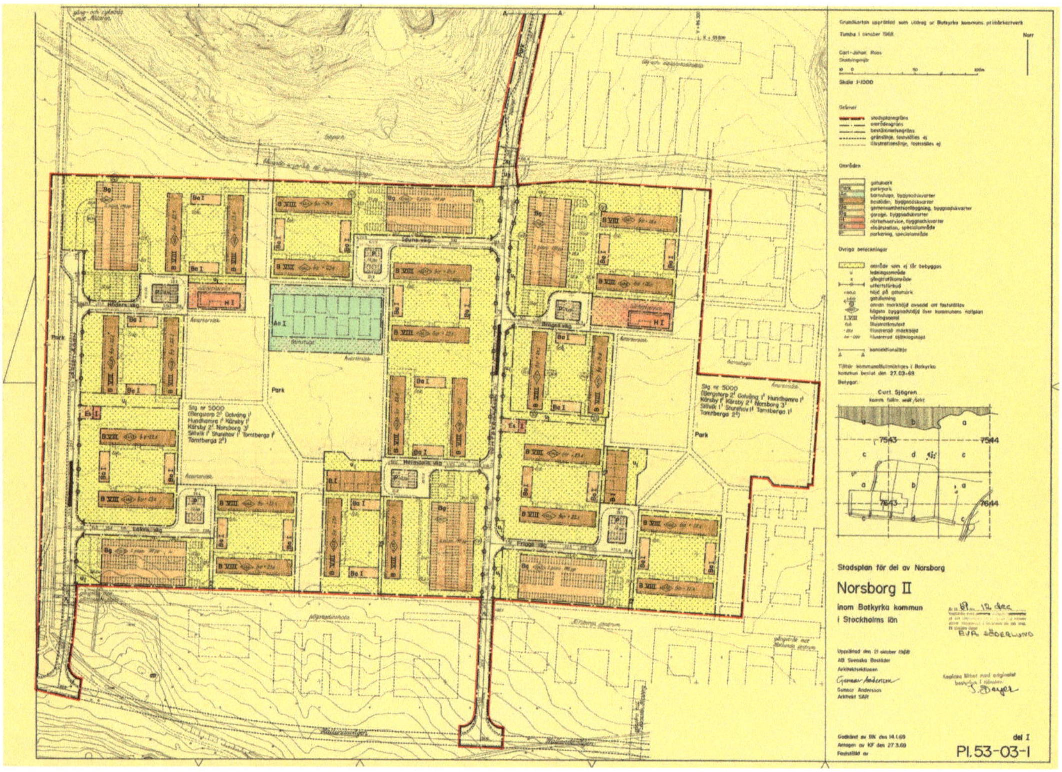

Plan of part of the neighborhood of Norsborg.

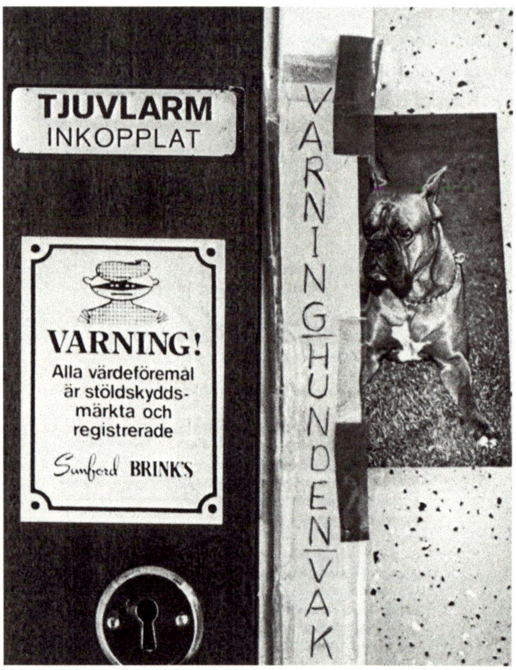

The sign outside an apartment in Norsborg from the 1970s reads: “Burglar alarm activated. Warning: All valuables are anti-theft marked and registered. From *Kvinnoliv, Förortsliv*.

While we might simply understand this as dubious research or journalistic entertainment, the production of reports like these had lasting effects on how the general public—who often never visited the suburbs firsthand—understood these neighborhoods and their social and physical conditions during the 1970s. More alarmingly, the pattern of disparagement in these reports and the almost-immediate understanding of these landscapes and housing as failed products of architectural hubris produced a sense that no redemption was possible. Narrative snapshots were taken of architecture and landscapes in progress, places that were actually in the process of being finished. This static view removed any sense of a dynamic progression or ongoing development of and in the neighborhoods, either architectonically or socially. Schwartz and Sjöqvist suggested that Norsborg could never achieve the beauty, friendship, and everyday public life of older urban centers and thereby implicated the Million Program and its many new town neighborhoods across Sweden, at large.

CONCLUSION: A STUBBORN STORY

Was the Million Program a mistake? This Swedish national project that invested countless crowns and used wide swaths of unbuilt land to build new neighborhoods for modern citizens of the mid-twentieth-century welfare state, and the public wanted to know. Journalists of the 1970s set out for the neighborhoods of Million Program to find answers, with their excursions taking on the quality of a safari. The story they told proved to be a stubborn one.

In all three reports, the authors present only an anemic discussion about how these snapshots of 1970s life in Skärholmen, Norsborg, or Tensta actually represent an *early* phase for these neighborhoods. That they were new towns built from the ground up is presented as an act of violence or hubris, with even the five years of development for Norsborg compared with the 500 needed for Halmstad, being used to suggest that Norsborg can be judged upon its present—and future—merits at the five-year mark. The time that bushes and trees and flowers need to develop, for example, is completely omitted. The emphasis on the non-human designers and "rationalized" designs suggest how this may all be part of the plan. In this sense, the reports are both unequivocal and unforgiving.

Instead, the authors freely assess new suburbs in comparison with older neighborhoods—where trees may have been growing since the last century or longer, and where the fine tuning of urban designs over many decades have made adjustments to residents' experiences—as a scientifically sound analytical act. Furthermore, when visual judgments of modernist designs and the welfare they promised are made, they occur *during* the construction of the Million Program or shortly after its construction, when vegetation was still growing and, in places like Tensta, active building projects were ongoing.

Nonetheless, investigators for reports about the early years of the Million Program were confident in their assessments. They suggested through their disparaging words that one could rightly expect Million Program new towns to become perfect specimens of neighborhood living overnight and that anything less meant that the project at large was misguided and misanthropic: too "rationalized" in its designs made by probable nonhumans. In my interpretation, the writers presented problems in the neighborhoods as intrinsic to the designs, not as temporary hiccups nor as possible frameworks upon which a better future could be built. This "story" was not just one representation, but the only tale it was possible to tell.

Panning the results of the Million Program at the start thus entrenched them. These assessments became a stubborn story, rather than being merely analytical snapshots of a passing moment—that has since made it difficult for Million Program neighborhoods to be understood in any other way. At breakneck pace, journalists and researchers appraised life in half-completed Million Program neighborhoods. Melodramatic depictions (both textual and photographic) conveyed a hellscape of monolithic concrete housing blocks, deserted and dangerous outdoor spaces, eccentric residential behaviors and alcoholism, pervasive social problems and unemployment, women's feelings of depression and abandonment, a lack of infrastructure, and tedious landscapes. Authors of reports in the 1970s thus engrained this stubborn story for good; this Million Program was eternally beyond control.

Psychologists, ethnologists, journalists, photographers, and others all claimed an expertise in the analysis of social conditions, yet all of them included as evidence of the projects' "failure" lurid and often-incendiary subjective descriptions and portraits. They describe misguided architectural theories as materialized in inhumane (concrete) form and repeatedly highlight the struggles of people on the social margins.[30]

In fact, since the 1970s, it has been next to impossible to impart any alternative or positive visions of these modernist suburbs. Today, the ontologies of the 1970s remain visible in the many calls for radical renovations of Million Program neighborhood infrastructures and housing blocks, which are always regarded as in need of intervention. More chillingly, some politicians and planners in Sweden and in nearby countries like Denmark have departed from notions of failure that leave demolition as the only solution to suburban problems, a new form of "ontological politics."[31]

Today, the 1970s reports themselves have largely been forgotten. Yet the authors' prose and choice of analytical frameworks were far from neutral or ephemeral. When their words and photographs demonstrated that compassionless machines and rationalized architecture had apparently defined a human life that was not worth living, these evolved into unruly ontologies. Such ontologies continue to color perceptions of Million Program suburbs into the present day, while circumscribing many decisions made about the futures of these neighborhoods and their residents. Suburbs in progress were treated as results forever, producing both immediate and enduring, obdurate narratives of catastrophe: a stubborn story.

30 Margareta Schwartz went on to become an advisor to the national government on questions of gender equality. See "Till minne: Margareta Schwartz," Dagens Nyheter, April 27, 2021, https://www.dn.se/familj/till-minne-margareta-schwartz.

31 Mikko Joronen and Jouni Häkli, "Politicizing Ontology," *Progress in Human Geography* 41, no. 5 (October 2017): 575.

Parking lot in Norsborg, 1970s, published in *Kvinnoliv, Förortsliv*.

Children playing in Norsborg, 1970s, published in *Kvinnoliv, Förortsliv*.

Christina Pech

THE GREAT BETRAYAL

A Swedish Critique of Welfare State Architecture

Writing in 2024, it's been more than fifty years since a thorough historical assessment of the modern architecture associated with the welfare state commenced. But still today, long after it was called into question and much of its welfare framework was dissolved, modern architecture stirs up sentiments in contemporary architecture discourse. The phenomenon "Arkitekturupproret" (the architecture uprising) dates ten years back to 2014 when it started as a Facebook group, counting among its members students from the KTH School of Architecture in Stockholm. With the explicit aim to fight modern (and neo-modern) architecture and the "uglification"[1] of cities, and to do so in the name of the public interest, the movement has spread to neighboring Nordic countries and the Baltic Sea region. The group focuses almost exclusively on aesthetic and visual qualities, targeting, with the vocabulary of a raging press, predominately selected examples of building stock from the late 1960s and 1970s, and heralding a short moment of architecture and planning from the 1920s. By considerable media coverage and polemic polls (rating, for instance, the "most beautiful" to the "ugliest" building), the movement has raised public awareness around architecture in general and modern architecture in particular.

A similar tendency to critique modern architecture has lately also become evident in a number of popular science publications, which have been disseminated widely by established publishing. In 2016, medical doctor Gösta Alfvén wrote about how the design and building practice of modern architecture had created "unhealthy" environments. The physiognomy of the right angle was critiqued as "anti-human" in a narrative that linked Le Corbusier with extensive postwar demolitions of historic Swedish town centers and the Million Program,[2] while promoting a historic, varied townscape.[3] A couple of years later, similar trajectories surface in Per I. Gedin's award-winning *När Sverige blev modernt* (When Sweden became modern), a biography of Gregor Paulsson (on whom more below). Perhaps more than a biographic portrait, it describes Swedish modern architecture as an amalgamation of scientific racism, and, again, the influence of Le Corbusier that led to demolitions, new urban schemes, and the Million Program.[4]

Without wanting to debate Alfvén's and Gedin's contributions in detail—the topic of this article brings us elsewhere—the point I wish to make here is that theirs is a criticism that equals a specific architectural design with a specific ideology. However, it tends to stop at the level of ideas and does not take actual implementation into consideration; nor does it consider the other actors and the politics—the *society*—that fostered the built environment of the postwar years. Architectural historian Eva Eriksson rightfully mentions the eerie feeling of an unnamed scapegoat in-between the lines of Gedin's book, referring to Social Democracy or even the welfare state as a whole.[5]

1 Arkitektupproret, "About," accessed February 3, 2024, https://www.arkitekturupproret.se/om-au/about-english/.

2 *Miljonprogrammet* (The Million Program) was a large public housing program implemented in Sweden between 1965 and 1974 to boost the availability of affordable housing. The goal was to construct one million new dwellings in ten years which was achieved.

3 Gösta Alfvén, *Ohälsosam arkitektur: En annan sida av funktionalismen* [Unhealthy architecture: Another side of functionalism] (Stockholm: Balkong förlag, 2016).

4 Per I. Gedin, *När Sverige blev modernt. Gregor Paulsson, Vackrare vardagsvara, funktionalismen och Stockholmsutställningen* [When Sweden became modern: Gregor Paulsson, Better things for everyday life, and the Stockholm Exhibition] (Stockholm: Albert Bonniers förlag, 2018), 10.

5 Eva Eriksson, "Myten om Sveriges rasistiska arkitektur," *Svenska Dagbladet*, February 19, 2019.

6 Thomas Paulsson, *Det stora sveket* [The great betrayal], radio broadcast, Swedish national radio P1, May 28, 1972. Excerpts from the show were published in *Arkitekttidningen* 2 (1972): 7 and commented on by Göran Ekblad. See Göran Ekblad, "Vilka är ansvariga för 'det stora sveket'" [Who is responsible for "the great betrayal"], *Arkitekttidningen* 2 (1972): 8.

7 Original phrases in Swedish: "den folktomma skräckens betongvärld," "sveket" and "skönhetstro," Paulsson, *Det stora sveket*.

8 Researchers such as Kristina Grange, Johan Rådberg, Ulf Sandström, and Lisbeth Söderqvist are among those who have analyzed responsibilities in Swedish postwar architecture more recently. Despite some variability, their work supports a reading that is similar to Paulsson's, arguing that many Swedish architects followed the prevailing conditions without voicing notable objections or experiencing conflicts. This is also confirmed by various writings in which architects are heard, such as Claes Caldenby's book about the offices A4 and ELLT or Ragnar Uppman's "professional memoirs." See Claes Caldenby, ed., *Arkitektur i förändring: A4, ELLT, Coordinator 1954–91* [Architecture in transition: A4, ELLT, Coordinator 1954–91] (Stockholm: Svensk byggtjänst, 2000); Ragnar Uppman, *I arkitektens öga: minnes- och debattbok* [In the eye of the architect: a book of memories and debate] (Stockholm: Carlsson, 2006).

The disputes of the present-day debate are not new. In putting the responsibility on the architect, questioning the entire profession's *raison d'être*, and presenting a genealogy of modernism which immediately links politically radical ideas from the early twentieth century with a negative assessment of the building stock of the 1960s, they echo arguments from both the 1930s, and the late 1960s and early 1970s, which were equally harsh and irreconcilable. This text will revisit a politically invested debate from the 1970s, to shed some light on the arguments surrounding the physical environment of the postwar welfare state, and the commencement of the historicization of modern architecture in Sweden.

1972: THE GREAT BETRAYAL

Det stora sveket (The great betrayal) was the title of a radio show broadcast on Swedish national radio on May 28, 1972.[6] The show would debate Swedish architects' actions in virulent terms, putting a finger on one of the most burning points of discussion in the contemporary debate: the architects' responsibility for developments in Swedish architecture and urban design since the 1930s, and results that were considered undesirable, especially in postwar housing.

The radio program was produced by the art historian Thomas Paulsson, who criticized what he described as a denial of the city and the street, broadly speaking, and the environmental shortcomings of this neglect in postwar community building. Paulsson spoke of "the horror of the deserted concrete world" and put the play, the children, and the inhabitants in focus. And this is where "the betrayal" comes in: according to Paulsson, the architects, and their profession at large, had betrayed the actual clients, the people who were to live with and live in postwar Swedish architecture. And, furthermore, not only were the citizens let down, but architecture as a field of knowledge was betrayed. Paulsson pointed to shortcomings in architects' education and described how visions were lacking and architecture's "aesthetic credo" had been sidelined.[7] According to Paulsson, architects seemed willing to carry out whatever the client had ordered without reflection or objection, regardless of who it happened to be.[8] In this agitated tone, parallels were drawn all the way to an Albert Speerian technocracy and the Third Reich.

There are various reasons for examining *Det stora sveket* in the context of welfare state architecture. Firstly, the radio program illustrates clearly the rejection, established in the early 1970s, of the large-scale housing and community-building projects of the 1950s and 1960s. Perhaps less obvious, but nonetheless significant, is Paulsson's way of explicitly connecting the problems of contemporary architecture to architectural modernism or "functionalism," which is the preferred term in Swedish, established in the 1930s. In other words, it links the formative years of the welfare state with its mature present-day (early 1970s) condition. Evidently, Paulsson's overall analysis of the course of events in architecture was negative. Moreover, Paulsson's reasoning resonates with the overtly political nature of Swedish modern architecture: he argues that the political radicalism of the 1930s was watered-down, resulting in postwar environments that had very little to do with the social incentives of modern architecture and left citizens to tackle a very different situation regarding their environments, where other interests were at stake. In the midst of this crossfire stood the architect, who, by abandoning the social ideas of modern architecture, as well as the aesthetic creed of the architect, had let people down and *betrayed* them.

ARCHITECTURE AND POLITICS BEFORE THE WELFARE STATE

Thomas Paulsson was the son of Gregor Paulsson, one of the leading figures and ideologues of modern Swedish design and architecture. An art historian and critic, Gregor was director of Svenska Slöjdföreningen (the Swedish Society of Craft and Design, today Svensk Form) during the interwar period. The organization was strongly influenced by the Deutsche Werkbund's work to improve the quality of industrially produced utility items. Alongside its active effort to enhance standards, Slöjdföreningen acted to establish collaborations between artists and manufacturers as well as educate the public. The social and radical dimensions of the Werkbund's program strongly engaged Paulsson, and he developed the notion of *social aesthetics*—how to make art, design, and architecture available to the largest number of people—in response. According to Hans Pettersson, for Gregor Paulsson, this was ultimately a political question: industry, trade, housing, and social conditions were to be refined through political work and the enhancement of society.[9] Paulsson's and Slöjdföreningen's activities embraced multiple aspects of the domestic environment, including architecture, and their influence on the housing production of the welfare state would become significant. In 1930, Gregor Paulsson acted as Commissioner General of the Stockholm Exhibition, the event that is considered to have launched modern architecture more widely in Sweden and the Nordic countries, and the following year, he contributed as one of six authors to *acceptera*, the closest we get to a manifesto for modern architecture in Sweden.[10]

As a prolific writer and critic of architecture and urbanism, Gregor's son Thomas would follow in his father's footsteps. At the time of the radio show in 1972, his engagement, especially in planning issues, was already long-established. His 1959 doctoral dissertation, "Den glömda staden" (The ignored city), which deals with Swedish urban planning in the early 1900s, marks his position as a hardline interrogator of Swedish functionalism as a social project.[11] While taking a particular interest in urban form and its effect on inhabitants and citizens in the 1960s and 1970s, he targeted the ongoing demolitions of the historical building stock.[12] Father and son also collaborated in various publications and radio programs on several occasions.[13]

Paulsson's argument is characterized by an explicit social reading that directly connects his claims with objections that were introduced from the political left as early as the 1930s. The act of making such a linkage between the modern avant-garde and contemporary architecture was not unique among critics in the late 1960s and early 1970s, and authors debated whether there was a gap, or disruption, in theory and practice between modernism then and

9 Hans Pettersson [also known as Hans Hayden], entry in Svenskt biografiskt lexikon, https://sok.riksarkivet.se/sbl/Presentation.aspx?id=8074&forceOrdinarySite=true; see also the doctoral dissertation: Hans Petterson, "Gregor Paulsson och den konsthistoriska tolkningens problem" [Gregor Paulsson and the problem of interpretation in art history] (PhD diss., Uppsala University; B. Östlings bokförlag. Symposion: Esløv, 1997).

10 Gunnar Asplund et al., *acceptera* (Stockholm: Tiden 1931).

11 Gregor Paulsson, "Den glömda staden: svensk stadsplanering under 1900-talets början med särskild hänsyn till Stockholm: idéhistoria, teori och praktik" [The ignored city: Swedish town planning at the beginning of the twentieth century particularly regarding Stockholm: history of ideas, theory and practice] (PhD diss., Stockholm University, 1959).

12 Paulsson reported on architecture on national radio and produced several themed shows during the 1970s. See, for example, *Det var på 30-talet* [That was in the '30s], broadcast on Swedish national radio P1, January 23 and 29, 1972, or the series *Den nya staden* (The new city), which was broadcast in nine episodes between 1979 and 1980.

13 See, for example, Thomas Paulsson and Gregor Paulsson, *Ny stad: människans miljö* [New city: people's environments] (Stockholm: Almqvist & Wiksell/Geber, 1958); Gregor Paulsson, *Vägar till konsten: från målarkonst till stadsmiljö* [Roads to art: from painting to urban environment], radio broadcast on P1, January 23, 1972; and Gregor Paulsson's autobiography: Gregor Paulsson, *Upplevt* [Experienced] (Stockholm: Natur och kultur, 1974).

now. Similar inquiries also became prevalent in the historical and scholarly accounts that emerged in the late 1960s and early 1970s.

To illustrate this critical political perspective, which proposed deviating from the ideals of the 1930s already at that time, architect Gun Sjödin's 1936 article "Funktionalismens dilemma" (The dilemma of functionalism) can serve as a case in point. The article was originally published in *Kulturfront*, the journal of a socialist and anti-fascist association of the same name.[14] In 1972, it was reprinted in a facsimile version in *Ord & Bild*, one of Sweden's oldest cultural journals that operated as an influential platform for the intellectual left in the 1960s and 1970s.[15] However, Sjödin's article was published one more time, in 1993, in an anthology on twentieth-century Swedish architectural criticism, which points to its relevancy not only for the contemporary discourse but for historiography more generally.[16] Alongside other Swedish contemporaneous accounts such as the keystone publication *acceptera,* Sjödin's article illustrates the politically charged positions at the time of Swedish modernism's implementation. Sjödin's critique centered on what she described as modern architecture's "political dilemma"—namely, the discrepancy between its social aims and conditions of production; functionalism, she writes,

> was created as part of the capitalist rationalization efforts, but it is based on principles that consistently applied can be implemented first in a society organized according to the principle of need—in a *socialist* society.[17]

The blurring of the line between modern architecture on the one hand and industrialism and metropolitan culture on the other, she argued, veiled the fact that modern architecture was linked to a particular trajectory within capitalism: namely that of *rationalization*, a global process dependent on colonial exploitation. The profit-driven escalation to simplify and cheapen turns "necessity into virtue," thus creating modern architecture, Sjödin claimed. Entrepreneurs, soon realizing the commercial value of the new "style," called everything between heaven and earth, fresh and fabulous "funkis," disregarding whether it was rational or not, and the public soon followed suit. In the same ardent tone, she explained how resistance to modern architecture was to a large extent a *chimera*, as an alleged scapegoat called "the traditionalist" was made up only to be revealed.[18]

But what about the architects who were accused of betrayal forty years later? Gun Sjödin argued that the socially progressive young architects of her own generation were also caught up, knowingly or unknowingly, in this capitalist architectural machinery. According to Sjödin, the new design principles attracted many architects who sought more personal designs than the classicist schemes allowed—these architects' work was often characterized by sheer artistry. At the same time, others so passionately adopted rationalization that they reduced everything to fundamental facts. Housing and urban planning became particular targets in such problem solving.[19] For this reason, rationalization was made into a guiding star on the wrong merits, Sjödin argued. Soon, a whole generation could witness how their progressive housing ideas remained on paper since:

14 *Kulturfront* (published 1935–38) gathered several renowned culturally progressive thinkers, artists, writers, and architects. Architects Sven Markelius and Gun Sjödin, who worked at Markelius' office at the time, were both members of the board. Gun Sjödin, "Funktionalismens dilemma" [The dilemma of functionalism], *Kulturfront* (1936).

15 Gun Sjödin, "Funktionalismens dilemma," *Ord & Bild*, no. 1–2 (1972).

16 Peter Sundborg, ed., *Svensk arkitekturkritik under hundra år* [100 years of Swedish architectural criticism] (Stockholm: Arkus, 1993).

17 Original quote in Swedish: "Den tillkom som ett led i de kapitalistiska rationaliseringssträvandena, men den bygger på principer som konsekvent tillämpade kan genomföras först i ett samhälle organiserat enligt behovsprincipen – i ett *socialistiskt* samhälle." Sjödin, "Funktionalismens dilemma," in *Svensk arkitekturkritik under hundra år*, ed. Peter Sundborg (Stockholm: Arkus, 1993), 119.

18 Sjödin, "Funktionalismens dilemma," 117.

19 Sjödin, "Funktionalismens dilemma," 117–18.

Architect Gun Sjödin's 1936 article "Funktionalismens dilemma" (The dilemma of functionalism), initially published in the anti-fascist magazine *Kulturfront*, was given renewed attention in the politically charged debate on modern architecture in the 1970s.

Viewing platform for the press at the 1930 Stockholm Exhibition. The history of this exhibition that launched modern architecture in Sweden was primarily written in the 1960s and figured frequently in debates on the condition of postwar architecture.

> The rent is an equation based not on building costs but on revenue; in other words, the housing question that they [the architects] consider a technical problem and sought to solve within the framework of capitalist society and with capitalist methods is actually a social problem, and a question of distribution.[20]

Writing in the 1930s, this political contradiction in modern architecture was obviously a tangible and dangerous one that threatened to overthrow capitalist society's stability. Sjödin pointed to the developments in early 1930s Germany, where the advancement of modernism was halted under Nazi rule. She did not detail the German situation further but argued that the solution for democratic nations like Sweden had become a more subtle political neutralizing of modern architecture. She observed how the task of the architect-designer was becoming increasingly apolitical, how modern architecture was not practiced fully, and how architects retreated to formalism. So-called social aspects were added to all sorts of tasks only to prevent the young architects from engaging with modern architecture's most burning issue: housing.[21] Sjödin's conclusion is deeply pessimistic, stating that as modernism was undermined in this way, the movement's capitalist foundations were increasingly difficult to reveal, ultimately leading to the impossibility of modern architecture as a project.

FUNCTIONALISM THEN AND NOW

At the time of Sjödin's article in 1936, Swedish society was still to introduce the social democratic welfare state—Socialdemokraterna (the Social Democratic Party) came to power in 1932[22]—and her account still reflects the politically charged nature of the late 1920s, of which the fierce debating of the Stockholm Exhibition was part. However, the political complexities of modern architecture were no less acute in the lead-up to the 1970s. As Sweden's forceful responses to the housing crises (including increased mass production and standardization) started to materialize in the mid-1960s, attention again turned to architecture's underlying ideology and politics. The professional press paid the situation a great deal of attention, frequently drawing parallels to the 1930s: "Their problems are ours, their debate is ours," stated a 1969 editorial in *Arkitekten*, the architects' union's magazine.[23] These political aspects were not least brought up in a critical revisiting of the Stockholm Exhibition and reminders that support for the exhibition and its modern architecture mainly came from the conservative press. The architects' societal loyalties were thus scrutinized, and previous generations' bourgeois values were recapitulated in a tone that could be both agitated and rhetorical: one article said it was probably the architects of the 1930s who had passed the ball to the production system of big business: "a pass between elites."[24]

Architecture was also highly present in the daily press throughout the 1960s and 1970s, where critique was voiced not only by specialized architecture critics but also by way of evaluations of architecture made by diverse cultural actors. With the establishment of the Swedish Museum of Architecture in 1962, a whole new public institution for the dissemination of architecture was

20 Original quote in Swedish: "hyran är en funktion inte av byggnadskostnaden utan av avkastningsprocenten; kort sagt, att bostadsfrågan, som de betraktar som ett tekniskt problem och sökt lösa inom det kapitalistiska samhällets ram och med kapitalistiska metoder, i själva verket är ett socialt problem, en fråga om fördelningen." Sjödin, "Funktionalismens dilemma," 118.
21 Sjödin, "Funktionalismens dilemma," 119.
22 Socialdemokraterna formed a minority government between 1932 and 1936. From 1936, they were in power until 1976, in periods in coalition with center-conservative Bondeförbundet (Farmer's union). During the Second World War, a government of national unity was led by social democratic prime minister Per Albin Hansson.
23 Original quote in Swedish: "att dess problem är våra, att dess debatt är vår." Editorial, *Arkitekten* no. 8 (1969): 217.
24 Original quote in Swedish: "En passning mellan eliter." Kurt Bergengren, "Arkitekterna – hur dribblar dom?" [The architects: how do they dribble (the ball)?], *Aftonbladet*, August 8, 1972.

installed. Founded by the Swedish Association of Architects (SAR), the museum soon became a beacon of debate, especially casting a critical eye on urban development and the substantive demolitions of the historic building stock. Importantly, this contemporary critique went hand-in-hand with the historical analysis of the early stages of modern architecture in Sweden, making the critique a historiographical project as well.[25]

Among the more scholarly accounts, art historian Per G. Råberg's research stands out as one of the first and arguably still most thorough investigations of Swedish modern architecture. Råberg's doctoral thesis and publication *Funktionalistiskt genombrott: en analys av den svenska funktionalismens program 1925–1931* (Functionalist breakthrough: An analysis of Swedish functionalism's program 1925–1931), examines the stakeholders, events, writings, and buildings leading up to the Stockholm Exhibition in 1930.[26] Råberg's analysis of the explicit intentions of Swedish architects and the actual results of their work, like Gun Sjödin's, demonstrated discrepancies between theory and practice in Swedish modern architecture. Contrary to what was claimed by the main protagonists themselves, the movement, he argued, primarily resulted in the launch of a new aesthetic. The social and rational motives that the actors strongly emphasized were, according to Råberg's reading, merely a rhetorical packaging to carry out an "intuitive visual discovery."[27] Råberg argues that despite an official rejection, the architects, in fact, retained much of a traditional artistic subjectivism. The resulting modern architecture was more than the consequence of a particular ideological conviction—rather, it was prompted by architects' adaptation to a new market dictated by technology and industry.[28] Again, this echoes Sjödin's concern from the 1930s: what was packaged as a social project of architecture with the users' interests in mind turned into a project of form and aesthetics that could not, or was never intended to, meet the users' needs.

In relation to our current concerns with historicizing welfare state architecture, Råberg's observation that the discrepancy between theory and practice had also cast a shadow over the prevailing historical studies is of particular interest. He describes available accounts of functionalism's breakthrough as "puzzling," arguing that the authors of those accounts neither reflected on nor abandoned a formalistic analytical approach. Rather, functionalism was treated as a style despite its pronounced "rationalist theories" and "anti-aesthetic programs."[29] In this respect, Råberg's research would point to a political lacuna in the historiography of modern Swedish architecture, exposing how the rhetorics of the architect-pioneers were taken for granted and not sufficiently analyzed. Indeed, this may have contributed to suppressing the politically heated debate of the 1930s later on, in a history that voices like Sjödin's can help to unpack and nuance.

Per G. Råberg's research would strongly influence ways of describing and analyzing functionalism in the 1970s. The thesis was first published by the Swedish Museum of Architecture and became an essential theoretical starting point for the museum's major critical review of Swedish functionalism, i.e., the traveling exhibition *Aufbruch und Krise des Funktionalismus: Bauen und Wohnen in Schweden 1930–80* (The breakthrough and crisis of functionalism: Swedish housing 1930–80), which premiered in Munich in 1976. By

25 Thordis Arrhenius and Christina Pech, "The Swedish Museum of Architecture 1962–1978: The Making of a National Museum of Architecture," *OASE* 99 (2017), 46–55.

26 The thesis was originally published by The Swedish Museum of Architecture in a simple edition in 1970. In 1972, it was published by Norstedts publishers with a new title: *Funktionalistiskt genombrott: radikal miljö och miljödebatt i Sverige 1925–1931.* The debate surrounding the Stockholm Exhibition was also analyzed in Råberg's 1964 licentiate thesis. See Per G. Råberg, *Funktionalistiskt genombrott: en analys av den svenska funktionalismens program 1925–1931* (Stockholm: The Swedish Museum of Architecture, 1970); Per G. Råberg, *Funktionalistiskt genombrott: radikal miljö och miljödebatt i Sverige 1925–1931* [The breakthrough of fuctionalism. Radical environment and the environmental debate in Sweden 1925–1931] (Stockholm: Norstedts, 1972); Per G. Råberg, "Stockholmsutställningen 1930: debatt och kritik" [The Stockholm Exhibition of 1930: Debate and critique] (licentiate thesis, Stockholm University, 1964).

27 Original phrase in Swedish: "intuitiv visuell upptäckt." Råberg, *Funktionalistiskt genombrott*, 204.

28 Råberg, *Funktionalistiskt genombrott*, 304–6.

29 Råberg, *Funktionalistiskt genombrott*, 11.

1980—the year of the fiftieth anniversary of the Stockholm Exhibition—the exhibition reached Stockholm, and the revised catalog remains a notable scholarly contribution to the history of Swedish twentieth-century housing. Neither book nor show is presented in more detail here, but they form an essential backdrop to the simultaneous architectural debate in the national media.[30]

A BETRAYAL OF WHOM? DEBATING ARCHITECTS' RESPONSIBILITIES

The above account has attempted to lay the foundation for a detailed discussion of the architectural discourse around 1972, which centered on the merits of Swedish modern architecture, its authors, and their responsibilities. Thomas Paulsson's radio program was followed by a debate in *Dagens Nyheter*, one of the major daily nationwide newspapers which would bring the issues to an even wider public and last well beyond the summer of 1972.[31] While contributors to the debate initially went on to address professional vocations and competencies, including education and artistic ability, it was the author and critic Torsten Ekbom who turned up the temperature by advancing the most combative opinions. This included Ekbom's call for a new Stockholm Exhibition as a kind of protest exhibition against the "betrayal of established architects." [32] He drew attention to the merits of early Swedish functionalism and highlighted the buildings along the street Askrikegatan in Gärdet district in Stockholm as exemplary and still "astonishingly fresh and modern." [33] According to Ekbom, the first generation of functionalists were too far-sighted and radical to have their ideas realized in their time. The original ideological aspects had been disregarded or even misinterpreted and misused by later generations.[34]

While Ekbom argued along the lines of Paulsson (and Sjödin), he would go back further than the Stockholm Exhibition to a time and place even more politically and aesthetically radical, proposing a connection to the Russian constructivism of the 1920s.[35] To find a way out of modern architecture's dilemma, he sought nourishment in an allegedly less ambiguous, more politically radical period. But was this the time for a reboot of functionalism, forty years later, to realize the visions that had not been realized? There, opinions differed sharply.

Architect and KTH professor Hans-Erland Heineman picked up on the idea of betrayal. Heineman—a longstanding critic at the other major national newspaper *Svenska Dagbladet*, who had been consistent in his emphasis of artistry as the architect's particular area of expertise—acquitted the architects by saying that the fault was not theirs but rather that of a society that didn't value creativity enough. He was explicit about the devastating social and cultural effects that the modernist architect's comprehensive role in planning had had on the environment.[36] However, the architect must also come clean about this professional vocation, and he later argued that it was time not to hide aesthetic arguments behind a "quasi-scientific vocabulary." [37]

Architect and urban historian Björn Linn relieved the architects, too, of responsibility, rather tracing the problem to an outdated view of the architect's role. In a historical exposé of changing conditions

30 See Christina Pech, "Arkitekturmuseets utställning Funktionalismens genombrott och kris: ett bidrag till historieskrivningen om svensk 1900-talsarkitektur" [The Swedish Museum of Architecture's exhibition "Functionalism's breakthrough and crisis: A contribution to the historiography of Swedish architecture in the 1900s], in *Forskning i centrum* [Research in the center], ed. Monica Sand (Stockholm: Arkitekturmuseet, 2014), 33–64.

31 The debate included the following articles: Torsten Ekbom, Motroten (column), *Dagens Nyheter*, June 5, 1972; Hans-Erland Heineman, "Är sveket arkitekternas?" [Is it the architects who committed the betrayal?], *Svenska Dagbladet*, June 8, 1972; Björn Linn, "Arkitekten kan inte lösa politiska problem" [The architect cannot solve political problems], *Dagens Nyheter*, June 21, 1972; Torsten Ekbom, "Skräckhusen – är det politikerna som har ritat dem?" [The horror houses: Is it the politicians who designed them?], *Dagens Nyheter*, June 27, 1972; Bengt O. H. Johansson, "Arkitektur – eller kosmetika?" [Architecture—or makeup?], *Dagens Nyheter*, July 4, 1972; Torbjörn Lundgren, "Hyvla inte bort naturen!" [Don't chisel away nature!], *Dagens Nyheter*, July 7, 1972; Hakon Ahlberg, "Arkitekturkris i den västliga välfärdsvärlden?" [Architectural crisis in the western world of welfare], *Dagens Nyheter*, July 11, 1972; Björn Linn, "Vem är den svenske arkitekten?" [Who is the Swedish architect?], *Dagens Nyheter*, July 14, 1972; Torsten Ekbom, "Arkitektens estetiska ansvar" [The aesthetic responsibility of the architect], *Dagens Nyheter*, July 20, 1972; Sune Lindström, "Visst kan arkitekten påverka!" [Of course architects can exert influence!], *Dagens Nyheter*, July 26, 1972; Kurt Bergengren, "Arkitekterna – hur dribblar dom?".

32 Original phrase in Swedish: "Etablerade arkitekternas svek." Ekbom, Motroten column.

33 Original phrase in Swedish: "förbluffande fräscht och modernt." Ekbom, Motroten column.

34 Ekbom, "Arkitektens estetiska ansvar."

35 Ekbom, "Arkitektens estetiska ansvar."

36 Heineman, "Är sveket arkitekternas?"

37 Original phrase in Swedish: "Kvasivetenskaplig vokabulär." Hans-Erland Heineman, "Arkitekt i föränderligt samhälle," *Svenska Dagbladet*, November 23, 1972.

Cover of the exhibition catalogue *Aufbruch und Krise des Funktionalismus*, 1976. This traveling exhibition, which premiered in Munich, was curated by the Swedish Museum of Architecture and offered a scholarly and critical account of developments in Swedish housing from the 1930s through the 1970s.

Highlights of 1930s housing were mentioned as exemplary in the 1970s polemical debate. Journalist Torsten Ekbom described Askrikegatan in Stockholm as astonishingly fresh and modern.

SVENSKA DAGBLADET Torsdagen den 8 juni 1972

Är sveket arkitekternas?

Den speciella egenskap som inte enbart är fantasi utan en ofta intuitiv kanalisering av intryck, erfarenheter och kunskaper i konstruktiva projekt gynnas inte av rådande meriteringssystem, som nästan automatiskt sållar bort den kreativa begåvningen, skriver arkitekt HANS-ERLAND HEINEMAN i ett bemötande av fil. dr Thomas Paulsson, som i radion under rubriken "Det stora sveket" givit arkitektkåren "en gruvlig salva".

Är samhällena bara "följsamt anpassade till bilarnas krav?

HANS-ERLAND HEINEMAN

VAD SVERIGE LÄSER

bridge

Det är inte arkitekternas fel att vi saknar ett humanistiskt präglat byggande, skrev arkitekt Björn Linn i ett debattinlägg. Det är det visst det, menar Torsten Ekbom i sitt svar. Arkitekternas rörelsefrihet var hårt kringskuren redan på trettitalet, men då fanns entusiasm, pionjäranda och opposition, allt det som i dag lyser med sin frånvaro.

SKRÄCKHUSEN – är det politikerna som har ritat dem?

Sheraton Hotel, den vidriga betongparken på Tegelbacken (t v), departementsbyggnaden intill Sheraton, etc... allt detta är ritat av inkompetenta arkitekter, totalt renons på all estetisk sensibilitet, skriver Torsten Ekbom.

TORSTEN EKBOM

The daily press also discussed the architects' responsibility in light of contemporary architecture. Hans-Erland Heineman, "Är sveket arkitekternas?" (Is it the architects who committed the betrayal?), *Svenska Dagbladet*, June 1972.

In the heated debate during the summer of 1972, rhetorical questions were often juxtaposed with pictures of concrete buildings and heavy car traffic, contributing to the arguments against contemporary modern architecture and the architects' role in it. Torsten Ekbom, "Skräckhusen – är det politikerna som har ritat dem?" (The horror houses: Is it the politicians who designed them?), *Dagens Nyheter*, June 1972.

during the 1900s, Linn painted a picture of a development whereby the freedom that architects enjoyed around 1930 had been increasingly curtailed. In 1972, he argued, architects were bound by different types of governance—legislation, production technology, and political goals—and since the problems were political, not aesthetic, the architect couldn't solve them.[38] In a reply, Torsten Ekbom objected to the split between politics and form, claiming that the architects could not abdicate responsibility. After all, it was not the politicians who had designed the "horror houses" in Stockholm, Ekbom pointed out.[39] After this round, the director of the Swedish Museum of Architecture Bengt O. H. Johansson sought to clarify the museum's position. The museum's critical activities were motivated by the fact that the power structure of society conditioned architecture, Johansson argued, explaining that this was why the museum devoted little space to "aesthetic issues, or utopian, politically naïve architects' dreams."[40] For the museum, it was important to criticize, among other things, housing policy and what Johansson described as commercial urban devastation. It also included fighting some "sham solutions" to the societal problems that the 1930s generation of architects had turned into "planning dogmas."[41] Johansson asked if Ekbom hadn't noticed that the modernist architects had actually achieved what they dreamed of and referred explicitly to the results in Per G. Råberg's thesis (i.e., that the 1930s generation were more interested in aesthetic exercises than reforming society with architecture).[42] The position of the Museum of Architecture was thus clear on the matter: functionalism was a dead-end, and for the future, there was hardly anything to be gained from the 1930s.

Ekbom's first article thus suffered a backlash in the following exchange, and the deliberately pointed claims opened an abyss in different interpretations of functionalism and its relationship to the architecture of the postwar welfare state. To what extent and in what way architects could be held responsible varied. But Ekbom's way of reconnecting with the 1930s to retrieve new visions met with little understanding at all. The sum total of several writers' analysis was rather that one would not search for alternatives in the 1930s if one disliked today's architecture. What had happened in Swedish architecture followed a logical but undesirable chain of development.[43]

After the first exchanges described above, which still addressed the overall (moral and political) question of social betrayal and the architect's power over the results of welfare state housing, the debate became more technical and retreated toward aesthetic concerns.[44] Key questions revolved around the architect's area of competence and *raison d'être* as an artist. It was debated whether architects had been given too little or too much power and if the lack of artistically adequate architectural projects had roots in structural, educational, or aesthetic shortcomings. Entries by architects Hakon Ahlberg and Sune Lindström, respectively, should be mentioned as they reveal a generational shift. Both were practicing modernist architects of the first generation (albeit with different careers) and contributed to the 1972 debate by acknowledging the huge responsibility resting on the architect while maintaining a more positive evaluation of the outcome of the modern architecture implemented in Sweden in the 1930s.[45] Ahlberg built a bridge to the 1930s when pointing out that Ekbom's objections to contemporary architecture

38 The article is an elaboration of a column in *Arkitekttidningen*. See Björn Linn, "Har arkitektyrket någon framtid?", *Arkitekttidningen* 21/22 (1971): 15; Linn, "Arkitekten kan inte lösa politiska problem."

39 The "horror houses" mainly referred to the 1960s government blocks around Tegelbacken, but the School of Architecture's new building in Östermalm (opened 1970) was also included. Ekbom, "Skräckhusen – är det politikerna som har ritat dem?"

40 Original phrase in Swedish: "estetiska frågor, eller utopiska, politiskt aningslösa arkitektdrömmar." Johansson, "Arkitektur – eller kosmetika?"

41 Original terms in Swedish: "skenlösningar" and "planeringsdogmer." Johansson, "Arkitektur – eller kosmetika?"

42 Johansson, "Arkitektur – eller kosmetika?"

43 Linn, "Arkitekten kan inte lösa politiska problem"; Ahlberg, "Arkitekturkris i den västliga välfärdsvärlden?"; Johansson, "Arkitektur – eller kosmetika?".

44 In a survey focusing on the assessment of 1960s multi-family dwellings in architectural press and architectural competitions, Kristian Berg has argued that articles and presentations focused on a wide range of societal and technical questions, and rarely on design matters or aesthetics. The content of Berg's study precedes the present text chronologically and the results form an interesting backdrop for understanding the change of criticism in the 1970s. Kristian Berg, "Ideal i arkitekturen" [Ideals in Architecture], in *Rekordåren – en epok i svenskt bostadsbyggande* [The Record Years—an epoch of Swedish housing], ed. Thomas Hall (Karlskrona: Boverket, 1999), 59–94.

45 Ahlberg, "Arkitekturkris i den västliga välfärdsvärlden?"

echoed the criticism once directed at 1930s modern avant-gardism in their underlining of a "lack of aesthetic sensibility."[46]

Beginning with Paulsson's description of a "betrayal," the 1972 debates in different media highlight how architecture, society, politics, rationalism, and aesthetics, or their more viable synonyms, entered an entangled relationship where positions are difficult to single out. The excerpts raised here show that opinions differed on the architects' responsibilities and the underlying reasons for what was described as a failure to respond to the actual clients' needs by Paulsson. But regardless of where debaters put themselves in terms of political, ideological, educational, or aesthetic factors, the overall lesson that can be drawn out of the debate is a shared sense of dissatisfaction with contemporary architecture and a sense of disciplinary crisis as we entered the 1970s.

POLITICS BECOME AESTHETICS

Over a strikingly short period after the Second World War, Sweden's rapid urbanization fundamentally changed living and housing patterns. The physical transformation of society engaged people far beyond the circles of architects and planners. Architecture and urban matters were more present in the public debate in the 1960s than they are today; debaters of culture, writers, and artists voiced their concerns in both national newspapers and the specialized press. Above all, the suburbs were put center stage, and the criticism was harsh—well-known authors described the spread of an experience of emptiness and loneliness in the idyll of *folkhemmet* (the people's home) and pointed out the shortcomings of the suburbs' architectural design.[47] And as the largest scale of postwar housing initiatives started manifesting in the late 1960s, some Million Program suburbs were met with irreconcilable disapproval. This critique was paralleled by a commitment to the cultural and historical dimensions of urban development, a position present in the extensive criticism that met the ongoing demolitions of historical buildings in town centers.[48]

In all, the discontent with contemporary housing and urban planning extended to modern architecture in general but grew progressively more complex and contradictory in the next decade. By the end of the 1970s, the pendulum had swung so that modern architecture is sometimes still singled out as a deterrent example but, intriguingly, more often hailed as a role model and solution for future practice.[49] The present brief excerpt from the discourse, which departed from a radio show in 1972, stops short at the threshold of these changes while trying to introduce two tendencies that came to affect the evaluation of modern welfare architecture: its historicization and aestheticization. The historicization was triggered through the critique of the contemporary to better understand the course of events. At that time this was still very much about analyzing what went wrong—and who did wrong, however, slowly but surely, the scrutiny and mapping of stakeholders, projects, policies, and discourses accumulated certain conclusions about modern architecture and whether it was possible or desirable to do modernism right, to make it a fully-fledged tool, also politically, for a welfare society. The relationships to earlier phases of modernism were looked at carefully and intriguingly several of

46 Original phrase in Swedish: "Bristen på estetisk sensibilitet." Ahlberg, "Arkitekturkris i den västliga välfärdsvärlden?" Ahlberg is not the most obvious representative of Swedish functionalist architecture. See, for example, Eva Eriksson's epilogue in *Den moderna staden tar form* which nuances the relationship between Swedish functionalism and classicism. Eva Eriksson, *Den moderna staden tar form: Arkitektur och debatt 1910–35* (Stockholm: Ordfront, 2001), 492.

47 Several writers followed with great interest the course of events in Swedish architecture, see, for example, the themed issue of *Arkitektur* 1 (1966), or P. C. Jersild's novel *Babels hus* and Lars Gustafsson's novel series *Sprickorna i muren*, both of which cast a critical eye over architecture as an expression for the contemporary development of society. Stig Claesson, "För arkitekter att läsa" [For architects to read], *Arkitektur* 8 (1965); P. C. Jersild, *Babels hus* (Stockholm: Bonnier 1978); and Lars Gustafsson, *Sprickorna i muren* (Stockholm: Norstedts 1984).

48 Emelie Eriksson's doctoral dissertation "Stockholm med modernismen i centrum. Cityomdaningen ur ett aktörs- och ett mediaperspektiv" [Stockholm with modernism in the center: The transformation of the city center from an actor and media perspective] (PhD diss., Stockholm University, 2004) provides valuable insight into attitudes toward urban redevelopment in Stockholm by studying articles published in *Dagens Nyheter* and *Arkitektur* between 1955 and 1973. According to Eriksson, the number of articles increase between 1967 and 1972 but decrease sharply after that. Initially, the attitudes toward urban rejuvenation are generally positive but toward the mid-1960s a shift is noted and the negative criticism culminates in 1969.

49 Christina Pech, "Arkitektur och motstånd: om sökandet efter alternativ i svensk arkitektur under 1970-talet" (PhD diss., KTH Royal Institute of Technology, Stockholm; Makadam: Stockholm and Gothenburg 2011).

the arguments and the political analyses that surfaced in the 1970s recuperated critical standpoints from the 1930s, here exemplified by the reprinted version of architect Gun Sjödin's article from 1936.

According to the Swedish debaters in the early years of the 1970s, modern architecture, and the architects' capacities to implement a socially equitable design appeared to have reached a dead-end. Political practice, be it market-oriented capitalism or a social democratic welfare state, was incompatible with the utopian impetus of modern architecture and the architects' role therein. So the question of betrayal surfaced: a betrayal of citizens, which followed from a betrayal of political ideas (be it insufficient political consciousness, lack of accurate tools, or lack of political willingness) that would negatively affect the architect's task to provide citizens with high-quality buildings, in this case, specifically housing.

Returning to 2024, we witness how, in public debates and popular history, aesthetics has become politics in the perception of modern architecture. Design that is considered undesirable is equaled with an undesirable political development. Such linkage was apparent already in the Stockholm Exhibition quarrels in the 1930s and echoed, as we have seen, in the 1970s' analysis of modern architecture's unfolding. Today's debate repeats the mistake of the 1970s of omitting the immediate postwar years in the historical analysis of causes and effects in modern housing production between 1930 and the late 1960s. And the debate doesn't seem to have learned the lesson from the 1970s: that the problem of modern architecture rested in the fact that the utopian and revolutionary rhetoric of the 1930s was taken for granted and insufficiently analyzed in the light of its actual political implications. Architecture's actual effects and real possibilities in reforming society were never exposed. What was left was an anomaly, a socialistic creed that relied on a capitalistic system, which solidified in a certain design aesthetic. The present text has pointed to an awareness and an interest in these political conditions of architecture that were soon lost.

Today, this connection between aesthetics and politics is complete: in Swedish architectural debate, the appearance of modern architecture is oftentimes equated with totalitarian political ambitions without any in-depth analysis of the political system that facilitated the aesthetics. And the idea of betrayal has returned full force when the architects are, more or less, alone held responsible for the shortcomings of Swedish architecture during the welfare state era. But the idea of betrayal seldom goes beyond the individuals, and never asks whether the architects ever wanted to or believed in the possibility of changing society through form in the first place. In relation to welfare architecture, much still remains to be done when it comes to examining the infrastructures of thought and the vectors of power that govern them.

Martin Braathen

CAUGHT IN THE NET OF SOCIAL DEMOCRACY

Norwegian Marxist-Leninism and Postwar Architecture

In 1970, Norwegian architectural discourse was shaken by the introduction of a radical ideological movement: Marxist-Leninism (ML). The Norwegian Marxist-Leninist movement developed out of 1960s counterculture, becoming an oppositional force in the cultural-political landscape of the 1970s. In general, it sent shockwaves through the political and cultural discourse in Norway, due to the movement's revolutionary agenda and its uncompromising analysis of Norwegian society and its entanglement with capitalist development. Its effects on architectural discourse were no exception, and the idea of the welfare state architect as an agent of positive change was in particular attacked as naïve and outdated. The architectural schools became important arenas for such analyses, and this chapter describes the formation of this movement in and around the Oslo School of Architecture.[1]

The late 1960s in Norway were politically turbulent, with Arbeiderpartiet (the Labor Party) losing power to a center-right coalition in the 1965 election, their first defeat since the Second World War. The first two decades after the war had been dominated by the construction and consolidation of the welfare state by Arbeiderpartiet and were broadly characterized by strong economic growth. From the late 1960s, political challenges sparked by globalization and unstable economy, as well as new generations of citizens and politicians with new political agendas, ushered in a new phase in Norwegian social politics.[2] The following years were a transitional phase in all parts of Norwegian society, accommodating a shift from the social democratic welfare state of the postwar years to the new political reality of neoliberalism and deregulation that arose in the 1980s.

The ideology of Arbeiderpartiet came under attack, not only from the political right, but also from the political left. Arbeiderpartiet had been promoting an industrialist society that would secure a predictable welfare system and continuous growth in the purchasing power of its citizens.[3] From the late 1960s, their political narrative of an ever-growing, empowered working class started to appear increasingly unrealistic to many, and the political left started to search for new ideological models—sparking the rise of the new left in Norway.[4] As early as 1961, a breakaway faction from Arbeiderpartiet had constituted a new and more radical socialist party, Sosialistisk Folkeparti (SF, the Socialist Popular Party). In the coming decade, SF represented a reformist, nonrevolutionary socialism which became an important political alternative for disillusioned Arbeiderpartiet members and oppositional 1968-ers alike.[5]

The Norwegian Marxist-Leninist movement had its roots in SF, beginning as a breakaway faction from SF's youth party, SUF, which named itself "SUF (m-l)" in 1969.[6] Adding the acronym "m-l" (Marxist-Leninist), SUF (m-l) signaled a turn toward Maoism, and Mao Tse-Tung's reading of Marx, Engels, and Lenin. Inspired by the

1 This chapter builds on parts of my PhD dissertation: Martin Braathen, "The Magician and the Shoemaker," (PhD diss., NTNU, 2019).

2 Francis Sejersted, "Norsk historie fra 1970 til 1990" [Norwegian history from 1970 to 1990], in *Store norske leksikon*, updated October 10, 2017, https://snl.no/Norsk_historie_fra_1970_til_1990.

3 Rune Slagstad, *De nasjonale strateger* [The national strategists] (Oslo: Pax, 2001), 431.

4 Slagstad, *De nasjonale strateger*.

5 In 1973, SF became a part of the parliamentary basis for the new government in a new constellation, Sosialistisk Valgforbund [Socialist electoral association], together with other leftist fractions, and in 1975, Sosialistisk Venstreparti (SV, the Socialist Party), was founded. See Sejersted, "Norsk historie fra 1970 til 1990."

6 Four years later, in 1973, this organization would develop into a full-blown Maoist party, Arbeidernes Kommunistparti (marxist-leninistene) [The workers' communist party (Marxist-Leninists)], or just AKP (m-l).

Chinese Cultural Revolution, the ongoing student protests were radically transformed into a campaign for building a revolutionary party, working toward the "dictatorship of the proletariat." The ML movement also reinstated Stalin as an important political thinker, and hence chose sides in the ongoing battle between China and the Soviet Union, attacking the current Soviet regime as rightist revisionists.[7] Within the uprisings around 1968, where the US had been the main enemy, now the Soviet Union, with its "social imperialism," also became a primary enemy.[8] Whereas the more short-lived Marxist-Leninist initiatives in neighboring Sweden and Denmark developed out of the Soviet-loyal communist parties, the Norwegian Maoists hence developed out of the New Left.[9]

SUF (m-l) gained a foothold among students and made its way into different parts of academia, including the architecture schools, from 1969. Over the next years, the movement efficiently spread its message and organizational tentacles in the architecture schools, magazines, and civic action groups. At the same time, the revolutionary rhetoric and political dogmatism gradually hardened, and a central issue of debate for the architectural branch of the movement was the role of architecture as discipline, as well as the architect as contributor to society, under capitalism.

The movement presented a strong critique of the fundamental self-understanding of the discipline, and especially the naïvety in the idea of architecture as a positive, transformative act. Rather, by understanding architecture as a professional field that had developed hand-in-hand with capitalism, actors of the movement posited that all acts of architecture—including optimistic ideologies such as techno-optimism and socially engaged welfare state architecture—contained false promises. It was only through proper analysis, including the methods of dialectics and historical materialism, that one could clearly understand the role played by architecture in society and the limitations of its actions. In order to understand how society was shaped by capitalism, and architecture's role within those changes, one needed to look at how architecture was actually produced, and not only how ideologies rhetorically framed it.[10] Performing such a turn, the image of the welfare state as a relevant framework for producing socialist architecture was shattered.

STUDIES IN PLANNING UNDER CAPITALISM

The seminal student project to be based on ML theory in Norway was "Studier i planlegging under kapitalismen" (Studies in planning under capitalism) from 1970.[11] Produced by students at the Oslo School of Architecture and Design (AHO), it was a comprehensive theorizing of Marxist-Leninism within architecture and planning. It became an important reference, both as an introduction to ML theory for architecture students, as well as an example of how that theory could be applied in an academic study.[12] The project clearly shows the disbelief in the political system in Norway, which despite its social democratic roots were understood as completely overtaken by capitalist, bourgeois interests.[13]

"Studier i planlegging under kapitalismen" was handed in as a theoretical work in four volumes before the summer of 1970, having

7 See, for instance, the use of Stalin as source in "Studies in Planning under Capitalism," later in this chapter. Also, the first issue of the ML newsletter (and later daily) *Klassekampen* stated in 1970: "Marxist-Leninists have always and will always defend Stalin as one of the communist movement's great leaders and as a great proletarian class fighter." Quoted in: Hans Petter Sjøli, *Mao, min Mao: historien om Akps vekst og fall* [Mao, my Mao: The story of AKP's rise and fall] (Oslo: Cappelen, 2005), 19.

8 Sjøli, *Mao, min Mao.*

9 Sjøli, *Mao, min Mao.*

10 A similar architectural critique was performed by Italian theorist Manfredo Tafuri, who, in his studies of the decline of the architectural profession, likened architectural ideologies to illusory tricks performed by a magician. In his allegory, the critic who wants to expose those tricks, must watch the magician from backstage, not from the front row. See Manfredo Tafuri, "L'Architecture dans le boudoir," in *Oppositions Reader: Selected Readings from a Journal for Ideas and Criticism in Architecture, 1973–1984*, ed. K. Michael Hays (New York: Princeton Architectural Press, 1998), 292–316.

11 Kalle Grude, Jan Wilhelm Løchstøer, and Knut Østby, "Studier i planlegging under kapitalismen," student project, Oslo School of Architecture (1970). One of the authors, Kalle Grude, describes how they printed and distributed the project widely. Kalle Grude, interview by author, Oslo, May 16, 2014.

12 Karl Otto Ellefsen, interview by the author, Oslo, December 12, 2012.

13 Grude et al., Studier i planlegging under kapitalismen," vol. 1, 50. Grude et al explains it as such: "The power is hidden behind a parliamentary democratic form of governance with formal freedom (free elections, free speech, freedom to congregate, etc.). This system is the best hiding place of the bourgeois." Original quote in Norwegian: "Makta skjules bak en parlamentarisk demokratisk styreform med formelle friheter (frie valg, meningsfrihet, forsamlingsfrihet, osv). Dette systemet er borgerskapets beste skjul."

Kalle Grude, Jan Wilhelm Løchstøer, and Knut Østby, Studier i Planlegging under kapitalismen (Studies in Planning under Capitalism), student project, Oslo: Oslo School of Architecture, 1970. All four volumes.

been developed through three semesters as a planning course for the town of Kongsberg by third-year students Kalle Grude, Jan Løchstøer, and Knut Østby.[14] The project spans the crucial years of 1969 and 1970 and hence tracks the transition of the movement into a more consistent, dialectical Marxist-Leninism. A passage in the work describes how political awareness was raised in this period, from a third way socialism into full-blown Maoism with the introduction of historical materialism:

> Our political stance when we started this project was undefined socialist, a slightly messy socialism without inner coherence and consequence. Through the work this has developed toward a more conscious and coherent historical-materialist view of society. This way of seeing represents for us today the only fruitful starting point for grasping and explaining the present society we are living in.[15]

This transitional character is present in several places in the work, and the authors write that it is necessary to go from merely pointing to a problem to analyzing it. One must not only "make clear the irrationality and manipulative qualities of society (Marcuse)," one must also "evaluate how this irrationality of capitalism and manipulation is being replaced by socialist rationality and the power of the people (Marx)."[16] Attacking the position of the third-way socialist, they write that it is no longer enough only to "describe the symptoms of illness without grasping their internal relations or their causes."[17] To grasp such relations, the whole creation of the architect in school must change radically. The authors blame their school's curriculum for not sufficiently training future planners to read their environment as it was actually produced, and look behind the veil of bourgeois ideology. Hence, in opposition to this, the students' primary work was to explore and elaborate a Maoist critique of architectural training.

"Studier i planlegging under kapitalismen" was developed as four thick volumes, each printed as a book of its own. The cover of each volume contains a visual pun, or subversive comment, on the commercial underpinnings of the architectural discourse in Norway. The cover photo appears as a documentation of a real "master planner" in action, a man with a moustache and a cigarette, with his hands leaning over a housing development model. But this particular image was well known to Norwegian architects, as it was taken from an advertisement for a producer of doors, which ran in every issue of the biweekly architecture magazine *Arkitektnytt*.[18] Hence, commercial interests, architectural discourse, and the idea of the autonomous professional, was mixed up in these collages.

In the introduction to Volume 1, the authors state that planning must be "totalized" ("Planning must … be seen as an economic, political, social, and cultural act") and politicized ("This means that it cannot be seen as neutral and objective, but as an expression of the ruling interests in society").[19] In the introduction, we find concerns about large-scale economic changes in society, from the downsizing of primary industries to international poverty. So far, their agenda does yet stand out as particularly radical, or incompatible with the Norwegian welfare state. The proof of a more rigorous Marxist-Leninist application of theories comes on the next page: "The main topic is to what degree the premises of planning cause

14 Grude et al., vol. 2, n.p.
15 Original quote in Norwegian: "Vår politiske holdning da vi startet denne oppgaven var udefinert sosialistisk, en litt rotete sosialisme uten indre sammenheng og konsekvens. Dette har i løpet av oppgaven utvikla seg mot en mer bevisst og sammenhengende historisk-materialistisk samfunnsoppfatning. En slik betraktningsmåte står for oss i dag som det eneste fruktbare utgangspunkt for å kunne gripe og forklare det samfunnet vi lever i." Grude et al., vol. 2, 78.
16 Original quotes in Norwegian: "utdype samfunnets irrasjonalitet og manipulasjonsevne (Marcuse)," and "vurdere hvordan kapitalismens irrasjonalitet og manipulasjon avløses av sosialistisk rasjonalitet og folkemakt (Marx)." Grude et al., vol. 3, 208.
17 Original quote in Norwegian: "beskrivelse av sykdomssymptomene ved kapitalismen uten å få tak i sammenhengen mellom dem eller årsaken bak dem." Grude et al., vol. 3, 208.
18 The company was Aall-Ulefos Brug, and the ad was for their door series "Drage."
19 Original quotes in Norwegian: "Planlegging må … sees som en økonomisk, politisk, sosial og kulturell handling." and "D.v.s. at at den ikke kan betraktes som nøytral og objektiv, men som et uttrykk for de herskende interessene i samfunnet." Grude et al., vol. 1, 1–2.

III HVA DENNE OPPGAVEN KONSENTRERER SEG OM.

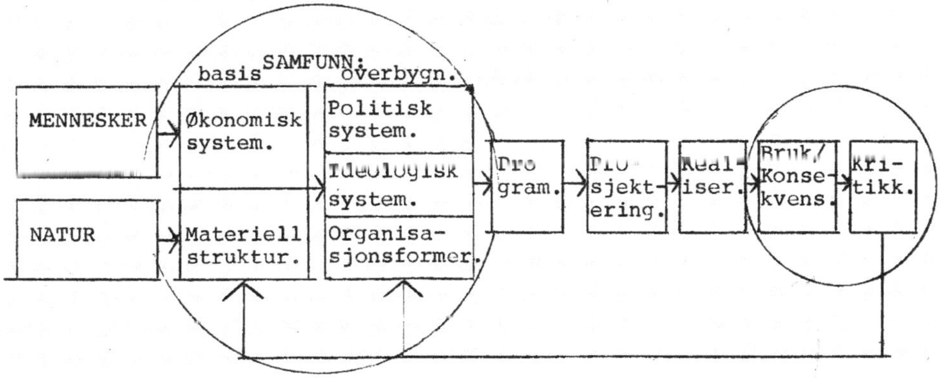

(A) PLANLEGGINGAS FORUTSETTINGER: (B) PLANLEG. PROSESS: (C) PLANLEG.- KONSEKVENSER.

- Vi vil i denne oppgaven beskjeftige oss med den rådende planleggingas konsekvens (C) og planleggingas forutsetninger (A). Hovedtemaet vil være å drøfte i hvilken grad planleggingas forutsetninger er årsak til planleggingas konkrete konsekvenser. Eller m.ao. i hvilken grad planlegginga i dag står overfor strukturelle problemer som krever strukturelle endringer i samfunnets rådende økonomiske og politiske system.
- Det er flere grunner til at vi har valgt en slik problemstilling:

  For det første måtte vi nå for vår egen del få en avklaring på de spørsmåla som problemstillingen reiser. Vi følte det personlig svært utilfredsstillende å drive planlegging og projektering, uten å ha et reflektert forhold til grunnlaget for vår virksomhet.

  For det andre er dette arbeidsområdet så godt som totalt forsømt både ved utdannelsesinstitusjoner som ved forskningsinstitusjonene og ved planleggingskontorene. Mener vi at planleggingsutdannelsen skal gjøre oss i stand til å anvise virkelige løsninger på de problemene vi i dag står overfor, må vi nå også konsentrere oss om planleggingas konsekvenser og forutsetninger.

  Vi har store hull å tette før vi har oppretta den helheten som en fullstendig planleggingsteori krever.

Grude et al., Planlegning under kapitalismen. Facsimile. Project Description, with a diagram visualizing the components of the project.

the concrete consequences of planning. Or, in other words, to what degree planning today faces structural problems that demand structural changes in the governing economic and political system of society."[20] The key is *structural changes*, opening the possibility that change cannot happen by intervening in the superstructure alone, but rather by going to the roots of the problem: exchanging the whole political-economic system of the welfare state.[21]

Due to the connection between capitalist relations of production and social relations, this view has important consequences for the architect: "A planner, architect, or other professional who doesn't have a basic understanding of the decisive meaning of economic relations for other social relations, but concentrates all his efforts on narrow professional problems such as form and function or sociocultural phenomena, can hardly reach outside the frames of thinking and action of bourgeois society."[22] Pure professionalism is definitely futile for making change, since architecture is deeply intertwined in bourgeois society and its capitalist relations. Rather, correct Marxist training is what is needed to come to such insights, and from there to be able to develop relevant strategies for architecture. It was exactly such training that the students were trying to achieve through this project, and by disseminating it, the architecture school could become a place where the illusions of the welfare state could be revealed.

In "Studier i planlegging under kapitalismen," the authors put up two main ideological enemies: the "social imperialism" of the Soviet Union on the one hand, and "the Western apparatus of exploitation" of American imperialism, NATO, and the EEC, on the other—the latter was not an external enemy, but had already infiltrated the Norwegian welfare state.[23] This position aligned with the view of the SUF (m-l) organization at large, as did the theoretical sources for the project, which were presented in Volume 2: namely, Stalin's *Dialectical and Historical Materialism*, Bo Gustavson's comments on Stalin's article, and Mao Tse-Tung's *On Contradiction* and *On Practice*.[24] The study of these sources stretches over twenty pages and includes a long introduction to historical Marxism, dialectics, and materialism. It ends in a set of "theses" and an index of terms taken from Stalin, Gustavson, and Mao.[25] All volumes contain the same concluding quote by architect and AHO teacher Jan Carlsen:

> The reckoning. I prepare for the revolution. The city will belong to the people, the city will become large enough to facilitate the people. It is large enough—if we break open the doors and fill the buildings with meaning. And the meaning is that the city will tell the truth. Oslo is a lie and we have to expose the liars ... everything that does not serve the majority shall fall, all buildings that don't liberate the people will be levelled or rebuilt, to make room for new actions.[26]

The city, according to this quote, is not only a site of intense contradictions—it is also the site of a future transformation into a different society, even a revolution.

Although the project serves as an introduction to ML thinking in general, it also contains a section where the theories are applied to planning. The authors analyze the General Plan for Kongsberg,

20 Original quote in Norwegian: "Hovedtemaet vil være å drøfte i hvilken grad planleggingas forutsetninger er årsak til planleggingas konkrete konsekvnser. Eller m.a.o. i hvilken grad planlegginga i dag står overfor strukturelle problemer som krever strukturelle endringer i samfunnets rådende økonomiske og politiske system." Grude et al., vol. 1, 3.

21 Grude et al., vol. 1, 3.

22 Original quote in Norwegian: "En planlegger, arkitekt eller annen fagmann som ikke har avgjørende innsikt i de økonomiske forholds avgjørende betydning for andre samfunnsforhold, men konsentrerer all sin innsats på å snevre faglige problemer omkring f.eks. form og funksjon eller sosial-kulturelle fenomener, vil vanskelig komme utenfor det borgerlige samfunns rammer for tanke og handling." Grude et al., vol. 2, 46.

23 Grude et al., vol. 2, 48, 50.

24 See the sections "En oversikt over den dialektiske- og historiske materialisme" [Dialectical and historical materialism: An overview] and "Noen teser om den norske kapitalismen" [Theses on Norwegian capitalism]. Grude et al., "Studier i planlegging under kapitalismen," vol. 2. Sources quoted: Josef Stalin, *Den dialektiske og historiske materialismen* [Dialectic and historical materialism] (Trondheim: Offsettrykk/SUF, 1970); Bo Gustavson, *Etter tretti år* [After thirty years] (Trondheim: Offsettrykk/SUF, 1970); Mao Tse-Tung, *Om motsigelsen* [*On Contradiction*] (Oslo: SUF-trykk, 1969); Mao Tse Tung, *Om praksis* [*On Practice*] (Oslo: Futura, 1968).

25 Grude et al., "Studier i planlegging under kapitalismen," vol. 2, 78.

26 Original quote in Norwegian: "Oppgjøret. Jeg forbereder meg på revolusjonen. Byen skal tilhøre folket, byen skal bli stor nok til å romme folket. Den er stor nok – hvis vi sprenger dørene og fyller bygningene med mening. Og meningen er: at byen skal si sannheten. Oslo er en løgn og vi må avsløre løgnerne.... alt som ikke tjener flertallet skal falle, alle bygninger som ikke frigjør menneskene skal jevnes med jorda eller bygges om, gi rom for nye handlinger." This passage, taken from Jan Carlsen's *Byen som medium* [The city as medium], is quoted on all final, unnumbered pages in each of the four volumes. Carlsen had been central in the socialist group Kanal, which was central as a proto ML group, and contained both later ML devotees but also third third-way socialist actors. See Braathen, "The Magician and the Shoemaker."

which "shows the general features of a centralistic, technocratic planning." [27] The main industry of Kongsberg was Kongsberg Våpenfabrikk, Norway's largest weapons factory. The students remark that the general plan is based solely on the expansion of the factory, and that "expansion and higher productivity is seen blindly as a positive development," being "based on the cornerstone business's own prognosis." [28] They criticize the lack of concern for the living conditions of people in the town, as well as the region, and understand the development as directed only by industry's interests: "The general plan draft shows how a large business controls and influences the whole planning apparatus." [29]

In showing how planning was a tool for privileging capital and creating a greater divide, the students claimed that architect-planners were stuck in a system from which they could not escape. Until a new social system is in place, the most important (and least destructive) tasks of the architect would be to make such analyses and to pursue critique.

Not dismissing the power of architecture entirely, the authors also allow for a certain space for "concrete operations," such as demonstrations and interventions. But they remark that these must be built on thoughtful analysis to avoid what they call "actionism," described as "actions for the sake of actions," demonstrating a cynical suspicion of non-ML agendas, and the urge of the ML movement consequently to get behind layers of political representation, to something that is real and rooted in material conditions.[30] They are suspicious about speculative student projects, warning that those pursuing "alternative projects" must be careful to "grasp the utopian character that most of these projects necessarily will have under capitalism." [31] But, given the right level of political consciousness, such projects could develop "powerful examples that grimly contrast with the irrationality and lack of humanity in capitalism." [32]

"Studier i planlegging under kapitalismen" marks an important shift in Marxist thinking, from New Left to Marxist-Leninism, and demonstrates how the Maoists' curriculum also could be applied to architecture, giving a theoretical toolbox for political-architectural analysis and a broad terminology that could be applied to discourse. The outline of a larger project of critique is drawn, one that pushes the vantage point of the critic further and further away from the idea of a neutral professional. This development would soon culminate in a manifesto of almost complete negation, which brought the ML theories out of the confines of academia and into the world of practicing architects and their magazines—even drawing out the theorist and editor Christian Norberg-Schulz to discuss the pros and cons of Marxism.[33]

A MANIFESTO FOR ML CRITIQUE

Although it was active in the architecture schools and in certain working and reading groups, explicit Marxist-Leninism emerged in the public discourse of Norwegian architecture in October 1970 when second-year architecture student Karl Otto Ellefsen delivered a fiery speech at the Oslo Association of Architects. Under the title "Omprioritering av arkitektyrket" (Reprioritizing the architectural

27 Grude et al., "Studier i planlegging under kapitalismen," vol. 3, 166.
28 Original quote in Norwegian: "En ekspansjon og produksjonsøkning betraktes blindt som en positiv utvikling...," and "... baserer seg på hjørnestensbedriftens prognoser." Grude et al., vol. 3, 166.
29 Original quote in Norwegian: "Generalutkastet viser hvordan en storbedrift kontrollerer og øver avgjørende innflytelse på hele planleggingsapparatet." Grude et al., vol 3., 166.
30 Original quote in Norwegian: "Det er viktig at dette ikke utvikler seg til aksjonisme, til aksjoner for aksjonens egen skyld." Grude et al., vol. 3, 206.
31 Original quote in Norwegian: "Forutsettinga for dette er at man erkjenner den utopiske karakter de fleste slike prosjekter har under kapitalismen." Grude et al., vol. 3, 207.
32 Original quote in Norwegian: "slagkraftige eksempler som stiller kapitalismens irrasjonalitet og mangel på menneskelighet i grell kontrast." Grude et al., vol. 3, 207.
33 Norberg-Schulz curiously plays a supporting role in Volume 3 of "Studier i planlegging under kapitalismen." By 1970, Norberg-Schulz was a main target of the architectural ML movement. Therefore, it seems peculiar that Grude et al. included quotes from Norberg-Schulz, taken from *Intentions in Architecture*, as epigraphs to each of the volumes. The first one reads: "The architect works in 'situations.' ... These situations consist of among other things economic, political, and social relations, of cultural traditions, of physical premises," and the subsequent one reads: "If a task is only partly defined, meaning: If only a part of the necessary poles are intended, we have to reject the solution, even if it is otherwise cleverly accomplished. This is often ignored today." Here, Norberg-Schulz's comments are taken out of context and taken hostage for a materialist understanding of the architectural task. This is probably pure mockery of the school's theoretical champion, ironically adopting him as an accomplice for a case he certainly despised. After all, only two years earlier he had urged the same students to "stick to their lasts" (stick to their own area of expertise), and not confuse architecture with politics. See Braathen, "The Magician and the Shoemaker," 7–8.

BORGERLIG DEMOKRATISME.

Demokrati for et forsvinnende mindretall, demokrati for de rike - det er demokratismen i det kapitalistiske samfunn.

Staten og revolusjonen
Lenin.

FOLKETS DEMOKRATISKE DIKTATUR.

Demokrati for det overveldende flertall av folket og undertrykkelse med vold, dvs. utelukkelse fra demokratiet, av folkets utbyttere og undertrykkere - det er den forandring demokratiet gjennomgår ved overgangen fra kapitalismen til kommunismen.

Staten og revolusjonen
Lenin.

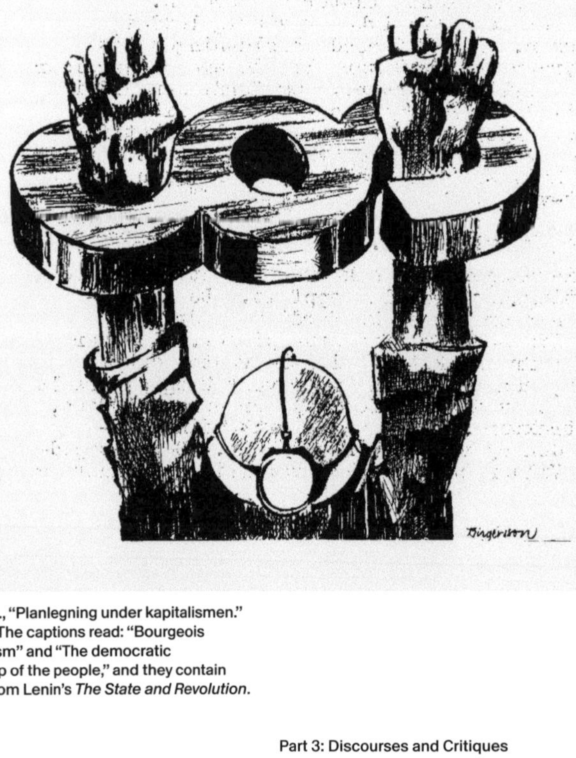

Grude et al., "Planlegning under kapitalismen." Facsimile. The captions read: "Bourgeois democratism" and "The democratic dictatorship of the people," and they contain excerpts from Lenin's *The State and Revolution*.

profession), he urged the architects to understand the limitations that capitalist development put on the profession, understanding "why what they do [has] unpleasant consequences for people," and "how the development of the capitalist economy makes things hellish."[34]

The lecture, transcribed over four pages in the news and debate magazine *Arkitektnytt*, is the most consistent analysis among the ML documents in print in Norwegian publications of the period, and is here understood as a manifesto with a program of Marxist architectural critique. The objective of the speech was to give a wake-up call to slumbering architects, providing a grave prognosis for the state and future of architecture, and urging them to realize the foundational reprioritization of the discipline that was happening before their eyes.

The background for Ellefsen's lecture was that architecture was perceived as being in a deep crisis as the Norwegian welfare state was entering a new phase of capitalism, with a fast-expanding building industry and the country facing a possible integration with the European markets through EEC.[35] Large-scale changes was necessary, according to Ellefsen, and "it is not about a reprioritization from design to programming ... from a kind of ambiguous creative endeavor to research work and social sciences," Ellefsen wrote.[36] No, in order "to solve the current problems facing architects," they cannot be naïve and think that they can only be good "technicians" or purely be socially engaged. Taking the future of the architecture student as an example, he predicted that the possibilities of working as a traditional design-based architect were close to zero. Now, "it is much harder than before to establish your own office," and it is hard "even for the architecturally highly skilled, younger people to get building commissions." Large-scale, interdisciplinary (and international) offices were on the rise and would change the very idea of how architecture was produced.

> The tendency of larger units will, for the architecture students, lead to a future as a normal wage earner—without specific influence on anything other than details in their work. The ideal of the lonely, creative individual making a synthesis of the considerations of specialists and conveying objective critique on the conditions to the expert, that ideal comes forth as absurd. It is not like that. This is not the situation that awaits you. Older, socially accepted architects, with a well-established office, can in the future experience the same.
>
> Companies such as Totalprosjekt A/S (Total Project Inc) have great competitive power. With great capacity, advanced computer equipment, and great ability to attract experts, it is in principle nothing for such companies—on the conditions of the capitalist system—to solve tasks better than anyone else. EEC will also open the way for mammoth continental offices.[37]

Here, Ellefsen's comments aligned with Tafuri's observations of how various tasks and responsibilities are taken away from architecture, and taken over by other actors in the market, as capitalist development proceeds. With the European market expansion as both symptom and force, the architect will be more and more like any industrial worker with a specialized and limited responsibility.

34 Original quotes in Norwegian: "...hvorfor det han gjør har ubehagelige konsekvenser for folk" and: "Hvordan utviklinga av den kapitalistiske økonomien gjør det jævlig." Printed a week later as: Karl Otto Ellefsen, "15-10-70: Omprioritering av arkitektyrket" [15-10-70: Reprioritizing the architectural profession], *Arkitektnytt*, annual volume (1970): 447.

35 In 1970, the Norwegian parliament decided to apply for EEC membership, and this kick-started a strong mobilization on the political left (as well as among populist centrists). For some years up until the vote in 1972, they battled side by side in what they called the United Front. When the vote was over, and the negative voices had won, over 120,000 Norwegians had joined the organized fight in Folkebevegelsen mot EEC [The people's movement against the EEC], and 25,000 had been part of the AKMED, Arbeiderkomiteen mot EEC og dyrtid [The worker's committee against EEC and high costs of living], which was the ML movement's own campaign. See Braathen, "The Magician and the Shoemaker," 64–66, and http://no.wikipedia.org/wiki/Arbeiderkomiteen_mot_EEC_og_dyrtid, read 23.05.14.

36 Original quote in Norwegian: "Det er ikke snakk om en omprioritering fra prosjektering til programmering. Fra en form for ullen kreativ virksomhet, til utredningsarbeid og samfunnsvitenskap." Ellefsen, "Omprioritering av arkitektyrket."

37 Ellefsen, "Omprioritering av arkitektyrket," 449. See the development of Norplan, which was happening at the same time. Original quote in Norwegian: "Tendensen til større enheter fører for arkitektstudenter med seg ei framtid som vanlig lønnsarbeider – uten særlig innflytelse i annet enn detaljspørsmål i arbeidet han gjør. Idealiet som det ensomt, kreative individet som kan lage syntese av spesialistenes betraktninger og føre objektiv kritikk tilbake på ekspertenes premisser, dette idealet står frem som absurd. Det er ikke slik. Dette er ikke situasjonen som venter en. Eldre, sosialt aksepterte ark. med godt innarbeidet kontor, kan komme til å merke det samme. Firma av typen 'A/S Totalprosjekt' har stor konkurranseevne. Med stor kapasitet, avansert datautstyr og store evne til å knytte til seg eksperter, så er det prinsipielt ingenting i veien for at slike firma – på premissene til det kapitalistiske systemet – kan løse oppgaver bedre enn andre. EEC vil også gi mulighet for kontinentale mammuttkontorer."

Hence, he predicted, the future status of architects in society will decline, and architects will (be forced to) understand themselves as proletarians:

> When the expectations about one's future career become absurd and one no longer feels that one belongs to a social elite, it will be easier to be in solidarity with other wage earners. In Marxist terms: It will be easier to be in solidarity with workers—against exploitation.[38]

To visualize the complete dead end architecture was facing, Ellefsen created a rhetorical gallery of Norwegian architect's roles, dismissing their futile ideological positions one by one. Ellefsen's cast of tragic characters consisted of the following: First came the artistic and confident architect with a capital A, seeing their work as autonomous and detached from social consequences: "Some are architects—'impartial, objective, professionals,' elevated above politics in the world of form. Those who know better."[39] Second were the "gently socially engaged": "Those who get indignant at Philip Johnson for placing the caretaker's apartment in the basement ... [and want] a friendly square as part of the new warehouse in Vika, or a Haukeland [sculpture] in front of the Storebrand [insurance] building."[40] This description could fit several sides of the political spectrum (and many of the regular visitors to the Oslo Architecture Association, where the lecture was held), describing a pragmatic and experienced architect with large-scale corporate projects, and with a view of social engagement as a symbolic representation of good intentions. Then came "the designers": "Buckminster Fuller, Victor Papanek, AD, Archigram (the group had a small, strong branch around NTH too). People who very strongly emphasize and overestimate the role of the designer ... [issues such as] over-production, consumption, ... the energy barrier between rich and poor countries. Everything can be solved with relatively easy means by the designer."[41] Here, all the techno-optimistic neo-avant-gardes were attacked for their blind belief in the power of design. The fourth group is the most problematic category, according to Ellefsen: the socialist architect who still believes in the welfare state. "I would like to dwell a bit on the fourth group: those who are so bloody socially engaged and concerned about the welfare of humankind. Joining this group has become the fashion among architects today. The talk about social underdogs, the new proletariat, worldwide class struggle ... the Norwegian worker exploiting the Indian farmer ... [Those who think they] are making a considerable political effort by drawing 'good' satellite towns."[42] Ellefsen rather cynically mocks the ignorance lurking behind the "arrogance" of these socialist architects, who believe that they can help the proletariat by "extending their living rooms by ten square meters." According to Ellefsen, these architects wrongly believe that "the state is actually good," and that it is just because of "a lack of will and/or over-administration in governmental departments" that things are not being changed for the better. Ellefsen hence paints a bleak picture of all architecture—formalist, mainstream, socially engaged, neo-avant-garde. These figures all represent the current prevailing ideologies of Norwegian architecture, all of them failing to see architecture for what it really is.

38 Original quote in Norwegian: "Når karriereforventningene blir absurde og en ikke lenger føler at en hører til en sosial elite, vil en ha lettere for å solidarisere seg med andre lønnsarbeidere. I Marxistiske termer: EN vil ha lettere for å solidarisere seg med arbeidsfolk – mot utbytting." Ellefsen, 449.

39 Original quote in Norwegian: "Noen er arkitekter – 'upartiske, objektive, fagfolk' høgt hvet [sic] over politikk – i formens verden. De som vet bedre." Ellefsen, 447.

40 Original quote in Norwegian: "De svakt sosialt engasjerte," "De som harmes over at Philip Johnson plasserer vaktmesterleiligheten i kjelleren ... Folkevennlig torg i Vika varehus, og Haukeland utenfor Storebrandbygningen." Ellefsen, 447.

41 See Martin Braathen, *Alt er arkitektur!: neoavantgarde og institusjonskritikk i Norge 1965–1970* (Trondheim; Tapir akademisk forlag, 2010). Referring to the young rebels at NTH, Ellefsen even implicitly includes his older architect brother Eilert Ellefsen among these; he was part of a neo-avant-gardist environment with ties to the British group Archigram and Reyner Banham through their teacher Per Kartvedt. Original quote in Norwegian: "En tredje gruppe – designerne: Buckminster Fuller, Victor Papanek, AD, Archigram (gruppen har hatt en sterk liten fløy rundt NTH også). Folk som til de grader understreker og overvurderer designerens rolle ... Overproduksjonen, kjøp og kast kulturen, ..., energikløften mellom rike og fattige land ... Alt kan løses med forholdsvis enkle håndgrep fra designeren side. Maktforholdet eksisterer ikke."

42 Original quote in Norwegian: "Den fjerde gruppen vil jeg dvele litt ved: De som er så jævlig sosialt engasjerte og bekymrede for menneskehetens ve og vel. Å slutte seg til denne gruppen er på mote blant arkitekter i dag. Snakket om sosiale underdogs, det nye proletariatet, klassekampen i verdenssammenheng ... den norske arbeider som utbytter den indiske bonde ... en voldsom politisk innsats ved å tegne 'gode' drabantbyer." Ellefsen, "Omprioritering av arkitektyrket," 447.

The most tragic of all architectural figures are the ones closest to a real political commitment, but who lack the proper Marxist-Leninist training to realize how they are doomed to fail. The (non-ML) socialist architects lack a dialectic approach and still believe in a "one-sided description of the symptoms of the disease of capitalism, without grasping the relations and causes."[43] In this analysis, the Norwegian welfare state could be understood as the greatest ideological veil of all, appearing as a socialist project and deceiving architects to believe that its system still worked, that it only needed revisions, and that they as architects could actually make a difference within it. But, there is really no hope for architecture in Ellefsen's program. Even bettering the living conditions of the proletarians was seen as counterproductive, as it was delaying the necessary revolts. If there was no architecture of the present that could solve those current contradictions, no architectural programs containing revolutionary potential, what else could ML architects do?

LEARNING FROM HISTORY: THE PLAN GROUP

The young ML architects, disillusioned with architecture's prospects and its role in changing the future, turned to history for precedents—if not for solutions (to return to another historical moment in that way would be deemed undialectical)—then at least to look for others who had faced similar dilemmas. To return architecture to a distant or not-so-distant past (most often in order to legitimize or reorient contemporary practice) was not only a project of the emerging postmodernist movement but had also been crucial to the neo-avant-gardes of the 1960s, who reconnected to the avant-gardes of the 1920s. Within Norwegian architectural history, there was really only one earlier group of hardcore Marxists: a constellation of socialist architects called *PLAN-gruppen* (the PLAN Group) who operated in the 1930s; they represented the core of the Marxist-Leninists' own dilemma: could a sincere Marxist project be integrated into the institution of architecture (even if PLAN's Marxism was not the same)?[44]

The PLAN Group were members of the Sosialistiske Arkitekters Forening (the Association of Socialist Architects), the architectural branch and one of the front organizations of the communist group Mot Dag (which translates to "Toward Day"). Mot Dag had an eponymous magazine as their official organ, and it was also the mother organization of other front organizations, such as those of medical doctors, teachers, and lawyers, in addition to the architects, mirroring the structure of the national ML movement.[45] Mot Dag was not, nor was it part of, a political party, but as the SUF (m-l) later, it was an organization whose aim was "recruiting intellectuals for socialism."[46] The Mot Dag group also gathered a huge number of leading intellectuals in Norway, from authors to leading politicians, many of whom would become influential politicians and bureaucrats in the postwar years—again mirroring the recruitment of intellectuals to the Marxist-Leninists of the 1970s.

The PLAN Group published four issues of the eponymous magazine *PLAN* in the period 1933–36 as an organ for Sosialistiske Arkitekters Forening.[47] The core of the PLAN Group was Eyvind

43 Original quote in Norwegian: "ensidig beskrivelse av hvordan sykdomssymtomene ved kapitalismen, uten å få tak i sammenheng og årsaker." Ellefsen, "Omprioritering av arkitektyrket," 447.

44 The Institutional Theory, understanding architecture as an institution within society, among law, medicine, or art, with its own discourse and ideologies, is central for understanding the dynamics of the oppositional ideologies studied in Braathen, *The Magician and the Shoemaker*. In this text, I have removed most references to this theory, as well as its connections to Manfredo Tafuri, but have chosen to keep it in a few places.

45 Johan Ditlef-Martens and Ketil Moe, eds., *Plan 1933–1936* (Oslo: Universitetsforlaget, 1983), 21.

46 Ditlef-Martens and Moe, *Plan 1933–1936*, 27.

47 See the 1983 interview with Eyvind Alnæs, Carsten Boysen, Gunnar Øvergaard Jørgen, Frode Rinnan, and Erik Rolfsen in: Ditlef-Martens and Moe, *Plan 1933–1936*, 21–39. Note that this anthology of *PLAN* was edited by two (former) ML-ers, still preoccupied in 1983 with the history of the group.

48 The interview occurred on March 14, the day of Karl Marx's death, something that the three interviewers—Jon Guttu, Johan Ditlef-Martens, and Magnus Nygaard—made a point of in the introduction.

49 Jon Guttu, Johan Ditlef-Martens, and Magnus Nygaard, "Rinnan og Rolfsen," *Fagavisa* no. 2 (1974): 20.

Alnæs, Carsten Boysen, Gunnar Øvergaard Jørgen, Frode Rinnan, and Erik Rolfsen, all important figures in postwar architecture in Norway. Rolfsen became the director of city planning in Oslo; Øvergaard would lead OBOS, the largest housing cooperative in Norway; Alnæs became the editor of architecture magazine *Byggekunst*; and Rinnan directed some of the largest postwar housing developments in Norway, became a president of the national architects' association, NAL, and even made a career within Arbeiderpartiet. All of the four founders were educated at NTH in Trondheim and had been active in student politics before embarking on the PLAN project. As young revolutionaries in 1933, they launched an ambitious agenda for their new magazine and an ambitious program for changing the role of the architect.

During the 1970s, the former PLAN members were still active. In the student magazine *Fagavisa* at AHO in 1974, two of them, Frode Rinnan and Erik Rolfsen, were interviewed, probably conscious of how their past was being framed within the current context of ML.[48] In a long interview over six pages, topics revolved around the relationship between the historical context of the PLAN group, the 1930s, versus the then-present, the early 1970s, comparing issues such as the change in housing policies, planning strategies, and capitalist development. The main challenge, the crux of the interview, was the transition that these architects had gone through: These former radicals were "theoretically trained very well" as Marxists in their younger days, according to the interviewers, but failed in their revolutionary agency and ended up in successful careers within the mainstream institution and even in mainstream politics. One could argue that they were now working for a corrupted welfare state which had become a carrier of bourgeois culture and partook in American imperialism. Hence, to the Maoists, they demonstrated the impossibility of merging political radicalism with professional work as architects.[49] The interview was supplemented with several original texts from *PLAN* magazine as facsimiles, focusing on the role of architecture in society, socialism as a "real," not utopian project, critique of the role of the architect, and so on. In order to understand PLAN, I will give a short introduction to this magazine and the group's manifesto, called "Vårt program" (Our program), to draw out the similarities of argumentation, a certain pattern of Marxist meta-analysis and critique, with that of the Marxist-Leninists forty years later.

CRITIQUE OF HOUSING AND SOCIAL PROGRAMS

Traveling back in time to the Norway of 1933, the year of the first issue of *PLAN*, was paradigmatic of the tendency of the 1970s to make historical returns in order to rediscover, learn, and project into the future. What the ML-ers found there was a country very different from the Norway of the early 1970s, especially financially, as Norway was struggling with the consequences of the recession. But it also resonated with their present in several respects. After the first wave of functionalism, which had taken place within a more prosperous economy than that of the mid-1930s, *PLAN* performed a strict critique of modernism and how it had developed, in their eyes, into a style-oriented minimalism without social agendas. The

Jon Guttu, Johan Ditlef-Martens, and Magnus Nygaard, "Rinnan og Rolfsen," *Fagavisa* no. 2 (1974) 20–21.

RINNAN OG ROLFSEN

Socialistiske Arkitekters Forening ble dannet i 1933. De studerte boligspørsmål og arkitektur med et marxistisk utgangspunkt. Foreningen la fram sine programmer og analyser i tidsskriftet "Plan" som kom i fire utgaver fra 1933 til 1936.

Etter at Fagavisa var kommet godt igang sist høst, fastsatte redaksjonen en del oppgaver som kunne gi interessant stoff til avisa. En av disse jobbene var å diskutere gamle og nye problemer med tidligere medlemmer av Socialistiske Arkitekters Forening.

Vi kontaktet Frode Rinnan og Erik Rolfsen. De spilte en sentral rolle både i Foreningen og i Plan, og har senere henholdsvis vart leder på arkitektkontoret Rinnan og Tveten, og byplansjef i Oslo.

Samtalen fant sted torsdag 14.3.1974 (91-årsdagen for Karl Marx død), den siste av noen soldager som fikk oss til å tro at våren var kommet. Vi satt under industrilampa på Guttus kontor med kaffe, peanøtter og eplemost.

Fagavisa (heretter F.):
I Plan ble det [illegible] til endringer av by- og boligplanleggingen. Dere ville bl.a. ha økt kooperativ, statsstøttet boligbygging, styrket beboermakt, kollektive anlegg i boligområdene som butikker, badeanlegg, vaskerier og barnehager, smale blokker med gjennomgående leiligheter og flere rom til hver familie, en leilighetsutforming som hindret utleiervirksomhet, bekjempelse av den uhygieniske "kjøkkenstuen" og sterkere byplaninngrep, i første rekke for å sanere eldre boligområder og utvide trafikknettet.

I hvilken grad mener dere at boligbyggingen og byplanleggingen etter krigen har rettet seg [illegible] gyldige fremdeles, og hvilke krav må i dag sees som feilaktige?

ROLFSEN:
Den kooperative boligbyggingen som vi sammen med mange andre så som en hovedsak, startet så vidt opp før krigen, men kom ikke skikkelig igang før etter 1945. Kommunen ble representert i styret fra 1936 og selskapet (OBOS) ble organisert som et boligsparelag. Prinsippet var at alle skulle spare, leilighetene skulle fordeles etter medlemsskapets alder, og ved loddtrekning.

F.:
I mellomkrigstiden kunne dere enten gå inn for å styrke leieboerbevegelsen og fremme en bygging hvor kommunen bygde og leide ut boligene, eller arbeide for en kooperativ boligbygging der beboerne gjennom et kollektivt organ ble eiere av boligene. Hvorfor satset dere alt på den kooperative byggingen?

RINNAN:
Vi hadde meget intim kontakt med det svenske miljøet. Mange av de ordningene de hadde opprettet i Sverige adopterte vi og gjorde til våre mål. I Sverige er det leieboerbevegelsen som har spilt den mest sentrale rollen i boligbyggingen. H.S.B. (Hyresgästernas Sparkasse och Byggnadsförening) har vert en politisk maktfaktor og en plattform for mange sentrale politikere innenfor sosialdemokratiet i Sverige.

20

Cover of Johan Ditlef-Martens and Ketil Moe, eds., *Plan 1933–1936* (Oslo: Universitetsforlaget, 1983), with the cover of *PLAN* 3/1935 as facsimile.

issue of social housing was also an urgent matter, and this was identified as the main challenge of Norwegian architecture by the PLAN group.[50] Their biting critique of architectural discourse in Norway and Europe in general came to the fore in the magazine, most explicitly in their program text "Vårt program."[51] Here, they scrutinized architectural production and architectural publishing from the viewpoint of young radicals to paint a picture of a servile and naïve profession with an uncritical professional press. In their dismissal of their contemporaries, their main criticism was that they lacked a proper analysis of the relations of production, foreshadowing the critique found in both Karl Otto Ellefsen's ML manifesto in "Omstrukturering" and "Studier i planlegging under kapitalismen."

The very first issue of *PLAN* already delved straight into the core of the professional-political dilemma: Is there a contradiction between political tendency and architecture? The editors orchestrated the question with a fictional monologue, wherein an old architect instructs a younger:

> And by the way, why should we architects be concerned with politics? We build, we have our destined duties in life, we are above the political parties, we are professionals employing our knowledge and Art in favor of both the worker and the millionaire. So, let the others mess around with that dirty politics.[52]

The fear of the unpolitical professional, the one preoccupied with the formalist tasks of the discipline without grasping the larger political context, was already haunting architecture, forty-one years before *Fagavisa*'s return. Against this unpolitical attitude, the PLAN Group carved out their own agenda in a historical-materialist manner:

> All intellectual life, all theory, is in its development conditioned by the present material and social basis. When a harsh battle of meanings occurs within a discipline, when there are sharp theoretical antagonisms, that is the result of a deep change within the social position of the discipline—in the material and economic basis for its production.[53]

They describe such changes in the conditions for creating architecture, where international functionalism responded to a strong social tendency, and as a result of that, put the architect (and the institution of architecture) in a privileged role:

> New social demands have forced the architect into a new mode of work that first and foremost rests on a scientific analysis of the functions to be filled, and of the constructive possibilities present. The architect has become the organizer of building activity.[54]

From an institutional standpoint, the observation of the architect as being in a fundamentally decisive role is interesting. Amid the anxiety of the 1970s about the future of architecture, ML returned to a point in Norwegian history where architects really understood themselves as having great influence on the material production of the built environment. This resembled Manfredo Tafuri's observation of other actors of the same period of the 1930s, with architects

50 See the facsimiles of housing issues in *PLAN*, reprinted in: Guttu et al., "Rinnan og Rolfsen," 22, 23, 26.

51 See facsimile in: Guttu et al., "Rinnan og Rolfsen," 25.

52 Pre-editorial, untitled text. *PLAN* 1, reprinted in Ditlef-Martens et al., *Plan 1933–1936*, 42. Original quote in Norwegian: "Og forresten, hvad skal vi arkitekter oppgi politikken efter? Vi bygger, vi har våre bestemte opgaver i livet, vi står over partiene, vi er fagfolk som yder vår viten og Kunst så vel til arbeideren som til millionæren. La så de andre rote med den skitne politikken."

53 Ditlef-Martens et al., *Plan 1933–1936*, 42. Original quote in Norwegian: "Alt åndsliv, all teoretisk tenkning, er i sin utvikling beting av det materielle og samfundsmessige grunnlag som er til stede. Når der innenfor en enkelt stand foregår en krass meningskamp, når der finnes skarpe teoretiske motsetninger, er det et resultat av at der er i ferd med å skje en dyptgående endring i standens samfundsmessige stilling – i det materielle og økonomiske grunnlag for dens virksomhet."

54 Original quote in Norwegian: "Nye sociale krav har tvunget arkitekten over i en ny arbeidsmåte som først og fremst hviler på vitenskapelig analyse av de funksjoner som skal fylles og av de konstruktive muligheter som foreligger." Ditlef-Martens et al., *Plan 1933–1936*, 42.

such as Martin Wagner and Ernst May taking up roles as "organizers" of building activity, made possible by "a new attitude toward the role that intellectual work may undertake in its efforts to remove the capitalistic contradictions in building and in the planned utilization of resources."[55] In Norway in the 1930s, those contradictions were highly present, and even unsolvable, according to the PLAN architects:

> But still, he is through his work on city planning confronted with the task of organizing the lives of humans. The unsolvable housing problem, the unsolvable problems of the urban plan within the frames of the existing society, have led many architects through their organizing activity away from the old professional isolation and into a continuously more conscious social activity.[56]

The situation is hence not so different from the picture drawn by Ellefsen, in which the unsolvable contradictions of the time had pushed many architects toward a socialist stance—and in Ellefsen's view, not a constructive one. The key to both is the question of what is understood by "conscious" social activity. The PLAN Group described how early functionalism was not purely a technical cleanup process, but a reaction—an "unconscious" reaction—against "planlessness in capitalistic society."[57] The problem of functionalism, in its first phase, was its "political neutrality" and the lack of a proper social theory to turn it into the social instrument it had the potential to become. Such a social "clarity" could be achieved only if the planner "sees himself as a link in the social whole," implicitly describing the need for materialist analysis.[58] Pointing to the rise of socialism in European architecture at large, the road to this second phase of functionalism is, according to PLAN, an "unbiased, professional debate, studies in socialism, and the active participation in the struggle of the working class."[59] Hence, the architect must become an active political agent, well trained in Marxism, acting in solidarity with the working class.

PLAN architects, although active as socialists with the aim of "standing clearly and without doubt on the ground of the labor movement," were clear that this did not mean an abandonment of the role of the architect, contrary to what we see with the 1970s' ML movement as a result of their deeply dialectical analysis of the role of architecture in society. Rather, "the profession of architecture is in reality in the very center of the transformational process happening in society," as the PLAN Group wrote.[60] In order to take part in that change, fundamental retraining and reorientation of the profession was necessary, toward achieving new knowledge.

> Our organizing work will, during the plan economy of the future, take as its premise a real understanding of the development laws of society, of the social structures of the city, of class relations, industrial conditions, of their relations and financial dependence on the countryside, and so on. One will demand that we be able to work anonymously, in cooperation with social economists and social hygienists, and that we actively take part in the socialist transformation process in the service of the working class.[61]

55 Tafuri, "L'Architecture dans le boudoir," 312.

56 Original quote in Norwegian: "Men samtidig er han gjennom sitt byplanarbeide blitt stilt overfor den opgave å organisere menneskenes liv. Uløseligheten av boligproblemet, uløseligheten av byplanproblemene innenfor det eksisterende samfunds rammer har ført til at mange arkitekter gjennom sin organiserende virksomhet er drevet bort fra den gamle faglige isolasjon, og over i en stadig mer bevisst social aktivitet." PLAN, "Vårt program," 42.

57 PLAN, 43.

58 PLAN, 43.

59 PLAN, 43.

60 PLAN, 43.

61 Original quote in Norwegian: "Vårt organiserende arbeide vil under fremtidens planøkonomi ha som en nødvendig forutsetning en virkelig forståelse av samfundets utviklingslover, av byenes sociale strutkur, klasseforhold, industrielle betingelser, av deres forbindelse og økonomiske avhengighet av landdistriktene, og så videre. Man vil forlange av oss at vi er istand til å arbeide anonymt, i samarbeide med socialøkonomer og hygienikere, og at vi aktivt deltar i den socialistiske omformningsprosess i arbeiderklassens tjeneste." PLAN, 50.

62 Original quote in Norwegian: "Den klassiske striden mellom revolusjonære og revisjonister mistet sin argumentasjonskraft i 30-åra. Grunnen var at vi stod foran en ny verdenskrig, og alle signaler i retning av at venstrekreftene måtte samles i en bredest mulig folkefront." Ditlef-Martens and Moe, *Plan 1933–1936*, 27.

63 Guttu et al., "Rinnan og Rolfsen," 23.

64 Guttu et al., "Rinnan og Rolfsen," 23.

Hence the architect could work toward the new society through architectural work. And they, as editors, could contribute by means of critique, highlighting and possibly heightening the tensions to enhance the coming crisis. As architects, they needed first and foremost to join the battle together with the proletarians—but they did not yet step down and see themselves as proletarians, a point that would be seen as undialectical from the vantage point of the 1970s.

A COMMUNIST AT HEART? PLAN AS A FAILED PROJECT

After the PLAN period, and as the Socialist Architects merged with Arbeiderpartiet, the radicalism of the group was slowly replaced by a new political pragmatism. As recalled by Rinnan in an interview in 1983:

> The classic struggle between revolutionaries and revisionists lost its power of argument in the Thirties. The reason was that we stood before a new world war, and all signals pointed to the left joining forces into a Popular Front as broad as possible.[62]

The dream of a revolution was replaced by the fear of a coming world war, which in turn would shake up the political landscape. When the architects returned to professional work after the war, their positions would change drastically, from the role of critical observers on the fringes to occupying power positions at very center of the institution. Looking from 1974, then, onto the PLAN project must have been both a depressing but perhaps also slightly triumphant sight: it certainly confirmed ML's theory of the impossibility of opposition from within architecture. The two interviewees in *Fagavisa*, Rinnan and Rolfsen, had gone from being critics to being complicit in shaping a social democratic society that had gone completely wrong in the eyes of Maoists. Confronting them with this paradox in 1974, the interviewers referred back to PLAN's original belief, that the housing problems of the working class could not be solved within a capitalist society. Now, as architects in positions directly involved in developing postwar housing policy, they asked, did Rinnan and Rolfsen still consider these claims as valid?

Rinnan answered the question as a man in such a position: According to a recent study that he had produced, the housing problem was not that bad, and larger apartments had become "cheaper and cheaper" over a long period of time. He compared Norway favorably to eastern Europe, claiming that the radical socialist solution of appropriating land had produced a "housing standard far lower than what one would dare to offer to anyone in western Europe."[63] Rolfsen agreed with Rinnan, ending in the cynical conclusion that "the housing problem actually cannot be solved, even within a socialist society."[64]

CONCLUSION—NOTHING LEFT BUT CRITIQUE

Such capitulation to capitalism—and even complete denunciation of the most radical solution—must have been shocking, but also deeply confirmative to the Marxist-Leninists. On the one hand, the PLAN project demonstrated a comprehensive critical project, based on socialist training and a revolutionary approach that had many similarities to that of the ML movement. On the other, it proved that the very belief in architectural socialism was undialectical: Throughout their careers, the PLAN members brutally demonstrated how they failed in "enhancing a crisis," demonstrating how working from within the system, or from the institution outward, had been futile and even counterproductive to the cause. As architect Jan Carlsen stated two years later, the "conditions [for PLAN's revolutionary project] were not ready yet," and they "ultimately were caught in the net of social democracy."[65]

By historicizing PLAN's project, there was nothing to learn from the history of the political avant-garde except the confirmation of one suspicion that had been there all along: For a Marxist-Leninist project, there was nothing beyond critique, neither in the present nor the past. Historical materialism was an approach that was quite the opposite of historicism; there was no "toolbox" of the past or stylistic catalogue to choose from. As long as the social democratic state in itself had become entangled in capitalism and different forms of suppression, it had become the very fundamental, structural problem in itself. Ideas of making the world better, or of performing class solidarity by designing better social housing, were signs of extreme naivety, or even cynicism. There were no solutions within the welfare state, no architecture which could fundamentally make changes. The only possibility was to learn to observe and to perform critique. The critique of the architectural establishment was, in the end, *total.*

65 Original quote in Norwegian: "… forholdene lå ikke til rette da, de endte i sosialdemokratiets garn til slutt." Jan Carlsen, "Arkitektene har ikke vinger," [Architects don't have wings] in *Arkitektnytt* no. 5 (1976): 93–97.

LIVING IN A SATELLITE TOWN

Ane Hjort Guttu

70

post

Living in a Satellite Town (2004) was an art project and an investigation into the conventions and rhetoric of architectural photography. Over a period of time in the early 2000s, I went through a large amount of documentation from newly built housing areas in Scandinavia, mainly in issues of the architectural journals *Byggekunst* (Norway), *Arkitektur* (Sweden), *Arkitektur* (Denmark), *Arkitektnytt* (Norway), and others, ranging from 1920 to 2000. Images of these areas are remarkably similar within certain periods of time, although periods differ radically from one another: one can identify specific conventions for photographing the suburbs in the 1960s and, for instance, the 1990s. Why are there so many children in the pictures from the 1970s? Why are there always trees in the photographs from the 1950s? And what are the clouds in the sky doing, for the 1925 viewer?

Exploring these types of questions—and seeing all the material from various time periods in the light of changing political agendas—made my own artistic photography feel ever more difficult, as if everything I did was trapped in photographic rhetoric situated in time and space. *Living in a Satellite Town* therefore marked the beginning of a different approach to photography for me, whereby I moved away from "my own" photographic expression to an interest in found footage, archives, and a greater problematization of the documentary image.

The images presented on the previous pages are selected from a larger series that recycles and mixes these photographic conventions. In addition to about 30 images, *Living in a Satellite Town* also included a text, which took a closer look at historical documentary footage from housing areas in Scandinavia, seen against the political context of their time.

Living in a Satellite Town was originally presented at the Young Artists' Society (UKS) in Oslo in 2004 and has later been shown in a number of art institutions and journals. The title is taken from the second report on the satellite town of Ammerud, "Å bo i drabantby," by Grete Bull, Torbjørn Hansen, and Ragnhild Haug, 1971.

*

Photos taken in Oslo: Haugenstua, Kalbakken, Furuset, Ammerud, Tveita, Trosterud, Bjerke, and Romsås.

4 RECONCEPTUALIZATIONS AND NEW FORMATIONS

Ellen Braae

FROM COMMONS TO PUBLIC SPACE

Relational Green Open Spaces in Danish Housing Estates

Landscape and welfare are tightly related. Landscape is literally molded into large-scale Nordic postwar housing estates, which provide plenty of green open space. These spaces are embedded with multiple welfare values and services aimed at the residents and their neighbors; moreover, they work as concrete spaces for encounters and shared uses among multiple people, regardless of ownership—that is, they are forms of *public space*. However, having mainly been conceptualized as the result of "neighborhood unit" planning and (modernist) spatial frameworks of "objects floating on a surface," these spaces go beyond the typical urban stereotypes of public space. Given the radical transformation of many Nordic postwar large-scale housing estates to mirror the ideal of *the mixed city*—that is the antithesis of the socio-culturally and economically segregated city[1]—and the pursuit of market-driven development, these formal frameworks and categories of spaces today need to be revisited.

All over Europe, cities and their public spaces—including the large-scale postwar housing estates—are changing rapidly.[2] While some of these transformations rely on more incremental processes of growth, decay, appropriation, and abandonment, others are more deliberate and more radical. In Denmark, the concrete social housing estates of the 1970s have had a bleak public reputation since their erection, despite being built for all social classes. Today, they stand as symbols of former ideals related to welfare and the mid-twentieth-century welfare state; they are also perceived as dull, monotonous, and even "failed architecture."[3] Such areas are often located near city centers and as a result of subsequent urban development and its often plentiful green open spaces, they also represent attractive new building opportunities for investors. In late 2018, the passing of the "Ghettoloven" (the "Ghetto Act") by the Danish parliament, which at the time was led by a right-wing government, created an opening for a significant politicization of the (already ambiguous) social housing sector, manifesting the processes of deliberately radical physical and socioeconomic transformation underway at that time. The Ghetto Act defines a so-called ghetto as "a physically cohesive social-housing area with at least 1,000 residents" and the potential classification depends on the employment, crime, education, income, and ethnicity/immigration characteristics of the people who live there. If these metrics are high, the number of social housing units in a given "ghetto" must be reduced by 60 percent by means of eviction, demolition, or privatization (including densification)—either individually or in combination.[4] This process of transformation was reaffirmed by the social democratic government installed the year after the Act's introduction, using "mixed city" ideals (which we will return to shortly). As such, no matter what strategy justifies them, in transformations of

1 The mixed city, in Danish "den blandede by," has within recent years become a generally accepted term used by politicians, architects, and the public yet it lacks a clear definition. However, the concept is mainly used in the context of socially vulnerable housing areas and not in rich districts albeit they are both segregated. The main tool put into use enhancing the mixed city ideal is diverse ownership forms.

2 Ali Madanipour, Sabine Knierbein, and Aglaée Degros, eds., *Public Space and the Challenges of Urban Transformation in Europe* (New York: Routledge, 2014).

3 Claus Bech-Danielsen and Mette Mechlenborg, *Renovering af almene boligområder: Evaluering af fysiske indsatser gennemført i perioden 2014–2016 [Renovation of public housing areas: Evaluation of physical efforts carried out in the period 2014–2016]* (Kongens Lyngby: Polyteknisk Boghandel og Forlag, 2017).

4 Regjeringen [Government of Denmark] (2018) *Ét Danmark uden parallelsamfund. Ingen ghettoer i 2030* [One Denmark without parallel societies: No ghettoes in 2023]. Økonomi og indenrigsministeriet, Copenhagen, https://im.dk/fejl/publikationsmigrering/et-danmark-uden-parallelsamfund-ingen-ghettoer-i-2030.

5 Ellen Braae, "Welfare Landscapes and Communities," in *Forming Welfare*, ed. Katrine Lotz et al. (Copenhagen: Danish Architectural Press, 2017).

6 Braae, "Welfare Landscapes and Communities."

7 Gøsta Esping-Andersen, *The Three Worlds of Welfare Capitalism* (Princeton, NJ: Princeton University Press, 1990).

8 Braae, "Welfare Landscapes and Communities."

this scale, the spatial structure will change significantly and the amount, structure, character, use, users, and classification of open spaces will be deeply affected.

The transformations that took place before the enactment of the Ghetto Act, and those that were fueled directly or indirectly by it (even with the aim of avoiding becoming a "ghetto"), stimulated many relevant arguments relating to demolition and displacement as a planning strategy. These include concern over the weakening of the constitutive role of Danish social housing, both in the Danish welfare city context and as part of the "Danish model"; the neglect of existing resources; the entailed CO_2 emission increase and applying the same scheme everywhere lacks logic. The more recent densification aims, which stem from the Ghetto Act, the ideal of the mixed city, and (private) investor-driven development have only added to these concerns. Important as these questions are, though, my focus here is on understanding the open spaces of such areas—their materialities, uses, and discourses—in terms of a physical and formal shift from acting as "commons" to being *quasi-public spaces*, with the latter aiming to invite in new users and promote new values. As such, I here ask: How can the socio-spatial divide which characterizes much of the research related to the open spaces of social housing be overcome? What happens to these now recommodified open spaces once large-scale private investors enter the field? And what ideals relating to welfare does this shift and social engineering entail?

WELFARE LANDSCAPES

From the 1960s onwards, the design of large-scale housing estates in Denmark—as elsewhere in Europe—rested on modernist spatial configurations of "objects floating on a surface." The estates were made using prefabricated concrete assembly constructions, and erected using cranes; the structure of their open spaces was affected by this production mode. These spaces were thus an integral part of how housing was thought of and made at the time.[5] The estates also materialized ideas about welfare as it related to open space and nature at large, taking inspiration from contemporary and historical international sources (for instance, the Garden City movement and CIAM planning) and translating those ideas into a Danish postwar architecture and planning context. In Denmark, welfare became specifically associated with the distribution and consumption of good and equal living conditions for every individual, from cradle to grave, and with the strengthening of community and democratic spirit.[6] Equally important, because of the Danish welfare state's design and use of its own "social housing association" model, which sought to keep the housing estates free from market forces, the open spaces were a de-commodified resource.[7] Welfare and landscape are thus held together in Denmark by a cluster of values involving strong communities and equal and free access to nature, health, and well-being for all, with special attention paid to children.[8] By emphasizing the collective role of green open spaces, the Danish postwar large-scale housing estates established a new set of human relationships and expanded notions of *welfare* and *public*

Four blocks were torn down to make room for a Paris-like boulevard as one of the main concepts to disrupt the estate's spatial Radburn-logic guiding the first radical Danish social housing estate transformation.

space; this made the landscape of the estates anything but a neutral backdrop for everyday life.

The estates were built on virgin, mostly agricultural, land. They were mainly, in line with international practice, planned as "neighborhood units" and were conceptualized as vehicles to stimulate people's sense of "community,"[9] "neighborhood,"[10] and a larger "public realm."[11] Set within a "floating" spatial framework, which placed buildings as solitary objects on a unifying ground or surface, the open spaces on these estates have been subjected to much criticism for their effects on public life.[12] The critics have argued in general ways that the open spaces, loosely defined by multistory concrete buildings and often characterized by a monotonous character and lack of human scale and experiences, left no room for individual expression and inhibited public life, even sustaining a sense of unsafety. Critics also maintain that the functionally segregated city, with its large car-based infrastructures and rationally produced large-scale housing estates, was unable to live up to its own optimistic idea of architecture as *social engineering*, which, in Denmark, involved providing good housing for everyone, and mixing social classes within a culturally and ethnically very homogeneous population. Among the most prominent critical voices, we find the American Jane Jacobs and the Dane Jan Gehl, who both instead advocated for pedestrian-friendly and human-scale principles in the design of public space.

Despite the criticism and their bleak public image, the postwar housing estates came to house an ethnically diverse population that was nonetheless less socially diverse than intended. Today, many of these estates' open spaces are the daily locus for multiple cultural encounters and have been recognized as public spaces that sustain public life.[13] Yet the ongoing transformations are more than an aesthetic makeover: the physical changes are fundamental in the sense that they impact upon uses, users, and embedded values. From a theoretical point of view, they highlight the need for new approaches to understanding and describing the open spaces in question. If we fail to conceptualize and theorize these changes, we lose our grip on one of architecture's most important roles: to enable social encounters and to sustain public life in a way that actually makes it happen, and, moreover, we may overlook the full consequences of the embedded and potentially incongruent intentions. Here, I argue that previous conceptual frameworks, including those of *the commons* and *public space*, no longer adequately mirror the complexity of open spaces being driven by the ongoing transformations of the postwar housing estates.

In what follows, the concept of *publicness* and its capacity to grasp these transformed open spaces is discussed. "Publicness" here denotes the interaction between physical spaces and people's ways of life; it informs a relational understanding of public space that can take into account non-material, yet highly embedded aspects, and do so over time. Public space is often handled as either a spatial concept *or* a social concept, thereby mirroring disciplinary demarcations, but thinking in terms of publicness provides a way to transgress these epistemic boundaries. The concept is therefore integral to a cross-disciplinary framework, combining aspects of heritage, policy, practice, democracy, and informality—all of which, both individually and together, may inform us about

9 Serge Chermayeff and Christopher Alexander, *Community and Privacy: Towards a New Architecture of Humanism* (New York: Doubleday, 1963).

10 Kenny Cupers, *The Social Project: Housing Postwar France* (Minneapolis, MN: University of Minnesota Press, 2014).

11 Tom Avermaete, Klaske Havik, and Hans Teerds, *Architectural Positions: Architecture, Modernity, and the Public Sphere* (Amsterdam: SUN Publishers, 2009).

12 Jane Jacobs, *The Death and Life of Great American Cities*. New York: Random House, 1992 [1969]); Jan Gehl, *Life Between Buildings: Using Public Space* (New York: Van Nostrand Reinhold, 1987).

13 Ali Madanipour, *Public and Private Spaces of the City* (London: Routledge, 2003); Anne Tietjen, ed., *Public Space in European Social Housing (PuSH)*, Copenhagen: Copenhagen Architecture Festival, 2022. Published in conjunction with an exhibition of the same title, curated by Anne Tietjen and presented at the Copenhagen Architecture Festival (CAFx), April 21–May 1, 2022. www.pushousing.eu.

14 Ali Madanipour, "Rethinking Public Space: Between Rhetoric and Reality," *Urban Design International* 24, no. 1 (2019): 1.

tensions between, for example, the individual and the collective, public and private interests, and informal and formal institutions or legal frameworks. The strategies applied at the shared open spaces in the Farum Midtpunkt estate, a social housing complex from the 1970s in Northern Zealand in Denmark worked as a model for reconfiguring the common spaces in other Danish social housing estates to public spaces, forming a point of reference for the ambitions of the later Ghetto Act and thus indirectly for conceptions of the mixed city. The concept of publicness helps to reflect on and understand the shifts at work in this particular case. It is important to note that the transformations wrought upon Farum Midtpunkt did not include the 60 percent ownership changes designated in the Ghetto Act, which would have resulted in demolition or intensive densification. This fact allows for the open space alterations made here—and their effects in a mixed city ideal—to be analyzed closely. While changes directly stemming from the Ghetto Act tend to be driven by municipalities inviting in private investors and using key open spaces as "an instrument of delivering investment and maximizing rewards,"[14] the changes witnessed at Farum Midtpunkt have been carried out by a collaboration between the housing association and a private foundation, thereby decreasing the commodification seen in Ghetto Act-driven transformations. As postwar housing estates are a widespread phenomenon, and similar transformation processes are occurring elsewhere in the Nordic countries and beyond, this case also has international relevance.

Farum Midtpunkt is an iconic case due to its remarkable appearance, yet it is also a representative case due to its distribution of welfare goods and its recent transformation mainly turning a central green area into an "activity square" addressing users coming from outside the estate and adding new public pathways throughout the estate. The 1,650-unit estate was built in the early 1970s in the town of Farum, situated about 25 kilometers north of the Copenhagen city center. The buildings were designed by Fællestegnestuen (Jørn Ole Sørensen, Viggo Møller-Jensen, and Thyge Arnfred) and the landscape by Edith and Ole Nørgaard. The estate is structured around 24 terraced, parallel, four-story apartment buildings, subdivided into four clusters. All buildings have parking areas on the terrain level and terraced apartments on the upper three levels, linked by elevated, partly outdoors, partly indoors infrastructure. The apartments have large individual terraces facing west or balconies facing east; they are accessed via wide corridors, which serve as shared spaces as much as entrance areas. The estate holds various open spaces in a fine-grained, multi-scalar network consisting, besides the private terraces, of small squares, neighborhood squares, pedestrian pathways, an elevated pedestrian high street, parking areas, and a surrounding green area. Consisting of the housing blocks, shops, and a school, the estate is situated on a 31-hectare large shell-shaped parcel of land, spatially enforced by green open spaces and a forest-like perimeter plantation. Within the area, many public and shared facilities are located on and next to the elevated pedestrian street, which serves as a backbone for the estate and provides access to the apartment buildings and the common open areas via perpendicular streets, which also connect the estate to the town of Farum.

15 David Harvey, *Rebel Cities: From the Right to the City to the Urban Revolution* (New York: Verso, 2012), 73.

16 As formulated by first Clarence Perry in *The Neighbourhood Unit* [1929] (Reprint London: Routledge/Thoemmes, 1998), 25–44, and then by Lewis Mumford, "The Neighborhood and the Neighborhood Unit," *Town Planning Review* 24, no. 4 (January 1954): 256–70.

COMMONS, NEIGHBORHOOD, PUBLIC SPACE, AND THE TERMS' LIMITS

Various theoretical frameworks have guided the sociospatial development of postwar housing estates and thus their open spaces: most notably, ideas about common space, community planning, the neighborhood unit, and ideas about public space in addition to categories such as parks, open and closed gardens. The commons can be understood as a social practice of governing a resource by a community of users, who self-govern the resource through the institutions they create.[15] In this sense, the concept of commons ranks among the main aims embedded in the mixed city, as common space may become central to sustaining the ideal of the democratic citizen. Since the Danish social housing sector owns or has a long-term lease on the land of the estates, and their governance moreover is characterized by tenant democracy, the estates' spatial appearance and governance converge into the traditional understanding of a commons made up of large parcels of lands collectively managed. The housing estate's common spaces form part of a larger web of shared welfare resources such as schools, libraries, and sports facilities encompassing open spaces too. However, these institutions and their spatial entourage do not provide access to direct decision-making. This complicates how an estate's open spaces can be characterized: despite the shared goals of welfare provision, they should, rather, be considered public space.

Ideas of community planning may relate directly to commonly used space, and in large-scale Danish postwar housing estates, such ideas merged with modernist design principles. Here, the US-born idea of the neighborhood unit pointed specifically to centering the school, placing arterial streets along the perimeter, designing internal streets, restricting local shopping areas to the perimeter, and dedicating at least 10 percent of the neighborhood land area to parks and open spaces, thereby creating places for play and community interaction.[16] These strategies, in combination with modernist principles of admitting daylight into the housing blocks (a practice sustained also by the montage crane logic), placed new buildings in a syntax of parallel lines, with all open space operating as a unifying floor or surface. A new open space paradigm thereby emerged. In general, this denoted a paradigmatic shift in urban design away from conventional public spaces such as streets, squares, and galleries and toward a city of "public landscapes," which are extensive, open, and traversable. It also denoted a new balance between open and built, and green and petrified, as well as between public and privately owned spaces in the city. Moreover, in Denmark, the neighborhood unit and the common green area also merged with the green tissue that linked the blocks together and provided them with egress. Later, this spatial distribution—which materialized the "Radburn principle" of a cellular street pattern, with a ring road linking the cul-de-sac roads serving the housing units, situating the shared open green area in the car-protected center of the housing estate—increased the public perception of the estate as introverted and private, and the green center as being for residents only. In other words, divided by large infrastructures, this new shared open space paradigm partly appeared as detached islands of which one part—the one owned

Farum Midtpunkt is an iconic Danish social housing estate characterized by stacked terrasse flats in parallel rows with lush green in-between areas.

The new Activity Square is located next to the main pedestrian arteria and has replaced green in-between space.

The plan shows the clustering of parallel row houses within a green framing. The Activity Square is located next to the main entrance to the estate.

by the housing association and governed by the tenants—worked as a common.

However, the resulting spatial framework sustained social and cultural encounters, and hence sustained a kind of public life across the estate. Public life refers to the many and diverse ways that "people rub along, or don't, in the public spaces of a city."[17] The related concept of public space is widely understood as those places where public life unfolds.[18] Public space is a very prominent concept, and outdoor meeting places—often associated with classical urban places, such as boulevards, urban squares, and metropolitan entertainment or commercial districts—are seen as defining spatial characteristics of European cities, implying a certain normativity within the concept. However, urban public space goes beyond typical urban stereotypes and that which is publicly owned.[19] It also does not relate to collective government. As places of public life, public space also includes the open spaces of social housing areas, even if formally these are semi-public in the sense that their ownership, use, and governmental structures are closely linked to the tenants. While constituting public spaces, the open spaces of postwar social housing estates do not resonate with the traditional public space typologies and their structural distribution.

The ideal steering the ongoing transformations is that of the mixed city. This concept has in general terms been advanced by prominent urban theorists such as Richard Sennett, Doreen Massey, David Harvey, and Ash Amin.[20] They highlight it as key for sustaining social cohesion through social contact between different social groups, for its potential for openness, for its use and sharing by all, and for its capacity to integrate and support the coexistence of social and cultural difference. In other words, the mixed city ideal holds the promise of remedying the negative social and cultural consequences of increasing inequality, spatial sorting, and social segmentation (which, incidentally, is far more prevalent elsewhere than in Denmark). In practical terms, the mixed city promotes social and cultural interaction via a spatially framed "thrown-togetherness" of people,[21] ensuring peaceful coexistence.

However, the mixed city does not in and of itself maintain a coherent consensual formula concerning the scale at which mixing should take place. If we are to judge from the ongoing transformations, we can conclude that the scale of the 1970s social housing estates apparently justify for an ideal mixed city district unit, as the estates are deliberately chosen to form such future mixed city districts. Nevertheless, while the mixed city is an undisputed ideal, its meaning is unclear. What is the size of the mixed city's units, how are they structured, and what means can be applied to achieve a mixed city? These are all unanswered questions. It is thus surprising that these non-explicit ideals apparently turn out to fit precisely with the size of postwar large-scale developments and their location in the larger urban landscape, and that the mixed city is supposedly achieved by lowering the proportion of social housing to a maximum of 40 percent. Moreover, the current realization of the mixed city ideal within the framework of social housing estates is somewhat of a paradox, since the aims of today's mixed city to a huge degree mirrors the aims of the past, echoing the postwar neighborhood unit ideal in its aim of bridging social and cultural differences; as such, it aspires to provide equal access to welfare

17 Sarah Watson, *City Publics: The (Dis) enchantments of Urban Encounters* (London: Routledge, 2006), 2.
18 Ali Madanipour, ed., *Whose Public Space? International Case Studies in Urban Design and Development* (London: Routledge, 2010).
19 Madanipour, *Public and Private Spaces*.
20 Richard Sennett, *The Conscience of the Eye: The Design and Social Life of Cities* (London: Faber, 1990); Doreen Massey, *For Space* (London: Sage, 2005); Harvey, *Rebel Cities*, Ash Amin, "Collective Culture and Urban Public Space," *City* 12, no. 1 (2008): 5–24.
21 Massey, *For Space*.

goods and services *for the second time in exactly the same area*. Here it is worth noticing that the criticized spatial framework of "floating" open space (open space as a surface) has already proven itself capable of enabling social interactions and being both inviting and accessible, so how much should be changed to widen the user group? Process-wise, the mixed city introduces another paradox, as two of the large-scale postwar estates' main challenges—its gigantic scale and "once-and-for-all" planning ethos—are to be repeated: the full-scale entity of the housing estate will once again become subject for a once-and-for-all masterplan.

PUBLICNESS AND THE INTERACTION BETWEEN PEOPLE AND PLACES

How can the pitfalls of open spaces of large-scale housing estates be avoided when discussing their past, present, and future, and their role in the wider urban context? We are in dire need of concepts that can help us to understand, assess, and consider how to intervene in these complex spatial, social, and cultural contexts. The concept of *publicness* may help to conceptualize these transformed open spaces while retaining a focus on the intersection of people and places, as well the core values that informed their construction; it may also assist in going beyond the simple social engineering that drove the conceptualization of the first large-scale housing estates built on virgin land. In the "PuSH" research project, publicness worked as a starting point for a multidisciplinary exploration of how large-scale postwar housing estates act as sites of public life, and as active co-producers of cultural encounters across social and material domains.[22]

In Farum Midtpunkt, the estate's main open space was subject to a significant transformation between 2012 and 2016, and changes included a new "activity park" for play and sports, a new pedestrian infrastructure, and some small-square makeovers. All of these places can be analyzed as potential sites of publicness where people and places may interact. The aim of the transformation was to open the estate to its adjacent areas and to people living nearby, and the more subtle open space changes can be regarded as the first step in a mixed city initiative.

Interrogating public space beyond the architectural object, the notion of publicness is one way to address the new and complex entity of the former social housing estate as it transitions toward a mixed city ideal. Publicness builds on a relational conception of space that helps us understand the material and immaterial aspects of different urban development phenomena, its spatial, cultural, and temporal normativity. In the words of Tornaghi and Knierbein, "relational space approaches involve concepts that define 'lived space' as phenomena that can only be explained by their social, political, and cultural context and by the relations between people and objects, both at a given moment in time and in the course of history."[23] Publicness is thus a working concept that helps us to think about the relation between public life and public space and not a fixed characteristic determined by the main function of a space. It focuses on spatial and social processes, as well as on their cultural and political contexts and inequalities, over time.[24]

22 PuSH, "Public Space in European Social Housing," was a three-year HERA funded research project led by myself and conducted by four national teams from Denmark, Italy, Norway, and Switzerland. Farum Midtpunkt was the Danish case. For an introduction, see Ellen Braae et al., "Examining the Publicness of Spaces on European Social Housing Estates: A Position Paper," *ARQ: Architecture Research Quarterly* 27, no. 2 (June 2023): 143–57. https://doi.org/10.1017/S1359135523000155.

23 Chiara Tornaghi and Sabine Knierbein, eds., *Public Space and Relational Perspectives: New Challenges for Architecture and Planning* (London: Routledge, 2016), 4.

24 Tornaghi and Knierbein, 6.

The Activity Square is programmed with hard surfaces sustaining mainly skating and soccer.

25 Braae et al., "Examining the Publicness of Spaces on European Social-Housing Estates."
26 Madanipour, *Public and Private Spaces.*
27 Madanipour, *Public and Private Spaces.*

In order to address the combined social, political, and cultural contexts at work within specific moments and over longer time-frames, four analytical categories or lenses can be applied to the concept of publicness—namely, heritage, policies and practices, informality, and democracy. Each category represents a sphere of fluid and context-specific relations which allow negotiations and an ever-changing meaning of publicness that can transgress normative definitions given by location, form, regulation, or function alone.[25] Moreover, this combination of analytical categories also works as a cross-disciplinary framework bridging the gap between social and spatial professions, between place and people, and grasping the tensions and crossing the epistemic boundaries that traditionally hamper public space discourses.[26]

The first aspect, heritage, is here understood as lived heritage, starting at the local level—that is, starting from the histories, concerns, and values of residents and other local actors. Regarding large-scale housing as heritage in this way reveals unique local interactions between lives lived and their material framework, and potentially holds an empowering aspect. The Farum Midtpunkt heritage analysis addressed a local and much-contested site of publicness: the internal semi-public corridors that, in later becoming semi-private, pushed the public life and circulation system to areas not originally intended for such uses (ground-level parking areas that many residents have experienced as lacking security partly due to drug dealing). It also revealed that the long-term residents shared positive memories of the communities constituted by past everyday life in the corridors, and that some of the decentered open spaces have been domesticated by dog owners, and some by gardeners, in both cases constituting much-debated yet also important meeting places for various subgroups. The lived heritage outside the individual dwellings mainly concerned nearby areas and past and ongoing domestication battles, the sense of insecurity, and the demarcation between private, semi-private, and semi-public zones.

The second aspect, made visible through the lens of policies and practices, supports a long-term sociospatial perspective of space as something that is relational and socially produced. A housing complex can be seen as an open system connected to everyday life and experiences as well as to public and individual narratives. Over time, policies and practices shape place and space in a dynamic and performative manner.[27] From the Farum Midtpunkt analyses, it became clear that the relationship between policies and spatial practices at Farum Midtpunkt cannot be reduced to a mere opposition between top-down and bottom-up. In some places, practices and policies have brought about ways of sharing places where a variety of interest groups have gained the right to use specific places through formal policies and regulations by the tenant board and the municipality; in other places, specific groups (such as the already mentioned dog owners and gardeners) have occupied underused spaces over time until they became habitual and accepted.

This also touches upon the third aspect, which focuses on democracy; this lens is related to social interactions intertwined with physical space and its embedded qualities and ways of sustaining politics. These embedded and sustaining factors/elements may be found in the distribution of spatial resources (who gets to

28 Madanipour, *Public and Private Spaces*.
29 Madanipour, *Public and Private Spaces*.

use which spatial resources, when, and how?), in decision-making processes (who decides and who is represented?), and in spatial practices (how is space adapted, performed, perceived, and used?).[28] In Farum Midtpunkt, the aforementioned domesticating groups, along with the lack of sense of security when going to the parking level, demonstrated the way in which not everyone is welcome. Moreover, the tenant board is dominated by white, elderly persons who have lived at the estate for many years and are reluctant to include new voices.

Informality, our final aspect of publicness, is a concept based on an implicit divide established by an authority that sets normative standards and opposes anything that falls outside its realm or does not conform to its precepts. This may be examined through planning laws (through which we can detect unplanned/spontaneous/illegal land uses); cultural, moral, and religious norms (by which something can be judged as anomalous, non-belonging/alien, even harmful); design codes and rules (through which we can distinguish unexpected affordances of objects); and state welfare regulations (through which we can detect the self-provisioning of collective goods and services).[29] Some places in Farum Midtpunkt, like the parking areas, have gradually come to be used in ways that they were not planned for, in reaction to some of these often rigid spaces or spaces with designated uses defined by the tenant board. While other sites intended to "invite users in" from outside the estate by means of material upgrade and a higher level of maintenance were not, for instance, used at all.

The four aspects of publicness—heritage, policies and practices, informality, democracy—came together when examining Farum Midtpunkt's newly formed Activity Square and the new circulation system. The transformation was based on the two aims of opening up Farum "to increase the experience of community and the perception of safety" by fostering activity in the outdoor common spaces, and of better connecting the housing estate to the surrounding town of Farum. The new Activity Square, as a pronounced renewal site for publicness, introduced a materiality, an aesthetic, and a conceptual take that departed boldly from the existing 1970s architecture. The strong visual contrast to the architecture, and the immediate decoding of its heritage, can be seen as evidencing a disregard of what was there already. The spatial order of the estate has been reconfigured with this significant centralization of the estate's largest and spatially most integrated public space, and its appearance in a structure of otherwise decentralized and distributed shared spaces, which were located close to clusters of residents' homes. By enhancing the hierarchy of the internal infrastructure and facilitating the use of key entrance areas by people from inside and outside the estate, the sense of security and accessibility has increased in these areas while other areas (the parking areas, and smaller, less central open spaces) are experienced as even more "remote" and inaccessible. However, a new system of boardwalks placed within the lush green areas at ground level and located between the parking areas has reopened and made accessible—and thus public—the longitudinal infrastructures of the estate that were terminated when the wide interior corridors and entrance areas working as semi-private space for the block's residents and walk-throughs for non-residents were closed off. The materiality of the boardwalks corresponds with the rusted Corten steel on the facades, and they weave in and out of the parking areas, introducing new functions such as ping-pong and inviting new users in.

One of the social consequences of the new Activity Square design lies in the tendency for one group or activity to be dominant, as much of the equipment is only suitable for one activity or age group at a time. Playable structures such as a climbing wall, a street basketball court, trampolines, skating areas favor physically active children, that is, most often, tweens and young teenage boys. While maintaining the historical focus on children's play, focus is now on performative modes of being. The open space now works as a public event.[30] While some types of equipment and the spatial setting invite diverse groups of users, specific design features may indirectly continue to exclude specific groups—for example, the elderly, who might be discouraged to sit on uncomfortable benches, or those who don't play soccer or pingpong. Another challenge lies in a new tension between generations promoted by a clash between the long-term goal of demonstrating that the estate is attractive for children and young people and the needs of the currently dominant tenant group of elderly people, who find the Activity Square too noisy. The changes thus also shed light on the core aspect of the commons—that is, as a social practice that governs a shared resource for the tenants. With the new design, people coming from the adjacent areas are equally users of the Activity Square as a public space, yet it is governed by a semi-private institution, that is, the housing association, which is mainly ruled by a white, elderly group.

The transformation was initiated in 2014 as a collaboration between Realdania, Denmark's largest philanthropic association for the built environment, the local housing association, Furesø Boligselskab, and residents' representatives. The tenants' democracy—a key feature of the Danish housing association tradition—was thus partly in play, yet was also questioned, given that this new area was aimed at both the tenants and people living outside the estate and no option was given to decline the transformation initiative. In this case, the area is still formally owned by the housing association and thus the tenants, while in other ongoing transformations such as that occurring at the iconic housing estate Tingbjerg, which is being driven by the Ghetto Act, the land is being sold off to private investors and open spaces will be reconfigured for a new target group of buyers. In the latter case, the concept of the commons is no longer valid and collective government is being dismantled. While the concept of the commons is no longer fully adequate, the concept of the neighborhood unit and its embedded welfare values may still, however, be valid as long as proximity to green open space with a high degree of publicness to schools and other public institutions is maintained. For better or worse such spaces maintain the messiness and entanglement of everyday interactions that make up lived heritage, and through the various user groups, top-down and bottom-up policymaking, and everyday practices, aspects of democratic expression and involvement, and some room for informality, remains. It is extremely important to examine the results and experienced consequences of ongoing transformations in detail, and to discuss them in the context of the

30 Bettina Lamm and Svava Riesto, "Farum Midtpunkt / Renewal of Shared Spaces," in *Public Space in European Social Housing (PuSH)*, ed. Anne Tietjen et al., Copenhagen: Copenhagen Architecture Festival, 2022, 136. Exhibition catalog. www.pushousing.eu.

The lush green areas between the parking lots at ground zero have provided space for a new pedestrian infrastructure since the corridors were closed off.

The programming of the covered parking areas beneath the apartments has been expanded so that the parking areas are perceived as less unsafe.

The interior corridors were planned as both a semi-private/semi-public area and part of the estate infrastructure. Yet they were soon closed off to work for the residents in block only.

31 Noortje Marres, "Issues Spark a Public into Being," in *Making Things Public*, ed. Bruno Latour and Peter Weibel (Cambridge, MA: MIT Press, 2005), 208–17.

significant number of welfare-imbued public space transformations taking place in the Nordic countries. The goal is not a seamless society—there will always be tensions and frictions—yet we must learn how people and places interact to sustain productive and enriching encounters.

CONCLUSION

Social and cultural encounters in shared open space are key to the ideal of the mixed city. However, when the mixed city takes form in Danish social housing estates—either through tough means (demolition and densification) or lighter methods (such as the redesign pursued in Farum Midtpunkt)—while ideas of public life and many key welfare values might be maintained, where ownership shifts, traditional concepts such as common, community, public space, and public life are inevitably challenged.

The need to better understand public space, beyond only its spatial or only its social aspects, calls for relational thinking, which involves a series of re-conceptualizations. Ideas of spatial identities, everyday uses, planning practices, and policy environments must be revised and viewed as being built relationally and contextually: they must be understood as highly entangled. The concept of publicness and the four analytical categories of publicness introduced in this text—heritage, policies and practices, democracy, and informality—bring in various disciplines and theoretical framings. Individually and in combination, they enable an examination of how interactions between people and the spaces they share create sites of public life (albeit of a more performative kind of public life), how the interaction between space and people changes over time, how spaces become a public concern and "spark a public into being,"[31] and how such spaces might make living with others (who are different from oneself) possible. Bringing together the social and the spatial, they help reveal sites of publicness within the spatial and conceptual reconfigurations and ongoing transformations of the Danish social housing estates, beyond general questions of what spatial, infrastructural, and social paradigms are "preferred" or rigid ideas of public space and social engineering. Transformations deeply affect the embedded values, uses, and users of open spaces and unlike the virgin land development of the postwar period, a multitude of places, people, practices, memories, and rules are already in place in Denmark's housing estates. As a heuristic concept and tool, publicness may also help us understand how embedded welfare values are being twisted and challenged, traditional concepts of commons and public space exhausted, evaporated, and replaced—despite the fact that the areas continue to be conceptualized with the "floating" space paradigm of an earlier modernism. The shift from commons to relational public space has changed the relationship between the enlarged group of citizens and the open spaces as a consequence of the transformations aiming for mixed-city districts. This means commodifying the housing and their open spaces and inviting new users in, potentially resulting in an alienation of the open spaces in terms of a sense of heritage, democracy and practices, as they are no longer a shared responsibility of the people using them.

Erik Sigge

THE WORTH OF WELFARE

Who Benefits from Market Models in the Public Sector?

In recent years, a lively debate has occurred around the Swedish deregulation of welfare sectors such as education, healthcare, childcare, and care of the elderly. Prompted by new headlines referring to "large profits in the welfare sector" and "welfare billionaires," Swedish citizens have begun to ask how their tax money could be generating personal wealth for a select few while public services struggle to stay afloat.[1] If room exists for huge profits to be made in the privatized welfare sector, does this mean that the publicly run services are inefficient? Or is the quality of services compromised in the profit-run companies? Where are these revenues coming from?

In increasing their shares of the healthcare sector, private healthcare companies such as Capio, Attendo, Aleris, and Humana have simultaneously increased their profits.[2] In education, the four largest corporate groups—Academia, Engelska skolan, Thorengruppen, and Kundskapsskolan—together made 1.3 billion SEK (Swedish crowns) in profit during 2021 and over 4.6 billion SEK over the last five years.[3] Over the last ten years, we have seen a similar privatization of municipally owned housing. While companies in health and education strategically establish themselves in affluent areas, servicing healthy and well-educated inhabitants, housing transactions have primarily occurred in poorer and socioeconomically weaker areas, that in addition also have badly maintained building stocks. What are the incentives to invest in these buildings? The simple answer is that the marketization of housing has allowed for increases in property values that have not only given new opportunities to borrow more money for new acquisitions, but also meant higher returns for the companies, as the increased value could be reported as profit. Many municipalities are thrilled by the opportunity to fund new investments and other parts of their operations, and at the same time to get rid of the burden of maintaining a run-down building stock.[4] Despite lofty promises of long-term strategies with sustainable and affordable renovations, private real estate companies have been quick to sell to other companies—often international venture capital companies with headquarters somewhere far away—at large profits.

One Swedish company that assures us that it is in it for the long run is the private company Samhällsbyggnadsbolaget i Norden, SBB, which is a listed corporation that owns buildings in Sweden, Denmark, and Norway, whereof a majority lies in so-called "welfare buildings" while the rest is in housing.[5] SBB's model is simple: buy buildings from municipalities that need to free up capital for other expenses or investments, then sign long rental agreements with the same municipalities. The risks are almost non-existant, as the tenants are stable and public tax money ensures that the payments will be made. The opportunities for value increases are enormous.[6] The most spectacular example of SBB's expansion is perhaps the

1 Academia's return on equity is 13.2 percent which is comparable to SEB, one of Sweden's largest banks. This debate has taken place in a recent series of articles, for instance "Välfärdsmiljonärerna," published in the daily newspaper *Dagens Nyheter* during the summer of 2022 and as a three-part podcast. See Björn af Kleen, host, Välfärdsmiljonärerna (podcast), August 5, 2022, https://www.dn.se/sverige/valfardsmiljardarerna/.

2 Margaretha Levander, "Vårdjättarna ökar sina vinster," *Dagens Samhälle*, June 8, 2017, https://www.dagenssamhalle.se/samhalle-och-valfard/sjukvard/vardjattarna-okar-sina-vinster/.

3 https://www.svt.se/nyheter/inrikes/skolvinsterna-4-6-miljarder-pa-fem-ar.

4 "Alby är inte till salu" ("Alby is not for sale") is perhaps the best-known public critique of this development, for which the tenants of public housing in Alby, in Botkyrka municipality outside of Stockholm, organized themselves to protest the municipality's sale of public housing to private companies, around 2012.

5 Andreas Cervenka, *Girig-Sverige* (Stockholm: Natur och Kultur, 2022), 117. SBB has quickly become the fifth largest real estate company in Sweden, see "Största fastighetsägarna 2022" ["Largest property owners"], *Fastighetsvärlden*, March 30, 2022, https://www.fastighetsvarlden.se/analys-fakta/topplistor/storsta-fastighetsagarna-2022/.

6 During the last five years, SBB raised the values of their building stock with a total of 29 billion SEK. Cervenka, *Girig-Sverige*, 118.

Sara Culture House in Skellefteå in northern Sweden. SBB bought the building complex, which was initiated and constructed by the municipality of Skellefteå and also includes a hotel and apartments, in 2018 for 1 billion SEK whereafter the municipality signed a lease contract worth 45 million SEK per year for 50 years.[7] The calculations do not add up in the municipality's favor, as the total bill after 50 years will be more than 2 billion SEK. Skellefteå had its specific reasons to free up capital for other investments and it is difficult to make a general judgment regarding their choice. What is clear, however, is that what we see all over Scandinavia is a massive transfer of wealth from the public to the private sector. In 2020 alone, welfare buildings were sold in Sweden for 40 billion SEK.[8]

After its founding in 2016, SBB grew rapidly, and in 2021 it was Sweden's fifth-largest real estate company with a total value of properties of 149 billion SEK, an increase from 90 billion SEK the year before.[9] With the recent rise in inflation and interest rates, SBB's business model has proved to be extremely vulnerable, as a majority of the rapid acquisitions have been financed through loans based on newly raised property values. During 2023, SBB was forced to sell buildings for about half of its total value and today continues to sell off their "welfare buildings" to other private companies, but also, increasingly, to municipalities that now "buy back" buildings such as schools, nursery homes and homes for elderly. SBB continues to have problems with short-term liquidity and long-term overindebtedness, and financial experts believe that the company needs to bisect its property holdings once again to reach a feasible balance.[10] Although there has been a public debate about the political morale and economic advantages of selling—and now buying back—public buildings, the current situation has not changed the reasoning around welfare policies or the practices of welfare. One of the main arguments for selling has been that it is good public management to distribute the risks of ownership to other, private actors, who are also thought to be more efficient as real estate owners. Although SBB is now blamed for its risky behavior, the general verdict is that it is not the privatization of public property or the marketization of building management that is the problem, but the risks taken by SBB in expanding faster than their economic gains.

The recent privatizations point to a condition in which citizens are misled to believe that publicly run companies and welfare are a burden that need to be slimmed, reformed, outsourced, or abandoned. How have we arrived at this conclusion? This text focuses on the ownership and management of public buildings, through a closer investigation of the state-owned real estate company Akademiska Hus, and argues that the models and rationales behind our current welfare allocation and distribution could be revealed in the financial and managerial instruments that are employed in publicly supported operations. Such instruments not only succeed politically in initiating deregulation and marketization, but arguably push the objectives of welfare policies beyond the interest of individual citizens and the common good. Although the worth of welfare is always under negotiation, and such negotiations in turn form both the means and ends of many policies and programs, few public explanations are given regarding how changes in *means* affect the final *worth* of our welfare society. The following is an attempt to provide a description of current welfare logics.

7 Marcus Derland, "Skellefteå om affären med SBB: 'Ska finnas ett större syfte'" ["Skellefteå on their Deal with SBB: 'There should be a greater purpose'"], *Dagens Nyheter*, August 8, 2022, https://www.dn.se/sverige/skelleftea-om-affaren-med-sbb-ska-finnas-ett-storre-syfte/.

8 Cervenka, *Girig-Sverige*, 120.

9 Mårten Arwidsson, "LISTA: Här är landets största fastighetsbolag 2022," *Fastighetsnytt*, June 15, 2022, https://www.fastighetsnytt.se/ekonomi-och-finans/finansiering/lista-har-ar-landets-storsta-fastighetsbolag-2022/.

10 "Affärsvärlden bedömer SBB kan behöva halvera fastighetsbeståndet ytterligare en gång," *Affärsvärlden*, November 14, 2023, https://www.affarsvarlden.se/aktierekar/affarsvarlden-bedomer-sbb-kan-behova-halvera-fastighetsbestandet-ytterligare-en-gang.

School of Architecture of the KTH Royal
Institute of Technology, Stockholm, Sweden.
Built 2013–15. Architects: Tham & Videgård.

Akademiska Hus owns, develops and manges properties for universities and colleges. It is the largest company in this real estate segment, and currently the sixth largest overall in Sweden. In September of 2015, Akademiska Hus announced that it would be paying a dividend of 6.5 billion SEK to its shareholder, the Swedish Government—1 billion SEK more than the company's yearly revenue from rentals. This is after the government had given new owner directives and instructed Akademiska Hus to raise the value of its properties by 5 billion SEK. Behind the directives was the government's demand that the company lower its solvency in order to achieve a more "efficient capital structure."[11] The announcement led the leaders of Swedish universities to protest the government's new owner directive, which had been harshly criticized even before the change.[12] Critics talked about a "covert taxation" of higher education, as an increasing part of the state budget allocated to higher education would now go directly to rent, in turn leaving less and less money for the core activities of education and research.[13] Akademiska Hus assured its tenants that the extra payment to the government would not affect the company's rents, and that they instead borrowed money for the dividend.[14] The statement could certainly be questioned, as reassessments of properties' value, whether up or down, normally influence the rents correspondingly. Although there were no immediate rent increases that could be directly tied to the special payment of 2015, the increase of building values created an opening for sharper increases of rents in the future.[15]

In 1993, the existing state premise provider, the National Board of Public Building (Kungliga Byggnadsstyrelsen, KBS), the governmental agency in charge of providing premises by maintaining existing buildings, renting out spaces, and constructing new buildings,[16] was dissolved and its duties reconstructed in three different entities: the National Property Board (Statens fastighetsverk), which administers historical buildings, land, and state properties abroad; Vasakronan, which is a strictly commercial property owner that primarily rents out commercial spaces for office and retail, and up until a few years ago the largest real estate company in Sweden; and Akademiska Hus, which according to the owner directives should "own, develop and manage properties for universities and colleges, with a primary focus on educational and research activities."[17]

The division into three "enterprises" should firstly be seen in the light of an attempt to clarify the economic strategies of the state's dealings with building rentals, building maintenance, and building construction, in which the directives for Akademiska Hus are clear: "The company's operations shall be carried out in a business-like manner and yield competitive profits by adapting our rents to the company's business risk."[18] From this perspective, Akademiska Hus is actually doing a great job of fulfilling its mission and delivering what it is asked to and more. However, the risks involved in providing premises for universities would seem very low compared to renting to other tenants. This risk is reduced further, as Akademiska Hus has a privileged position as the foremost provider of such premises, owning around 60 percent of the market share.[19]

From the citizens' point of view, the core of the problem is that less of the tax money allocated for education and research is going to these central functions of higher education, and is instead being used for the universities' so-called "overhead" expenses. In the

11 The Government issued new directives to Akademiska Hus in 2014 that strengthened the strict business management of the company and set a new solvency benchmark of 30–40 percent. Prior to the special dividend on October 2015, solvency was 48 percent, and after around 39 percent.

12 Rectors/Vice Chancellors at 30 Swedish universities and colleges published an article stating that "the state is draining the universities." See "Staten dränerar universiteten" [The state is draining the universities], *Dagens Industri*, October 15, 2015, https://www.di.se/artiklar/2015/10/15/debatt-staten-dranerar-universiteten/.

13 See, for instance, the article by Stellan Lundström, response by Kerstin Lindberg Göransson, and interview with Stellan Lundström: Stellan Lundström, "Högskolesektorn smygbeskattas via Akademiska Hus" [The covert taxation of the tertiary education sector by Akademiska Hus], *Fastighetsnytt*, October 28, 2014; Kerstin Lindberg Göransson, "Replik: Akademiska Hus" [Response: Akademiska Hus], *Fastighetsnytt*, October 30, 2014; and Christer Gummesson, "KTH:s hyror onödiga miljonkostnader" [KTH's rent an unnecessary cost of millions], *Campi*, November 24, 2014.

14 According to Jonas Ragnarsson, CFO at Akademiska Hus. See the interview: Sverrir Thór, "Lånar pengar till utdelningen" [Loaning money to the department], *Fastighetsnytt*, September 30, 2015, http://fastighetsnytt.se/2015/09/lanar-pengar-till-utdelningen/.

15 "Största fastighetsägarna 2022," 2022.

16 For a more detailed account of the work of Kungliga Byggnadsstyrelsen, see Erik Sigge, *Architecture's Red Tape* (PhD diss., KTH Royal Institute of Technology, Stockholm, 2017).

17 See Akademiska Hus, "Mission," accessed on September 1, 2022, www.akademiskahus.se Vasakronan was until 2021 Sweden's largest real estate company and dispite significant new acquisitions it is now the third largest, while Akademiska Hus used to be the third largest but is now only in place number six. For information on 2021 see "Största fastighetsägarna 2022," 2022, https://www.fastighetsvarlden.se/analys-fakta/topplistor/storsta-fastighetsagarna-2022/, and for information on 2023, see https://www.fastighetsnytt.se/fastighetsmarknad/forvaltning/hela-listan-de-ar-sveriges-101-storsta-fastighetsbolag/#.

18 Akademiska Hus, "Mission." The full goal reads "The mission of Akademiska Hus is to own, develop and manage properties for universities and colleges, with a primary focus on education and research activities. The company's operations shall be carried out in a business-like manner and yield competitive profits by adapting our rents to the company's business risk. Akademiska Hus shall work to promote a sustainable long-term development of university and college campuses." The mission was approved by the Swedish Parliament in December 2013.

19 Akademiska Hus, "Mission."

case at hand, these include substantial revenues to the real estate owner. Tax money allocated to education and research travels far and takes many turns within the state system. The concentricity of the money flow is particularly telling. In a financial market economy, the flow of capital is essential, as capital should "work," regardless of whether it is owned or borrowed, restricted or unrestricted. In every transaction there is a potential economic surplus, which provides incentives to constantly optimize the financial structure of the holdings in relation to future prospects.

Sweden remains the international example *par excellence* of a society with robust social welfare in which social equality and equal opportunity are prioritized. Although these claims may still be true of welfare areas such as childcare and social insurances, as far as economic equality goes, Sweden's position as the champion of social welfare is long gone.[20] Since 1993, Sweden has deregulated many of its welfare services, with a majority of the privatization taking place after 2007. Among the deregulated sectors were postal services, national telecom, and railways, all in 1993. Incidentally, 1993 was also the year in which the state's premise provision was commercialized and Akademiska Hus was established. As a result of this reorganization, all state institutions became responsible for renting premises and covering the cost of market rents with their allocated budgets.[21] Around the same time, the government decided to implement strict "economic steering" of state institutions, and in 1998 the Agency of Economic Steering or *Ekonomistyrningsverket* (ESV) was established for this purpose.[22]

We know in general what *deregulation* and *privatization* mean with regard to changes in ownership structures and the basic view of the role of government, however, other, more hidden or silent, changes to the Swedish welfare state have occurred that go beyond the larger ideological, societal shift and the corresponding policy changes. From a historical perspective, we can see that in the late 1960s and early 1970s, the financial structure of public administration had already become more aligned with for-profit business management, and traditional budgetary management gave way to capital accounting systems with new bookkeeping techniques. Although the changes should be seen as an ideological shift toward marketization of public administration, it is also important to acknowledge that a general interest in business-like management existed, accompanied by a widespread belief that it would make economical and managerial improvements. The most tangible change that prompted the dissolution of KBS in 1993 and its reincarnation as Vasakronan, the National Property Board, and Akademiska Hus could be traced all the way to 1967, when the government implemented a new budgetary system at KBS. Called Program Budgeting, this new system introduced performance and evaluation concepts into budget planning. In the statement following this decision, KBS's Director General Sixten Larsson predicted that KBS would become a "commercial agency" within five years—a commercial public enterprise operating as a business, "that buys, produces, rents, and sublets premises of all kinds."[23] It may come as a surprise that the new methods of administration were such that KBS saw the entirety of its operations change with the change in bookkeeping, but it attests to the significance of what sociologist and philosopher Maurizio Lazzarato calls "accounting machines," to which I will return later.

20 The internationally acknowledged Swedish "middle road" was built on equality and mutual understanding, commonality, and belonging, and reforms and agreements that were to be drafted on the widest possible consensus and provide general welfare for all, i.e. universal, tax-financed, and publicly provided welfare. This economic policy has long since vanished and Sweden is instead intertwined in European economic policies and global affairs. See Bo Eriksson, *Sveriges historia* (Stockholm: Nordstedts, 2012), 458–64; and Erik Lundberg, *The Development of Swedish and Keynesian Macroeconomic Theory and its Impact on Economic Policy* (Cambridge: Cambridge University Press, 1993), 49–53.

21 Förordning (1993:528) om statliga myndigheters lokalförsörjning.

22 Ekonomistyrningsverket, ESV was established in June 1998. Before this, economic steering and control within the state was managed by Riksrevisionsverket (RRV).

23 As we now know, this change of operation did not happen until 1993. For "the prediction" that KBS would become a commercial enterprise—a statement made by Sixten Larsson in 1968—see Byggnadsstyrelsen, *Byggnadsstyrelsen*, offprint, *Arkitektur* 9 (1968).

24 Sweden has experienced rapid deregulation, which, according to some research is the fastest of all "Western countries." See Göran Eriksson, "Den liberala revolutionen" [The liberal revolution], *Svenska Dagbladet*, March 24, 2012, https://www.svd.se/a/29975a60-c157-3ad1-90c3-f99d853f866b/den-liberala-revolutionen.

25 Michel Foucault, *The Birth of Biopolitics: Lectures at the Collège de France, 1978–1979* (New York: Picador, 2008), 131.

26 Foucault, 146.

What is at stake here are political decisions about welfare policies, and with those decisions, the mechanisms of public choice. If Sweden's earlier welfare policies were founded on an economic policy in which the decisions were based on collective choice through state programs, welfare policies since the 1970s have been increasingly based on individual choice determined through a market of demands (i.e., competition). The longstanding problem of being able to make decisions regarding policies and programs on the basis of social needs—the classic problem of a welfare economy—has been depoliticized and formalized into questions of efficiency and competitiveness. Formerly, the drafting of welfare policies was based on the consideration of social needs in relation to the costs of welfare programs; it was thus a matter of political decisions based on cost-effectiveness and cost-benefit analyses. However, this has now, in Sweden as in other places, been replaced by the neoliberal idea of "market justice," whereby social needs are only acknowledged if they can appear as viable demands on a market, and then determined as profitable enough to justify the supply (the background analyses, however, are still cost-effectiveness and cost-benefit). How, then, can we understand Sweden's historical development from champion of welfare economics to Europe's most rapidly privatized country?[24]

In his genealogy of government, Michel Foucault describes how governments operating on the basis of *raison d'état*, the reason of the state, in which the good government was determined on its capacity to be just in relation to the law, changed toward the evaluation of a government's legitimacy according to the truth of the market. We can observe European state capitalism, which, after a period of strong social policy during the Keynesian welfare state government (1930s–1960s), became increasingly accepting of neoliberal ideas about what a government should be and do. According to Foucault, what is at stake with the rise of neoliberalism in the 1960s is the fact that the exercise of political power "can be modeled on the principles of the market economy" and thus, "it is not a question of freeing an empty space but of taking the formal principles of a market economy and referring and relating them to, of projecting them onto a general art of government."[25]

Foucault highlights three fundamental responsibilities of the new art of government: it should ensure the creation of markets, construct a competitive order, and facilitate the multiplying of enterprises. He states these concerns in relation to how the conceptualization, instrumentalization, and principle of social policies in a welfare economy would be structured. First, a neoliberal government should "make the market possible" by introducing "market regulation as [a] regulatory principle of society" not through the "exchange of commodities" but as "mechanisms of competition."[26] The key difference from a welfare economy is that the government should not implement social policies of "relative equalization" that smooth out the differences—which would be "anti-economic"—but instead make markets possible by letting inequality function. This leads us to the second point: competition. The mechanism of competition as a regulator of markets (and society) is that "the price mechanism," in the words of Foucault, "is established through fluctuations that only perform their function and only produce their regulatory effects on condition that they are left to work, and left to work through differences."[27] Thus, we should accept that we cannot not strive for equivalence, but instead allow for inequality so that competition can "ensure economic rationality."[28] The third and final point is an extension of points one and two: the neoliberal government should help diffuse and multiply the number of enterprises, as a society subject to "the dynamics of competition" is an "enterprise society."[29] The government should facilitate the multiplying of enterprises because a program of "economic rationalization" is what connects "the basic units" of individuals, families, communities, properties, and businesses into a "social fabric," with the form of an enterprise. This network of enterprises entails that everyone and everything connected to it falls under the regulation of the market. In Foucault's reading of neoliberal governmentality, the market, competition, and the enterprise constitute "the formative power of society."[30]

An intriguing part of Foucault's theorization of the art of government lies in the link he draws between new neoliberal ideals and the abandonment of pre-welfare-state liberal dreams of a laissez-faire government. Instead, a neoliberal government should intervene, not "let go": interventions should be made, provided that they do not interfere with the game of the market and rather instead facilitate the market's improved function. The focus is on competition, which is the key factor for ensuring that the market can do its "fair" and "just" job. The "justice of the market" (or efficiency through competition) replaces "justice of the law." Efficiency thus becomes what political scientist Mark D. White describes as "the predominant factor shaping the rules, procedures, and institutions of the common law" because the most widely accepted position is that "efficiency is [a] defensible criterion in the context of judicial decision-making because 'justice' consideration, for which there are no academic or political consensus, introduce unacceptable ambiguity into the judicial process."[31] In accepting this position, the state should refrain from making considerations based on value rational decisions and instead make formal rational decisions that strictly assess the system's efficiency.

In the case of public administration in the 1960s, the introduction of capital accounting techniques was a trigger for marketization; KBS provides one example of such a move. If we bring the logic of capital accounting principles to the question of the rent of buildings under public administration—anticipating the practices of KBS and later Akademiska Hus—welfare-supported tenants (such as schools, hospitals, etc.) are not necessarily able to pay "market rents." An example of the new public administration profit-logic (i.e., the marketization of welfare services) would be a municipal social services department: while this department would usually rent office space from the municipality itself, in the new simulated market, this office space would be located in a building owned by a municipal business enterprise (i.e., a for-profit public company). The rent should—according to the capital accounting techniques—be market-based to comply with the municipal corporation's accounting system and ensure the efficient management of its business.

The real problem with this type of arrangement is that the allocation and distribution of tax money not only serves the social purposes for which it was earmarked—i.e., the cost of social welfare. Instead, a large percentage goes directly back to the "profitable" part of the municipal organization. Regardless of the landlord,

27 Foucault, 142–43.
28 Foucault, 119.
29 Foucault, 147.
30 Foucault, 148.
31 The quote is from philosopher and political scientist Mark D. White's *Theoretical Foundations of Law and Economics* and refers to the Chicago School of Economics' development to dominance regarding the concepts of efficiency and competition in relation to rationality and reasoning in law, economics, and politics. Mark D. White, *Theoretical Foundations of Law and Economics* (Cambridge, MA: Cambridge University Press, 2009), 42.

Campus Valla of Linköping University,
with Studenthuset (2019) in the middle.
Architects: White.

certain expenditures are openly displayed for any public administration's office—not only the direct cost of welfare support but also the salaries and social expenses of staff, various administrative expenses of running an office, and the cost of renting an office. The visible use of tax money obviously rises with the increasing cost of any of the expenses. Most readers would, instinctively, interpret the rising cost (deficit) of a department of social services as a result of increasing administrative costs for social services—although it could in fact be caused by increased rent and consider it evidence of the excessive bureaucratic organization. This is also the logic of most of today's privatized or market-tailored welfare services: more and more money is spent on welfare programs (the cost of running welfare programs), while less and less money goes directly to welfare. Sadly, proponents of deregulation have been very successful in their campaigns, which identify excessive bureaucracy as the only problem and hence privatization as the only solution.

The real test of implementing market rules for public services is to reveal the "unprofitable" parts of public administration, and consequently to identify the most costly and least self-supporting units. Plainly speaking, following this reasoning: the simulation of market economy in public services is intended to reveal the most poorly-run organizations with the least healthy business plans; a glance at the numbers is to expose the unrealistic scope of an organization's activities and ultimately the ineffectual nature of state bureaucracy. Max Weber astutely acknowledged that it is only possible to produce profitability for markets in which people can afford to pay. Public funds (tax money) can certainly provide that profitability for privatized welfare services, but it is quite obvious that these "welfare markets" are not going to provide social services or other welfare services in sparsely populated or poor areas in the field of health or education, unless the government creates "profitable fees" for doing the job.

The notion that profitability can be manipulated is a cornerstone of the neoliberal view of the role of government. Foucault's description of the role of a neoliberal government as one that can intervene in the environment through the making of markets, the construction of a competitive order, and by facilitating the multiplying of enterprises is crucial for understanding the deregulation of welfare service. Opening a previously closed area of public services for profit enables the realization of the points identified by Foucault. But we also understand that the government immediately has to abandon previous goals of welfare service, as its new prioritized task will not be to provide welfare services but to provide markets, ensuring competition and creating possibilities for the establishing of enterprises in order for *others* to provide welfare service. The difference is colossal.

In this respect, the impossibility of the continuation of state-provided welfare services is due to the lack of clarity in these questions, and the real problem is in the lack of counterarguments to the order of competition. Upon accepting the new neoliberal role of government, one is seemingly caught in a Catch-22: if the government continues to regard the provision of welfare services according to a state services model and structures them accordingly, competition is not ensured and the market does not function as a competitive market. Similarly, if the opening up of a market

32 Foucault, *The Birth of Biopolitics,* 172.
33 Maurizio Lazzarato, *Governing by Debt* (South Pasadena, CA: Semiotext(e), 2015).
34 Lazzarato, 42–43.
35 Lazzarato.

to generate profit for businesses also includes the retention of public providers—i.e., public schools and public healthcare institutions—government intervention will be required to regulate and protect those providers (or, depending on one's perspective, *to protect private welfare providers from the dominance of the public providers*). These interventions will in turn hinder fair competition among *all* providers. Inevitably, there will also be neoliberals who criticize the government's (in)ability to secure markets and competition.

At the heart of the political problem is the impossibility of a plan. Foucault says that "the Rule of Law will have the possibility of formulating certain measures of a general kind, but these must remain completely formal and must never pursue a particular end."[32] Therefore, we can see the *means* of an earlier "planned" era remaining—for example, the quite specific means of rationalization and efficiency—being retained but for very unspecific ends. General welfare turns into general efficiency, whilst rationalization accelerates at an even faster rate than before, because these kinds of processes are supported by the old system of welfare economics as well as by the newer neoliberal ideas.

Changes have been made to bookkeeping within public administration, rendering it more similar to the practices of businesses. In Sweden, this shift began in the late 1960s. If we study these changes more carefully, we realize that they bring significant alterations to the objectives and evaluation of the performed activities. Maurizio Lazzarato has explained the historical shift in "accounting machines" whereby they move from measuring "labor time" to measuring "financial rent," introducing a new focus on "the valuation of investment opportunities" in addition to a more traditional attention to "profitability."[33] Economic performance is measured in many ways, but arguably the most common and useful of these is "Return on Equity" (ROE). Used in the private corporate world since the beginning of the twentieth century, ROE's importance in the public sector grew through the implementation of new budgeting and procurement systems in the 1960s. In extending these designations so that the different phases of capitalism also have different structures and programs (including different methods for allocation, appropriation, distribution, etc.), Maurizio Lazzarato identifies "three apparatuses of capture" that in turn represent "three accounting machines that evaluate, measure, and allocate value and surplus value in a specific way."[34] Thus, "each capture apparatus has its criteria for evaluation and comparison, its own measurements, and its own property regime, all of which coexists, while their hierarchy changes according to the political context."[35] If we view the systematic and programmatic changes made to the administrative apparatus of Akademiska Hus and its predecessors in terms of these categories, we could relate the new instruments and their accompanist practices to a broader logic of political change.

A first phase in this process can be identified in the welfare state of 1945–1970, when a direct relation between profit and labor existed. For Lazzarato, who draws on Deleuze and Guattari, this means that "the capture apparatus for 'profit' carries out the evaluation of 'activities' to be 'compared, linked, and subordinated to a common and homogeneous quantity called labor." In contrast, in

36 Lazzarato, 44.
37 Chris Meyer and Julia Kirby, "End the Religion of ROE," *Harvard Business Review*, October 20, 2011, https://hbr.org/2011/10/can-we-end-the-religion-of-roe.
38 Meyer and Kirby.

the second phase—i.e. the neoliberal—profit "is no longer founded on the valuation of 'labor' but on the valuation of investment opportunities and the profitability of corporations." The third phase, which for Lazzarato began with the 2008 debt crisis, is still based on the evaluation of investment opportunities but extends to more creative financial exercises. All in all, the changes in "apparatuses of capture" require new "accounting machines" to measure the economic value of the activities. Lazzarato explains: "Return on Equity (ROE) is the 'measurement' of a corporation's economic performance from the shareholder's point of view," where "appropriation is no longer handled by the entrepreneur but by the creditor. The hegemonic regime of property remains private, but it is now based on the ownership of capital securities."[36]

As a type of measurement entirely free from the direct correlation of "activities" to "labor," ROE instead addresses shareholders' equity. Thus, attention that was earlier focused on activities and performances declines, as the most important measure turns out to be the return itself. Should there be some interest in activities and performances, these are no longer valorized in relation to labor or professions, but once again, in relation to the return. The greatest fundamental shift in the use of ROE as a business measurement was not in the 1970s, but rather already in the 1920s, with the particular invention of the so-called DuPont Formula. ROE has been the driving principle for maximizing profits ever since. The change identified by Lazzarato came about as ROE—which, in the example of DuPont's Ford, was running on equity capital—was increasingly run on equity debt, i.e. on financial investment rather than industrial investment. It is here that we can begin to understand what is happening at Akademiska Hus and with its generous payment to its shareholder, the Swedish Government. To acquire a more "efficient capital structure," the government is urging Akademiska Hus to lower its solvency and take loans (equity from debt), rather than using its own investments. Hence, the move from Return on Equity to Return on Equity Debt.

In an article in the *Harvard Business Review*, written soon after the 2008 debt crisis, Chris Meyer and Julia Kirby call to "end the religion of ROE."[37] The authors depict the historical invention of Return on Equity, identifying the current immorality of the old management equation with sarcasm:

> In the case of ROE, spurred on by the DuPont equation, society came to suffer from ... entrenched corporate runaways. In their pursuit of margin, marketers sought market power even to the point of monopoly, requiring antitrust laws to cry stop at the last moment of the end game. Similarly, production engineers treated their factories royally and their labor as expendable, until unions and labor laws intervened. Financial managers, supported by their bankers, increased their debt-to-equity ratios until capital requirements were imposed—oops, we mean until there was a catastrophic financial crash and a depression. Then banking regulations were imposed.[38]

They further take a clear stand against ROE in relation to social welfare, pointing to its inadequate capacity in considering necessary distribution of resources, or: the societal worth of business.

39 Meyer and Kirby.

> The lesson: Return on Equity, … is a very poor guide for allocating resources. It fails for two reasons. First, fixating on ROE fails to maximize the benefit of business to society because it measures value in terms of returns to only one stakeholder; second, it allocates human resources as if maximizing the efficiency of financial capital were critical to growth of social welfare.[39]

In the case of Akademiska Hus, we could argue that the "one stakeholder"—the government—*is* society, and we would therefore all benefit from this arrangement. The crux of the problem here however is not that the state receives revenue (which is good), but that the business of Akademiska Hus departs from the allocation of resources for education and research.

One real threat to welfare services is ROE's analytic tendency to locate the underperforming parts of organizations' operations. When ROE is used in public administration, the mechanisms of evaluating the social and societal worth of welfare services fall short, as the only prevailing evaluation is economic performance. The specific example of governmentally or municipally-run real estate companies, supposedly established to ensure something other than profit, is particularly telling.

If we now try to explain how it is possible to cash out billions from Akademiska Hus, we see that Return of Equity has developed to become increasingly concerned with equity debt over equity capital. The dividend to the shareholder of the company is accordingly arranged through technical financial instruments of raising the value of properties, with the subsequent borrowing of money equivalent to that raise. The "covert taxation" argument made by critics of Akademiska Hus's high rents can thus be tied to Lazzarato's assertion that in the current debt crisis, debt is not paid through revenue but through taxation: both investments and mortgage payments are paid by someone external to the company (in the case of Akademiska Hus, the loans are provided by European funds, whereas the rents of mortgage are paid by the tenants).

In 2015, Swedish university leaders requested a change in ownership directives from the government or alternatively for the universities themselves to be made the primary owners of Akademiska Hus. The critique has weakened since, however, with no shockwave around the increases in rental fees that are currently taking place; the high rents, with their annual market increases, have been normalized as "a new reality." In the long run, it is highly unlikely that an alternative where the universities own Akademiska Hus will effectuate any changes to the problem of prioritizing economic development over developments of education and research, but it holds the potential of practicing collective choice for determining rents and long-term priorities of the company. Another model that has been discussed, and similarly has the potential of greater autonomy of higher education and research, would see universities themselves act as landlords of their facilities. Such organization runs the risk of creating similar financial steering of education, putting university departments into competitive races for the best performing and most efficient (which arguably already exists because university managements are also thinking like business managers) and into open fights with the university's real estate divisions.

In Sweden today, although we are continuously surprised by the political approvals of entrepreneurial innovations of public works, we face a situation where most of the welfare services that could be made profitable have been marketized or privatized and the unprofitable parts are publicly shamed for their ever-increasing costs that need to be covered by public resources. The burden is obviously not equally distributed as both economic and geographical differences have proved to put the poor and peripherally situated in unfavorable positions. The better situation you are in, the better deal you get. For municipalities in depopulating regions, there is little hope, unless there are ways to find or invent new values in old possessions that can booster the (economic) expectations of the future.

Real estate companies deal with speculation, in the traditional understanding of buying low and selling high, at least in the short term. Nonetheless, the majority of today's speculation is not primarily focused on smart transactions, but rather on financial inventions for optimizing efficiency, maximizing profit, and seizing the economic moment of potential new or higher revenues. None of the actors addressed here have any interest in slower increases of the market prices of real estate or land, nor in cooling off hotly expanding bubbles in the housing market: this would require growth to slow and result in decreased revenues. But if the market fails to deliver what the shareholders are asking for, there are always new possibilities to invent compensations for costs which are first postponed and then later reinvented as rents on someone else's bills.

Tom Nielsen

THE DANISH WELFARE CITY

The concept of *the welfare city* sets the political idea of *the welfare state* in relation to that state's *urban development*.[1] In a "welfare city," form and structure stand in direct relation to welfare policies. Whilst its origins can be traced to the early twentieth century, the Danish welfare state is a political narrative and system that still exists and continues to develop and transform in the present.[2] In many ways, the urban development and architecture of the Danish welfare cities is similar to what is found in the development of other cities of the late-twentieth and early-twenty-first centuries—even those that developed under other political systems. Its origins, after all, lie in the great acceleration experienced by industrialized western societies in the postwar period, a moment that was not unique to places with distinct welfare policies. As a product of the Nordic version of the welfare state that emerged in the Nordic countries—specifically, Norway, Sweden, and Denmark, which share a number of cultural and linguistic characteristics—during the postwar period, the Danish welfare city is similar to its counterparts in the other Nordic countries. Exceptions are for example the role of regional policy (Denmark is far smaller and much more densely urbanized than Sweden and Norway) and the relation to economic cycles (the Nordic countries differ in their focus on industrial sectors as a result of varying access to resources). In the following chapter I present a concise, linear history of the concept and built reality of the Danish welfare city; this history is structured in terms of three distinct phases (the planning and building of the welfare city, 1950–70; the crisis of the industrial model of the welfare city, 1970–90; and the welfare city in the competition state, 1990–2020).[3] Following this overview, I also engage in a brief discussion of the future of the Danish welfare city in light of possible adjustments demanded by pressing issues of sustainability (resource scarcity) and social equity.

PLANNING AND BUILDING THE DANISH WELFARE CITY (1950–70)

After the Second World War, welfare states were built in many democratic and capitalist European countries, including those of the Nordic region. These states shared a number of features, including a focus on the construction of economically prosperous industrial societies; attempts to balance the interests of individuals, civil society, and the market; and the deployment of the modernist architecture and urban planning principles initially developed in the 1920s and 1930s, as concrete tools in the rebuilding and expansion of cities.[4] The Nordic countries followed similar paths in building their welfare states.[5] The ideology behind the Nordic welfare states

1 The first mention in a Danish context was in Jens Kvorning, "Velfærdsbyen" [The welfare city], *Landskab* no. 4 (June 1996): 74–77. In 1997, "Velfærdsbyen" was the title of a research project at The Aarhus School of Architecture which resulted in the publications Poul Bæk Pedersen, *Arkitektur og plan i den danske velfærdsby 1950–1990. Container og urbant raster* [Architecture and plan in the Danish welfare city 1950–1990. Container and urban grid] (Aarhus: Arkitektskolens forlag, 2005); Niels Albertsen and Tom Nielsen, eds., *Welfare City Theory*, special issue, *Nordic Journal of Architectural Research*, no. 2 (2004); and Tom Nielsen, *Gode intentioner og uregerlige byer* [Good intentions and unruly cities] (Aarhus: Arkitektskolens forlag, 2008). Recently the welfare city has also been understood as a contemporary phenomenon. See, for example, Signe Sophie Bøggild, Pernille Maria Bärnhein, and Kristoffer Lindhardt Weiss, *Welfare City in Transition: A Compilation of Texts and Images 1923–2020* (Copenhagen: Danish Architectural Press, 2020), and Kirsten Marie Raahauge, Deane Simpson, Martin Søberg, and Kathrine Lotz, eds., *Architectures of Dismantling and Restructuring* (Zurich: Lars Müller Publishers, 2022).

2 For the development of "The Welfare Space" see Niels Grønbæk and Runa Johannessen, "Introduction: The Welfare-Space Nexus," in *Architectures of Dismantling and Restructuring*, ed. Kirsten Marie Raahauge, Deane Simpson, Martin Søberg, and Kathrine Lotz (Zurich: Lars Müller Publishers, 2022), 30–44.

3 This periodization and several formulations in this chapter builds on Tom Nielsen, *Byen Danmark* (Copenhagen: Danish Architectural Press, 2023), primarily chapters 3, 4, 5, and 12. That book will be published in English as Tom Nielsen, *The City Denmark* (Copenhagen: Danish Architectural Press, 2025).

4 Mark Swenarton, Tom Avermaete, and Dirk van den Heuvel, eds., *Architecture and the Welfare State* (London; New York: Routledge, 2015) or, for a more general history of modern urban planning, see Peter Hall, *Cities of Tomorrow. An Intellectual History of Urban Planning and Design Since 1880.* Fourth edition (Hoboken, NJ: Wiley Blackwell, 2014).

5 See Braae, *Urban Planning in the Nordic World*, 17–29.

can be described as a form of marriage between *social democracy* and *social liberalism* (as defined by John Stuart Mill), where the goal was one of balancing individual freedoms and providing support for those disadvantaged by a market-driven society. This has also often been described in terms of what Jeremy Bentham, another liberal thinker, expressed as "the greatest possible happiness for as many as possible." [6]

The Nordic model focused on a strong state and on universal access to welfare benefits (i.e., not linked to income or family status), which went well beyond securing basic human rights (housing, food, medical care, etc.) to also deal with access to culture, education, work, leisure activities, mobility, recognition as a citizen, and democratic participation.[7] In Denmark, the welfare state was developed as a *dannelsesprojekt* (cultivation project)[8]—an ideal of a society living together with shared values that derived from equal rights and delivered almost equal possibilities for all.[9] Material aspects, including housing for all, well-functioning cities with high-quality amenities, and—not least—well-designed educational institutions (from kindergartens to universities and public libraries) were key to realizing this cultivation project. An emphasis on the high quality and democratic character of physical environments was therefore positioned as one of the core aspects of the Nordic welfare city.

The welfare state also arose in Denmark as the result of a political agreement between the political parties representing the bourgeoisie, the farmers, and the workers, after various shifts in the balance of power in the period between the First and Second World Wars. As such, what came—in the 1950s—to be labeled "the welfare state" [10] was established by way of pragmatic political deals.[11] By stretching what metaphorically was understood as a "safety net" that would support the working class, the leading parties hoped to secure themselves and the nation against the electoral landslides toward fascism or communism that were seen elsewhere in Europe in the 1930s. It worked.

The postwar welfare state, with its orientations toward both growth and consumption, was, to a large extent, a tax-financed project. The postwar wave of industrialization made it necessary to extend existing urban areas in order to house the expanding urban population, as people moved from rural areas to work in industry and the growing public service sector.[12] Already by 1950, two thirds of the Danish population were living in cities.[13] This proportion increased in subsequent decades, which were characterized by a general population increase and the postwar baby boom. From the initial phase of the welfare state, housing policies were deemed a central component in the endeavor to construct a modern and just society. These early housing policies tended to focus on building as many homes as possible as quickly as possible everywhere they were needed (primarily in and around existing Danish cities). The high volume of new homes being produced were supported through interest rate policy and public subsidies for non-profit construction, as well as state-guaranteed loans for building housing.[14] Policies for full employment meant that a great number of women began to enter the labor market. This in turn meant that children and the elderly lost their primary caretakers, and it became necessary to create institutions and spaces to care

6 See Hans Fink, *Samfundsfilosofi* [Philosophy of society] (Aarhus: Aarhus Universitetsforlag, 2003), 109–12, 150.

7 See Niels Albertsen, "Transformations of the Welfare City in Denmark 1960–2016. Five socio-spatial panoramas" (paper presentation, Velfærdsbyen i forandring, Arkitektskolen Aarhus, September 2016).

8 "Dannelse" is a Danish word which translates into German "Bildung," but not into English. The idea is that there are moral and ethical aspects and ideas of raising the character through education of the individual to a higher and more civilized state.

9 The Danish Welfare state is without an actual definition. The social democratic party's political program from 1945 *Fremtidens Danmark* (Denmark of the Future) is an example, where full employment, social security and efficiency, and democracy in industrial production are key goals. See, for example, Niels Wium Olesen, "Planer for velfærd. Sammenlignende studie af de nordvesteuropæiske socialdemokratiers efterkrigsprogrammer," in "Den nationale velfærd? Den danske velfærdsstat i international belysning," ed. Johnny Laursen et al., special issue, *Den Jyske historiker*, no. 82 (December 1998): 62–91.

10 The terms *velfærd* and *velfærdstat* (welfare and welfare state) seem to have been introduced in Denmark in 1952 in Jørgen Paldam, *Planlægning for velfærd* [Planning for welfare] (Copenhagen: Forlaget Fremad, 1952). See Preben Etwil, "Velfærd nu og i fortid," *Samfundsøkonomen,* no 4 (2005): 10–13.

11 Kanslergadeaftalen (The Kanslergade-agreement) from 1933 is often mentioned as the deal that put the project on track.

12 The public administration and service grew as part of the building of the welfare state. The number of jobs increased from 200,000 in 1957 to 500,000 in 1973. See Mogens Rudiger, *Oliekrisen* (Aarhus: Aarhus Universitetsforlag, 2019), 25.

13 See *Befolkningen i 150* år [The population in 150 years], Danmarks Statistik (2000), 16.

14 See, for example, Erik Nygaard, "Boligmangel og billige statslån," [Housing shortage and cheap state loans] chap. 1 in *Tag over hovedet* [Roof over your head] (Copenhagen: Arkitektens forlag, 1984), 17–24.

for these groups. Homes for the elderly and kindergartens were built in even the smallest urban communities. Together with educational facilities, public administration buildings, and housing, these functional typologies became the building blocks of the welfare city. Industrial parks with large plots of land and space for expansions were laid out, farmland was bought by municipalities and housing associations for park housing or as plots for detached houses. These changes included extensive redevelopment projects (in effect demolitions) in the existing city, which also formed an important part of the development of what was expected to be rational, zoned cities according to the functionalist principles of separation and connection formulated in the Athens Charter.[15]

The architects of these new parts of the cities drew on a number of sources for their inspiration, although they rarely described these references explicitly. The idea of the garden city and the new town movement in England, the German *Siedlung*, and concepts in other Nordic countries (most notably, the "ABC" new towns in Sweden) clearly served as inspirations. The idea of "the functional tradition"—in its Danish version formulated by Kay Fisker—is the closest we get to a theoretical backdrop for the early stage of the welfare city.[16] The idea here was that of a *regional modernism*, devoted to sensible solutions in a downplayed formal language, which drew upon historical form and used local materials such as brick and wood in order to create atmospheric and emotionally suggestive environments with simplistic and legible functional qualities. This approach resonated deeply with what evolved in the other Nordic countries and what in the British journal *Architectural Review* was, in the years around 1950, dubbed "New Empiricism."[17] In relation to urban development, the functionalist approach was characterized by an ideal that envisaged the architect as creating meaningful relations between the house, the district, and the regional plan, employing principles of simple organization and legibility in order to work across multiple scales.

The welfare cities were thus slowly established as a result of the rolling out of the welfare state policies of the early 1950s. From the 1960s onwards, an economic boom meant that an increasingly complete version of the welfare state could be realized. The prosperity of the Danish state doubled between 1950 and 1970. The overall effect of this emphasis on material aspects of building society was an overwhelming restructuring of cities and the countryside. Development took place around the big cities, the market towns, and the station towns. Stimulated by government subsidies and policies that sought to promote even development, villages situated close to larger cities also began to develop, with the result that earlier, preindustrial distinctions between urban and rural began to collapse. The welfare city was built in all parts of the country.[18]

The utopian, modernist visions that were conceived of and drawn by architects and planners[19] in the interwar period fit well with the welfare state's growth paradigm and its mindset of equality. The roll-out of this first, industrial version of the welfare city was, however, based on a generalized notion of "the citizen" and as such there was little adaptation to individual needs. This approach was an extension of an ideology that held that everyone should be given equal opportunities within Danish society, an ideal that was

15 See the description of the Danish welfare city as architectural typology and structure in Poul Bæk Pedersen, *Arkitektur og plan i den danske velfærdsby 1950–1990. Container og urbant raster* [Architecture and plan in the Danish welfare city 1950–1990. Container and urban grid] (Aarhus: Arkitektskolens forlag, 2005).

16 See Knud Millech and Kay Fisker, *Danske arkitekturstrømninger 1850–1950* [Danish architectural currents 1850–1950] (Copenhagen: Østifternes Kreditforening, 1951, repr. 1985), 321–[illegible].

17 See Nils-Ole Lund: *Teoridannelser i arkitekturen. Arkitekter og ideer fra 40'erne til i dag* [Theory formations in architecture. Architects and ideas from the 40s to today] (Copenhagen: Arkitektens forlag, 1985), 31–46.

18 See the account of urban planning during the postwar period in Arne Gaardmand, *Dansk byplanlægning 1938–1992* [Danish urban planning 1938–1992] (Copenhagen: Arkitektens forlag, 1993).

19 For example Le Corbusier's Ville Radieuse/Ville Contemporaine, Ludwig Hilbersheimer's New City, and Frank Lloyd Wright's Broadacre City.

The suburban development outside the medieval core of the merchant town Elsinore, shown in this aerial view from 1960, is an example of how sports facilities, schools and daycare centers were built simultaneously with the many new homes.

dependent on an industrial logic for its realization: large numbers of similar units would be produced for a market that could absorb them. The idea of functionally separated cities was the dominant concept, but it was complemented by a number of other rationales and agendas: love of high-rise buildings and dense urbanity, love of cars and extensive "American suburbia," nostalgia for the half-timbered houses of market towns and villages, and Cold War fears of nuclear war and the accompanying logic of thinning that such fears promoted. These differing ideas and understandings of how the material form of the welfare state should be structured and what it might look like related to the slightly different architectural and planning ideals at play at this time. In combination with a lack of overarching planning controls, this resulted in a relatively heterogenous urban form. The cities in Denmark were quite small; as such, building the welfare city became a step-by-step task undertaken by a diverse array of actors including small municipalities, entrepreneurs, housing associations (which, outside of the main cities, were all rather small local entities), individual investors building private homes for themselves, and businesses building for themselves. The pragmatic, bit-by-bit approach and aforementioned lack of central planning controls meant that large-scale developments and satellite towns, echoing international references, were not regular features of the welfare city, with the only examples of such settlements being in proximity of the largest cities (Copenhagen, Odense, and Aarhus).

A built reality emerged out of all of these projects, ideals, and models that was significantly less ideal, and significantly messier, than anyone had wished. The welfare cities did not have clear and unambiguous forms like the villages, market towns, or station towns that preceded them. Instead, the welfare city was a hybrid, full of clashes between the new and the old, with parts that promised efficiency and radiated future optimism often built in direct adjacency to parts that were remnants of past times and other economic and technological logics. In the period 1950–90, more buildings were built in Denmark than in any other period in history. As a result, the welfare city was at least half-modernist, but it was also somewhat collectivist and in part at least centered around more conservative ideas of the family and the private house. It was generally quite low density, with some exceptions.

CRISIS OF THE INDUSTRIAL MODEL OF THE WELFARE CITY (1970–90)

New ideals started to reshape the welfare city at the end of the 1960s: modernist architecture and welfare planning began to be met with increasing criticism and, as the international oil crisis of the early 1970s set in and the momentum of the second wave of industrialization began to subside, a paradigm shift took place. The welfare state was not just hit by an economic crisis and the politically very difficult problem of removing benefits that had been introduced under more favorable economic conditions. The very belief in progress had begun to wane. Two critical positions on the welfare city drove the resulting transformation. The first was a basic critique of the relationships between the individual and the

20 See Tom Nielsen, "Velfærdsstatens krise og interessen for individet," [The crisis of the welfare state and the interest in the individual] chap. 3 in *Gode intentioner og uregerlige byer* [Good intentions and unruly cities] (Aarhus: Arkitektskolens forlag, 2008), 55–72.

21 See, for example, Eric Allardt, *Att ha, att älska, att vara: om välfärd i Norden* [To have, to love, to be: on welfare in the Nordic countries] (Lund: Argos forlag, 1975).

22 Jane Jacobs, *The Death and Life of Great American Cities* (New York: Random House, 1961) was a major inspiration for community groups. An influential Danish example was Jan Gehl, *Life between Buildings. Using Public Space* (New York: Van Nostrand Reinhold, 1987; original edition *Livet mellem husene* published in 1971).

collective, and between planning and freedom.[20] The second lay in the discovery that the historic city was not so bad after all. The top-down, industrial, homogenizing, and universal approach to planning thus became subject to criticism from those who were not directly involved in making the decisions—first from an intellectual elite, and then ever so slowly from the people that the city was meant to serve.

Critics pointed out that the planned parts of the welfare city—the large-scale housing developments with their concrete and asphalt surfaces and windblown green lawns—appeared alienating.[21] Addressing the "rational" modernist aesthetic, which was seen as homogenizing, repetitive, and cleansed of recognizable symbols and forms, this critique did not reject the idea of the welfare state but rather aimed at including perspectives that, a couple of decades into the development, seemed missing. One of these missing elements was "community," which modern urban planning had somehow forgotten or abandoned as a consequence of its own (justified) critique of the poor health conditions that accompanied the very dense early industrial cities. Lowering densities and dispersing urban functions had, it was realized, negative consequences for social life. Studies of how communities formed around the classic street, with its sidewalks and shops and street-life, started to appear.[22] These ideas resonated with a young generation, which, inspired by the 1968 student revolts, found the old and partly abandoned city an attractive alternative to modernism's high-rises, park buildings, lawns, and asphalt, which did not—in their view—allow for communities to thrive. Hippie dreams evolved into metropolitan nostalgia and the counterculture gradually began to divert attention away from the suburbs and newly built parts of the welfare city. Spearheaded by an alternative youth culture, fragments of the old city were transformed into districts for a renewed consumer culture, which emerged amongst young people who had grown up in the suburbs but found the opportunities there too limited. In the centers of the largest cities, which had developed as central business districts as a consequence of the focus on housing in suburban areas, there was free space to unfold. Discos, cafes, subcultural shops, and meeting places began to appear, first in Copenhagen and later in the big market towns such as Aarhus, Aalborg and Odense.

This interest in the aesthetic and social qualities of the historic city led urban development actors (including politicians, investors, housing associations, architects, and urban planners) to perform a 180-degree turn, shifting their attention from the fields around the cities back to the dilapidated city centers that were now to be re-urbanized. This renewal approach, in contrast to the "sanitation" projects (in reality demolitions) of the 1950s and 1960s, meant that housing conditions and urban environments were now to be preserved. Focus shifted to acts of renovation: installing bathrooms and merging smaller apartments, lowering building densities by clearing courtyards and adding outdoor facilities in connection with the apartments. Citizen involvement and public consultation became a legal requirement through the planning law reforms in the early 1970s, and—with the sudden end of the frantic period of the 1960s, which was characterized by a whole lot of action and vastly less reflection—more began to be said and discussed than drawn and built. The economic crisis and what turned out to

This aerial view from 1989 from Kolding shows a heterogeneous totality: the sum of planned but never fully aligned patches of urban development after the expansion period of the welfare city after the Second World War.

The so-called freetown of Christiania in the 1970s. Christiania and Sofiegården in Copenhagen or the Sjællandsgade-neighborhood in Aarhus were examples of the new "self-made" urban quarters defined by youth culture and the idea of community that developed in inner cities from the 1970s.

be an oversaturation of the housing market (especially for rented apartments) at the start of the 1970s severely lowered construction levels. The development of new parts of the welfare city slowed markedly. Some new housing continued to be built, either in the form of single-family houses or as "dense-low" architecture that mimicked the village and the self-built environment, and was a result of the modernism-critical "environmental debate."[23] With this, planners and architects hoped that the same close community that had traditionally existed could emerge again through this new way of building the city. Dense-low became a dominant local Danish version of the renewed interest in the historic cities that had arisen in the south and central Europe. Where in Germany, Italy, and elsewhere, the focus was on the reconstruction of the urban block of the metropoles, wherein neo-rationalism and postmodernism were guiding design principles, in Denmark it was largely an idealization of the village and a desire to reconstruct traditional communities that motivated this position.

THE WELFARE CITY IN THE COMPETITION STATE (1990–2020)

Individualism and liberalism, which were now seen as having been suppressed by egalitarian welfare state ideology, reappeared and gradually became dominant figures within political, but also urban, thinking. The belief in the great societal visions of new cities was over, and the small and close-knit community and the individual were now seen as necessary focal points for societal development. Against this background and with the end of the Cold War and the subsequent rise of globalization, from around 1990 *neoliberalism* emerged as a dominant ideological and political concept, which started to influence *realpolitik* and urban development of the Danish welfare city.[24]

Neoliberalism's core idea, "the minimal state," which was coined by American philosopher Robert Nozick[25] in the 1970s, was thus introduced and flagged as an alternative to the Danish welfare state.[26] Based largely on market forces and an extensive degree of individual responsibility, the minimal state stands in direct opposition to the welfare state. In the new situation of global competition which emerged in the 1990s, whereby both capital and labor moved much more easily than before and were no longer bound by national borders, Denmark was understood to no longer be able to raise taxes to finance increased welfare or new needs. On the contrary, demands for tax cuts were made, based on the argument that to be globally competitive, jobs, export earnings, and international investment would have to be contended for. The individual—not the collective—was seen as being most capable of making rational and just choices and as a result, individual consumer intelligence was seen as more fair than mediated markets.

In relation to urban development, neoliberalism pointed to deregulation and the easing of planning requirements as a way to transform cities in a new, post-industrial reality where financial sectors, experience economics, and service jobs would become central.[27] Emphasis was placed on what the market, understood as investment capital, wanted. In 2001, with the shift of power to a

23 See Kim Dirkinck-Holmfeld, "Den menneskelige dimension," [The human dimension] in *Den menneskelige dimension*, Ingrid Gehl et al. (Copenhagen: Danish Architectural Press, 2021), 425–66.

24 When these issues were raised in the 1990s and resonated also with the social democratic party, Denmark embarked on the same path—the third path between hard liberalism and socialism, which also characterized politics in other European countries like the UK and The Netherlands in the 1990s. Third-way politics were formulated as a practical opportunity for political reform after the crisis of the welfare state in the 1970s. This was taken up, among others, by the sociologist Anthony Giddens, who was an adviser to New Labor and Tony Blair in the 1990s. It was perceived as an option to operate between two poles: the great social democratic welfare state and the liberal minimalist state.

25 Robert Nozick, *Anarchy, State and Utopia* (New York: Basic Books, 1974).

26 Most prominently, this was taken up in the 1990s by the later (2001–2009) Prime Minister Anders Fogh Rasmussen of the Liberal Party (Venstre) in Anders Fogh Rasmussen, *Fra socialstat til minimalstat: en liberal strategi* [From welfare state to minimal state: a liberal strategy] (Copenhagen: Samleren, 1993).

27 The London Docklands project (from 1981 onwards), with its partial deregulation and deliberately created state of exception, provided a model that was later used and developed in many other parts of the world.

Aerial view of Blangstedgård, 1988. Dense-low settlements carried ideas of urban reconstruction and the village community into greenfield developments. They supplemented the single-family house with smaller and more compact dwelling types.

28 Kaare Dybvad, "Boligområdet er vigtig værdipolitik," August 15, 2019, https://www.altinget.dk/by/artikel/kaare-dybvad-boligomraadet-skal-igen-vaere-vaerdipolitik.
29 Ove Kaj Petersen, *Reaktionens tid. Konkurrencestaten mellem reform og reaktion* [The age of reactions. The competitive state between reform and reaction] (Copenhagen: Informations forlag, 2018).
30 Petersen, *Reaktionens tid*, 11.
31 See Holger Bisgaard, *Københavns genrejsning* [Copenhagen's rebuilding] (Nykøbing: Bogværket, 2010).

liberal, right-wing government in Denmark, the old social democratic and welfare state bastion of the Ministry for Housing was shut down. Housing policy was placed under *Erhvervsministeriet* (Ministry for Industry and Business), signaling that housing was now seen as a matter of business, rather than welfare provision. Following this move, urban and landscape planning was also moved to the Ministry of Industry and Business.[28] Political ambitions were no longer, as in the decades following the Second World War, directed toward goals like "housing for all," "jobs for all," "education for all," or the provision of built infrastructure to support those goals. Instead, politics attended to the task of raising enough money to maintain the welfare state and the welfare cities that already existed and making them economically sustainable. Whilst this seems to be a conservative project, it resulted in a restructuring process that had a very direct physical impact on Danish cities of a magnitude that resembled the construction of the early welfare city. The Danish professor of political economy Ove Kaj Pedersen has used the term "competition state" to describe the new understanding of the state's role in relation to citizens and the surrounding world which emerged in the period following the end of the 1980s.[29] The "competition state" was not the "minimal state" of neoliberalism. It was the result of a forced marriage between neoliberalism and the welfare state.[30] The welfare state thus survived, but with a new ideological extension. As the original twentieth-century reasoning behind the welfare state moved toward the ideals of a society driven by liberalism and was marked by the unplanned consequences of this move, this forced marriage became a contradictory, complex, and conflict-filled pairing.

Global integration created a new framework for understanding Denmark as part of the world. Initially, this meant that from the beginning of the 1990s, investments were made in rebuilding Copenhagen as Denmark's only bid for a major city in Europe that could attract investment and labor in the new knowledge-driven economy.[31] It was no longer agriculture or industry alone that made money: research and development became increasingly central to industry as well as agriculture. Workplaces became more knowledge intensive. People with a university education tended to stay around the cities where their social life and professional networks had formed and the university cities developed into gravitational points in the transforming landscape of welfare cities, with Copenhagen as by far the largest and strongest node. Accessibility through infrastructure, attractive living environments, and exciting cultural experiences (leisure) became important competitive parameters globally. In Denmark, these parameters could be built on the foundations of good welfare services, a high degree of trust, and commensurate high degree of security—all of which had been established through the postwar welfare state. The welfare state was thus a precondition for the success of the competition state. When, after the turn of the millennium, the strategic investment in Copenhagen began to prove its worth, such planning spread to market towns and other aspiring big cities, which sought to develop and grow according to the same template.

The built heritage of the period from 1850 to 1950, constructed during the first wave of industrialization—which in the 1970s and 1980s was seen as polluted and a problem for both property owners

32 Danish author Lars Olsen has in numerous books and articles cast light on the inequality and new version of the class society that has developed in Denmark after 1990. See, for example, Lars Olsen et al., *Rige børn leger bedst* [Rich kids play best] (Copenhagen: Gyldendal, 2021).

33 Hans Skifter Andersen, Hans Thor Andersen, and Thorkild Ærø, "Social Polarisation in a Segmented Housing Market. Social Segregation in Greater Copenhagen," *Danish Journal of Geography* 100, no. 1 (2000): 71–83.

34 Petersen, *Reaktionens tid.*

35 The large modernist housing estate of Gellerup is an example. See Sidse Martens Gudmand-Høyer, Karen Olesen, Tom Nielsen, Inge Vestergaard, Kari Moseng, Birgitte Geert Jensen and Rune Chr. Bach, *Gellerup* (Copenhagen: Danish Architectural Press, 2021).

36 The agreement was called Fælleserklæringen af 8 december 1987 (The Joint Declaration of 8 December 1987), https://danmarkshistorien.dk/vis/materiale/faelleserklaeringen-af-8-december-1987. The first obligatory payments from the salaries of the workers into the pension funds began in 1991 and were originally modest (0.9 percent) but are today (2024) typically 12 percent, or even higher.

37 Deane Simpson, "Copenhagen under the Metric Regimes of the Competetive and Attractive City," in *Atlas of the Copenhagens*, ed. Deane Simpson et al. (Berlin: Ruby Press, 2018).

and municipalities—slowly, from 1990 onwards, became viewed as an asset for urban development. Port areas, railway areas, and larger industrial areas, which had been completely or partially abandoned as part of the deindustrialization and the outsourcing of manual labor first to eastern Europe and later to southeastern Asia, rose like phoenixes from the ashes. Seaside locations became a top priority for urbanites and thus a value to be priced and marketed. The more it cost, the more attractive it became, both as a place to settle and as an investment. The formerly polluted and abandoned backsides of the city became new enclaves for the better-off.

The 1990s witnessed the emergence of growing class divides, which after a period of time began to become visible in Danish cities. The middle class were those who were firmly attached to the labor market, and the new underclass formed amongst those who were not.[32] The latter also included many of the immigrants who had arrived, or were arriving, in the country as refugees or job-seeking migrants. Cultural and educational differences made it difficult for many of these people to enter and maintain attachment to the labor market. The same was true for many without a medium or higher level of education. This led to increasing differences that ultimately resulted in more unequal or polarized cities than a few decades earlier. The polarization became evident both in the larger cities[33] and in the smaller cities around the country. The differences between the opportunities for owners and renters, and those with stable savings for the pension and those without, had become greater.[34] This meant that, for example, the large housing estates built by housing associations—the crown jewels of the welfare city—which had already started to become poverty enclaves in the 1980s maintained that role, as economic incentives for home ownership, along with the value of property, steadily increased.[35] It is also important to note that as a result of a political agreement made at the end of the 1980s, an obligatory private pension fund for workers had been established, which was integrated into salaries (labor market pensions); these funds gradually grew, positioning fund managers as strong investors in Denmark.[36] As the pension funds, and thus the workers, became influential players in urban development, the *pension-fund building* emerged as a concept (oftentimes comprising of housing, but also institutions and commercial buildings). In this way, this new incarnation of the welfare state was still influenced by the trade union movement and a working-class majority, but on a liberal and market-oriented ideological basis. They were now investors.

With a focus on competitiveness both at the national level and in the municipalities, it became important for cities to stand out. This was in contrast to the early postwar phase of the welfare state and the welfare city, where the goal was rather that cities would become as similar as possible (even across significant differences in size), providing the same services and thus a comparable and compatible framework for the opportunity to live a "good life." With competitiveness as a somewhat vaguely defined goal, "benchmarking" and "best practice" as well as the ranking of strong, attractive, and popular cities also became important.[37] Politicians had to know what unique competitive advantages their city had in a field of—in many ways very similar—Danish cities. Differences,

38 The UN report *Our Common Future* (1987), also known as "the Brundtland report," marked a point where the sustainability discussion was put upfront in the international development debate.

not equality, were now emphasized. Special parts of the city (often the leftovers from industrialization that had begun development earlier, as mentioned above) were now seen as important pieces, as *assets*, in a greater game. Not only attractive residential areas or business clusters, but also new institutions could deliver what came to be called "core welfare" at the highest level: schools, hospitals, educational institutions, libraries, and cultural centers.

This core welfare was not only evaluated and understood *quantitatively* (as welfare had been treated in the original early welfare state) but also *qualitatively*. It was now possible to not only see if there was a school or a hospital available, but also how those institutions performed. In line with this new understanding of welfare, a new role was allocated to the built environment and architecture. Rather than the "correctness" of the functionalist tradition of the 1950s, a no-less-important representative and iconic role was accorded to architecture in the competitive welfare city. As a result, clearly differentiated versions of the welfare city emerged, which could be distinguished not only in terms of their size, but also their growth potential and relative attractiveness. Not all cities came out on top in this process. The cities, towns, and villages furthest away from the university cities, which in the initial phases of the welfare policies had grown and were equipped to be able to offer the same basic opportunities as the large cities, were plunged into crisis, losing population, investment, and jobs to the larger cities.

While planners and architects after the millennium were busy designing new homes for new "mixed" urban neighborhoods in former industrial areas and engaging in the renewal of the major modernist housing projects, urban growth begun to emerge again in the fields surrounding the "winning" cities. New neighborhoods of detached houses, new dense-low enclaves, and new industrial areas for large, "big-box" production and storage facilities began to be constructed, continuing to follow modernist dogmas about the zoned city, which remained more or less unchallenged regulatory tools to be used to organize life in the welfare city.

THE FUTURE OF THE WELFARE CITY: SUSTAINABILITY

The latest phase of the welfare city is, like its predecessors, just as much characterized by what did *not* happen there as what it achieved. The sustainable transition promised in recent decades—and in particular its subsequent failure to materialize—is, at the end of the present period of city development, i.e., the 2020s, an elephant in the room (and in the welfare city at large). In the 30 years between 1990 and 2020, the sustainability agenda failed to exert a significant influence on urban development or thinking, even though it was clearly present from the end of the 1980s onwards.[38] The Danish welfare city is unsustainable because it is based on a model that demands continuous growth to be economically stable, and because of the relative prosperity of the society which means that Danes consume much more than the planet and their territory can offer them on a long term.

Sustainability has to some degree been part of the implementation of many changes in Denmark's cities in recent decades—primarily through certifications and minimum standards in relation

The Iceberg housing development (SeARCH, Louis Paillard, JDS Architects, CEBRA). was built on the former container terminal in the port of Aarhus, which since the late 1990s has been undergoing transformation into a new district: Aarhus Ø. The Iceberg is an example of an iconic building that, in its form and architectural expression, communicates a clear identity. The investor was a pension fund owned by over half a million Danish workers. It was completed in 2013 and was already sold to a property fund in 2014. Housing became an investment and a commodity.

Dokk1 (Aarhus, 2015, SHL architects) is an example of a welfare institution of the competition state. It is built on a prime waterfront location and houses the public library and other amenities and facilities, for example "Citizen Service," the main point of contact between the administration and the residents.

to new buildings. On an urban level, sustainability was primarily translated into "densification" with reference to the in-principle lower CO_2 emissions per capita of people living in large, dense cities. Sustainability thus became an argument for the replacement of older parts of cities through massive construction projects and in some cases for the overutilization of building plots in the largest cities—development that would have happened in any case as the result of the dominant market thinking that characterized the period. The sustainability argument that "the higher the density, the better" was used to make (always) unpopular urban densification easier to swallow.

The difficult discussion about how to rearrange and develop cities on the basis of the natural resources that exist beneath, above, and around them is yet to be had. The future of the welfare city will involve questions about how people can live directly from local food and energy production. This challenge will probably lead to a different way of addressing issues of urban densification and urban growth. Dealing with the basic questions of creating space for water and space for species other than humans and livestock, for instance, would mean drastically reduce the area reserved and planned for industrial agriculture (today around two thirds of the Danish territory). If food production, further, is converted from animal-based to plant-based sources due to changes in demand, and furthermore becomes an urban industry with production of vegetables in vertical production sites close to consumers, this will not only transform the cities but also the territory they are embedded in, possibly leaving space for natural processes. Such transformations will potentially open up for a new version of the welfare city, which is more entangled and metabolistically integrated in the whole territory.

THE FUTURE OF THE WELFARE CITY: SOCIAL JUSTICE

The Danish welfare city developed as an equalizing, homogenizing, and uniform habitat, which took a range of different forms, from the capital city Copenhagen to smaller metropolitan centers, merchant cities, stations towns, and villages. Modernist planning principles, building technologies and formal architectural expressions made it uniform, but also in many ways distinct. Adjustments to a more competitive economy and new technologies, which created links between the welfare city and the world, made the differences between its parts clearer.

It can be discussed whether the welfare state succeeded in providing equal opportunities for all through planning. In some ways and areas, such as the healthcare and education sectors, the welfare state and welfare supply, which are still universal and free to all citizens today, are bigger and stronger now than they ever have been. Denmark is one of the countries with the highest "quality of life" when measured and benchmarked in international studies in the spirit of the times.[39] The country is very close to being ruled by principles of democracy and meritocracy. This could be an answer to the goal of "the good life" that is embedded in the idea of welfare.

On the other hand, as the result of increasing mobility, the network structure, and the real possibility that everything can take place everywhere, greater differences and greater inequality develop within

39 Political scientist Francis Fukuyama introduced the concept of "getting to Denmark" to describe how Denmark, as a societal construction, was used as an icon for certain principles of state building which was seen as not ultimately but relatively successful and attractive. It might as well have been called the "Nordic welfare state." The concept and discourse surrounding it became an important part of the political discussion in the USA. See Francis Fukuyama, *Origins of Political Order: From Prehuman Times to the French Revolution* (New York: Farrar, Straus and Giroux, 2011)

40 This process was described by Graham and Marvin using the concept of "splintering urbanism." See Stephen Graham and Simon Marvin, *Splintering Urbanism: Networked Infrastructures, Technological Mobilities and the Urban Condition* (London; New York: Routledge, 2001). The segregational processes and level of splintering and polarization to be fund in Denmark are generally less dramatic than what was described here, but the trends following liberalization and market developments are similar.

41 Emilie Aagaard, "Se kortet: Børn fra Lolland har fire gange større risiko for at dø end børn fra Frederiksberg, "4 May 2020, https://www.dr.dk/nyheder/viden/kroppen/se-kortet-boern-fra-lolland-har-fire-gange-stoerre-risiko-doe-end-boern-fra. Accessed January 2024.

42 The controversy was primarily related to the use of the word "ghetto," which was removed later. From 2021 on, the areas affected by the policy were referred to as accommodating "parallel societies" and the concentration of ethnic minorities in these areas was used as one of the criteria for definition. "Regeringen vil gøre op med parallelsamfund," 1 March 2018, https://www.regeringen.dk/nyheder/2018/ghettoudspil/. Accessed January 2024.

43 *Almene boliger* in Danish means "housing for all" echoing the universalistic character of the Danish welfare state. This is quite different than the English "social housing" which is for the socially disadvantaged and belongs to another idea of welfare.

the welfare state.[40] Children born on Lolland, the southernmost part of Denmark and a municipality that ranked as "low income" in 2020, have four times as high a risk of dying as children born in the high-income municipality of Frederiksberg.[41] Money and education level still matter. This is a sign of how specific urban qualities and the attractiveness of places mean more than they did earlier and how the welfare city has become geared to producing differences. One of the most significant and controversial attempts to counter segregation has been the so-called "Ghetto-law" (the full name of the political agreement being a little more true to its goal: *One Denmark without parallel societies. No ghettoes in 2030*) from 2018 addressing the issue of developing poverty islands and what politically was addressed as "parallel societies" of the underclass.[42] This specifically addressed the "poverty islands" that some of the large housing estates of the early welfare city had developed into. From around 2010 onwards, fundamental structural transformations began with demolitions and construction of new types of housing for a diversified economic and social class between the concrete blocks. The "Ghetto-law" has the goal of reducing the amount of *almene boliger* (affordable housing) in these areas from often 100 to 40 percent in order to thwart social segregation.

In early 2021, when appointed as the new Minister for Domestic Affairs and Housing, social democrat Kaare Dybvad referred heavily to classic welfare state planning. By bridging the two ministries, moving planning back from the Ministry of Industry and Business, and further reviving the Danish Housing and Planning Authority (which was dissolved in 1993), Kaare Dybvad retrieved a series of tools and a line of rhetoric from before neoliberalism, with its policies of slowly dismantling regulations and its "competition state" (and concomitant impacts on the distribution of tax-financed welfare institutions and services). Housing policy should again become important in securing social mobility and the public sector should again support the construction of thousands of new affordable housing units in the country's larger cities.[43] In the cities, high land values were seen as incompatible with the provision of affordable housing, the construction of which was almost totally halted as a result. This turned out to be a brief flashback, and a political parenthesis. From late 2022 on, a new social-liberal government once again went back to the combination of a total reassertion of the welfare state as the guiding political narrative, but in the version known from the last 30 years of competition state and marked-driven development.

PERSPECTIVE: THE TRANSFORMING WELFARE CITY

In the field of urban studies, with its focus on the relation between political ideology and urban development, the concept of the (Danish) welfare city offers insights into how over almost a century, the continuing evolution of an ideological foundation for the development of society has had an impact on the development of that society's physical territory.

The above description offers only a glimpse into the interplay between shifting political paradigms and shifting urban paradigms. The general characteristics that I describe here also apply to aspects of other Nordic countries. Acknowledging these similarities, it would be interesting to compare the development of welfare cities in other Scandinavian countries with corresponding cultural spheres and a similar pursuit of universal welfare state models from the mid-twentieth century onwards.

The welfare city transformed the industrial city into a hybrid, which was between industrial urban forms, the preindustrial fragments embedded in those, and the modernist architecture of the 1950s, 1960s, and 1970s. The adjustments and renewal of both industrial and modernist parts of the city, which has been a driving force in the latest phase has further transformed the Danish welfare cities into something new but maybe also increasingly specific in international comparison. Every transformation, despite being a local version of developments taking place in many places in the world, has local qualities. Multiplying these over many years gives some kind of depth to what is here called “the Danish welfare city.” A further study of the issue of specificity, and links between these increasingly hybridized urban forms and international examples, would also help cast light on not only the Danish welfare city but also on the relation between politics and architecture that lies at its core.

Leonard Ma

QUALITY CRITERIA AND THE NEOLIBERALIZATION OF CITY LIFE IN HELSINKI

Architecture and planning have played prominent roles in the postwar formation of the Nordic welfare states. As the art historian Kirsi Saarikangas observes, in Sweden and Finland, "the reorganization of everyday life and the rearrangement of architectural dwelling space culminated in the pre- and postwar period when new architectural aesthetics became an ethical as well as political project."[1] By virtue of its accessibility and its need to address an ostensible "public," the prominence and cultural legacy of Nordic architecture and urbanism continues to hold particular currency as a means of embodying social democratic values in the built environment. However, with the neoliberal market-oriented political reforms of the Nordic states in the 1980s, the role of architectural and urban expertise necessitates reconsideration in relation to the changing welfare state. Through a case study in Helsinki, Finland, this chapter will consider the ways through which the expertise of architects and urban professionals is deployed in the service of the market development following the state-driven development in the first decades after the Second World War. Rather than reasserting the potential of architecture and urbanism in defending the values of the welfare state, the rise of technocratic expertise in the built environment calls for consideration in relation to asset-based welfare policies and the new dynamics of class that such expertise entails.

In 2016, the City of Helsinki commissioned a study on pedestrian environments in the capital region. Utilizing the "Twelve Quality Criteria" developed by the Gehl Institute, the study sought to develop a comprehensive understanding of key pedestrians environments using qualitative and quantitative criteria.[2] First elaborated by Jan Gehl and Birgitte Svarre in the book *How to Study Public Life*, the Twelve Quality Criteria draw on Jan Gehl's decades-long *Cities for People* agenda, advocating for pedestrian-friendly and human-scale principles in the design of public space.[3] Entitled "Qualitative Assessment of Pedestrian Research," the 2016 study was conducted by Harris-Kjisik Architects and handled by a steering group composed of members of the Urban Environment Division from the City of Helsinki.[4] The study was initiated as an opportunity to reassess the quality of public spaces in Helsinki, and to "overcome individual biases and preconceived notions in urban decision making."[5] Conducted over a period of two weeks, with an additional two weeks reserved for supplementary work, the study established a relatively direct translation of Gehl's Twelve Quality Criteria into Finnish and was undertaken by five expert evaluators with backgrounds in architecture, and urban, landscape, and traffic design. Thirty-two sites in central Helsinki were studied, along with 14 sites in the greater capital region. Additional quantitative data was gathered by four members of the Harris-Kjisik team. Tasked with observing and recording users on each site, the team recorded

1 Kirsi Saarikangas, "The Policies of Modern Home: Organization of the Everyday in Swedish and Finnish Housing Design from the 1930s to the 1950s," in *Models, Modernity and the Myrdals*, ed. Pauli Kettunen and Hanna Eskola (Helsinki: Renvall Institute for Area and Cultural Studies, 1997), 81.

2 Harris-Kjisik Architects, *Helsingin jalankulkuympäristöt: Jalankulkututkimuksen laadulliset arviot vuonna 2016* (Helsinki: City of Helsinki, 2016), 1, https://www.hel.fi/hel2/ksv/julkaisut/los_2016-8.pdf.

3 Jan Gehl and Birgitte Svarre, *How to Study Public Life,* trans. Karen Ann Steenhard (Washington: Island Press, 2013).

4 Harris-Kjisik Architects, *Helsingin jalankulkuympäristöt*, 1.

5 Harris-Kjisik Architects, *Helsingin jalankulkuympäristöt*, 2.

6 Harris-Kjisik Architects, *Helsingin jalankulkuympäristöt*, 22.

7 Gehl Architects, "Twelve Quality Criteria," https://gehlpeople.com/tools/twelve-quality-criteria/. Accessed March 20, 2022. The worksheet is adapted from the quality criteria published in Gehl's Cities for People. Jan Gehl, *Cities for People* (Washington: Island Press, 2010), 239.

8 Gehl Architects, "Twelve Quality Criteria."

9 Gehl and Svarre, *How to Study Public Life*.

10 Bengt Lundsten, "Kortepohjan rivitalokorttelit," https://docomomo.fi/kohteet/kortepohjan-asuinalueen-rivitalokorttelit.

observational data using a series of site diagrams, noting the number of users engaged in activities such as sitting, walking, or "other active activities." [6]

There are several key methodological distinctions that should be noted between the Helsinki study and the Gehl Institute's worksheet. Originally designed as a user and stakeholder survey, the Gehl Institute's Twelve Quality Criteria worksheet was intended as a low stakes tool for community engagement and initial research on a particular site. Presented as a simple worksheet that is distributed as a survey, the Twelve Quality Criteria are organized around three themes: protection, comfort, and enjoyment. Survey participants are asked to observe a given site for approximately five minutes, and then to assign a happy, neutral, or a sad face for criteria such as "Protection against traffic and accidents, or the experience of aesthetic qualities and positive sensory experiences." [7] The Gehl Institute notes that the results of the study are "always subjective, since they are based on the perceptions of surveyors in a particular public space. Therefore, the evaluation data is not meant to be compared quantitatively to surveys done in other places." [8] The Helsinki study, on the other hand, utilized a team of expert evaluators across several sites. Instead of the three-point smiley-face scale, the evaluation criteria were assessed across a five-point scale of plusses and minuses. To further add an air of objectivity to the results, the average score of the expert group was used as the final value. The role of the quality criteria was therefore not to engage with stakeholders, but rather seen as a way to overcome *individual* biases in the group, and thus to bolster the group's existing expertise by offering more objective insights into public space.

Despite the City of Helsinki's newfound interest in observational analysis for urban decision making, the methodology has a long legacy within the fields of architecture and urban design. Indeed, in *How to Study Public Life*, Gehl and Svarre trace an extensive genealogy extending back to the early 1960s. Pioneered by figures such as Jan Gehl, Jane Jacobs, and William H. Whyte, amongst others, "public life studies" sought to address the shortcomings of modern architecture. For these figures, "machines for living"—characterized by modernist towers with access to light and air—lacked a concern for the life they purported to support; in contrast, these commentators encouraged a deeper concern with the interaction between city life and space.[9] Such principles similarly found a home in Finland, for example in Bengt Lundsten's pioneering plan for Kortepohja in Jyväskylä, which marked a radical shift in postwar planning in Finland.[10] In place of the loosely arranged blocks set in natural environments that characterized Finnish planning of the postwar period, Lundsten's 1964 proposal integrated research from sociologists and landscape designers early on in the design process. Privileging the "compact, contact" environment of traditional Finnish wooden housing towns, the project marked a shift to compact pedestrian-oriented grid plans in suburban Finland.

The Twelve Quality Criteria, and the City of Helsinki's newfound interest in them, reveal a parallel development in urban policy since the turn of the millennium. On the one hand, we witness the design of public space being prioritized, with the life *between* buildings nominated as the central focus of urban professionals; on the other hand, we can observe the continuing development of urban tools

11 Wendy Brown, *Undoing the Demos* (New York: Zone Books, 2015), 35.
12 Harris-Kjisik Architects, *Helsingin jalankulkuympäristöt*, 58.

and criteria to serve as the benchmarks for those designs. Though on the surface such shifts appear politically progressive, promising a more "livable" city by way of objective analysis and user feedback, they are also symptomatic of the hollowing out of the welfare state through neoliberal reform. The neoliberalizing welfare state no longer governs primarily through planning and building, but rather turns to subsidies, grants, tax breaks, and other financial incentives to direct market development. As the life *between* buildings grows more prominent as the site of state intervention and the public good, decisions about the life *in* buildings is increasingly offloaded to the market and framed as a matter of economic policy. Assessment tools and criteria such as the Twelve Quality Criteria therefore play an increasingly prominent role in neoliberal governance, serving to bolster what political theorist Wendy Brown describes as a "sophisticated common sense, a reality principle remaking institutions and human beings everywhere it settles, nestles, and gains affirmation."[11] From this perspective, the role of architects and urban professionals in the changing welfare state extends beyond the production of architectural and urban form and into the benchmarks and criteria that support this change.

Within the context of the neoliberalizing welfare state, there are particular consequences of the Helsinki study that extend beyond a concern for the quality of public space. By assigning an expert ranking—rendered objective through the methods of observational analysis and criteria of the Gehl Institute, multiple sites in both urban and suburban contexts were brought into comparative analysis and ranked. Tennispalatsinaukio—located in the center of the busiest commercial area in Helsinki—ranked highest. Particular significance was given to the feeling of safety and protection offered by the surrounding pedestrian streets. The second-highest-ranking site was Esplanadi (affectionately referred to as "the Champs Elysee" of Finland), which was recognized by the expert group as a significant green oasis in the city. The positive assessments of the highest-ranked sites were seen as evidence of the importance of parks and pedestrian-friendly environments in the urban structure, and the need for the city to invest in them.

The objective claims of the study, however, are inevitably limited by methodology that privileges observational analysis and data. By focusing on spaces "as they are," such studies risk overlooking how a site and its use may be socially or historically determined. The normalizing tendency of pedestrian criteria for urban quality is particularly evident when we consider the negative assessments in the Helsinki study. For example, Herttoniemi, a postwar neighborhood about 10 kilometers east of Helsinki's city center, was assessed particularly negatively. The study noted that the views of the traffic interchange over the highway were "not interesting," and identified the presence of drunks as contributing factors to the negative qualities of the site.[12] By focusing on a narrow set of parameters and criteria, systemic issues of class, race, and gender are glossed over and further deepened. Much can and should be said about the objective claims of the Helsinki study and the Twelve Quality Criteria. Though there could be opportunities to further expand and develop the study, to simply fine-tune or replace the criteria with other options would be to overlook the role of criteria in neoliberal governance in the first place.

View of Tennispalatsinaukio, the highest rated site in a large 2016 study of more than 40 locations in the Helsinki region. The square is bordered by pedestrian streets which contribute to the feeling of safety.

View of Esplanadi, a park in the center of Helsinki, described as a significant green oasis in the Helsinki study.

For a seemingly innocuous study conducted over a particular two-week period in the spring of 2016, the study has other far-reaching effects. Harris-Kjisik Architects, the office that conducted the study, is among the most established urban design and planning offices in Finland. Both of its founding partners are highly esteemed professor emeriti in the country, and their involvement lends the study considerable weight with both students and practitioners. The results of the study have also been enshrined on the City of Helsinki mapping service, and are accessible alongside data on property divisions, land reserves, and other demographic data. As observed by Wendy Brown, neoliberal rationality governs as a soft power, "drawing on consent and buy-in, [rather] than through violence, dictatorial command, or even overt political platforms."[13] The nature of the Helsinki study allows the expert group to simultaneously conclude that the Gehl method is not completely scientific or objective, yet this is a positive aspect, as it "leaves room for personal interpretation, empathy and the feelings of each evaluator."[14] Designed to simply 'test out' the efficacy of Gehl's work, the study is shielded from critique as it contains no concrete policies or objectives for further action that can be directly challenged.[15] Further iterations of the assessment criteria have also been developed and applied to Malmi and Kannelmäki, districts in northern Helsinki that are slated for planning revisions. The new assessment criteria build on the 2016 version and add elements from earlier research by Panu Söderström, a researcher at the Finnish Environment Institute.[16] Published just before *How to Study Public Life*, the ten-point 2012 "Living City Center's" criteria nonetheless draw heavily on Gehl's *Cities for People*, albeit with a distinctive Finnish flavor. The outcomes of the new studies are less ambiguous, with areas labeled "good," "poor," and "bad" on the city mapping services.

There is a long chain of expertise that disseminates across borders, disciplines, departments, and institutions. From Jan Gehl and his eponymous practice in Copenhagen to the Gehl Institute—the shuttered non-profit organization based in New York that develops open-source tools and reports using Gehl's principles—to the members of the Urban Environment Division at the City of Helsinki, who were taking the survey material and commissioning a local office to translate and apply those criteria on to existing sites. From the results of those assessments being placed on the City mapping service, enshrined as examples of "best practices" for prospective developers and investors looking for available lots, to those developers and investors commissioning architects to tacitly comply with the criteria—the Twelve Quality Criteria are another part of the "soft power" that is crucial for the apparatus of neoliberal urban governance.

13 Harris-Kjisik Architects, *Helsingin jalankulkuympäristöt*.
14 Harris-Kjisik Architects, *Helsingin jalankulkuympäristöt*, 70.
15 For example, the main outcome of the study was to identify the need for a comprehensive lighting plan, the need to improve the areas around the central railway station as "the gateway to the city" and the potential of holding an architectural competition to generate ideas.
16 Panu Söderström, *Elävät kaupunkikeskukset: Kaupunkiympäristön monipuolisuus ja laatu verkostokaupungin keskuksissa* (Helsinki: Suomen ympäristökeskus (SYKE), 2012).

CHANGING WELFARE

It is of particular significance that the success of Gehl's agenda is grounded in his Danish roots. The appeal of the narrative of *Cities for People* is that it is able to simultaneously anchor the narrative of urban livability, while drawing on the qualities of pragmatism and equality of the Nordic welfare state. For critics of neoliberal reform, the "Nordic model" is often invoked as a bastion of social democratic welfare. During the 2016 Democratic primary in the US, Senator Bernie Sanders proclaimed, "I think we should look to countries like Denmark, like Sweden, and Norway and learn from what they have accomplished for their working people."[17] However, for historians of the welfare state, the Nordic model of welfare is a flexible and contested concept. Welfare policies in Nordic countries are seldom the same, to the point that they are referred to as "one model with five exceptions."[18] Jani Marjanen, Johan Strang, and Mary Hilson further recognize that the positive connotations of "the Nordics" have made it an extremely valuable brand, noting that:

> The rhetoric of Nordicness is often used to distinguish particular features of the region, but it can also be an appeal to something higher or universal. Talking about the welfare state as Nordic rather than Norwegian or Swedish gives it the character of being something more eminent than a contingent result of a series of domestic political decisions. It becomes a "model" which, paradoxically, is at the same time culturally anchored and universal, and as such replicable by others.[19]

In a report prepared for the Nordic City Network, Gehl Architects outlined the agenda for "Welfare City 2.0," whereby "the new visions for the Nordic welfare cities now center around ideas of attractiveness and experience of urban living. The city is no longer perceived as a system that is the result of a plan and ideology, rather the focus is on people and their lifeworlds."[20] Gehl's *Cities for People* is therefore able to generate considerable goodwill, drawing on the political legacy of the social democratic welfare state, while emptying it of any political concern and casting it as a replicable model of timeless qualities at the human scale. Claims to serve the interests of "the people" are particularly seductive in the defense of the neoliberalizing welfare state. Hard-won through the struggle between the interests of capital and the interests of labor, the social democratic welfare state was a decidedly ideological and political project. *Cities for People* is able to draw on the legacy of that political struggle, while lending a distinctly Nordic spin to the neoliberal narrative for livable cities. Though "the people" may appear as a suitable stand-in for labor, in the dichotomies of Labor vs. Capital and People vs. Cars, cars make a poor substitute for the interests of capital.

Today, "neoliberalism" has gained great popularity as a pejorative term used to describe the privatization of public services and institutions of the welfare state. However, neoliberal reforms are perhaps better understood not as the result of an external force that replaces the welfare state, but rather, as Melinda Cooper notes, as tending to "*repurpose* rather than dismantle the institutional legacy of the twentieth-century welfare state."[21] As Sanford F. Schram further describes, "instead of repealing the welfare state, neoliberalism involves marketing welfare state operations so they run more like a business in the name of getting everyone in them, policymakers, program administrators, and clients to act in market-compliant ways."[22] Like Brown, Cooper, Schram, and a long list of thinkers drawing on Foucault's *Lectures on Biopolitics 1978–1979* at the Collège de France, we should consider neoliberalism, therefore, not simply as acquiescence to the demands of the market, but as a

17 Nick Gass "The best quotes from the first democratic debate," Politico, October 14, 2015 https://www.politico.eu/article/the-best-quotes-from-the-first-democratic-debate.

18 See Jani Marjanen, "Nordic Modernities: From Historical Region to Five Exceptions," *International Journal for History, Culture and Modernity* 3, no. 1 (March 2015): 91–106, doi:10.18352/ 22130624-00301005; Niels Finn Christiansen and Pirjo Markkola, "Introduction," in *The Nordic Model of Welfare: A Historical Reappraisal*, ed. Niels Finn Christiansen, Klaus Petersen, Nils Edling, and Per Haave (Copenhagen: Museum Tusculanum Press, 2006), 9–29.

19 Jani Marjanen, Johan Strang, and Mary Hilson, eds., *Contesting Nordicness* (Berlin/Boston: Walter de Gruyter, 2021), 20.

20 Nordic City Network, *Nordic Cities in Transition*, October 20, 2014, https://issuu.com/gehlarchitects/docs/1837_nordic_cities_in_transition, 6.

21 Melinda Cooper, *Family Values: Between Neoliberalism and the New Social Conservatism* (New York: Zone Books 2017), 314.

22 Sanford F. Schram, "Neoliberalizing the Welfare State: Marketizing Social Policy/Disciplining Clients," in *The SAGE Handbook of Neoliberalism*, ed. Damien Cahill, Melinda Cooper, Martijn Konings, and David Primrose (London: SAGE publications, 2018), 311.

TWELVE URBAN QUALITY CRITERIA

LOCATION:

☺ = **YES**
😐 = **IN BETWEEN**
☹ = **NO**

Protection	**Protection against traffic and accidents.** Do groups across age and ability experience traffic safety in the public space? Can one safely bike and walk without fear of being hit by a driver?	**Protection against harm by others.** Is the public space perceived to be safe both day and night? Are there people and activities at all hours of the day because the area has, for example, both residents and offices? Does the lighting provide safety at night as well as a good atmosphere?	**Protection against unpleasant sensory experience.** Are there noises, dust, smells, or other pollution? Does the public space function well when it's windy? Is there shelter from strong sun, rain, or minor flooding?
Comfort	**Options for mobility.** Is this space accessible? Are there physical elements that might limit or enhance personal mobility in the forms of walking, using a wheelchair, or pushing a stroller? Is it evident how to move through the space without having to take an illogical detour?	**Options to stand and linger.** Does the place have features you can stay and lean on, like a façade that invites one to spend time next to it, a bus stop, a bench, a tree, or a small ledge or niche?	**Options for sitting.** Are there good primary seating options such as benches or chairs? Or is there only secondary seating such as a stair, seat wall, or the edge of a fountain? Are there adequate non-commercial seating options so that sitting does not require spending money?
	Options for seeing. Are seating options placed so there are interesting things to look at?	**Options for talking and listening/hearing.** Is it possible to have a conversation here? Is it evident that you have the option to sit together and have a conversation?	**Options for play, exercise, and activities.** Are there options to be active at multiple times of the day and year?
Enjoyment	**Scale.** Is the public space and the building that surrounds it at a human scale? If people are at the edges of the space, can we still relate to them as people or are they lost in their surroundings?	**Opportunities to enjoy the positive aspects of climate.** Are local climatic aspects such as wind and sun taken into account? Are there varied conditions for spending time in public spaces at different times of year? With this in mind, where are the seating options placed? Are they located entirely in the shadows or the sun? And how are they oriented/placed in relation to wind? Are they protected?	**Experience of aesthetic qualities and positive sensory experiences.** Is the public space beautiful? Is it evident that there is good design both in terms of how things are shaped, as well as their durability?

3

The Gehl Institute's Twelve Quality Criteria Worksheet.

KESKUSTA KOOSTETAULUKKO

LAADULLISTEN KRITEERIEN TOTEUTUMINEN KESKUSTASSA
ASIANTUNTIJARYHMÄN MUKAAN

	SUOJA			MUKAVUUS						NAUTINNOLLISUUS			KAIKKI KATEGORIAT KOHTEITTAIN	
	Suojelu liikenteeltä ja onnettomuudelta	Suojelu rikoksia ja väkivaltaa vastaan	Suojaus epämiellyttäviä aistituntemuksia vastaan	Kävelymahdollisuudet	Mahdollisuus seisomiseen tai jäämiseen	Istumismahdollisuudet	Mahdollisuudet nähdä	Mahdollisuudet kuulla tai jutella	Mahdollisuudet leikille tai tapahtumille	Mittakaava	Mahdollisuus nauttia ilmaston positiivisista puolista	Esteettinen laatu tai positiiviset aistikokemukset		
1. KAIVOKATU	- -	+-	+-	+-	-	-	+	-	- -	+-	+-	-	-8	+1
2. TENNISPALATSINAUKIO	++	++	+	+	++	++	+	++	++	++	++	++	0	+21
3. KAMPIN METROASEMA	+-	+	+-	-	-	- -	+-	+-	-	+-	-	-	-7	+1
4. SALOMONKATU	+	+	+	++	++	++	+	+	+-	+-	+	++	0	+14
5. URHO KEKKOSEN KATU JA ANNANAUKIO	-	+	-	+-	-	- -	+	+-	- -	+-	-	-	-9	+2
6. NARINKKATORI	++	+	-	++	++	+	+	+	+	+-	+	+	-1	+13
7. SIMONKATU JA SIMONPUISTIKKO	+-	+	-	+	+-	+-	-	-	+	+	+-	+	-3	+5
8. MAUNO KOIVISTON - JA PAASIKIVENAUKIO	-	+	- -	+-	+-	-	+	- -	-	+-	+-	+-	-7	+2
9. MANNERHEIMINTIE	+-	+	-	+	-	- -	++	-	-	+	+	+	-6	+7
10. KOLMEN SEPÄN AUKIO	+	+	-	++	++	+	+	+-	+	+	+	+	-1	+12
11. EROTTAJANAUKIO	+-	+-	-	+-	-	-	+-	-	-	-	+-	-	-7	0

4

In place of the simple 3-point scale of the Gehl Institute version, the Helsinki study utilized a 5-point scale of plus and minuses. To further add an air of objectivity to the results, the average score of the expert group was used as the final value.

"governmentality," or an *art of governing*.[23] Distinct from liberalism, neoliberalism is a form of governmental reason that recasts the liberal *homo economicus* as the self-interested partner of exchange, an owner of their own "human capital." This shift aligns the interests of labor (workers) with that of capital: formerly socialized concerns, such as defined benefit pensions, public healthcare, and social housing, hard-won through decades of labor struggle, could now be cast as strategic investments into one's own capital and therefore individualized with the objective of seeking the highest returns possible.

It is worth here returning briefly to the core of the neoliberal project—its critique of planning. Directed in particular toward the figure of the public official, this critique called into question the presumed objectivity of the elite bureaucrats and their supposed service to the public good. For neoliberal critics, the public official was too easily swayed by special interest groups such as unions or lobbyists, risked "buying votes" with favorable policies, and doing more harm than good in interfering with the price signals of the market.[24] Opening up the Keynesian welfare state to competitive markets was therefore seen as a means to keep these institutional elites in check. However, as Will Davies notes, the paradox of neoliberalism's anti-elite project was that it would require its own vanguard of elites, "a type of flexible, post-jurisdictional elite, which is waged against the jurisdictional elites of state bureaucracy, academic disciplines and professions." [25] These neoliberal elites would exercise "a type of elite power which interprets what is on the screen, explains what it means, converts it into narrative, but possesses no authorship or authority over it." [26]

The neoliberal reforms of the late 1960s reconfigured the organization of cities along a "grid of economic intelligibility." [27] In place of social housing and the state-led modernist planning projects of the postwar era, housing policy was enacted through housing finance, including home ownership incentives and housing subsidies. Couched in metrics such as GMP (Gross Metropolitan Product) and real estate prices, the organization of cities could become a concern not only for architects and urban planners, but a matter of economic policy. The economic paradigm of the neoliberal city would require a human face, one borne not from the authority of the masterplan, but from the narrative of "urban life." From Jane Jacobs to Richard Florida, Jan Gehl is among a line of urban elites that are distinct from the master architect and planner of postwar urbanism. For the "hooray urbanists," the ego and naïveté of the master architect was the source of urban decay, and only through the spontaneity of urban life would cities realize their full potential.[28] The "life" of cities therefore was something that could not be planned, but unleashed through strategic investments in parks, cycling infrastructure, and pedestrian environments.

It is not a coincidence that Gehl's ascent to success coincided with his office's work in New York during the Bloomberg administration.[29] Under the directives of Amanda Burden, the chair of the New York Planning Commission (herself a protégé of William H. Whyte), "well-designed, well-used public open spaces" can "be a catalyst for the economic and social well-being of a city, and actually change the entire perception of a city." [30] Noting the paradoxically compatible alignment of the Bloomberg slogan "Building Like Moses with

23 Michel Foucault, *The Birth of Biopolitics: Lectures at the Collège de France 1978–1979* (New York: Palgrave, 2008).
24 Michel Feher, *Rated Agency: Investee Politics in a Speculative Age. Near Futures* (New York: Zone Books, 2018), 13.
25 William Davies, "Elite Power under Advanced Neoliberalism," *Theory, Culture & Society* 34, no.'s 5–6 (September 1, 2017), 238.
26 William Davies, 4.
27 "This means that analysis in terms of the market economy or, in other words, of supply and demand, can function as a schema which is applicable to non-economic domains. And, thanks to this analytical schema or grid of intelligibility, it will be possible to reveal in non-economic processes, relations, and behavior a number of intelligible relations which otherwise would not have appeared as such," Foucault, *The Birth of Biopolitics*, 243.
28 See Maroš Krivý and Leonard Ma, "The Limits of the Livable City: From Homo Sapiens to Homo Cappuccino," in *Avery Review* 30, (2018).
29 Gehl Architects, *World Class Streets: Remaking New York City's Public Realm*, May 23, 2014, https://issuu.com/gehlarchitects/docs/issuu_561_new_york_world_class_stre.
30 Robert Krueger, "Amanda Burden on Creating Value with Urban Open Space," *Urban Land*, November 23, 2011, http://urbanland.uli.org/ Articles/2011/Fall11/KruegerBurdenVid.

Jacobs in Mind," Scott Larson observes that "design becomes a powerful means of enhancing real estate values and encouraging development that is reflective of a broader class-based planning ideology."[31] The timeless and ideology-free qualities of public space that urbanists espouse prove imminently compatible with neoliberal urban development. Though appearing as a "win-win" scenario, where the fostering of high quality and well-designed public space serves as an engine for growth, this process normalizes the consideration of public space in economically speculative terms, directing infrastructural investment not based on need, but to those who are best placed to capitalize on its growth.

WANING EXPERT POWER

Describing the sociopolitical shifts of the neoliberal era, Adkins, Cooper, and Konings introduce the concept of "the asset economy."[32] Unlike an economy of commodities, an economy of assets shifts the locus of value toward speculation, not toward exchange and use value, but rather *future* value. Housing, particularly the boom of homeownership since the 1970s, plays a vital role in this economy, broadly democratizing participation in the asset economy.[33] As previously mentioned, for Foucault, the concept of *human capital* was central to neoliberal governmentality in aligning the interests of labor with capital. In the contours of the asset economy, the appreciation of assets such as private homes, equities and pension funds became a key vehicle to realize human capital gains, such that strategic investments would accrue capital gains to those who "earned" them.[34] Welfare therefore could be deployed to serve the interests in capital as a form of "asset-based welfare" while clinging to the redistributive promises of social democracy.[35]

Deployed in the service of the "narrative" of market development, the irony of *Cities for People* is that it also advocates cities for capital. Paired with loosened economic policy and increasingly sophisticated financial instruments, the agenda for urbanization and densification has above all, helped to usher in decades of real estate capital growth.[36] As noted by Samuel Stein, "public improvements become private investment opportunities as those who own the land reap the benefits of beautiful urban design and improved infrastructure."[37] Livable cities, human-scaled, with abundant green spaces and safe pedestrian and cycling paths, become a very concrete way to appreciate real estate capital. Thus, investment in the space between buildings could also manifest gains for the life in buildings. Through loans on home equity and investment properties, the rise in real estate value for private homes did actually improve the quality of life for lucky homeowners and investors, not through higher wages or value in their labor power, but through capital appreciation.

Parallel to the 2016 study *Qualitative Pedestrian Environments*, the City of Helsinki released their strategic vision for 2017–2021: namely, to become "The Most Functional City in the World." In the foreword, the mayor of Helsinki, Jan Vapaavuori writes, "Helsinki pursues this vision by seeking to create the best possible conditions for urban life."[38] Alongside the "Nordic model of high-quality city services," it is from the clean and safe urban environment that the livability of Helsinki emerges. The three themes of the Twelve Quality

31 Scott Larson, *Building Like Moses with Jacobs in Mind: Contemporary Planning in New York City: Urban Life, Landscape, and Policy* (Philadelphia: Temple University Press, 2013), 13.
32 Lisa Adkins, Melinda Cooper, and Martijn Konings, *The Asset Economy* (Medford, MA: Polity, 2020)
33 Lisa Adkins, Melinda Cooper, and Martijn Konings, 50.
34 Lisa Adkins, Melinda Cooper, and Martijn Konings, 46.
35 See Rajiv Prabhakar, "A House Divided: Asset-based Welfare and Housing," *International Journal of Housing Policy* 19 (2019).
36 Neil Smith, "Toward a Theory of Gentrification A Back to the City Movement by Capital, not People," *Journal of the American Planning Association* 45, no. 4 (1979), 538–48. https://doi.org/10.1080/01944367908977002.
37 Samuel Stein, *Capital City: Gentrification and the Real Estate State* (New York: Verso Books, 2019).
38 City of Helsinki, *The Most Functional City in the World: Helsinki City Strategy 2017–2021* (Helsinki: City of Helsinki), https://www.hel.fi/static/helsinki/kaupunkistrategia/helsinki_city_strategy_leaflet.pdf.

Situated in the urban periphery, the district of Herttoniemi was one of the lowest ranked sites assessed in the Helsinki study. The expert group noted the presence of drunks and that the views were "not interesting."

Criteria—"protection, comfort, and enjoyment"—were particularly timely to the future political vision of the city. In taxonomizing and ranking sites across the city, there is the implicit promise to locate deficient sites and to improve them through technocratic expertise. As the Helsinki strategic vision points out, "the best economic and business policy is to be a functional city." That the most successful sites in the 2016 study also happen to be the most expensive ones only contributes to this narrative.

Helsinki mayor, Vapaavuori—the former housing minister of Finland—led the coalition between the center-right National Coalition (Blue) Party and the center-left Green League that has dominated Helsinki politics since the elections in 2000. The alliance found surprising compatibility in directing policy to increase the supply of new construction, as advocated by the Blues, while pursuing the compact, sustainable, and lively city promised by the Green League. It was during this tenure that Pentti Murole observes that "pushing green political policies found a connection to brutal construction." [39] The simmering tension between "the most functional city" with the growing strength of the real estate industry came to a boil with Vapaavuori's exit from city politics in 2020. Vapaavuori announced to significant public backlash that he would be taking on a position with the Danish real estate company NREP (Nordic Real Estate Partners) as a special advisor.[40] Vapaavuori is not the first mayor that NREP has hired, having appointed the former mayor of Copenhagen Jens Kramer Mikkelsen as Director of Urban Development in 2018.[41]

When property values rise and wages stagnate, the redistributive promise of a democratic society of homeowners becomes available to an increasingly select few. As the authors of *The Asset Economy* write:

> The enduring catastrophe of the global financial crisis stems from the fact that it complicated what had long seemed the easiest route to asset-based democracy—upward mobility through home ownership. In recent years, it has become clear that private housing has itself come to serve as a major generator of inequality. [42]

Acute issues of housing affordability and inequality have considerably weakened the claims of neoliberal urban elites promising to make livable cities for people. Phenomena such as the "bike lash" have started appearing around the world, with popular protests to improvements to cycling infrastructure, and pedestrian environments.[43] Within the context of the asset economy, such projects are often "met with resistance as some longtime residents felt that greening was not an end in itself, but only a means of capital accumulation and gentrification." [44] The anger is not directed toward the bike lanes per se, but rather that urban expertise is unable to deliver the outcomes it promises.

As design and quality criteria have taken on a more prominent role in the built environment, they have also further entrenched the logics of home ownership and the asset economy and obscured what form housing and urban welfare policies can take. In Finland, the housing regime "is based on the presupposition that households satisfy their housing needs mainly by relying on sources other than the public provision of housing." [45] Housing policy is therefore

39 This post, written by professor emeritus Pentti Murole, just months before his death, is particularly significant as he was the pioneer of the "compact/contact" city that he then expressed some regret for. Pentti Murole, "Kun kaupunkisuunnitteluun tuli mittakaavavirhe, hurma nousi, henki hävisi!," *Kuntalehti*, November 23, 2020, https://kuntatekniikka.fi/penan-blogi/2020/11/23/kun-kaupunkisuunnitteluun-tuli-mittakaavavirhe-hurma-nousi-henki-havisi/ (In Finnish).

40 Katja Kuokkkanen, "Nrep houkutteli pormestari Vapaavuoren riveihinsä ravintola Savoyn kabinetissa: Tällainen on pohjoismainen kiinteistöjätti, joka etsii sijoitusrahalle kohteita Helsingissä," *Helsingin sanomat*, May 13, 2021, https://www.hs.fi/kaupunki/art-2000007974503.html (In Finnish).

41 NREP, "Nrep hires the former Mayor of Copenhagen as Director of Urban Development," *NREP*, August 24, 2018, https://nrep.fi/news/nrep-hires-former-mayor-copenhagen-director-urban-development/.

42 Lisa Adkins, Melinda Cooper, and Martijn Konings, *The Asset Economy*, 50.

43 See Amy Lubitow and Thaddeus R. Miller, "Contesting Sustainability: Bikes, Race, and Politics in Portlandia," *Environmental Justice* 6, no. 4 (2013).

44 Cedric Goossens, Stijn Oosterlynck, and Lieve Bradt, "Livable Streets? Green Gentrification and the Displacement of Longtime Residents in Ghent, Belgium," *Urban Geography* 41, no. 4 (April 20, 2020): 556. https://doi.org/10.1080/02723638.2019.1686307.

45 Marja Elsinga, "Home Ownership beyond Asset and Security: Perceptions of Housing Related Security and Insecurity in Eight European Countries," *Housing and Urban Policy Studies* 32 (2007): 72.

delivered primarily in the form of tax subsidies and home ownership incentives. Social housing in the form of state-subsidized affordable rentals, however, only accounted for a relatively brief period in Finland during the major urbanizations of the 1950s, when state backed ARAVA loans provided conditional financing in exchange for subsidized rents for dwellings. This policy was crucial in expanding the supply of housing when mortgage financing was limited to deposit banks with repayment periods of less than ten years. Beginning in the mid-1980s, financial reforms opened up the mortgage market, allowing for 25–30-year mortgage cycles and market rates, which coupled with interest rate subsidies opened up pathways to homeownership for many. As noted by John Doling, since the late 1970s direct subsidies and loans have steadily decreased as a percentage of public expenditure.[46] Public expenditure is increasingly spent indirectly in the form of tax relief tied to ever larger loans or allowances for rental housing.

With the challenges of postwar housing shortages eradicated, housing policy directed by state subsidized loans shifted away from housing tenure and toward questions of quality, addressing concerns of design, energy performance, and material and construction.[47] The boom and bust of the Finnish real estate market in the 1990s precipitated a drastic shift in attempts to safeguard home asset values. A new market for housing was created by expanding the private rental market which was supported with interest rate deductions and the abolition of most rent control by 1992, ensuring profitable returns for a new class of private investors.[48] The means of deploying housing welfare also had considerable implications in relation to rental markets. Over the 2015–19 period, 39 percent of households received some form of housing allowance in Finland (in practice the number is even higher as this excludes assistance provided for students).[49] Over 2 billion euros of housing benefits are paid out annually, with over half of this figure going to private landlords. In this manner, housing subsidies serve not just to provide housing for those in need, but by ensuring an average of 300 euros of housing assistance, they also serve to secure a constant return on capital for asset owners by establishing a price floor in the rental housing market. The economist Aki Kangasharju puts it plainly: "one additional euro of housing allowances leads to an increase of 60–70 cents in rent paid by claimants."[50]

By focusing on the life between buildings, the flourishing of urban life is not shared equally, and this is particularly challenging within a Nordic context. Home ownership fractures society along asset-owning (and often generational) lines, a problem that is compounded as real estate prices rise.[51] The pressure to secure constant returns for investors is fraught with tension as strong social security provisions also result in other forms of asset economy participation through pension and unemployment funds, many of which are among the largest institutional investors in real estate and are often behind the most ruthless rent expansion processes.[52] In the asset-based welfare society, appeals to the timeless design qualities of the human scale therefore limit the scope of what is possible in how we might imagine the design of cities today.

Expanding on the tradition of postpolitical thinkers,[53] Hochuli, Hoare, and Cunliffe—authors of *The End of the End of History*—observe that with the ending of the Cold War, the triumph of liberal

46 John Doling, "Housing Finance in Finland," *Urban Studies* 27, no. 6 (December 1990): 954. https://doi.org/10.1080/00420989020080931.

47 John Doling, "Housing Finance in Finland."

48 G. Geoffrey Booth, John L. Glascock, Teppo Martikainen, and Timo Rothovius, "The Financing of Residential Real Estate in Finland: An Overview," *Journal of Housing Research* 5, no. 2 (1994): 206.

49 Jaakko Eskola and Antti Halmetoja, "General Housing Allowance—Overall Reform of 2015, Development of Benefit Expenditure, and Employment of Benefit Recipients," *VTV National Audit Office of Finland*, April 2023. https://www.vtv.fi/en/publications/general-housing-allowance-overall-reform-of-2015-development-of-benefit-expenditure-and-employment-of-benefit-recipients/.

50 Aki Kangasharju, "Housing Allowance and the Rent of Low-Income Households," *The Scandinavian Journal of Economics* 112, no. 3 (2010): 595–617. https://doi.org/10.1111/j.1467-9442.2010.01615.x.

51 Between 2001 and 2008, house prices in Finland rose by over 42 percent. However, during 2010–19, prices dropped in Finland 8.2 percent, while rising 5.8 percent in Helsinki, lending further credence to the neoliberal urban policy.

52 The Norwegian Sovereign Wealth Fund, for example, is one of the main holders in shares of corporate landlords. See Manuel Aalbers, Rodrigo Fernandez, and Zac J. Taylor, "In Real Estate Investment We Trust: State De-Risking and the Ownership of Listed US and German Residential Real Estate Investment Trusts," *Economic Geography* 99:3 (January 1, 2022): 312–35. https://doi.org/10.1080/00130095.2022.2155134.

53 See, for example, Chantal Mouffe, *On the Political* (London: Routledge, 2005); Slavoj Žižek, "How to Begin from the Beginning," in *The Idea of Communism*, ed. Costas Douzinas and Slavoj Žižek (London: Verso, 2010), 209–26.

democracy and market economy, neoliberalism had limited the horizons of politics. Building on Francis Fukuyama's "end of history" thesis, the role of the state was merely to ensure the market's proper functioning, "the big questions, about what is produced and who gets how much, were settled."[54] In its place was *postpolitics*, "a form of government that tries to foreclose political contestation by emphasizing consensus, 'eradicating' ideology and ruling by recourse to evidence and expertise rather than interests or ideals."[55] As design and quality criteria takes on a more prominent public role in the direction of policy, it operates increasingly as a veneer on the capitalist forces shaping the city.

Far from an urban utopia founded on the values of the social democratic welfare state, there is a need to recognize Gehl's *Cities for People* for what it is: a technocratic populism designed to generate consensus and narrow the scope of political contestation. There is an opposite symmetry between Gehl and Fukuyama. For the latter, the triumphant model of liberal democracy was not the United States as the winner of the Cold War, but rather it was about "Getting to Denmark."[56] Yet for the authors of *The End of the End of History*, the popular political upheavals of the past decade have only further exposed the failures of managerial technocracy to deliver the outcomes it promises.[57] There is a very real danger as "the people" is invoked across the political spectrum to critique the neoliberal order, that *Cities for People* finds a home with the nationalistic authoritarian right. In early February 2022, the notable New Urbanist Andres Duany appeared on Tucker Carlson Today.[58] In an interview with the alt-right pundit, Duany effused the merits of walkability and that cars were the most awful part of American life. One of the great dangers of *Cities for People* is that it is also easily subsumed by those wanting cities for "the right type of people," as seen by the growth in far-right parties utilizing rhetoric blaming foreigners for rising housing costs.[59]

However, if there is a redeeming quality of Jan Gehl's *Cities for People* agenda, it is that it continues to remain a powerful galvanizing force within the fields of architecture and urbanism. It is a source of optimism that the built environment can help us live in more just, equal, and sustainable ways. But if there is to be a renewed welfare urbanism, it must contend with a radically altered governing apparatus of the welfare state. In the face of the failed distributive promise of an asset-owning democracy, the waning power of technocratic expertise calls for an ethical and political architectural project that can no longer luxuriate in its presumed objectivity. It must once again imagine anew the dynamics of class and the compromise between labor and capital today.

54 Alex Hochuli, George Hoare, and Philip Cunliffe, *The End of the End of History: Politics in the Twenty-first Century* (Winchester, UK: Zer0 Books, 2021), chap 1, iBooks.
55 Hochuli, Hoare, and Cunliffe, *The End of the End of History*.
56 See Francis Fukuyama, *The Origins of Political Order: From Prehuman Times to the French Revolution* (New York: Farrar, Straus and Giroux, 2011).
57 Hochuli, Hoare, and Cunliffe, *The End of the End of History*.
58 Kira Mautone, "Urban Planner Details how we can Design Cities for a Better Quality of Life," *Fox News*, February 18, 2022, https://www.foxnews.com/media/urban-planner-cities-design-quality-of-life.
59 In a 2024 report, the UN special rapporteur on housing recommended the need for governments to "actively counter incitement of hatred against foreigners who have been blamed for the housing crisis." See United Nations, General Assembly, "Report of the Special Rapporteur on adequate housing as a component of the right to an adequate standard of living, and on the right to non- discrimination in this context, Balakrishnan Rajagopal." A/HRC/55/53/Add.1 (Feb 28, 2024), https://www.ohchr.org/sites/default/files/documents/hrbodies/hrcouncil/sessions-regular/session55/advance-versions/A-HRC-55-53-Add1-AUV.pdf.

A CONVERSATION

Helena Mattsson and Deane Simpson

TOWARD AN ARCHITECTURE OF PLANETARY WELFARE

A number of publications have, in recent years, reflected on architecture and welfare; many of these have focused on the Nordic region. This is not surprising, given rapid changes seen in the contemporary political landscape. Not only is the relationship between the built environment, the state, and the citizen being rearticulated but the conditions under which the built environment is constructed have shifted. The discourse on architecture thus confronts the question: What is architecture and its role?

While the Nordic countries have been, and continue to be, considered "welfare states," many welfare institutions have been dismantled or restructured; housing policies have been increasingly challenged by global capital; housing assets, housing companies, and public or common infrastructures have been sold; and housing affordability has been reduced. Many of these changes are closely linked to neoliberalization processes, which have been observable in various forms across the Nordic countries over the past forty years; some are also the result of cultural shifts in how we understand the welfare paradigm and the welfare subject through, for example, the emergence of terminologies such as "livability" and "the livable city." Recent research has addressed how we should understand architecture in relation to these processes and how we should manage the built heritage of a very different era, when architecture had a different role in the construction of society.

We accepted the task of reflecting on the content of this publication out of a desire to say something about where we stand today and how we might think about the future when it comes to research on architecture/built environment and welfare. If we compare the present with the time around 2013 when the Scandinavian research network on architecture and welfare—which forms the academic background of this book—was established, things looked very different. Today, the democratic welfare state itself is under threat. Ideas about a bygone welfare state, together with nationalism, protectionism, and xenophobia, have created fertile ground for a growing right-wing populism with undemocratic overtones.

Questions and developments like these set the scene for our conversation, suggesting the necessity to revise perspectives regarding the identification, problematization, and interpretation of architecture and the built environment's relation to welfare and the welfare state. As the editors state in the introduction, this book goes beyond the concepts of *the social democratic regime* and *the Nordic Model* as they are understood from the outside. Instead, this volume examines the welfare state in formation through multiple perspectives from within the broad geography of Scandinavia. We take this critical position as a starting point for our conversation, which circulates around a series of themes that we understand as essential to future research on the developing spatialities of the

1 Francis Fukuyama, *The Origins of Political Order: From Prehuman Times to the French Revolution* (New York: Farrar, Strauss, and Giroux, 2011), 431.

welfare state, namely: geographical exceptionalism, the universal welfare subject, and—maybe most important—a planetary perspective.

GEOGRAPHICAL EXCEPTIONALISM

Deane Simpson (DS): Perhaps we could start our conversation with the theme of *geographical bounding*, which has come up frequently in our previous conversations—the geographical distinctions between the Nordics and the world, between the Nordic countries themselves, and between regions and neighborhoods within the nations which the various chapters in this volume touch upon in different ways.

Helena Mattson (HM): Yes, we might talk about this in terms of *geographical exceptionalism* and the contradiction between, on one hand, the specificity of borders and closed spaces, and on the other the concept of welfare as a human right which is ubiquitous (and thus unrelated to borders). It is risky to exaggerate the status of the Nordics or Scandinavia as the exception because this plays into today's growing nationalism. I think architecture's role in this emerging discourse is not something we should underestimate.

DS: I very much agree. In reflecting on the framing of a geographical exceptionalism, it is relevant to reflect on distinctions between how the Nordic welfare model is idealized from the outside, and how it is interpreted from within the Nordic countries. One of the more iconic external idealizations of the Nordic welfare model is Francis Fukuyama's notion of "Getting to Denmark"—framing a mythical space of political and economic stability and democracy, high economic prosperity, low inequality, low levels of corruption, high degrees of social mobility, and so on.[1] Looking at the Nordic states today, it is evident that they are functioning relatively well, according to Fukuyama's metrics and in terms of others such as quality of life, subjective well-being, livability, etc. But while much of this narrative is reinforced by those outside the Nordic countries, within the Nordics there are more differentiated debates going on about the dynamics of diverse changes in welfare states and welfare spaces. In the Danish context, for example, state political initiatives such as *Tættere på II* (2021) have steered housing association resources into expanding the common housing sector and affordable housing in the larger cities. The so-called "Blackstone Law" has been directed toward halting housing speculation in the large cities by global capital firms. While at the same time, as Ellen Braae addresses in her contribution, the Danish government has imposed legislation that has led to the eviction of several thousand residents in vulnerable common housing areas and the demolition or sale of housing within those areas to private investment firms. This suggests that there is not necessarily one singular consistent or coherent thread of welfare architecture transformation within these contexts, or across the Nordic countries—we are given a more complex picture than that suggested by external perspectives of singular Nordic welfare exceptionalism. This is where I think this publication plays a role.

HM: The notion of Nordic welfare exceptionalism is also based on architectural historiography. In the postwar situation, the Nordic sphere, especially Sweden, was showcased as an idealized site of "good architecture." Sweden was the country standing outside the war, and of course, that made the whole difference. But, as both Frida Rosenberg and Espen Johnsen shows in this book, even this history must be rethought: rather than a place for developing typical Swedish architecture, Sweden was an arena for transnational ideas and cooperations during the war. This demonstrates how important it is to keep a critical eye on historiography when it supports today's nationalistic ideas of exceptionalism.

DS: This ties to an exceptionalism functioning in temporal rather than geographical terms—in relation to past "golden ages." The danger of the idealization of historical periods, the romanticizing of a past that never existed, and the lament of its loss—these seem to be the great traps of our time. Whether this applies to a "golden age" of the universal Nordic welfare, or a constructed notion of pre-modernist nationalist identity, there is a link between nostalgia and emerging forms of exclusion.

HM: It is remarkable that only around 2015, the discussion on who was outside and who was inside the welfare state looked so different. One of the key topics today is to rethink this relationship. Welfare for whom and what kind of welfare? For sure, not only are the geographical delimitations decisive but also the social aspects, such as background and ethnicity. This is a spatial and an architectural issue, both as a conceptual figure and as a material question. How are borders constructed in bricks and mortar, both inside the welfare state and toward its surroundings? The tendency to stress policies of anti-solidarity was evident in the 2024 EU election when Swedish political parties competed in reframing Trump's terminology of The Wall. The bluntest phrase was stated by the right-wing populist party Sverigedemokraterna (Sweden Democrats): "Our Europe is building walls." So, in this new Europe, architecture has a topical role in building borders and secluded zones but also, in a very twisted and contradictory way, building what is called "integrated" societies through demolishing housing and drawing up new borders inside the national borders—I am considering here the policy of labeling housing areas as "vulnerable" or "parallel societies." This strategy takes its starting point in the narration of certain areas as failures, which in this book is discussed through three different thematic and geographical perspectives by Guttorm Ruud, Mikkel Høghøj, and Jennifer Mack.

FROM UNIVERSAL WELFARE TO COMPETITION

DS: The shift toward competition-oriented spatial planning, for example, in the Danish context in the 1980s and 1990s saw a strategic focus on Copenhagen and the capital-region as a growth engine for Denmark. As Tom Nielsen touches upon in this book, competition-oriented spatial planning's contribution to the spatial centralization of resources and other dynamics, including ongoing urbanization dynamics, saw an increasing differentiation of welfare subjects within an uneven geography of welfare at a national scale.

2 Carsten Jensen, *Welfare*, trans. Heidi Flegal, Reflections (Baltimore, MD: Aarhus, Denmark: Johns Hopkins University Press; Aarhus University Press, 2023), 53.

3 Peo Hansen, *A Modern Migration Theory: An Alternative Economic Approach to Failed EU* (Newcastle upon Tyne: Agenda Publishing, 2021).

Here, we can think of the depopulation and peripheralization of provinces, welfare institution closings, the thinning out and distancing of welfare amenities in the periphery. While there has been political pushback against this centralization process in a Danish setting, with the decentralization of some governmental agencies or public educational institutions, it might represent another kind of differentiated welfare subjectivity compared to that occurring in Norway, where considerable efforts and resources have been directed toward maintaining a dispersed population and amenity access across the country's varied geography. Here in Denmark we have seen large investments and elevated welfare conditions promoting the attractiveness of living in the "periphery."

Denmark's Parallel Society Act from 2010, which was applied to vulnerable housing areas, can be linked to another scale of differentiated welfare subjectivity—within cities, at the scale of the neighborhood. The Parallel Society Act's application of eviction orders and tougher legal penalties against residents is based on the metrics of the "Ghetto List," which includes the percentage of residents from "non-western" backgrounds, irrespective of whether they are Danish citizens or not. The intention of the Parallel Society Act to produce a "mixed" neighborhood by introducing more "resourceful" residents, and displacing more vulnerable residents has been widely criticized within Denmark and internationally from human rights and housing politics perspectives. It is these supposedly "unworthy" welfare subjects, to use Carsten Jensen's framing,[2] that are increasingly the focus of a biopolitical form of spatial planning and architectural practice driven by popularist nationalistic anti-migrant politics.

HM: Totally. The political scientist Peo Hansen has written very interestingly on what he calls "the migration myth" and how the contemporary welfare state relies on migrants.[3] Without people transgressing the national borders, the welfare state apparatus, including healthcare and elderly care, would not work. Hansen is basing his arguments on post-Keynesian thinking and New Monetary Theory and shows how the contemporary debate is more or less turned upside down. Instead of acknowledging that without immigration, we would not be able to keep up our welfare, despite politicians, experts, and commentators continuously arguing that immigration is a societal burden and something we have to pay for. To me, Hansen's perspective is extremely interesting and inspiring because it opens up for new strategic thinking regarding the welfare state and immigration. And it holds something positive, something that we can build new knowledge on that rests not on repression but rather construction. So, you know, this perspective radically changes how we perceive the foundations of the welfare state. This becomes urgent today when the notion of a welfare state is used in protective and conservative politics.

Today, we can notice a radical conservative use of *the welfare state* whereby the concept itself shifts meanings and gets new associations. One can compare this to ideas used in the 1968-movement and how they later tied into neoliberalizations. The discourse was slightly transforming into something else, the same concepts, but used in a new context. Now we can see a similar discursive shift regarding the welfare state as a concept.

DS: This is really relevant in its potential to reorient the conceptualization of welfare toward more positively framed ends—challenging narratives that are now ingrained in the political discourse and that are predominantly oriented toward conservation and preservation, and focus on saving and maintaining a "threatened" and economically vulnerable welfare state. Perhaps this points to a possible reconnection to some of the more emancipatory narratives that we might associate with the earlier welfare project and its architecture and planning—whether they have been fully realized or not, which have also been entwined with the democratic project. The emancipation of the working class from the inhuman conditions of the factory system and the industrial city; the emancipation of women from the domestic environment with their movement into the workforce; or the potential emancipation of other groups excluded across local, but also wider geographies.

HM: Yes, I think questions of emancipation in relation to the built environment and the welfare state are crucial. Built structures, such as theaters, public spaces, kindergartens, and libraries, aimed at both liberation and control. Early welfare state policies had the goal to emancipate workers, and partly also women, but many other groups were, as you said, excluded. I would like to return to the notion of being "inside" or "outside" the welfare state. Today, there are vivid discussions in Sweden on doing tests, such as language tests, before you are allowed into the Swedish welfare state community. And a Swedish "cultural canon"—whatever that means—is under construction by the initiative of the government. To become a Swede, you must be a "democratic" welfare state citizen, which can mean almost everything but often means *not* being a Muslim. So, in this way, concepts such as democracy and welfare play into what can be called a new racism, which is not based on biological race but more on language, religion, values, and culture. There has been a tendency to connect ideas of universal welfare to earlier periods with lower immigration and what is thought of as a more homogenous population. So, in that sense, nostalgic ideas about lost welfare can support desire for a "universal" welfare subject, where universal vaguely means something Swedish. To avoid this conservative trap, it's important to think outside the notion of a limited welfare state and instead talk about planetary welfare. But how to think about the role of architecture and built environment in a landscape of planetary welfare?

PLANETARY WELFARE

DS: The planetary perspective involves a range of dynamics that continue to challenge the dominant spatial units of the welfare state—the nation state and the municipality. Anti-migrant national policies and discourse, and the hard bordering of the welfare state have intensified in recent years as one of the main impacts of climate change, climate migration, is only expected to increase—as are the demographic imbalances associated with population ageing. Addressing these challenges requires alternate models of thinking, and alternate narratives capable of engaging more optimistic and solidaric outlooks at the planetary scale.

More generally, the polycrisis foregrounds the relevance of planetary urbanization as a conceptual framework to understand contemporary urbanization processes—and also places the anthropocentric focus of the welfare project in greater relief. In a moment increasingly defined by the necessity to come to terms with the ruins of the "urbanocene," the perspective of limitless resources and uncontained growth that drove it are increasingly in question. Does it make sense today to consider welfare as a dominant agenda that should coexist with urgent priorities of addressing the environmental dangers which threaten human life on the planet? Can welfare become a productive concept if expanded beyond human welfare dispensed at the scale of the municipality or nation state, into the welfare of other species, ecosystems, or the welfare or the faring-well of the earth system as a whole? Could this suggest possible expanded forms of spatial welfare practices?

Clearly, this sketches a conflictual space defined by opposing politics, and spatial logics—on the one hand, one foregrounding an anthropocentric-oriented welfare state conservation agenda focused on the cultural and economic narratives that you mentioned—and on the other hand, others that might prioritize environmental, climate, and biodiversity concerns. I am interested in what this might imply for a more expanded conceptualization of welfare—and if it might reinforce welfare as a still relevant concept.

HM: Yes, I totally agree with you that we have one of the most urgent conflicts here. However, I guess we—humankind—are forced to understand that the conflictual space holding, on the one hand, anthropocentric-oriented welfare and, on the other environmental and climate concerns depend on each other and must be thought together. This will, of course, have a radical significance for the notion of the welfare state. Another thing I want to bring up in relation to this theme has to do with rhetoric. I think we need to be watchful that concepts of environmental welfare, or more-than-human welfare, might support protective and conservative ideas about the local that are legitimized by traveling restrictions and local production. Therefore, it is even more critical to find new ways to connect socially and engage in different geographic, cultural, and social contexts without polluting the environment. So, I guess the role of infrastructure and mobility must be a priority in contemporary discussions about architecture and welfare.

DS: I agree, it is tricky. There is obviously not one answer to what a more-than-human welfare or an environmental welfare-oriented architecture and planning, might be. But perhaps there are relevant weak signals existing, that may not necessarily be immediately incorporated into a regressive popularist discourse: alternate scales of the bounding of planning such as the bioregional scale, a watershed for example; expanded legal rights for ecological systems, granting legal personhood to non-human spatial environments; expanded geographic bounding of the evaluation of environmental impact and externalized costs, mapping of extraction implications of new urban development projects; or planning with economic instruments focused on revaluing of nature contributions; etc., etc. We might consider these kinds of developments as corresponding to an expanded concept of welfare.

4 Cedric J. Robinson, *Black Marxism: The Making of the Black Radical Tradition* (Chapel Hill, N.C.: University of North Carolina Press, 2000 [1983]).

THE ROLE OF ARCHITECTURE

HM: It is critical to consider the role of architecture in a broader sense. For example, how has architecture's role shifted in relation to the four pillars of the welfare state (i.e., health care, housing, education, and social security)? Today, architecture is still part of a state policy with its roots in these pillars but now very different. Instead of aiming to support solidarity, architecture is mainly used as a strategy in a repressive policy, as a way to displace groups of the population using concepts such as parallel societies or vulnerable areas.

DS: I think the analytical filter of the pillars is interesting. Perhaps the pillar linked to the built environment that has undergone the most dramatic changes in a Danish context is that of housing. While the common housing sector is still a considerable proportion of the housing stock—housing approximately one in six Danes—the production of new Almene housing effectively collapsed during the 1990s, and has not since revived due to, amongst other factors, high land prices. Various other milestones include the forced selling off of rental housing assets by the municipality of Copenhagen in the 1990s, the cultural emergence of the private developer in Denmark around that period; the intensified financialization of housing; the increasing unaffordability of the housing market, particularly within larger cities, etc. Tom Nielsen's chapter touches on some of these developments and more. I could imagine that in a Swedish context, you could describe many of those transformations and perhaps even more extreme versions.

HM: Yes, absolutely! In Sweden, housing policy collapsed, or even ended, in the early 1990s, and thereafter a market logic has been governing the housing market. The financialization of architecture, not only housing, in the public sector is also something Erik Sigge discusses in this volume. I guess we can see the same development in the rest of Europe, and also in many other places in the world. But of course, when this transformation toward the market takes place *inside* the public housing sector, the effects become obvious and dramatic. Another effect of welfare being lost and sold is the retrenchment of social services in many areas—for example in suburbs where citizens from various cultural and ethnic backgrounds live, and thus as a symptom of racial capitalism.[4]

DS: It could also be relevant to reflect on the shift in the logic of planning and the production of architecture and urban development from a more evenly universal distributed approach to spatializing welfare—within the logics of the managerial planning ethos of predict and provide—toward more reactive or corrective approaches to intervention, according to more strategic or acupunctural logics of intervention. This might be interpreted as more pragmatic than utopian—whether directed toward addressing a social challenge, or exploiting an economic opportunity. A shift from a new school here and kindergarten there into more strategic investments such as the neighborhood uplift project, or a bridge. Identifying more vulnerable areas where more resources would be focused to try to address local challenges, would have both positive impacts on those specific communities, but also challenging outcomes such as gentrification. But at the same time, having also more focused welfare, not something only delivered evenly, but something addressing local problems, or sort of focusing problems, some of those more politicized than others, both for good and bad. On the one hand, we see how these neighborhood uplift projects are highly effective in engaging participation from the community, and on the other hand, we see new development area projects, by By og Havn for example, that are heavily criticized for their non-democratic character.

HM: Yes, as you say, acupuncture planning of welfare has replaced universal planning strategies. I would argue that these strategies clearly have reinforced class differences and made some into winners and others into losers. And absurdly, these projects often rely on one individual capacity to take initiative and approach the authorities.

DS: In a Danish context, these developments are often initiated by the state, municipality, or state-owned enterprises. We can discuss how they are influenced by a changed role of the state in relation to welfare—where welfare is a condition to support the competitiveness of the state, and its attractiveness to business. We can see how this ties into the concept of urban livability, its origins, and its competitive metrics—something my colleagues and I tried to address in *The Atlas of the Copenhagens*. We can see aspects of this unfolded in Leonard Ma's chapter.

HM: What you bring up here—that welfare becomes a service to support attractiveness that could enable investments—is crucial. It was a figure of thought that took form with the Third Way policy in the 1990s and Anthony Giddens described in *The Third Way* a new mentality of governance, a way of getting more out of less, which means that one investment should also support others. This new strategy contributed to understanding architecture as a discipline delivering "value." Within this new, aestheticized perspective, the architecture discipline became an important strategy to attract capital. In this context, one should also recognize how human capital (social competence, knowledge, and experiences) becomes a key asset in the production of welfare. This is a history that ties into Martin Søberg's text on playgrounds.

OPENING UP TO THE FUTURE

HM: Let's go back to our initial task: where do we stand today and how should we think about the future? We must focus on how to create hope and believe in future alternatives. How can we encourage radical fantasies of tomorrow? This also bring us to the topic of utopia. Today, we can notice the backlashes of the critique of modernist utopianism and see the effects of the lack of radical ideas of a future world. There are of course researchers and thinkers, for example, feminist scholars, who stress that kind of utopianism, but they have not won a platform in mainstream political thinking.

DS: Yes. I think that this is a really, really important discussion to have around welfare as a concept today. Does it, or can it still, hold utopian promise? Can it be relevant and operational, and progressive, today? For some of the reasons you point to, we clearly suffer a deficit of imagination in constructing alternatives to the systems and realities that we're in. And this recurring question as to whether welfare is something that has to be maintained and conserved or whether welfare has to be something dynamic, and responding to the changing conditions that we face, is key. It would perhaps necessarily involve a combination of both, for example, a reengagement with notions and spatialities of solidarity, which have been weakened by the increasing fragmentation and polarization of society. And at the same time, there's obviously the necessity to develop progressive, optimistic, novel spatial and societal imaginaries that address the specific challenges we face today. This is actually one of the key areas to which the discipline of architecture can contribute.

HM: I also think this discussion relates specifically to architecture. Today, there is little belief in architecture having the capacity to present and construct new utopias of a future welfare. This involves the profession and other actors, such as politicians, journalists, and individuals who all form the public debate. One can ask if architecture is part of the welfare project on a political level today. Thinking in these terms, it is urgent to show how architecture as a discipline carries utopian thinking and holds the possibility to imagine new worlds.

DS: That is an important challenge to the practitioners of today. To what extent are they operating in a form of utopian space or a space in which there is an attempt to push the existing boundaries of a system that—as you described—is increasingly dominated by market logics and private clients. I think we can start to see signs of some interesting examples of novel practice forms.

HM: Yes, it is crucial to articulate architecture as a field for play, experimentation, and social thinking where new conceptual figures can take form. In this space, we find the powerful overlap between the aesthetic and the political and the understanding of how designed spatial situations can impact the social sphere. That is a fertile ground of new notions of architecture and what it can do in society. You can rethink politics, come up with new social reforms and how to organize society, but to concretize these ideas, you need to have an architectural idea how to turn this radical fantasy into material form.

INDEX

ILLUSTRATION CREDITS

Front cover: Grantoften, Ballerup. Photo by Aage Strüwing © Jørgen Strüwing.
Back cover: Navestad, Norrköping. Photo by Lennart Jansson, 1971. Courtesy of Hyresbostäder i Norrköping.

1: Elverhøjens Skole, Herlev. Photo by Aage Strüwing © Jørgen Strüwing.
2: Retirement home in Enskede, Stockholm. Photo by Sune Sundahl, 1955. Arkdes collection.
3: Romsås, Oslo. Photo by Frits Solvang, 1974. DEXTRA Photo, CC BY-SA 4.0.
4–5: Hässelby, Stockholm. Photo by Sune Sundahl. Arkdes collection.
6: Tåsen, Oslo. Photo by Atelier Rude, 1971. Oslo Museum, CC BY-SA 4.0.
7: Grantoften, Ballerup. Photo by Keld Helmer-Pedersen © Jan Helmer-Petersen.
8–9: Hökarängen, Stockholm. Photo by Sune Sundahl, 1951. Arkdes collection.
10: Grantoften, Ballerup. Photo by Aage Strüwing © Jørgen Strüwing.
11: Romsås, Oslo. Photo by Frits Solvang, 1974. DEXTRA Photo, CC BY-SA 4.0.
12–13: Lambertseter, Oslo. Photo by Leif Krohn Ørnelund, ca. 1956. Oslo Museum, CC BY-SA.
14: Stovner, Oslo. Photo by Leif Krohn Ørnelund, 1970. Oslo Museum, CC BY-SA 4.0.
15: Malmö. Photo by Sune Sundahl, 1953. Arkdes collection.
16: Solbjerg Have, Copenhagen. Photo: Keld Helmer-Pedersen © Jan Helmer-Petersen.

MONUMENTALITY AND MASS HOUSING IN SWEDEN, 31–59

32 t, b: Photographer unknown, 1968. Courtesy of Hyresbostäder i Norrköping.
38: Photo by Sune Sundahl, 1964. Arkdes collection.
39: Photo by Lennart Jansson, 1969. Courtesy of Hyresbostäder i Norrköping.
42 t, b: Photos by Lennart Jansson, 1971. Courtesy of Hyresbostäder i Norrköping.
43, 44: Photos by Lennart Jansson, 1972. Courtesy of Hyresbostäder i Norrköping.
48–49: Photo by Joackim Kröger, 2000.
50 t, b: Photo by Pär Eliaeson and Nilsson Samuelsson, 1998.
55 t, b, 56: Photos by John Håkansson, 2023.
59: Gunnar Asplund et al., *acceptera* (Stockholm: Tiden, 1931).

DANISH PLAYGROUNDS AND THE FORMATION OF THE WELFARE CITIZENS, 61–73

62: Photo by Helle Nebelong.
65 t: Photographer unknown. Kbhbilleder.dk.
65 b: Photo by C. Th. Sørensen, 1965. The Royal Danish Academy Library.
68 t, b: Photo by C. Th. Sørensen. Not dated. The Royal Danish Academy Library.
73: Photo by C. Th. Sørensen. The Royal Danish Academy Library.

CABIN CONTROVERSIES, 75–96

77: Photo by Kristian Bech, 2023.
78 t: Photo by Olav Johannes Bøthun, 1996.
78 b: Photo by Hermann Christian Neupert, 1909–1932. Nasjonalbiblioteket.
81 t: Photo by Are Carlsen, 2002.
81 b: Drawing by Knut Knutsen, probably 1949. Photo by Børre Høstland. Stiftelsen Arkitekturmuseet, Arkitektursamlingene.
82 t: Photo by Jens Andreas Selmer, 1965–1980. Architects: Wenche and Jens Selmer. Stiftelsen Arkitekturmuseet, Arkitektursamlingene.
82 b: Cover of *Bonytt* 11–12 (1956). Bonytt/Story House Egmont.
85 t, b: *Byggekunst* no. 8 (1952): 144. Architect: Vilhelm Reinhard.
86 t: *Byggekunst* no. 1 (1976): 6. Architect: Robert C. Esdaile. Photo by Esdaile, Horgen og Bjærtnes.
86 b: *Byggekunst* no. 1 (1976): 6. Architect: Robert C. Esdaile.
89 t, b: Erik Langdalen and Karl Erikstad, *Plan i fjellet. Hytta på fjellet* (Oslo: A/S Byggtjeneste, 1966), 2, 4. Drawings by Erik Langdalen.
92: Kommunal- og distriktsdepartementet, 1966.

FRAGMENTS, WHISPERS, AND MATERIALS IN SPRING, 97–111

Photos by Aysha Amin.

LOCAL AGENCY AND TRANSNATIONAL COLLABORATIONS, 99–135

118: Photographer unknown, 1947. ArkDes collection.
119 t: Cover of G. E. Kidder Smith, *Sweden Builds*, rev. ed. (New York: Reinhold Publishing Corporation, 1957).
119 b: Kidder Smith, *Sweden Builds*, 33.
123 t: Photo by Annar Bjørgli. The National Museum, Oslo.
126 t: Cover of Harald Hals, ed., *Boliger og samfunnsbygg. Erfaringer fra Sverige* (Oslo: Johan Grundt Tanum, 1946).
126 b: Cover of Harald Hals, *Plan og Planlegging* (Oslo: Johan Grundt Tanum, 1946).
128: Harald Hals, *Plan og Planlegging*, 8.
131 t: Erik Rolfsen, *Generalplan for Oslo* (Oslo reguleringsvesen, 1950), 63.
131 b: Photographer unknown, 1964. Arbeiderbevegelsens arkiv og bibliotek (Arbark).
134–135: Photo by Annar Bjørgli. The National Museum, Oslo.

CATHERINE BAUER, 136–154

136: The Museum of Modern Art.
139 t: Photo by Sune Sundahl, 1953. Arkdes Collection.
139 b: Photo by Sune Sundahl, 1958. Arkdes Collection.
140: Photo by Sune Sundahl, 1957. Arkdes Collection.
143, 152: Courtesy of the Catherine Bauer Wurster Papers, The Bancroft Library, University of California, Berkeley.
145 t: Photographer unknown. Arkdes Collection.
145 b: Photo by John Stjernström, Arkdes Collection.
146: Photo by Oscar Halldin, 1930–1948. Arkdes Collection.
148, 149: HSB Archive, Centre for Business History.

A WELFARE STATE ON THE DRAWING BOARD, 156–173

156: Cover of *Plan*, no. 3 (1935). Nasjonalbiblioteket.
160: Cover of Gunnar Øvergaard Jørgen, "Bo bedre," *Teknisk-økonomiske småskrifter* 4 (Oslo: Det Norske Arbeiderpartis forlag, 1936). Arbeiderbevegelsens arkiv og bibliotek.
163: Cover of Teknisk Forening av D.N.A, "Boligbygging i Norge," *Teknisk-økonomiske småskrifter* (Oslo: Det Norske Arbeiderpartis forlag, 1937). Arbeiderbevegelsens arkiv og bibliotek.
167: Cover of *Det 20de Århundre*, no. 4 (1937). Arbeiderbevegelsens arkiv og bibliotek.
170: Cover of *Det 20de Århundre*, no. 8 (1937). Arbeiderbevegelsens arkiv og bibliotek.
173: *Det 20de Århundre*, no. 8 (1937): 303. Arbeiderbevegelsens arkiv og bibliotek.

MATERIAL NETWORKS, 175–192

177 t: Photo by Carl Nesjar, 1963. Stiftelsen Arkitekturmuseet, Arkitektursamlingene. © Nesjar, Carl/BONO.
177 b: Photo by Uppsala-Bild, 1967. Skarne collection, Erik Stenberg's Million Program Archive.
180 t: Photo by Jan Gustavsson Cogg, 1966. Skarne collection, Erik Stenberg's Million Program Archive.
180 b: Photographer unknown, 1957. Kurt Månsson collection, Erik Stenberg's Million Program Archive.
183 t: Photo by Arne Persson. Kurt Månsson collection, Erik Stenberg's Million Program Archive.
183: Pamphlet titled "Råslättprojektet – projektering produktion," Erik Stenberg's Million Program Archive.
185 t: Undated, likely 1967/1968. Skarne collection, Erik Stenberg's Million Program Archive.
185 b: Printed by Östlundh & Kühlhorn/ Bohuslänningens Boktr. AB, Uddevalla, 1988. Skarne collection, Erik Stenberg's Million Program Archive.
186 t: Cover of exhibition catalog *Konst i betong* (Stockholm, Moderna Museet, 1964).
186 b: Exhibition catalog *Konst i betong* (Stockholm, Moderna Museet, 1964).
187: Photographer unknown, 1957. Stiftelsen Arkitekturmuseet, Oslo, Arkitektursamlingene.
189, 192: Photographer unknown, 1963–1964 Sjöberg Bildbyrå.

CONCRETE SUBURB, 193–208

Photos by John Håkansson.

CHILDREN IN CRISIS, 211–225

213 t, 214 b: Photo by Fjellanger Widerøe, 1972. Oslo byarkiv, CC BY-SA 4.0.
213 b: Photo by Atelier Rude, 1969. Oslo Museum, CC BY-SA 4.0.
214 t: Byplankontoret, 1967. Plan- og bygningsetaten (saksinnsyn).
217 t: Cover of Terje Gammelsrud, ed., "Barn i krise," special issue, *Sinnets helse: Tidsskrift for mentalhygiene*, no. 5 (1975). Voksne for barn.
217 b: Gammelsrud, "Barn i krise," 13–15. Voksne for barn.

220: Cover of Odd Aksum et al., "Stovnerboere spør stovnerboere: En undersøkelse om res[s]urser, behov og Stovner sentrum" (1972).
225 t, c: NRK, 1975.
225 b: Photo by Svendsen-Foto, 1976. Arbeiderbevegelsens arkiv og bibliotek, CC BY-NC-ND 4.0.

DANGEROUS YOUTH, 227–237

228 t: *Ekstra Bladet*, January 7, 1974. JP/ Politikens Hus. https://jppol.dk/
228 b: Brabrand-Århus Local History Archive
231 t: Scanbox Entertainment Danmark A/S
231 b: *Ekstra Bladet*, December 31, 1976. JP/ Politikens Hus. https://jppol.dk/
234: Photographer unknown. Odense City Archives.

DADDY IS A COMPUTER, 238–255

238: Photo: Lars Nyberg. Margareta Schwartz and Suzanne Sjöqvist, *Kvinnoliv, Förortsliv*. (Stockholm: Gidlunds, 1978).
243 t, b, 244 t, b: Photo: Jan Delden. From Olle Bengtzon, Jan Delden, and Jan Lundgren, *Rapport Tensta*. (Stockholm: PAN/ Nordstedts, 1970).
248 t: Hans Gordon and Peter Molin, eds., "*Man bara anpassar sig helt enkelt.*" *En forskningsrapport om människor i Skärholmen* (Stockholm: PAN/Nordstedts, 1972).
248 b: Gordon and Molin, eds., "*Man bara anpassar sig helt enkelt*," 6–7.
250 t, b, 252 b, 255 t, b: Photos by Lars Nyberg. From Schwartz and Sjöqvist, *Kvinnoliv, Förortsliv*, 71, 30, 36, 27, 81.
252 t: Botkyrka Municipality

THE GREAT BETRAYAL, 257–269

261 t: Cover of *Kulturfront* no. 1 (1936).
261 b: Photo by C. G. Rosenberg, ArkDes collections.
265 t: Cover of *Aufbruch und Krise des Funktionalismus* (Stockholm, Arkitekturmuseet, 1976).
265 b: Photo by Sune Sundahl, ArkDes collections.
266 t: Svenska Dagbladet, June 8, 1972.
266 b: Dagens Nyheter, June 27, 1972.

CAUGHT IN THE NET OF SOCIAL DEMOCRACY, 271–287

273, 275, 278: Kalle Grude, Jan Wilhelm Løchstøer, and Knut Østby, *Studier i Planlegging under kapitalismen*, student project (Oslo: Oslo School of Architecture, 1970).
283 t: Jon Guttu, Johan Ditlef-Martens, and Magnus Nygaard, "Rinnan og Rolfsen," *Fagavisa* 2/1974: 20–21.
283 b: Cover of Johan Ditlef-Martens and Ketil Moe, eds., *Plan 1933–1936* (Oslo: Universitetsforlaget, 1983).

LIVING IN A SATELLITE TOWN, 289–303

Photos by Ane Hjort Guttu.

FROM COMMONS TO PUBLIC SPACE, 307–322

309, 313 b, 317 t, 321 c: © Cristina Ferraiuolo.
314: © The Danish Agency for Data Supply and Efficiency (SDFE).
321 t: © Ellen Braae.
321 b: © [illegible].

THE WORTH OF WELFARE, 325–337

327: Photo by Arild Vågen, CC BY-SA 4.0.
332: Photo by ErikAnd30, CC BY-SA 4.0.

THE DANISH WELFARE CITY, 339–355
342, 345, 348: Det Kgl. Bibliotek, Copenhagen.
346: Photo by Steen Eiler Rasmussen. Arkitektskolen Aarhus.
352 t, b: Photos by Tom Nielsen.

QUALITY CRITERIA AND THE NEOLIBERALIZATION OF CITY LIFE IN HELSINKI, 357–370

360 t, b, 367: Photos by Leonard Ma.
363: Gehl Architects.
364: Helsinki Urban Environment Division, https://www.hel.fi/kaupunkiymparisto/en.

CONTRIBUTORS

Aysha Amin is a Danish artist and curator. She founded the hybrid gallery for art, culture and architecture Andromeda 8220, located in the Aarhus suburb of Gellerup, where she grew up. Aysha is a jury member at Realdania Underværker 2024–2027 and was a jury member and one of the curators behind the Spring Exhibition 2024 at Kunsthal Charlottenborg. She has exhibited works at Den Frie (2023), Arthub (2021) Nikolai Kunsthall (2022), Berlin Biennale at Hydrocapsules DNA (2020), and Venice Biennale at the American Pavilion (2018). She is also an architecture student at Aarhus School of Architecture, owner and project manager of [Smag] à la Gellerup, project manager of the educational program *Vi Fællesskaber Vores By* (We co-create our city), and correspondent for *The Funambulist* magazine.

Thordis Arrhenius, professor of architecture at the School of Architecture, Royal Institute of Technology (KTH) Stockholm, is an architect and researcher with a strong engagement in contemporary architectural and urban practice and their theories. Recent research projects investigate the role of the architectural exhibition in the reception of modern architecture in Scandinavia, the historiography of conservation, the strategy of re-use, and its architectural and theoretical implications. Publications include *The Fragile Monument: on Conservation and Modernity* (Artifice books on Architecture, 2012); the co-edited anthologies *Place and Displacement* and *Exhibiting Architecture* (Lars Müller Publishers, 2014); and *Experimental Preservation* (Lars Müller Publishers, 2016).

Matthew Ashton is an architect, writer, and researcher based in Stockholm. He is currently completing a PhD through RMIT University Melbourne, researching material flows, landscapes of extraction, and walking as a creative research practice. Matthew has previously taught at KTH School of Architecture in Stockholm, and his work has been exhibited at Kulturhuset Stockholm, Malmö Form and Design Centre, and Röhsska Museum in Gothenburg.

Ellen Braae has been Professor of Landscape Architecture Theory and Method at the University of Copenhagen, Denmark, since 2009, where she heads the research group "Landscape Architecture and Urbanism." Her research bridges design and humanities, and over the recent decade she has focused on welfare landscapes: postwar open spaces planned by and for the public. She has led the collective research projects *Reconfiguring Welfare Landscapes* (2017–2022), funded by The *Danish Council for Independent Research*, Culture and Communication, and the HERA-funded project *PuSH, Public Space in European Social Housing* (2019–2022). She has published widely on landscape and heritage related matters including *Beauty Redeemed: Recycling Post-Industrial Landscapes* (Ikaros Press/ Birkhäuser, 2015), *Routledge Research Companion to Landscape Architecture* (Routledge, 2018) (co-edited with Henriette Steiner) and *Urban Planning in the Nordic World* (Wisconsin University Press/Aarhus University Press 2022).

Martin Braathen is an architect and Senior Curator of Architecture at the National Museum, Oslo. Holds a PhD in Architecture history and a Master of Architecture from NTNU, Norway. Educated at NTNU, Whitney Independent Study Program in New York, and Universität der Künste Berlin. Formerly editor-in-chief of architecture magazine Arkitektnytt, acting director of Oslo Architecture Triennale, and co-director of Projekt 0047 in Berlin. Many years of experience as freelance writer, critic, and editor, and was curator of the Nordic Pavilion at the Venice Biennale 2021.

Aslak Gurholt is a graphic designer, artist, author and curator. His practice is mainly focused on books, exhibitions and work with cultural institutions. Gurholt is the author of several books, ranging from conceptual picture books for children to artist's publications. As an integral part of his practice Gurholt works with research on graphic design and art history. His work is held at the Norwegian National Museum of Art, Architecture and Design, Oslo. In 2015, he was awarded "Bokkunstprisen" (the Norwegian honorary award for book design). He is currently a PhD candidate at Leeds Beckett University.

Ane Hjort Guttu is a Norwegian artist and filmmaker based in Oslo. She works in a variety of media, but has in recent years mainly concentrated on film and video works, ranging from investigative documentary to poetic fiction. Among the recurrent themes in her work are the relationship between freedom and power, individual and public space, social change and limits of action. Guttu is also a writer and curator, and she is a professor at the National Academy of the Arts, Oslo. Her most recent project is the full feature film VOICE, released in 2023.

Mikkel Høghøj is a cultural historian specialized in Nordic urban and welfare history. He is a project senior researcher at the National Museum of Denmark and holds a PhD from Aarhus University. In his research, he has explored the history of housing, urban planning, infrastructure, landscapes and resources to understand the historical connections between urban space, welfare, citizenship and everyday life in the modern city. Høghøj has been a guest researcher at the Centre for Urban History at the University of Leicester and Leibniz Institute for Research on Society and Space. In 2022, he received the *Planning Perspectives Prize* by International Planning History Society (IPHS).

John Håkansson is a Swedish photographer and artist. He earned his degree in Photography from the University of Photography in Gothenburg and furthered his studies at the Academy of Photography at Konstfack, Stockholm. His work is rooted in an interest in urban living and construction as well as the impact of human activity on nature. Landscape and architecture are thus common motifs, and suburbs are recurring subjects. He has participated in several exhibitions, received grants, and published three books: *Small: Mountains* (Bam Boom Books, 2020), *I närheten* (Trema, 2014) and *Vita husen* (Trema, 2014).

Espen Johnsen is professor in art history, IFIKK/University of Oslo. His research and teaching focus is on 20th-century Norwegian and Scandinavian architecture. Particularly concerned with modernism, procedural studies, avant-garde and network theories, welfare, and the relationship between architecture and visual arts, and architecture and nature/environmental studies. Earlier research projects dealt with the design and architectural history from the interwar period, followed by a focus on the postwar period. His most recent books were *Erling Viksjø. Eksperimenter i form og betong* (Pax, 2020) and *PAGON: Scandinavian Avant-Garde. Architecture 1945–1956* (Bloomsbury Publishing, 2023). He has ongoing book projects on "Sverre Fehn and Geir Grung" and "Knutsen and the Knutsen-School."

Anne-Kristine Kronborg is associate professor at the Norwegian University of Life Sciences, NMBU, and holds a PhD from the Oslo School of Architecture and Design. Her research interests lie in the intersection of architecture and politics, especially in the history of housing and urban planning in the welfare state. She has previously worked as an historian at the cooperative housing association OBOS. In her current position at NMBU she teaches the history of urban and regional planning and the history of the planning profession.

Beata Labuhn studied Architecture at TU Delft and L'EPFL Lausanne, as well as Philosophy at Leiden University. Currently, Labuhn is a Doctoral Research Fellow at The Oslo School of Architecture and Design (AHO), where she researches the entanglements of architecture and environmentalism in Norway between 1960 and 1980. Labuhn wrote in *Nordic Design Cultures in Transformation, 1960-1980* edited by Kjetil Fallan et al. (Routledge, 2023), in *Images of Egypt* edited by Mari Lending et al. (Pax, 2018), as well as in *Future Anterior, kritische berichte, Global Built Environment Review, de Architect*, and *Yearbook of Landscape Architecture and Urbanism in the Netherlands*.

Leonard Ma is a Canadian architect based in Helsinki. He is a member of New Academy, and currently teaches Urban Studies and Architecture at the Estonian Academy of Art. His research focuses on neoliberalism, financialization, and the legacy of the welfare state, and has been published in e-flux, The Avery Review, Drawing Matter and AA Files. He is the co-editor of Urbanizing Suburbia (Jovis 2023), which considers the turn to asset-based welfare, and processes remaking the outer European city since the financial crisis. Leonard is a practicing architect and leads PUBLIC OFFICE.

Jennifer Mack is Associate Professor and Docent at KTH and a Pro Futura Scientia Fellow of the Swedish Collegium for Advanced Study. Broadly, Mack's research links architectural history and anthropology to investigate culture, politics, and ecology in the built environment. Mack's book, *The Construction of Equality* (University of Minnesota Press, 2017), received the Margaret Mead Award. She has co-edited the anthologies *Rethinking the Social in Architecture* (Actar, 2019) and *Life Among Urban Planners* (University of Pennsylvania Press, 2020). Mack is an elected member of The Young Academy of Sweden and serves on the editorial boards of *Housing, Theory and Society, Human Organization*, and *Thresholds*.

ACKNOWLEDGMENTS

The research for Architecture and Welfare—Scandinavian Perspectives builds on the network meetings and seminars of the Scandinavian Research Network for Architecture and Welfare, initiated in 2013 by the Norwegian Institute for Cultural Heritage Research (NIKU), through Rikke Stenbro and developed over the years through lively exchanges among architectural institutions and research projects across Denmark, Norway, and Sweden including: Reconfiguring Welfare Landscapes, UCPH; Spaces of Danish Welfare (Royal Danish Academy); Restoring the Welfare State, AHO, KTH; Forming Welfare (Royal Danish Academy); Architecture in the Making, Chalmers, KTH, LTH; Architecture in Effect, KTH; and The Architecture of Deregulations, KTH.

In 2018, the research network received funding from the Joint Committee for Nordic Research Councils in the Humanities and Social Sciences (NOS-HS) for the workshop project Exploring Nordic Models of Architecture and Welfare. As a collaborative effort, six architectural institutions were represented: in Sweden, KTH School of Architecture, through Thordis Arrhenius and Helena Mattsson, and ArkDes, through Christina Pech; in Denmark, the University of Copenhagen, Landscape Architecture and Planning (UCPH), through Ellen Braae, and the Royal Danish Academy, Architecture, Design and Conservation, through Deane Simpson; and in Norway, the Oslo School of Architecture and Design (AHO), through Guttorm Ruud, and the University of Oslo, Department of Philosophy, Classics, History of Art and Ideas (UiO), through Espen Johnsen. Between 2018 and 2019, three workshops organized by the partners—held in Oslo, Copenhagen, and Stockholm—explored the complex relationship between architecture and welfare. This publication disseminates a cross-section of this extensive research environment.

We want to thank all the members of the network and workshop participants for their contributions and commitment throughout the process. Special thanks to Deane Simpson for his guidance in the early stages of this book project and to the anonymous reviewer for the thoughtful perspectives on the book's structure. We also thank Matthew Ashton for his editorial support and our copy editor, Helen Rix Runting, for carefully refining the language and arguments. Our gratitude goes to graphic designer Aslak Gurholt for his creative approach to the book's design and to Birkhäuser commissioning editor Ria Stein for her dedication and guidance.

Finally, we gratefully acknowledge the support of KTH Royal Institute of Technology, The Danish Arts Foundation, Helge Ax:son Johnsons stiftelse, Stiftelsen AA Palmérs minne, Letterstedtska föreningen, and Stiftelsen Thuréus, whose generous funding made this publication possible.

Graphic design: Aslak Gurholt
Copy editing: Helen Rix Runting
Copy editing for the publisher and project management: Ria Stein

Published with the support of the Royal Institute of Technology and the Danish Arts Foundation.

Danish Arts Foundation

Production: Anja Haering

Paper: 90 g/m² Kamiko Fly, 130 g/m² Magno Gloss
Printing: Beltz Grafische Betriebe GmbH, Bad Langensalza
Lithography: Repromayer GmbH, Reutlingen

Cover photographs: Aage Strüwing (front), Lennart Jansson (back)

Library of Congress Control Number: 2024901743
Bibliographic information published by the German National Library
The German National Library lists this publication in the Deutsche Nationalbibliografie; detailed bibliographic data are available on the Internet at http://dnb.dnb.de.

ISBN 978-3-0356-2796-1
e-ISBN (PDF) 978-3-0356-2799-2 Open Access
DOI: https://doi.org/10.1515/9783035627992

The book is published open access at www.degruyter.com.
Printed on acid-free paper produced from chlorine-free pulp. TCF ∞

Printed in Germany

9 8 7 6 5 4 3 2 1
www.birkhauser.com

MIX
Paper | Supporting responsible forestry
FSC® C089473

Helena Mattsson is Professor of Theory and History at KTH School of Architecture. Her research focuses on recent history and the interdependency between politics, economy, and spatial organizations. She is the co-editor of *Swedish Modernism* (Black Dog, 2010); the themed issue "Architecture and Capitalism: Solids and Flows" (*Architecture and Culture*, 2017); *Neoliberalism on the Ground* (Pittsburgh University Press, 2021), and the author of the monograph *Architecture & Retrenchment: Neoliberalization of the Swedish Model across Aesthetics and Space, 1968–1994* (Bloomsbury, 2023). She is on the editorial board of *Journal of Architecture*.

Tom Nielsen is an architect and professor of urban and landscape planning at the Aarhus School of Architecture, where he has been teaching landscape architecture, urban design and urban planning since 2004. His research focuses on the transformation of the Danish welfare city. This has included research into urban landscapes and public space, suburban transformation, urbanizing territories and the relation between urban concepts and values and ethics of contemporary urban transformation. Books available in English includes *Gellerup* (co-authored 2021), *Earthly Cities* (2024) and *The City Denmark* (forthcoming 2025).

Christina Pech is an architectural historian and senior lecturer at the University of Oslo. Her PhD was awarded by the School of Architecture in Stockholm (KTH) in 2011. She has held a position as a research coordinator at the Swedish Centre for Architecture and Design and is editor of *SITE Zones*. Christina's research revolves around architectural discourse in the 1970s and 1980s, in particular institutions and exhibitions in the Nordic countries. She is currently working on a project about the Norwegian Museum of Architecture. Her writings have appeared in journals and edited volumes such as *The Routledge Companion to Architectural Drawings and Models* (Routledge, 2022) and *Valences of Historiography* (Routledge, 2024).

Frida Rosenberg is an architect and teacher at KTH Architecture School. Her research interests focus on co-housing, co-living, and collective housing and also on the transfer of ideas in urban planning and housing between Sweden and the United States in the 20th century. Her essays have appeared in *Domus*, *PLAN* and *Footprint*. She is the co-editor of *Perspecta 40:Monster* and *Arkitektur och Modernitet*. She holds a Bachelor of Science from University of Texas at Arlington, a Master of Architecture from Chalmers and a Master of Environmental Design from Yale University. Her PhD thesis was on "The Construction of Construction: The Wenner-Gren Center and the possibility of steel building in postwar Sweden."

Guttorm Ruud is a Norwegian architect and independent researcher. He holds a PhD from The Oslo School of Architecture and Design—with a dissertation on the Norwegian critique of the planning of satellite towns around 1970. His research focuses on the relationship between architecture and welfare policy in the end of the post-war period, with a particular focus on political, economic and social aspects of the planning and design of urban environments. He teaches and lectures on architectural history, planning history, urbanism, academic writing, and design research.

Erik Sigge is an architectural historian and preservationist, a lecturer in theory and history of architecture and Head of Unit of Form Design Culture at the Department of Architecture and the Built Environment, Lund University, Sweden. During 2020–2021 he was a postdoc fellow at MIT, Cambridge, Massachusetts. Erik gained his PhD in architectural history from KTH, Stockholm. Prior to that, Erik was Director of Educational and Cultural Programs at Scandinavia House in New York City, where he led the public programs of The American-Scandinavian Foundation. He holds a master degree in Historic Preservation from Columbia University, New York, and a bachelor degree in Integrated Conservation of the Built Environment from University of Gothenburg, Sweden.

Deane Simpson is Professor of Architecture, Urbanism and Planning at the Royal Danish Academy, where he leads the master's program *Urbanism and Societal Change*. His research addresses the problematics of contemporary urban spatial practices, including urban spatial imaginaries, such as the liveable, compact, sustainable, welfare, smart, blended, and regenerative city. Publications include: *Young-Old* (Lars Müller Publishers, 2015); *The City between Freedom and Security* (Birkhäuser, 2017); *Forming Welfare* (Arkitektens Forlag, 2017); *Atlas of the Copenhagens* (Ruby Press, 2018) and *Architectures of Dismantling and Restructuring* (Lars Müller Publishers, 2022). He was educated at Columbia University and the ETH Zürich, and previously taught at the AA London and the ETH.

Martin Søberg is a Danish art historian and associate professor at the Royal Danish Academy's Institute of Architecture and Culture. He is cofounder of the Academy's Cluster for Housing Research and currently works on a research project on Danish housing ideals 1930–1960. He is author of *Kay Fisker: Works and Ideas in Danish Modern Architecture* (Bloomsbury, 2021) and coeditor of *Architectures of Dismantling and Restructuring: Spaces of Danish Welfare, 1970–Present* (Lars Müller Publishers, 2022), *The Artful Plan: Architectural Drawing Reconfigured* (Birkhäuser, 2020), and *Refractions: Artistic Research in Architecture* (Arkitekturforlaget, 2016). He is chair of the Danish Association of Art Historians and chair of Docomomo Denmark.

Erik Stenberg is an architect and Associate Professor at the KTH School of Architecture. For the past 25 years, he has been engaged in the practice, research, and politics of restructuring the large-scale postwar modernist housing areas of the Million Program era in Sweden. Stenberg has redesigned apartments, organized a housing fair, exhibited archival material from his collection, started an introductory architecture school in one of Stockholm's largest modernist housing areas, and lectured extensively. He has written "D4-gruppen 1955–1961" for the book *Flying Panels* (DOM Publishers, 2019) accompanying the exhibit of the same name at ArkDes, Sweden's national centre for architecture and design. In 2021–2025, Stenberg headed the Swedish part of ReCreate, an EU Horizon 2020-funded research project that focuses on the reuse of prefabricated concrete elements that were not intended for disassembly.